# OPTIMAL MANAGEMENT OF HEALTH CARE ORGANISATIONS

# OPTIMAL MANAGEMENT OF HEALTH CARE ORGANISATIONS

*Edited by*

**A.I. Irinoye**

**Spectrum Books Limited**
Ibadan
Abuja • Benin City • Lagos • Owerri

*Spectrum titles can be purchased on line at*
*www.spectrumbooksonline.com*

*Published by:*
Spectrum Books Limited
Spectrum House
Ring Road
PMB 5612
Ibadan, Nigeria.
*e-mail: admin1@spectrumbooksonline.com*

*in association with*
Safari Books (Export) Limited
1st Floor
17 Bond Street
St Helier
Jersey JE2 3NP
Channel Islands
United Kingdom

*Europe and USA Distributor*
African Books Collective Ltd.
The Jam Factory
27, Park End Street
Oxford OX1, 1HU, UK



First published, 2004



ISBN 13: 978-9-7802953-70

## DEDICATION

This book is dedicated to a rare gem, an indefatigable achiever, an accomplisher who has demystified all forces of evil in his domain. He doubles in many ways. He is:

- a successful military and civilian leader
- a two-time State Leader – first, as a Military Administrator of Lagos State and currently, the Civilian Governor of Osun State
- an astute administrator and excellent manager of human resources
- a motivator and human dynamo
- a pathfinder and pacesetter
- a royal prince and role model
- a Christian and good sportsman.

This multitalented man is His Excellency,
**Prince (Dr) Olagunsoye Oyinlola** (*RTD. BRIG. GEN.*) *DIP.* (*Inter. Rel.*), *M.Sc.* (*Defence*), *M.Sc.* (*Strategic Studies*), *LLB* (*UK*), *F.W.C.* (*Abuja*), *LL.D* (*Honoris Causa*).

## CONTENTS

*Dedication* *v*
*Acknowledgements* *xi*
*Foreword* *xiii*
*Preface* *xvii*

***Chapter 1***
Categorisation of Health Care Organisations
*Irinoye, A.I.* 1

***Chapter 2***
Population Dynamics and Health Provision in Nigeria
*Ebigbola, J.A. & Ogunjuyigbe, P.O.* 5

***Chapter 3***
Medical Ethics in Medical Practice and Medical Education
*Adebolajo, S.O.* 24

***Chapter 4***
Doctor/Client Relationship: Communication in Clinical Settings
*Adegoke, A.A.* 46

***Chapter 5***
Formulation and Implementation of Strategic Management in Health Care Organisations: An Industrial Sociologist's Perspective
*Ogunbameru, O.A.* 66

***Chapter 6***
Health Financing in a Developing Economy
*Oribabor, P.E.* 87

***Chapter 7***
Hospital Information System (*HIS*) Model in a Nigerian University Teaching Hospital
*Daini, O.A., Makanjuola, R.O.A. & Ojo, O.* 101

***Chapter 8***
Pharmacy Information Needs and Priorities
*Ilesanmi, L.A.* 108

***Chapter 9***
National Health Insurance Scheme: The Need for Optimisation and Mass Participation
*Irinoye, A.I.* 117

***Chapter 10***
Health Management: Marketing Perspective
*Egbuwalo, M.O.* 136

***Chapter 11***
Factors of Health Human Capital Accumulation in Nigeria
*Adebayo, A.A. & Oladeji, S.I.* 159

***Chapter 12***
Patient Therapy and Drug Control in Health Care Organisations
*Afolabi, M.O.* 182

***Chapter 13***
Stress and Stress Management
*Ogunlade, O.* 211

***Chapter 14***
Older Adults and Gerontological Nursing
*Fajemilehin, B.R.* 235

***Chapter 15***
Recreation in Medical Management
*Adeyanju, S.A. & Olorunsola, H .K.* 272

***Chapter 16***
Security Issues in Health Institutions
*Rotimi, A.* 282

***Chapter 17***
Legal Aspects of Health Care Organisations
*Orifowomo, O.A.* 294

***Chapter 18***
Human Health and the Environment
*Fajewonyomi, B.A & Bamgboye, A.P.* 314

***Chapter 19***
Globalisation and Its Implications on Health
*Irinoye, A.L. & Odebiyi, A.l.* 334

***Chapter 20***
Health Sector Reform
*Irinoye, A.I., Ogunbunmi, P.I., Aderounmu, A.O. & Abdulahi M.* 360

*Afterword*
*Ogunbameru, B.M.* 378

*Index* 379

## ACKNOWLEDGEMENTS

First and foremost, I am most grateful to the Almighty God, who is the Source of my health, knowledge, wisdom and inspiration.

I acknowledge all my teachers and colleagues for assisting me to discover myself.

For firing the enthusiasm in me to work on the manuscripts of this book, my profound appreciation also goes to the following people:

| | |
|---|---|
| • Olakunle Ogunbameru, | Department of Sociology and Anthropology, Obafemi Awolowo University, Ile-Ife. |
| • P.Ehi Oribabor, | Department of Management and Accounting, Obafemi Awolowo University, Ile-Ife. |
| • J.A. Ebigbola, | Department of Geography, Obafemi Awolowo University, Ile-Ife. |
| • Rufus Amusan, | Produce Merchant, Ipetumodu, Osun State. |

I also thank Ms. Olukemi Asiyanbi, who typed the original manuscript and Mr Steve Eyeh for his editorial contribution. I also acknowledge different authors whose ideas have been galvanised in this book.

Finally, I am indebted to my wife and children for their understanding, encouragement and support while working on this project.

## FOREWORD

*Optimal Management of Health Care Organisations* is written by an array of competent Nigerian scholars and health care practitioners to address important issues relating to health care organisations and their management.

The old saying, *Health is Wealth*, is still relevant till date. To be considered a normal person, first, an individual has to be in a very good state of health. This book has not only focussed on the issues involved in health care, but also examines the relevance of the proper management of health care organisations.

Although there exist some extensive literature on hospitals, management and organisations in general, literature on health care, especially health care management, is visibly scarce in Nigeria. This book of twenty chapters is published at an appropriate time to fill this yawning gap.

The book brings together, exploits and experiences of some well-known medical practitioners, health care providers, legal luminaries, sociologists, economists, demographers, psychologists, policy formulators and human resources experts to address a galaxy of issues relating to health care so as to meet the need of stakeholders in health care institution at this time.

The emphases of the book are multidimensional. A cursory look at the chapters show the following:

*Chapter One* follows the sociological tradition, using the system approach to explain the categorisation of health care organisations.

*Chapter Two* uses demographic paradigms to discuss the relationship between population and health in Nigeria.

*Chapter Three* examines the ethics involved in medical practice and medical education.

*Chapters Four, Seven* and *Eight* discuss the role of communication in health care management.

*Chapters Six, Ten* and *Eleven* analyse health care management from economic/marketing perspectives.

*Chapter Five* discusses the formulation and implementation of strategic management in health care management from an industrial sociologist's perspective.

*Chapter Nine* enumerates the need for optimisation and mass participation in the National Health Insurance Scheme in Nigeria.

*Chapter Twelve* thoroughly explains the role of pharmacists in the medication use process as well as drug utilisation.

*Chapter Thirteen* provides detailed account of the meaning, causes and management of stress as an omnipresent phenomenon in all human organisations.

*Chapter Fourteen* uses the gerontological approach to explain the relationship between the socioeconomic and socio-demographic variables of individuals and health care.

*Chapter Fifteen* focuses on the essence of recreation in medical management.

*Chapter Sixteen* specifically discusses the state of security in general, especially in Nigeria, relates this to what obtains in health care organisations and identifies the roles of security outfits in health care institutions.

*Chapter Seventeen* examines legal aspects of health care management with specific focus on the relevant constitutional provisions.

*Chapter Eighteen* focuses on human health and the environment which is an integral part of health care.

*Chapter Nineteen* accounts for the implications of globalisation on health.

*Chapter Twenty*, the last chapter, has done an extensive examination and analysis on the current efforts of the Federal Government of Nigeria in the reform of the health sector.

This compilation, written in simple and comprehensive language, is useful for health administrators, government officials at all levels, medical students, social scientists and researchers as well as individuals involved or interested in the study and running of health care organisations.

Finally, one cannot but commend the collective efforts of all the contributors and the editor of this book.

Professor Emmanuel E. Ekandem is a Consultant Paediatrician and he is currently, the Chief Medical Director of Federal University of Uyo Teaching Hospital, Uyo, Akwa Ibom State.

# PREFACE

Health care is a basic human need and effective management ofhealth care organisations is significant to human existence. The fact that we are all stakeholders in the management ofhealth care organisations, is a motivating factor in the collection of manuscripts for this book.

The objective ofthis compilation is not only to highlight the relevant areas in health management but also to show multidisciplinary and interdependence of factors in management ofhealth care organisations. The book has twenty chapters. The first chapter introduces and stratifies the health tree, while chapter two examines the relationship between population and the health status of the citizenry. The third chapter presents ethical issues in medicine and medical practice. These are so varied and multifaceted that they require some form of guidelines and general principles for seeking out more detailed ethical directives in solving such problems. The fourth chapter deals with health care provider-client interaction and the important role good and effective communication plays in this process. The fifth chapter discusses the formulation and implementation of strategic management with specific reference to health care organisations.

While the sixth chapter focuses on the crucial role of financing health in a developing economy like Nigeria, the seventh chapter discusses the importance of computerised hospital information technology in comprehensive health care management. Chapter eight identifies hospital pharmacy information needs from the viewpoint of informatics as essentially relating to drug supply management and drug use control. Chapter nine discusses health insurance as a means of obtaining a substantial part of the funds for urban health services from employers and employees, both private and public, so that taxes realised from contributions can be released for preventive and promotive action, and for primary health care where coverage is now inadequate or absent. The tenth chapter addresses the relationship between economic growth and health. It underscores the need for making conscious efforts to market health care/medical services to the citizenry.

The eleventh chapter examines the investment in health and other health related environmental factors critical to health human capital accumulation. The twelfth chapter presents drug utilisation studies or drug monitoring programmes as control strategies designed to enhance the standard of medical treatment at all levels of health care delivery system. The thirteenth chapter discusses stress and stress management as an integral aspect of health care management. The fourteenth chapter is on the elderly population, which is increasing more rapidly than the rest of the population, and the reduction in working hours with its resultant effect on health care management. The fifteenth chapter explains the role of recreation in medical management. The sixteenth chapter deals with security issues in health institutions. The seventeenth chapter treats legal issues in health care management. Chapter eighteen deals with human health and the environment while chapter nineteen reviews the impact of globalisation on health. The last chapter examines and recommends holistic reform of the health sector.

*Optimal management of health care organisations* illuminates the health networking systems which will guide all health care practitioners and consumers of health care services. However, in any health care setting, while we act locally, we should start thinking globally. This is the holistic approach to health care management.

**Dr A.I. Irinoye**
**2004**

*Chapter 1*

# CATEGORISATION OF HEALTH CARE ORGANISATIONS

*Irinoye, A.I.*

## INTRODUCTION

From the international level to the private rudimentary level, health care organisation comes in various forms, either as a complex system, sub-system or an open system. Some health care organisations are borne out of emergency or necessity, for instance, an organisation established to curb the spread of HIV/AIDS. Such organisations have localised frame of operation and a rapid vertical line of communication. Eradication of such diseases makes such organisations go into extinction. Emergency medical relief organisations are also formed during the periods of wars and natural disasters such as earthquakes, floods, famine, etc.

### Health Care Organisation As a Complex System

The achievement of the overall purposes of a human health organisation will involve a wide range of activities which are interconnected to form a system, such that, changes in the pattern of activities in one unit will initiate related changes in other units of the system.

### Health Care Organisation As a Sub-system

The health care organisation as a system is made up of three principal sub-systems: health care providers, technical system and social system.

The health care providers are the medical and paramedical workers. The technical system is made up of such element as equipment in use, while the social system consists of the relationship patterns between people who work in the organisations, i.e., health workers and the patients. In designing health care organisations, regard must be given to both the need to adapt the structure to the technical system and to provide health for the structure which makes for a satisfying pattern of human relationships.

The structure of any health care organisation is a product of many interrelated factors including its culture, the society where it exists and the policies guiding it.

### Health Care Organisation As an Open System

The existence of any health care organisation depends on some processes of exchange of services and goods with other organisations, social units or individuals in its environment. Health care organisations cannot survive if they are managed exclusively in a way that meet the needs of their clients only. Health care management is, therefore, partly the process of achieving a delicate balance between the expectations and needs of such internal stakeholders as shareholders, employees, managers and pensioners on the one hand; and the demands and constraints imposed upon the organisation by its catchment area, its trade unions, pressure groups of various kinds, strategies and tactics of the competitors on the other hand. Maintaining a balance therefore, calls for the continuous monitoring of the health care organisation's environment and the will to bring about appropriate responses on the part of the organisation.

The best way to organise a health care system is that the most rewarding system of health care organisations must continuously adapt its organisation to meet the demands of changing circumstances.

## STRUCTURE OF HEALTH CARE ORGANISATION

Each hierarchy in any form of health care organisation has three main "sub-systems", namely:

i. The "executive system" which is responsible for directing and controlling the organisation.
ii. The "operating system" which does the health work; and
iii. The "representative system" through which consultations and negotiations are made with stakeholders in the organisation.

At the apex of the health team is the international body which is known as the World Health Organisation with its headquarters in Geneva (Switzerland). The flowchart is as shown below:

World Health Organisation (W.H.O)

↓

Regional Health Organisations

↓

National Health Organisations

↓

State or Sectorial Health Organisations

↓

Local Health Organisations

↓

Community Health Organisations

↓

Private Health Organisations

↓

NGO's | Private Clinics | Mission Health Organisations | Faith Healing Homes | Traditional Healing Homes

Basically in any nation, health care organisations can be classified into three:

- Primary Health Centres
- Secondary Health Centres
- Tertiary Health Centres

Information materials and referrals flow in the same pattern.

Primary Health Organisations

↓

Secondary Health Organisations

↓

Tertiary Health Organisations

The primary health care organisations are the smallest of the group. This is where private health care organisations belong. In developing countries like Nigeria, there is in existence an illegal group of health care practitioners called the "Quacks". They pose a threat to all members of the health team in particular and the entire society in general.

Small health care organisations are characterised by entrepreneurial drive, adaptability, creativity and innovation unlike the bureaucratic systems of administration and control which is peculiar to large health care organisations. Health care management at any level in the categorisation is therefore, a process involving a mix of rational, logical decision-making, intuitive judgment and problem-solving activities.

# Chapter 2

# POPULATION DYNAMICS AND HEALTH PROVISION IN NIGERIA

*Ebigbola, J.A. & Ogunjuyigbe, P.O.*

**About the Contributors**

Ebigbola is a Professor of Demography and Social Statistics in Obafemi Awolowo University, Ile-Ife. His areas of specialisation are Reproductive Health issues, Census Methodology, Mortality Estimation, Population and Development. He is currently an external examiner to some Nigerian Universities; University of Ghana and Fourah Bay College, Sierra Leone. He has several published works both in national and international peer-review journals.

Dr Peter Olasupo Ogunjuyigbe is a senior lecturer in the Department of Demography and Social Statistics, Obafemi Awolowo University,Ile-Ife. His areas of specialisation include Reproductive Health, Male and Female Reproductive Behaviour, Adolescent Sexuality and Reproductive Behaviour and gender-related issues. He has published many articles and works in national and international peer-review journals.

## INTRODUCTION

Nigeria is the most populous country in Africa and among the ten most populous countries in the world. According to the 1991 Census, Nigeria had a population of about 89 million. The estimated population in year 2003 is about 126 million (NPC, 2003). The possibility of population explosion in Nigeria is so real that as far back as 1984, government realised that:

> Something has to be done to ensure the galloping population growth rate and over urbanisation which do not eclipse efforts being made by government to improve the economy and enhance the quality of social services available for the people (Buhari, 1984).

One of the important social services that the government was referring to was the health provision, and by 'health' it means a personal state of well-being, not just availability of health care services but a state of health that enables a person to lead a socially and economically productive life.

An important development goal of the government is to provide adequate health care for the entire population by the year 2000 but recently changed to 2010 (NPC, 2003) through the expansion of primary health care, improved services at secondary and tertiary health care delivery levels, implementation of alternative health financing through National Health Insurance Scheme and finally, the integration of trado-medical practice into orthodox health system. Thus, governments believe that there should be 'health-for-all' by the target dates. 'Health- for-all' implies the removal of the obstacles to health which include the elimination of malnutrition, ignorance, contaminated drinking water and unhygienic housing; and proffering solutions to the purely medical problems such as lack of sufficient doctors, hospital beds, drugs and vaccines. 'Health-for-all' means that health should be regarded as an objective of the overall development and not merely as one of the means of attaining it.

However, for most developing countries of the world including Nigeria, 'health-for-all' remains a dream and it will remain a dream so long as the dream is formulated in big hospitals deficient of high qualified doctors and nurses, drugs, vaccines and equipment as well as lack of appropriate measure to put rapid population increase under control. As the population expands rapidly, it will become more and more difficult to provide sufficient personnel, facilities and financial resources to maintain and improve health services and standards. As rightly pointed out in the National Population Policy (NPC, 2003), the rapid increase in the number of children under five years of age and women in their childbearing years (the groups with the greatest health care needs) will result in increased pressure on the health system. Provision of health services is being confronted with a number of problems among which are: too few resources which are being invested in the health sector; the attraction of highly qualified health professionals who are trained at the country's expense to the richer countries; little control of the ordinary people over their own health; and inability to regulate population growth rate especially of the groups in greatest need of health services.

It can be deduced from the above that health and population are closely interwoven. Health largely depends on the provision of clean water, good housing, safe sanitation, adequate nutrition, immunisation and other products of development process. Accelerated population growth retards development and overburdens health infrastructures. The fruits of development quickly dwindle in the face of rapid population increase; health services and facilities become overwhelmed and unable to meet all the needs of the poor and rural sections of the society. Therefore, the main thrust of this chapter is to examine the relationship between population and the health status of the citizenry.

## POPULATION DYNAMICS

Population growth rate is determined by three main factors: fertility, mortality and migration. International migration has played very insignificant role in determining population growth in Nigeria. Therefore, the high population growth rate Nigeria has been witnessing is the product of fertility and mortality trends.

While birth rates have remained high in Nigeria, death rates have come down although still relatively much higher than what obtain in developed countries. Life expectancy at birth rose from about 36 years in 1963 (NPB, 1963) and close to 48 years in 1980, 50 years in 1990 and 53 years in 1991 (NPC, 1998). The death rate – the number of death in each year per 1000 persons in the population – fell from

27 to about 17 over the same period. Females have a higher life expectancy (53.8 years) compared to males (52.6 years) in 1991. With life expectancy of about 53 years reflecting a very high infant mortality rate of about 120 per 1000 live births, health conditions in Nigeria are among the poorest (97th position) out of 103 countries studied. Though the increase in the life expectancy reflects the reduction in death rate over time, it is pertinent to note, however, that WHO, in its World Health Report (2000), reported 46.8 years and 48.2 years as life expectancy at birth for males and females in Nigeria respectiveiy for 1999, indicating a possible decline in life expectancy between 1991 and 1999.

The combination of historically high birth rates and declining death rates meant that the rate of population growth in Nigeria has increased over time. During the early 1950, the population was probably growing considerably between 2.0 and 2.5 percent per year. The country experienced a growth rate of 2.8 percent per annum between 1952 and 1991 (NPC, 1991). At present, the population is most likely to be increasing by more than 3 percent per year. The Nigerian population is currently estimated to be growing by about 2.9 percent per annum (NPC, 2003). And by this rate, Nigeria is one of the fastest growing populous countries in the world. The growth rate is not expected to change drastically in the short run. At that rate, the population would double about every 25 years. Given a continuation of high birth rates, Nigeria would have a population of almost 163 million in year 2000 and 281 million in 2015. The high population growth rate is essentially due to persistently high fertility in the face of decreasing mortality. Between 1960s and 1980s, total fertility rate (TFR) had remained high at about 6 children per woman (UN, 2000) while the crude death rate (CDR) had decreased from 27 to 15 deaths per 1000 population within the same period. The infant mortality rate (IMR) also declined from 187 to 90 deaths per 1000 live births between 1960s and 1980s. According to 1991 Population Census, the TFR was 5.89 and the CDR was 14 deaths per 1000 live births, while the IMR was 93 per 1000 live births and the child mortality rate was 64 deaths per 1000 live births. Factors associated with the high fertility rate include early age at first marriage, low literacy rate especially among females, low utilisation of modern contraceptives (CPR of 8.6 percent in 2000 (NPC, 2000)), and socio-cultural factors that have pronatalist leaning.

As pointed out by Ebigbola (1999), the general opinion concerning mortality level in the first four decades of the 20th century is that, mortality rate was very high while fertility rate was relatively low. For instance, Ayeni (1979), reported an infant mortality rate of 215 per 1000 live births and an expectation of life at birth of 31.87 years for Nigeria in 1931. Jones and Turner (1932), reported high infant mortality rates for Northern and Southern Provinces of Nigeria. Jones reported an estimated infant mortality rate of 128 per 1000 live births for Northern provinces while in the Southern surveys, Turner reported an infant mortality rate of 330 per 1000 live births in Abeokuta, 233 for Arogbo. Turner in his conclusion suggested, "a fair estimate for Southern Nigeria would appear to be among 300 per 1000 live births".

International migration does not contribute significantly to the growth of the population in Nigeria. The migrant population has grown by 5.5 percent between 1963 and 1991. Foreigners constitute only 0.5 percent of the population. Internal migration, especially from rural to urban areas, is increasing significantly. Also, a lot of Nigerians, particularly the well-educated ones in the productive ages, are known to be emigrating from the country as a result of economic difficulties and limited opportunities for professional actualisation.

The demographic transition model also places Nigeria in the mid-transition period and would probably be trapped there for a long time unless some measures are taken to curtail the birth rate.

## STATE OF HEALTH

In Nigeria, health interests have received a low priority because of the following reasons:

i. Public health programmes have been blamed for the population explosion witnessed in Nigeria because they have reduced death rates while fertility and birth rates have been sustained at high level.

ii. The appealing prospect, for reasons of prestige and status on the part of leading political and intellectual leaders, of advanced technologies and educational methods of acute curative, urban hospital-based medicine is practised in the developed countries in spite of unreliable information about their efficacy, utility, need or impact. Furthermore, the health power structure of Nigeria is overwhelmingly in favour of urban hospital-based science and technology and fails to relate these facilities to type, scale or distribution of the burden of illness experienced by the population.

iii. The lack of a suitable infrastructure with which to reach rural and some urban populations with needed health education and services – whether in terms of transportation, communication, electricity, and health managers. Majority of these people are illiterates and justifiably suspicious of those insensitive to their needs, beliefs and cultural practices and who are dependent chiefly on traditional practitioners.

iv. The failure of most experienced people in contemporary public health and community medicine teaching and practice, to influence substantially ministries of health and planning, heads of funding agencies and political leaders.

v. The conventional wisdom that economic development *per se* will 'trickle down' and improve health by raising standards of living and ultimately reduce birth rates.

vi. Significantly, many Nigerians do not place health above jobs, security and food.

However, in the recent times, health interests have been found to be on ascendancy. Nigerians have come to realise that erosion of human capital through death, disability, pain, depression, and other forms of suffering results in enormous waste of human resources; slows the speed of development; interferes substantially with educational attainment and helps to maintain high fertility rates. Nigerians have recognised that development prospects are enhanced by concurrent attention to economic and social development, nutrition, family planning, and reduction in morbidity and mortality rates.

Some socioeconomic correlates of development are determinants of the health status in a country (Ebigbola, 1999; Ogunjuyigbe, 2002). These socioeconomic determinants include access to health services, drinkable and pipe-borne water, electricity supply, shelter, etc, which are important ingredients to a healthy society. In the past two decades, these socioeconomic factors seem not to be in proper shape in Nigeria to guarantee 'a healthy mind in a sound body' because of the economic crisis and political strife that plagued the country. The percentage of households with electricity supply in 1993/94, for example, was 33.6 percent while households with flush toilet in the same period accounted for only 3.5 percent. The percentage of households with access to pipe-borne water and borehole in the same period was 31.7 percent and 66 percent of the populace had access to health services (FOS, 1996).

Health services in Nigeria and other African countries have their historical origins, on the one hand, in curative services geared mainly towards the administration and those related directly to it, and missionary services which were largely curative; and on the other hand, public health programmes mainly aimed at containment of endemic diseases. The medical technological advancement opened up a whole new promise of mass disease control by the 1950's. Just at this period, notions of economic development were technocratic, so were notions of health care development. There were proliferations of vertical programme (single-purpose programmes focused on specific diseases like smallpox, malaria and tuberculosis) for disease control. However, in 1970s, it was becoming apparent that this approach contained several limitations and inefficiencies. At the same time, the development debate had shifted from technocratic preoccupation with investment in large-scale production as the key to everything to one which focused on the nature of poverty.

An important component of the Nigerian health care system has traditionally been private medical practice. Health care provided by organisations and individuals outside the state sector is a major constituent in the total sum of health care provision. An estimated 60 percent of health expenditure in Nigeria comes from private sources

(World Bank report 1994). The missions, non-governmental agencies and voluntary organisations fall into this category. Orubuloye (1999), observed that Christian medical missions operated several clinics and hospitals across the country before they were taken over by the government in the late 1970s. In 1996, there were 3851 health facilities affiliated with the Christian Health Association of Nigeria operating in Nigeria, 84 percent of which were in the Central and Northern regions (World Bank, 1996). These health facilities included hospitals, maternity centres, mobile clinics and leprosaria. The Mission hospitals not only take care of the most needy and the poor, they also operate a flexible pricing policy according to the ability of the family to pay. Although the government has deregulated the health care system as one of the conditions for the World Bank – IMF program, there have been mixed responses from the Christian missions. Some have reopened their hospitals and clinics, while the majority, especially in Southern Nigeria, is apprehensive of the government's inconsistent policies.

The proliferation of private hospitals and clinics in the last few years has done serious damage to private medical practice in Nigeria. People without medical qualifications established many hospitals and clinics and their operations became a nightmare to the government and the people. Attempts were made by the government to close illegal and substandard hospitals and clinics and prosecute their owners but a few still operate clandestinely. Private individuals operate clinics and hospitals side by side with government hospitals across Nigeria. Most of the services are in the urban areas, especially in the densely populated areas of the cities and large towns. A few are found in the rural areas and small towns. Private health facilities operate flexible services, have friendly staff and provide drugs for their clients but they are more expensive than government health facilities where fees are subsidised.

The advent of the African syncretic and Pentecostal churches led to the emergence of faith and spiritual healing. This group now accounts for nearly one-half of all Christians in Southern Nigeria (Orubuloye, 1998). Nearly all now have maternity homes attached to the churches managed by church members with medical training where pregnant women receive obstetric care almost free of charge. Faith healing is growing in importance in the Nigerian medical care system. A small but increasing number of modern medical personnel now combine modern medicine and faith healing as did the early Christian missionaries. Many people patronise traditional healers for treatment of major ailments because of the inadequacies of the health facilities such as long waiting period and lack of drugs, and poor interpersonal communication skills of health workers, among others.

Traditional medical practice and its practitioners are widely spread across Nigeria. The practitioners draw their clients from wide sections of the society, both literate and illiterate (Maclean, 1965; Ademuwagun, 1978; and Uyanga, 1979). Although the practice suffered a serious setback as a result of intensive Westernisation and Christianisation; and association with witchcraft, it has remained an important component of the Nigerian health care system. As observed in a study of selected communities in Nigeria by Orubuloye (1998), between 8 and 32 percent of women reported using traditional health care providers during the most recent reported illness episodes. The general belief in the efficacy, cheapness and nearness to the users were the dominant reasons for using traditional health facilities.

The widespread use of radio and television in many Nigerian homes has magnified the effect of faith healing churches on the general population. Paid advertisements and spiritual healing services are broadcast on the radio and television extensively, especially in Southern Nigeria, where the leaders of these churches minister and demonstrate their healing powers to the public. The number of the adherents of the new faith increases daily at the expense of the orthodox Christian and the Muslim populations. The economic crises facing many families have further exacerbated the situation. The proliferation of faith healing churches and spiritual homes is a recent phenomenon related to the current economic difficulties, which have driven a significant proportion of the population to seek their support (Orubuloye, 1999). Uyanga (1979), pointed out that the users of faith healing churches and spiritual homes represented the whole spectrum of the Nigerian society. The faith healing and spiritual churches do not only provide cheap health care services to their members but also provide economic support.

Some of these churches have become refugee camps for the poor and the homeless who cannot afford to feed themselves. Nevertheless, the proliferation of the new faith healing churches and spiritual homes of the last few years has eroded the confidence of most people in their uses.

Apart from groups of health providers; pharmacy operators, small medicine stores and drug-peddlers also serve as another group of health care providers in Nigeria. In a census of health facilities conducted in 1962, the patent medicine vendors accounted for 60 percent of fixed health facilities in Nigeria and the registered pharmacies for 5 percent (World Bank, 1996). There is the evidence of preference for the use of these health outlets in Nigeria because of the spread of consultation and treatment, efficacy and convenience (Igun, 1987). Similarly, mothers now use patent medicine stores as an alternative to government health facilities because they offer flexible pricing and free consultations to their customers (Adetunji, 1991). The drug peddlers are found in large numbers across Nigeria, selling their medicines in 'dry drug' stalls (Igun, 1987), along the roadside and from house to house. The medicines they sell range from painkillers to malaria suppressants and antibiotics of various types. Drugs obtained on doctors' prescriptions elsewhere may be found on sale at the roadside and marketplaces. The drug peddlers have large distribution networks and they continue to be relevant in the Nigerian health system because of the poor state of the health facilities.

There was an overlapping in the use of the various health care providers because of the tendency to consult different health care providers concurrently in the course of one illness episode (Orubuloye, 1999). Nevertheless, between one-third and 72 percent of women across the regions reported that they used government health facilities and providers during the most recent illness episode in their families. The proportion of users of government health facilities was higher in the Central and Northern regions than in the Southwest and Southeast regions. The proportions of users were also higher in the urban than the rural areas across the regions, and higher for children's illness episodes than those of the mothers. The reasons why women used the government health facilities during their most recent illness episodes and those of their children include their belief in the services and because is always cheaper than private health facilities,

Before the introduction of structural adjustment programme (SAP) in 1986, the cost of treating an attack of malaria in a government health facility was less than thirty naira. In 1993, it was estimated at about one hundred naira. By January 1998, it was costing about one thousand naira to treat the same illness (Orubuloye, 1999). Treatment of the same illness will, at present, cost between 1500 and 2000 naira in government hospitals. The health sector suffered severely in Nigeria during SAP era. For instance, there was massive brain drain of professional and technical people especially from health-related fields in search of greener pastures. Hence, all the existing medical and health institutions were poorly equipped with staff and drug. And because of restriction on importation, there was widespread prevalence of fake drugs which are harmful to the health of the masses. Similarly, there was an embargo on recruitment, hence, those who left could not be replaced.

In view of the negative socioeconomic changes in Nigeria in the last two decades, with the attendant degeneration of health and social facilities and increasing inability of people to pay for health services under user pays principle, health status and mortality situation have worsened in recent times (Harrison, 1997).

These consequences of SAP were considered unhealthy and inimical to the welfare of the masses. Hence, majority of Nigerians were compelled to seek health care outside the orthodox medical institution. For instance, the WHO reported that over 70 percent of Nigerians have shifted procurement of health care services from orthodox medicine to traditional medicine mainly because of an outrageous rise in the cost of health services. Presently, traditional medicine and spiritual healing homes are booming in all nooks and crannies of the country. Therefore, an increase in the number of health establishment does not necessarily indicate an increase in health coverage.

The impact of other sectors of the economy on the purchasing power of the people to procure health services cannot be overemphasised. For example, the performance of manufacturing sub-sector in the 1990s has progressively worsened. The capacity utilisation has reduced from 75.4 percent in the 1975-1979 to an all-time low of about 30 percent in the 1990s (Ebigbola, 1999). According to Manufacturer Association of Nigeria (MAN), 1996:

> The economy is thus caught in a vicious circle of weak consumer demand, low production and weak economic performance, no growth (unemployment), low income and weak demand.

MAN assertion clearly portrays the weak disposition of the masses in procuring health services and other basic needs over the past two decades in Nigeria.

## POPULATION AND HEALTH

Population trend may contribute to the aggregation of health problems. For example, overcrowding pressure on the basic necessities of life especially food, poor environmental sanitation, increased risk of sexually transmitted infections, inadequate water supply and urban stress leading to psychological problems are some of the outcomes of the uncontrolled population increase. There is increased risk of occurrence of diseases associated with overcrowding such as tuberculosis, meningococcal meningitis and scabies (Lucas and Gilles, 1979). With scarcity of food for the teeming population, there will exist a high proportion of illness-prone children or aged persons. Poor quality water can give rise to diseases such as cholera, typhoid, dysentery, and infective hepatitis with their attendant high morbidity and mortality. Internal migration, necessitated by increased population growth rate may force women to prostitution as an economic strategy with its attendant risk of sexually transmitted diseases (STD's) such as gonorrhoea, syphilis and AIDS.

High parity is known to directly affect the health of children. The risk of stillbirth, infant mortality and child mortality are high with first births, following which they decline, only to increase again after the fourth birth. Also, the length of birth intervals is very important to the health of the mother and child. Chances of foetal loss, stillbirth, prematurity and early childhood death are very high for intervals less than one year and to a lesser degree, intervals between one and two years.

Careful longitudinal studies have revealed an increasing incidence of common respiratory infections and gastroenteritis with larger family size, presumably because of greater exposure. There are also studies showing an increasing prevalence of diabetes mellitus with increasing parity. Cancer of the cervix is also associated with high parity.

Besides the immediate health implications of high fertility, rapid population growth also affects the ability of the country to develop adequate and comprehensive health services in terms of infrastructure, financial and manpower resources.

The effect of internal migration is seen most in the change in the traditional role of caring for the aged. More often than not, the aged in both rural and urban areas of Nigeria are experiencing neglect and loneliness because of the gradual breakdown in the extended family structure largely brought about by the rural-urban migration.

Health affects and is affected by population growth. Health status directly affects mortality; and morbidity level affects fertility level both directly and indirectly and has a considerable influence on migration. Better health has many direct effects on population trends and the most obvious being a reduction in mortality. Better health also appears to increase fertility in the absence of family planning by elimination of diseases that reduce fecundity, such as tuberculosis and venereal diseases. Better health can also increase fertility by reducing the incidence of disease that interfere with the completion of pregnancy such as infectious hepatitis, malaria, tuberculosis, rubella etc. Malnutrition may contribute to maternal mortality, foetal loss, low birth weight and faulty lactation. The reproductive period may be increased by better health and nutrition and the total reproductive period may also increase following a decline in adult mortality.

## HEALTH AND POPULATION POLICY

Policy issues are also of considerable importance in the context of health improvement and having quality population. There is no doubt that Nigeria has a lot of relevant policies in existence and one may be tempted to say that the population and health problems we are facing in Nigeria is not lack of policies but of effective implementation of existing policies. Nigeria has a number of policies that address various areas in the population and health field. The National Population Policy launched in 1988 and recently reviewed has a particularly important place in this respect. In order to curb the exploitation of the numbers of people, population policy will have to become central to development planning. The ultimate goal of such policy is to improve the quality of life. Population policy addresses fertility, mortality and migration as well as interrelationship between population and overall socioeconomic development. The health policy is another relevant policy particularly in the area of maternal and child health and family planning. A draft of reproductive health policy has recently been produced and is awaiting presentation at the National Council of Health meeting for necessary approval. The Government of the Federal Republic of Nigeria in 1997 adopted a national policy on HIV/AIDS and STIs. This policy, which was designed to limit the spread of HIV/AIDS in the country, was revised in 2003 to take care of the multi-sectoral effort to control the epidemic and its effects. Also, the national policy on women has been recently approved; and an economic policy, which takes cognisance of population-related issues such as life expectancy and maternal mortality in national development, was also launched early in 2000.

On the whole, Nigeria's policies in population-related areas are fairly adequate. However, there are a number of policy issues that need to be addressed to provide appropriate framework for sectoral and national development. Some of the existing policies are outdated and need to be revised and updated in line with internationally agreed conventions and protocols. Also, a number of the existing policies have contradictory targets and strategies, and thus, such policies need to be harmonised and made more widely available to stakeholders. Currently, there are many policies in existence that are unknown to and unseen by large proportion of critical stakeholders.

## CONCLUSION

In this chapter, attempt has been made to highlight the relationship between population and health provision in Nigeria. Health has been shown not to be an end itself but rather one of the essential means to achieve socioeconomic development and improve quality of life of the populace.

As noted in the discourse, with the capital-intensive profile of the private sector, the health care of the poor is bound to be inferior to that of the rich. In recent times, the government is considering very seriously and is actually taking step to shift responsibility for health services to consumers through insurance schemes, like Taiwan Universal Health Insurance Programme launched in 1995, so that the healthy individuals would contribute to the cost of health care of the sick.

The chapter, therefore, recognised that an increase in budgetary allocation to the social sector in order to improve the coverage of services and overall quality of life of Nigerians is fundamental. It has been advocated at international level (UN, 1998) that a minimum of 20 percent of total expenditure should be allocated to social services. Therefore, in order to effectively stimulate human development and combat poverty alleviation, the Nigerian governments should commit not less than 20 percent of their budgets annually, for a ten-year period, to social services, particularly targeting the achievement of seven priority targets in the key areas of health, education and population (UNDP, 1998). The targets in the health sector are: universal access to primary health care and sanitation; immunisation of all children; reduction of maternal mortality by half; and complete elimination of severe malnutrition and reduction of moderate malnutrition. The percentage recommended by WHO for effective health services provision is 14 percent of the total government expenditure whereas only 3 percent of federal government expenditure is allocated to health. The target advocated for in the population field is access to family planning by all interested individuals and couples. Political stability and ability to sustain socioeconomic development matter very much in the efficiency of health care delivery system in Nigeria. These will affect the proportion of government expenditure allocated to health.

Reduction in mortality rates requires that health and population policy should be integrated into development planning. To advance development, health issues need to be integrated into all aspects of planning. Health care services and facilities of good quality should be accessible to all segments of population in this era of HIV/AIDS epidemic. It is particularly important to ensure that vulnerable groups such as the rural and urban poor women, the aged and the very young are not neglected. For instance, it is estimated that 40 percent of deaths among the youths in South Africa are caused by HIV/AIDS while 27 percent of total deaths are ascribed to HIV/AIDS. Good health should be regarded as a democratic right. By integrating family planning programmes with systems of maternal and child health care in the context of primary health care, the scope of services and delivery can be expanded and strengthened. Whereas better health care has usually been considered a major source of population growth, it can also contribute to a more rapid fall in birth rates by increasing the practice of family planning.

Finally, since the last three decades of the 20th century, there had been a widespread of military incursion in body politics and civil wars in sub-Saharan Africa, Nigeria is not an exception. The military incursions and civil wars have virtually ruined the gains in the health sectors acquired during the colonial era. Hospitals and other health institutions were badly damaged. Hence, the health status of the populace reversed to its status in post-Second World War era. However, the 21st century has very good prospects if certain features can prevail in African continent in general and Nigeria in particular. Such include political stability, true democracy and sustainable development, which are indices of considerable improvement in the health sector. Similarly, improved and stable economy will go a long way in improving the quality of life of the citizenry.

## References

Ademuwagun, Z.A. (1978). "*Alafia*- The Yoruba Concept of Health- Implications for Health Education". *International Journal of Health Education* 10:35-39.

Adetunji, J.A. (1991). "Response of Parents to Five Killer Diseases Among Children in a Yoruba Community, Nigeria". *Social Science and Medicine* 32 (12): 1379-1387.

Ayeni, O. (1976). "Retrospective Estimates of Mortality From the Nigerian Medical Censuses of 1930-1932: A Research Note" *The Nigerian Journal of Economic and Social Studies* Vol.18, No.3, P.468.

Buhari, M. (1984). "Nigerian Family Planning: Plan of Action". *Mimeograph,* Federal Ministry of Health, Lagos.

Ebigbola, J.A. (1999). "The Link Between Mortality and Socioeconomic Development in Sub-Saharan Africa: An Overview", *The African Population in The 21st Century*, Union for African Population Studies, 6-10 December. P.273-288.

Federal Office of Statistics (FOS)(1996). *Socioeconomic Profile of Nigeria.*

Harrison, K. (1997). "Maternal Mortality in Nigeria: The Real Issue". *African Journal of Reproductive Health*, 1 (1), 7-13.

Igun, U.A. (1987). "Why We Seek Treatment Here: Detail Pharmacy and Clinical Practice in Maiduguri, Nigeria". *Social Science and Medicine* 24(8): 689-695.

Jones, J.G.S. (1932). *Census of Nigeria, 1931, Vol.V: Medical Census of Northern Provinces*, London, Crown Agents.

Lucas, A.O. and Gilles, H.M. (1979). *A Short Textbook of Preventive Medicine for the Tropical,* Hodder and Stroughton.

Maclean, U. (1965). "Traditional Medicine and Its Practitioners in Ibadan, Nigeria". *Journal of Tropical Hygiene* 238.

National Population Commission (NPC) (1998). *1991 Population Census of the Federal Republic of Nigeria* (Analytical Report at the National Level), Abuja, Nigeria.

National Population Commission (NPC) (2000). *1999 Nigeria Demographic and Health Survey*. Lagos.

National Population Commission (NPC) (2003). *National Policy on Population for Sustainable Development*, Abuja, Nigeria.

Ogunjuyigbe, P.O. (2002). "Reproductive Health Care and Maternal Mortality: Strategies for improvement in Nigeria" *Global Journal of Medical Sciences*, Calabar, Vol.2, No.2 P.177-186.

Orubuloye, I.O. (1998). *Health Transition in Nigeria: The Cultural, Social and Behavioural Determinants.* Canberra: Australian National University.

Orubuloye, I.O. (1999). "Health Treatment and the Perception of Health Care Facilities in the Period of Economic Crisis in Nigeria", *The African Population in The 21st Century*, Union for African Population Studies, 6-10 December. P.273-288.

Turner, J.G.S. (1932). *Census of Nigeria, 1931, Vol.V: Medical Census of Southern Provinces*, London: Crown Agents.

United Nations (UN) (1998). *Political Declaration Guiding Principles of Drug Demand Reduction and Measures to Enhance International Co-operation to Counter the World Drug Problem.* Special Session of the General Assembly Devoted to Countering the World Drug Problem Together 8-10 June 1998.

United Nations (UN) (2000). *Key Actions for Further Implementation of the Programme of Action of the International Conference on Population and Development*, New York, June-July, 1999.

UNDP (1998). *Nigerian Human Development Report 1998*. United Nations Development Programme, Lagos.

Uyanga, J. (1979). "The Characteristics of Patients of Spiritual Healing Homes and Traditional Doctors in Southeastern Nigeria". *Social Science and Medicine* 13A: 323-329.

World Bank (1994). *Better Health in Africa: Experience and Lessons Learned*. Washington, D.C.

World Bank (1996). *Nigerian: Poverty in the Midst of Plenty: The Challenge of Growth*. Washington, D.C.

World Health Organization (WHO) (2000). *World Health Report*, WHO, Geneva.

# *Chapter 3*

# MEDICAL ETHICS IN MEDICAL PRACTICE AND MEDICAL EDUCATION

*Adebolajo, S.O.*

**About the Contributor**
Dr Adebolajo holds MBBS(Ibadan), MPH(Leeds) and Ph.D. in Medical Sociology. He is currently the Head of Department, Consulting Unit, Health Centre, Obafemi Awolowo University, Ile-Ife.

## INTRODUCTION

Every new advancement in medicine these days seem to pose a new problem for medical ethics. This is because every step forward forces value decisions upon us, as stakeholders or as principal actors in the field of medical practice. These decisions arise for two major reasons; the first being that, advances in medical knowledge and technology greatly expands our powers of human control and secondly, our limited resources do not allow us to exercise all of these powers all the time. Therefore, we must make choices – ethical choices – as to what powers to exercise at a given time.

Concern with ethical problems in medicine is not entirely new. From time immemorial, health care workers have had occasions in which they have to make decisions that will affect the life of others. Such decisions as euthanasia of brain-damaged patients, use of foetal tissue in research, frozen embryos and artificial insemination – using sperms from free donors. Cloning for example, is an issue which has received enormous attention from both the media and the society at large. Logical reasoning and conclusion based on the Hippocratic Oath given to us by the ancient Greeks have had great influence on our way of thinking and approach to sensitive issues and the way we handle them. Illness and death have always been matters important enough to hold attention and to force agonising decisions. Yet in all these, the moral issues raised will often remain obscure. Many people, including health professionals, will find themselves more or less perplexed when confronted with the latest case problem. Even when they seem to be convinced that the position they are taking is the right one with regards to a particular case, they may still feel uncertain and perhaps unsure as to how their position might be rationally defended.

Enough doubts and confusions attend our reflections upon problems in medical ethics to suggest that we should, perhaps, reserve judgment and take no stand on these issues. But life does not always allow us the luxury of reserved judgments. For example, abortion may be a very difficult problem for us, but the problem does not go away simply because we do not want to face its difficulties. Either the laws permit or they forbid abortions; either public funds pay the cost of some abortions or they do not; either a pregnant woman has an abortion or she does not, we face what William James, a philosopher called a "forced option"; that is, if we reserve judgment, life goes on as if we did make a decision. Numerous problems in medical ethics present us with such forced options. We simply must struggle with these problems so as to take the most intelligent decisions that we are capable of making.

## GENERAL ETHICAL PERSPECTIVES AND PRINCIPLES

The problems presented by ethical issues are so varied and multifaceted that they require us to establish some form of guidelines and general principles for seeking out more detailed ethical directives in solving such problems. Although the principles offered here do not cover all of the possibilities, however, they are particularly fruitful in allowing us to apply some significant moral principles to problems in medicine. Admittedly, some principles may possess explicit religious foundations but that is not to say that the other principles are anti-religious or non-religious. They may also be justifiable on religious grounds as well.

While recognising the fact that ethical issues may have specific legal judgments applicable to them, we, as professionals and stakeholders at the centre of it all, must seek to arrive at moral judgments based upon the various ethical perspectives as presented below, we should not allow legal considerations to override such moral judgments.

## The Issue of Personality

The term personality simply means self-consciousness, that is, the concept of the self as a continuing subject of experience as well as awareness of being such a subject. Anything that exists without personality cannot have moral values or rights. What gives dignity and moral value to human life is the presence of personality. This is true and applicable even to special situations in which there may be temporary unconsciousness including mental illness, or types of mind control.

Anything that enhances the existence and development of personality is good, and treatment of beings with personality as though they were things, however is evil.

Ethical issues in medicine; and the controversies they engender are usually accompanied by assertions about rights. Thus, we hear about patients' rights to life, rights of the unborn, a woman's right to control her own body, rights of the retarded, rights of the mentally ill, right of death with dignity, and right to health care.

## Rights and Responsibilities

Rights are entitlements. They are not privileges for which we should give thanks. When we demand our rights, we only demand what others (persons or governments) are obliged to give. When we possess these rights, we are entitled to expect others to act accordingly. Hence, others are obliged either not to interfere with us or to provide something to us, in accordance with what those rights are.

When it comes to asserting basic rights, there seems to be no limit to such claims. However, getting general agreement or reaching a consensus about them poses a more difficult problem. With regard to practical application, rights of opportunity tend to be more vague and open-ended than rights of non-interference. Consequently in practice, rights of opportunity establish less clear-cut obligations upon others than rights of non-interference. Nevertheless, both rights should still be taken seriously especially in a nation like ours where potential resources abound.

Although the distinction between non-interference and opportunity is fundamental, situations arise where both kinds of rights require attention together. For example, the right to have abortion is basically a right of non-interference; yet its implementation is inseparable from a corresponding right of opportunity. A safe abortion requires well-trained medical personnel, adequate facilities and psychosocial support. Given these, a woman can have a genuine opportunity to exercise her right of non-interference. It would be strange and cruel to assure a woman the right to an abortion and deny her access to medical personnel, adequate facilities and psychosocial support. Therefore, it follows that a right of non-interference may exist along with an obligation to provide background conditions based on a right of opportunity.

At this point, at least, we know what a "right" means in medical ethics and what justifies it. Arguments about rights to abortion, sterilisation, death with dignity (using a "living will" as authorisation) deal with a right of non-interference. Rights of opportunity establish less clear-cut obligations than rights of non-interference. Thus, granted that a right to health care exists, we may still have considerable difficulty determining what we ought to do.

### *Relationships between Rights and Responsibilities*

Rights relate to responsibilities in several ways. If a person possesses a right, then, others have a responsibility to respect it. Possessors of a right also have responsibilities in the exercise of it. Although someone has a right to health care, we can reasonably demand that such a person take some responsibilities for keeping in as good health as possible to avoid unjust harm to others. Any person who violates either of these obligations or responsibilities must be ready to accept the consequences and to avoid wasting limited resources as a result.

Right is not an absolute or unlimited guarantee of anything. Other moral considerations and reality enter in. Within the area of medical ethics, we should recognise that the mere establishment of a right is insufficient. We also need to know what limitations and overriding moral obligations are applicable.

## TYPES OF ETHICAL PROBLEMS

### Abortion

Most controversy about abortion tends to rotate around one particular question. When does the conceptus possess the rights normally accorded a human being? There are some that fix the moment of conception on religious grounds or even upon the biological grounds that human life begins then and that genetic individuality exists then. Some other persons fix upon the twelfth week, when the brain structure is essentially complete, because they associate the brain's functioning with being a live human being. Still others fix upon the point of viability, because they think the conceptus is capable of existing independently outside the womb. And yet still others insist upon the existence of "personhood" (that is, conscious self-awareness) as the characteristic that makes us truly human. There are still other interpretations besides these. This fact further complicates the controversy. Thus, the controversy continues to rage on for the simple reason that there seem to be insufficient evidence on the issue to settle it in a clear-cut way. Instead, we rely upon various perspectives and moral principles that depend, to a large extent, upon both fundamental values and convictions about the nature of reality.

Certainly, everyone will not adopt the same principle or take on the same perspective on the issue of abortion in the near or perhaps even the distant future. We can only hope for greater agreement or consensus of opinion through a dialogue promoted by consideration of the different perspectives and also continuing attention to any relevant facts that may come up from time to time.

**The Morality of Abortion**

Paul Ramsey (1968) argues that abortion is morally acceptable only when continuing development of a fetus threatens survival of the mother. The threat, according to him may be physical or mental. However, in practice, only physical threats are sufficient to justify abortion at this time. Knowledge in psychology is too unreliable to determine with any assurance that a fetus constitutes an authentic threat to the mental survival of the mother.

Although Ramsey (1968) accepts the ethical position of "alien dignity" which stipulates that all human life is an expression of God's love and possesses infinite worth, he does not think that determination of the exact point at which the fetus becomes human or becomes a person has much to do with the ethical issues involved. He believes that it is precisely because the fetus is weak, innocent and helpless that we have a special obligation to protect this life which is an expression of God's love. Abortion is justifiable only when we must choose between the life of the mother and the life of the fetus.

Ramsey accepts the Roman Catholic position of the principle of double effect, which allows indirect therapeutic abortions. That is, if, in the process of rightly intending to save the mother's life from some physical threat unrelated to the pregnancy itself, the fetus dies as an unintended result, then, such abortion is morally acceptable. For example, if a woman has cancer of the uterus and the radical surgery necessary to save her leads to the death of the fetus, then the abortion comes under the principle of double effect. Such a procedure is a "right" means of seeking a "good" end in a tragic situation. In such a case, there is no motivation to want the death of the fetus, nor does one intend to directly attack and kill. He further contends that:

> The intention is directed toward the incapacitation of the fetus from doing what it is doing to the life of the mother, and is not

> directed towards the death of the fetus, as such, even in the killing of it. The child, of course, is only doing what comes naturally, that is, growing and attempting to be born. But this, objectively and materially, is aggressing upon the life of its mother.

Although the fetus is innocent of any aggression in the moral sense, the fetus is an aggressor in the material sense.

### *The Roman Catholic View*

There is a further stress upon natural law in the Catholic position. Any attempt to kill the fetus directly in order to save the mother's life is a direct attack upon an innocent human life, and such attacks are contrary to natural law. While conceding the fact that there are some tragic but natural risks and consequences in pregnancy that we must accept, Catholic view contended the fact that in direct therapeutic abortion, we use an evil means to accomplish a good end, namely, saving the mother's life. But since the end does not justify the means, these abortions are morally unacceptable.

From the Catholic standpoint, the fetus is not considered in any way "an aggressor", as Ramsey says – not even a material one. Moreover, there is a difference between taking a life and permitting death to occur.

The ethical issue involved in this viewpoint is the question of the direct taking of one innocent life or of merely permitting two deaths. In other words, there is question of one "murder" against two deaths. The Catholic standpoint is that of these two evils, the moral evil of murdering the fetus is far greater than the merely physical evil involved in allowing and doing nothing about the unavoidable deaths of both mother and fetus.

Gerald Kelly (1958), in his Medico-Moral Problems, denies that this position leads to preference for the life of the fetus over that of the mother. He further denies that more women die due to complications of pregnancy in Catholic hospitals, besides, that there are very few cases where therapeutic abortion is actually necessary to save the life of the mother.

### *Abortion and Infanticide*

According to Michael Tooley (1972), a being has a moral right to life if and only if that being is a person. Without conscious self-awareness, you cannot be a person. Since the fetus, is not a person because it lacks such a consciousness of itself as a continuing subject of mental states, it does not possess a moral right to life; therefore abortions should be allowable on demand – without violating any moral principle. On these same grounds, Tooley argues that infanticide is morally permissible until the infant becomes a person. Although he asserts that conscious awareness is not present during the first week after birth, he conceded the fact that there is some doubt as to when this occurs. However, as a practical matter, he concludes that a decision in favour of infanticide should be allowable during this first week, since the presence of gross deformities and the likelihood of severe handicaps are often evident at this stage, and since most people prefer to avoid the suffering associated with such deformities and handicaps, allowing infanticide can significantly increase the happiness of the society.

### *Freedom, Sanctity of Life and Abortion*

Daniel Callahan (1970) is opposed to highly restrictive abortion laws. He argues that they lead to many illegal abortions which are also quite hazardous, especially in underdeveloped countries. In most cases, such laws are "unenforced and unenforceable", hence they lower respect for law and do nothing to enhance respect for freedom of women. Nevertheless, Callahan opposes repeal of all abortion laws.

As for the moral foundation of this position, Callahan emphasises two principles:

(1) we should maximise individual freedom of choice, and
(2) we should respect the sanctity of life.

Thus, Callahan does not like abortion, and he refuses to trivialise it. But he also wants to assert a woman's right to make her own choice as well. And he recognises that situations arise where abortion is a morally correct choice for a woman.

Since legally compulsory abortions are repugnant and violate rights, he opposes them except in the unlikely extreme case where survival of the human race itself or of a whole people requires the superseding of individual's rights.

### *Utilitarian Perspective on Abortion*

This perspective is predicated on the fact that there are no universal ethical absolutes. Rather, there are ethical judgments based upon needs in particular situations.

Therefore in assessing needs, people should recognise that quality of life, not simply the quantity of it, is most important. Thus, mere presence of life provides no absolute justification for preserving it. We must differentiate between biological life and human life in particular. Nothing is truly human without personhood and the ability to survive separately. Personhood requires some minimal amount of intelligence and includes traits such as curiosity, affection, self-awareness, self-control, memory, purpose, and conscience. Hence, a fetus is not a human being; therefore no sound moral justification for compulsory pregnancy exists.

Thus, in making abortion decision, this viewpoint supports that whatever produces the greatest good for the person involved is the correct action. Factors such as health, survival, growth, joy, social interest, and self-realisation deserve consideration. For the most part, the persons most immediately involved – particularly the woman – should decide. According to Fletcher (1974), "pregnancy when wanted is a healthy process, pregnancy when not wanted is a disease". He presumes that persons can be trusted not to choose abortion for frivolous reasons. The decision also requires special attention to social responsibilities when the likelihood of a social burden – for example, birth defects causing some drain on society's resources – is evident.

As in most moral decision-making, a balancing of good and bad consequences is appropriate. And in situations where the balance favours abortion, it is a positively good course of action.

### *Medico-Legal Perspective on Abortion*

It has been argued that the fetus is a "person" and therefore possesses rights. However, there is no legal provision that enables us to apply the word "person" prenatally. Also, it has been argued that life begins at the moment of conception and that the state therefore has an obligation to protect life from that moment. This issue is a matter of controversy among experts in medicine, philosophy and theology. Hence, the court cannot decide for itself when human life begins.

In deciding this issue, one must also recognise a woman's right to privacy. This right to privacy is not unlimited, however, because of the State's legitimate interest in protecting potential life. Therefore, it can be concluded that the right of personal privacy includes the abortion decision, but that this right is not unqualified and must be considered against important State interest in regulation.

With regard to the State's interest in protecting potential human life, particularly in areas other than criminal abortion, the law has been reluctant to endorse any theory that life, as we recognise it, begins before birth or to accord legal rights to the unborn except in narrowly-defined situations and except when the rights are contingent upon life birth. Therefore, the State's important and legitimate interest in protecting potential human life becomes "compelling" at the point of viability – that is, when the fetus presumably has the capability "of meaningful life outside the mother's womb". The point of viability occurs between the twenty-fourth and twenty-eight weeks of pregnancy.

### Sterilisation

Among issues in medical ethics, sterilisation does not get much attention except when problems of coercion arise. However, as sterilisation becomes more popularly acceptable as a birth control measure, concern with ethical questions is also likely.

Sterilisation for women has always been a major procedure, whereas vasectomies for men are relatively simple. Traditionally, men have been reluctant to accept vasectomies and doctors have been reluctant to do them, although social attitudes are now changing.

According to Joseph Fletcher (1954), sterilisation may be

therapeutic, eugenic or compulsory, and all three are justifiable, if the proper conditions occur.

***Therapeutic Sterilisation***

Both direct and indirect sterilisation are acceptable for therapeutic reasons which include happiness, marital well-being as well as physical threats to health. Fletcher (1954) rejects the Catholic position. He argues that no clear evidence exists in early Christian literature, including the Bible, to show disapproval of sterilisation. Further, he rejects appeal to "natural law" on the ground that what nature "intended" about sexual union cannot be logically established since a very small percentage of such unions result in conception, hence conception does not necessarily follow sexual union so that any attempt to tie sexual love to procreation cannot be justified.

***Eugenic Sterilisation***

This is sterilisation, voluntary or involuntary for the purpose of eliminating the possibility of inheritable diseases. With regard to eugenic sterilisation then, some social responsibilities are necessary. It is believed that children should have a right to be born free of disease and defect. It is also obvious that the birth of feeble-minded children does not enhance personal integrity, therefore people should recognise the need to seek eugenic sterilisation voluntarily when medical indications show the likelihood of defective children.

***Compulsory Sterilisation***

The issue of compulsory sterilisation is an enigma. It defies all rational resolutions that could lead to a consensus. In cases of compulsory sterilisation, we must make decisions regarding whose interests warrant protection and whose rights take precedence. Does a handicapped person, particularly one severely-retarded, has the same constitutional rights as any other citizen? Do children have a right to be born free of disease and to be assured proper care, even when granting this right may close off the possibility of their ever existing? In other words, are some children better off without these rights, even though it means more handicaps and misery, because sterilisation as a preventive measure precludes their ever being born? If guardians or society must care for children of retarded parents, have they consequently a legitimate right to determine, in part at least, whether or not the children will be born?

The major purpose of a compulsory eugenics sterilisation programme is the elimination of children with severe birth defects. This being so, we must recognise that even the most avidly-pursued programme would not eliminate all these defects; because even "normal" parents sometimes have defective offspring. Moreover, since there are many more normal parents than retarded ones, normal persons as a whole produce a greater number of retarded offspring than do retarded parents as a whole. In considering all these facts, it becomes obvious why some people conclude that a compulsory sterilisation programme is not worth the threat to basic rights that it creates.

## Ethics of Genetic Control

The awesome potentialities of contemporary science and technology are more evident in the area of genetic control over the future of humanity. Programmes which aim at actual restructuring of human being's biological make-up become increasingly feasible. However, ethical issues arise from the realisation that with our present scientific knowledge, just about anything is possible in biological engineering – within the next ten to thirty years! (Joshua Lederberg, 1966). This fact poses genetic threat about the potential to change biological structure.

Advocates and critics have adopted different positions to the ethical issues involved. There are pessimists who want to avert a steady decline in the human race and optimists who want to develop a super race. There are some who find the prospects of clones and human-animal hybrids a dazzling scientific triumph. And there are others who merely want parents to have healthier babies. No matter what the alleged advantages, any proposal should be subjected to a full range of ethical evaluations.

### *Ethical Implications*

It is estimated that 20% of individuals conceived have a genetic defect that prevents their surviving to maturity or reproductive age. This process of natural selection eliminates individuals with extreme detrimental genes and counterbalances the production of these genes through harmful mutations. Modern medicine and technology, however, upset the balance because it is possible to make as many as 90 percent of these genetically defective individuals to live and perhaps reproduce. Since the society still make ethical commitment to saving these individuals regardless of the consequences, the genetic deterioration of human beings is certain. This gloomy prognosis for the future of humanity is further enhanced by the fact that the society fails to ensure that only the most favourable genetic material is passed on to future generations and because of the probable tendency of those with lesser genetic endowment to have the largest number of children, it becomes obvious that they consume more and more of society's energy and resources and yet contribute little or nothing in return. An extrapolation of this process to the distant future therefore, presents us with a vision of disaster. The ethical question then is what do we do?

There are enormous practical difficulties in identifying and mapping out individual genes, as well as knowing their internal constitutions and functions. Therefore, the idea of genetic surgery is rejected by Muller. Instead, he advocates genetic control over reproduction – through artificial insemination at first, then through artificial inoculation and cloning later. However, these options have ethical considerations as well. Artificial insemination – using sperm from storage banks – is the most feasible method presently. It offers the hope of passing on to future generations the genetic capabilities of men of the calibre of Albert Einstein, Louis Pasteur, Obafemi Awolowo or Nnamdi Azikiwe. Since spermatozoa can be safely stored almost indefinitely, Muller suggests a waiting period of some twenty years after death before making a relatively unbiased decision about a person's genetic potentiality. By selecting desirable traits such as intelligence, aesthetic appreciation, empathy, honesty, community loyalty, vigour, longevity and perhaps even a reduced need for sleep, human beings can avert genetic deterioration.

However, the conflict with moral values and the currently held superstitious beliefs on these proffered solutions may pose ethical dilemmas that may not be easily resolved. To achieve this conscious direction of human evolution, Muller pointed out how these solutions conform to acceptable human values, for example, to happiness, wisdom, brotherhood, the will to self-development and the general welfare of mankind. He did not think that compulsory social programmes will be necessary. He believed that once people recognise that the well-being of children and of subsequent generations is the main objective of reproduction, rather than the mere act of having children for self-glorification, then, they will want to act responsibly. Once they are aware of the genetic problem and its needed solution, they will welcome the promise of a better future and the opportunity to help create it.

## MORAL CAUTIONS ON ETHICAL ISSUES

There is a general recognition of responsibilities associated with recent advances in genetic knowledge. Already, considerable genetic knowledge exists and it is readily available to all through the use of scientific method. With respect to genetic control, scientists are ineffective in affecting policy decisions. They ignore social consequences, or they downplay any possible fears about genetic control. Actually, it is the society as a whole which should take responsibility for making decisions. Therefore, the scientific community should direct its efforts towards the community as a whole – by providing technical information about genetic knowledge, by laying out all the possibilities of genetic control before the public, and by encouraging people to engage in a dialogue appropriate to the making of decisions about these weighty value questions. Attempts to form judgments about genetic control are difficult, partly because of the biological knowledge necessary to make intelligent decisions. Some of this knowledge are available now, although everyone may not possess them, and some remain to be known. However, given the data and the available information reporting accomplishments and projections regarding genetic knowledge, do we have sufficient reasons for devoting serious thought to decisions about genetic control? Are there enough serious birth defects due to genetic diseases to warrant all the efforts on genetic engineering? Is diabetes for example, a serious genetic disease to warrant some effort to encourage diabetics to have fewer children? Should genetic counselling be required before marriage? Does the fact that traits such as intelligence and temperament not monogenic, and have any bearing on the issue of genetic control? Should further research be banned? Should public fund be denied of such a research? Or should research be allowed, but with prohibition of any applications in society? These are some of the ethical questions that call for moral caution in their consideration.

## Death and Dying

Everyday, all over the world, patients' relatives, doctors and nurses face agonising deliberation on whether or not to let someone die by withholding life-saving procedures. They wonder whether or not a respirator should be disconnected, electrical stimulation to "re-start" the heart applied, antibiotics for life-threatening infection withheld or surgery to correct heart defects withheld, from babies with Down's syndrome. Often, moral issues are called into play when taking such decisions because making ethical decision is pretty difficult. To resolve some of the dilemmas arising, attempts are made to reinterpret death in the light of new medical knowledge and technology.

The traditional definition of death as a discrete event in which there is cessation of breathing or heartbeat (otherwise known as the "last gasp", with stiffening of limbs) no longer prove adequate today because it is possible to sustain the functioning of organ systems with machines so successfully that those traditional signs of death can sometimes be postponed almost indefinitely. It has been argued that death is not a discrete event, as the traditional signs of death indicate, and that death is better described as a process. This process interpretation has added new dimension to the traditional perspectives by expanding the range of options available in critical situations.

## Death As a Process

Most controversies centre on the issues of "death with dignity" and euthanasia. Consequently, various positions on these issues are adopted by different people as to whether or not there can be a death with dignity, and whether or not there is dignity in hastening death to avoid further suffering be it physical, mental, social or economic. According to Robert Morrison (1971), we must be wary of our tendency to fix upon traditionally-abstract concepts of death as a discrete event which may introduce "artificial discontinuities into what are essentially-continuous processes". In the process of dying, we talk about death as if it were a discrete event. Yet we know, largely because of advances in medical technology, that various parts of the body, including organ systems and cell lines, can go on living long after that organisation which makes possible a quantitatively valuable human life has disintegrated. Hence, we must make judgments based upon the value of an individual human being, recognising that this value changes relative to other values according to time and circumstances. In other words, an individual's life may no longer be worth living once the person's ability to participate in the complexity and richness of human life deteriorates sufficiently.

## A Definition of Irreversible Coma

According to Harvard Report prepared by an ad hoc committee of the Harvard Medical School, irreversible coma is defined as conditions that establish a permanently non-functioning brain. These include:

(i) unreceptivity and unresponsivity to externally-applied stimuli even intensely painful ones;
(ii) absence of spontaneous movement or breathing for at least one hour;
(iii) no reflexes; and
(iv) flat electro-encephalogram (EEG).

Although the report deals mainly with medical matters, its ultimate purposes are ethical and legal as well. It establishes new criterion for death and makes clear when organs for transplant may be taken from a dead donor, to protect doctors from possible malpractice suits, and to aid families and hospitals in deciding whether extraordinary means should be used to prolong life. If these test conditions are satisfied at a particular time, and also satisfied twenty-four hours later, then death may be declared.

## Euthanasia and the Caring for the Irreversibly-ill Patient

The Roman Catholic Church views euthanasia as the direct killing of an innocent person and therefore, declares it as morally wrong. If the act is voluntary, then it is described as suicide; if involuntary, it is murder. The act is regarded as clearly contrary to both natural and divine law. For example, "The innocent and just man thou shalt not put to death" (*Holy Bible*, Exodus 23: 7). However, Kelly (1958) in his "Medico-Moral Problems" made it clear that easing pain and conquering disease are worthy acts for the Christian, although these aims do not justify euthanasia. The condemnation of euthanasia does not imply an insistence upon preserving life at all cost regardless of conditions. When a person enters irreversibly into the process of dying, care should be directed towards making the person comfortable and showing loving concern rather than toward preserving life.

To hasten the patient's death by administering the overdose is an act of euthanasia. If the patient suffers in such excruciating pain so as to be beyond comforting, then the use of a painkilling drug, which happens to also hasten the process of dying, may be acceptable. And if the patient is totally beyond consolation, as in the case of comatose patient for many months, then the measures to prolong life may be discontinued. It is harder morally to justify letting somebody die a slow and ugly death, dehumanised, than it is to justify helping him to escape from such misery. This is the case at least in any code of ethics which has a value system that puts humanness and personal integrity above biological life and function.

## Lawsuits and Informed Consent

A patient has the right to obtain from his physician complete current information concerning his diagnosis, treatment and prognosis in terms the patient can be reasonably expected to understand. When it is not medically advisable to give such information to the patient, the information should be made available to an appropriate person on his behalf.

The patient has the right to receive from his physician information necessary to give informed consent prior to the start of any procedure and/or treatment. Except in emergencies, such information for informed consent should include, (but not necessarily be limited to the specific procedure and/or treatment), the medically significant risks involved, and the probable duration of incapacitation. Where medically-significant alternatives for care or treatment exist, or when the patient requests information concerning medical alternatives, the patient has the right to such information.

The patient has the right to refuse treatment to the extent permitted by law, and to be informed of the medical consequences of his actions.

Doctors are liable to lawsuits if they fail to give sufficient information when obtaining informed consent for a medical procedure.

### The Right of Confidentiality

It is generally believed that the right to confidentiality is justified on the basis that it is necessary to establish trust in the doctor-patient relationship. However, on the other hand, the society also has a right not to suffer harm at the hands of the patients and patients have no right to cause themselves grievous harm. Therefore, there may be limits to the right of confidentiality.

## MEDICAL ETHICS IN MEDICAL EDUCATION

The issue of medical ethics in medical education, centres on moral issues involved in the philosophy concept and policy underlying the design, establishment and implementation of medical education. The relevance of traditional education of medical undergraduates to the essential needs of the community has been an issue of intense debate in Africa. One of the main objectives of basic medical education is to train doctors with strong orientation towards priority health problems and community programmes. How this is achieved appears to be inadequately specified in most of the curricula of medical schools, however, the issue at stake today is different. It is the political ideology employed in the planning orientation and implementation of medical education policy.

Today, medical education has become a big business. New Medical Schools are being established at an accelerated rate, while the existing schools are left to grapple with the ever-increasing annual student intake into, not only the same basic facilities that existed several decades ago at its inception, but also much more poorly-maintained old facilities. The health policy formulators and implementors are bound partly by their own values, partly by the values of the intended clients (that is, the society) and least by ethical or moral considerations. The dilemma therefore exists between what is politically desirable and what is morally binding. It is unfortunate that much of the debate and discussions on this issue have been dominated by the power politics between the administration, Universities and the Medical Colleges; all bent on protecting their vested interests.

In fact, there is reason to believe that our medical schools are in some ways producing the sort of persons we do not want. At present, they are producing fine young physicians who might be most competent scientists, anxious to diagnose and manage the most complicated and rare syndromes or driven to produce research papers to justify and/or earn their academic promotion. Most of them do not seem to be very interested in caring for or in fact good at caring for ordinary patients with ordinary day-to-day problems. They seem to have learnt to be proud of the knowledge they have accumulated. By far more appalling and distasteful characteristics of these doctors, are their lack of care, insensitivity, failure of communication or lack of human understanding and other similar traits displayed with such brazen impunity!

Professional callousness, negligence and sheer incompetence are age-old forms of malpractice. With the transformation of the doctor from an artisan exercising a skill on personally-known individuals into a technician applying scientific rules to classes of patients, malpractice has acquired a new anonymous, almost respectable status. What had formerly been considered an abuse of confidence and a moral fault can now be rationalised into the occasional breakdown of equipment and operators. Hence in a complex technological hospital, negligence becomes 'random human error', callousness becomes 'scientific detachment', and incompetence becomes a 'lack of specialised equipment'. Furthermore, the depersonalisation of diagnosis and therapy has turned malpractice from an ethical into a technical problem ...!

There is no doubt that both the efficiency and effectiveness of medical education can be substantially increased if we pay proper attention to what is already well-known about the education process and apply educational research methods. We can produce more doctors and certainly better doctors, possibly cheaper than we do at present. It is quite clear that a rigid and inflexible curriculum, which requires all the students to pass through the same sequence of teaching at the same time, will be less efficient in encouraging learning than one which encourages each individual to move at his own best rate through a course which presents him with a variety of educational facilities, from which he can choose those which most help him.

We must realise as basic principle, the adaptation of instruction to the individual students needs, rather than attempt to adapt the individual to the instructor's needs, or to administrative or departmental convenience. We should aim at, first, a clearly-defined flexible-care curriculum, taken by all students and containing all the information which every physician must have in order to practice medicine, and which should be conveyed with the use of all modern techniques available; and secondly, a free elective curriculum, the precise contents of which vary from student to student. Its content grouped into compulsory elements, free options and areas where a choice could be made between a series of limited alternatives. The planning and conduct of the curriculum needs to be handled by a curriculum committee, including senior and junior staff members, from pre-clinical and clinical departments, and medical students in effective and appropriate numbers. The committee must keep the course under constant review, and must be empowered to make suitable changes.

## THE ATTRIBUTES OF A GOOD PRACTISING PHYSICIAN

We can quite easily define some of the qualities we would hope to encourage in the student. Based on the knowledge he possesses, the young doctor should be able to make accurate observations, and be capable of making correct deduction from these observations and then choose an appropriate course of action. He should be able to form hypotheses which can be confirmed or refuted by experiment and observation. He will need physical and mental stamina to meet the demands that will be made upon him during and after his training and he should be a sincere and stable person. He should be able to speak with kindness and understanding. He must have been adequately prepared to continue learning throughout his life and be able to embark successfully on the programme of postgraduate vocational training in whatever field of medicine he chooses. He is not only learning things and behaviours, but he is learning how to become a different person and how to fulfil a very different role.

The basic question is: How can this observable behavioural change be achieved and also increase the likelihood that such behaviour will recur in appropriate circumstances?. We may conclude then that a detailed, realistic and behavioural statement of objectives is needed if we are to be able to have any reasonable expectation, that the courses are going to have the desired effect on our students. Objectives must be expressed behaviourally; in terms of what the student is to become and how we want him to behave when he has completed the period of training. A number of studies have demonstrated that educational objectives in specific behavioural terms may be drawn up without excessive difficulty and used to determine curriculum content (Spivey 1971). In this way, training can be adapted and tailored to community and national need.

**References**

Callahan, Daniel, (1970). *Abortion: Law, Choice and Morality,* New York: Macmillan, Ch. 9.

Fletcher, Joseph, (1974). *Morals and Medicine* (Boston: Beacon Press, 1960), Chs. and 7 – "The Ethics of Genetic Control: Ending Reproductive Roulette" Garden City, N.Y. Anchor Books.

Fletcher, Joseph, (1969). "Our Shameful Waste of Human Tissue," in Donald R. Cutter, *Updating Life and Death: Essays in Ethics and Medicine.* P. 1 - 30. Boston, Mass: Beacon Press.

Herman J. Muller, (1960) "The Guidance of Human Evolution," in Sol Tax, (ed) *Evolution After Darwin; Vol. II: The Evolution of Man.* P. 423 – 462. Chicago: University of Chicago Press.

James, Williams, (1948). *Essays in Pragmatism,* New York: Hafner.

Kelly, Gerald S.J. (1958). *Medico-Moral Problems* (St. Louis, Mo: The Catholic Hospital Association).

Lederberg, Joshua, (1968). "Experimental Generics and Human Evolution", *Bulletin of the Atomic Scientists* (October 1966), 4-9.

Michael A. Simpson, (1972). *Medical Education: A Critical Approach,* Butterworth & Co. Publishers Ltd.

Morrison Robert "Death: Process or Event?" *173 Science* (August 20, 1971), 694 – 698.

Ramsey, Paul, (1968). "The Morality of Abortion" in Edward Shils, *et al., Life or Death: Ethics and Options.* Seattle: University of Washington Press, 1968.

Ronald, Yezzi, (1980). *Medical Ethics: Thinking About Unavoidable Questions*, Holt, Rinehart and Winston Publishers.

Spivey, B.E. "A Technique to Determine Curriculum Content", *Journal for Medical Education*, 46, 269.

Tooley, Michael, (1972). "Abortion and Infanticide", *Philosophy and Public Affairs,* 2, No. 1, 37 – 65.

# *Chapter 4*

# DOCTOR / CLIENT RELATIONSHIP: COMMUNICATION IN CLINICAL SETTINGS

*Adegoke, A.A.*

**About the Contributor**

Adegoke is a lecturer at the Department of Psychology, Obafemi Awolowo University, Ile-Ife. He is an alumnus of the same University, and he has a Master of Science degree in Health Psychology. His areas of research are Health Promotion and Maintenance, Psychological factors in Health and Illness and HIV/AIDS prevention.

## INTRODUCTION

The term communication has been defined by Bennett (1976) as a process by which senders and receivers of messages interact in a given social context. Thus, no single aspect of communication can be meaningfully understood when parted from the other constituents of behaviour. For any communication to occur, there must be a sender and a receiver, and a message passing between the two. The process may fail at various points; the sender may not output the message or he may output it in a way that is unintelligible to the receiver; or the receiver may fail to input message or he may interpret the message wrongly; or the message may be interrupted or distorted in its passage from sender to receiver. The similarity between the message as the sender recognises it and the message as the receiver perceives it indicates the success of communication *per se*.

The study of communication and persuasion is concerned with understanding of the problem of "who says what, to whom, with what effect?" It is precisely this question that social psychologists have been attempting to answer for more than five decades. More specifically, they have been concerned with manipulating communicator variable (the who), message variables (the what) and audience variable (the to whom) in an attempt to understand their influence on various measures of reception and attitude change (the effect) (Fishbein, 1976). Fletcher (1973) has laid down certain principles of communication, and these principles are reproduced here for emphasis.

1. The purpose of communication is not just to deliver a message but also to effect a change in the recipient in respect of his knowledge, attitude, or eventually in his behaviour.
2. The value of a communication is to be judged not on its purpose or current but on its effect on the recipient. An elegant or witty communication may satisfy the communicator but leave the recipient uninformed and unmoved.
3. Good communication is difficult. Few can master it without special tuition and constant attention to its effectiveness.
4. Communication must be matched to the knowledge, social background, interest, purposes, and needs of the recipient. It requires empathy, which is "the power of projecting one's personality into, and so fully understanding, the object of contemplation'.
5. Communication is effected not only by words, which must have the same meaning for giver and receiver, but also by attitudes, expression, and gestures. This is especially relevant to a consultation where client and doctor are both givers and receivers.
6. If communication is to change behaviour, the required change in the recipient must be seen by him to have more advantages than drawbacks, otherwise it will not be made, or if it is made, will not

persist. New information resulting in a change of attitude is usually a necessary prelude to a change in behaviour.

7. To make sure that a communication has succeeded, information about its effects ('feedback') both immediate and subsequent is needed.
8. Communication demands effort, thought, time and often money. Effective communication between colleagues also demands willingness on the part of the giver to discover that more may be learnt than taught.

## THE NEED FOR BETTER COMMUNICATION AND EMOTIONAL SUPPORT

Doctors and indeed all health care providers need better communication skills to perform excellently in the process of diagnosis and treatment – ascertain client's concerns, worries and theories about illness – to give information to clients regarding their illnesses and treatments; and if any side effects, to be sure that clients' understood them and to give emotional support and care to clients and their families recognising their feelings, fears, distresses and anxieties. It has been noted that good health care provider-client interaction has positive effects on recovery from illness, decreasing clients' anxiety, improving compliance with treatment and reducing common causes of clients' complaints.

However, one major task of health cares is to provide reassurance and comfort for those in distress about their illnesses. There is also a need to provide the client with an explanation for illness as well as instructions as to how best to deal with it. The giving of such information and support is one of the most important tasks performed by the health care provider. Dissatisfaction with medical communication is one of the most common complaints of clients'. This has also been discovered to be the major factor why some clients choose other forms of help and treatment, such as alternative medicine, with its focus on directly involving the clients' in treatment and encouraging them to talk freely about their problems. (Corney, 1991).

As a result of illness, individuals concerns, preoccupations and worries shifted dramatically, centred around the presenting symptoms and have subsequent impacts on their daily life, careers and families. The physician need to be aware of these and attend to psychological factors and be alerted to the worries and distresses of the client. Failure to assess these problems objectively means that the physician and the client are addressing different priorities and with this, it is unlikely that good communication will ensure in the process.

## THE DOCTOR/CLIENT RELATIONSHIP

The doctor/client relationship does not just " happen". Both physician and patient go through a process of relating to one another, each negotiating for certain conditions, carrying out agreed-on tasks and then disengaging from the relationship. The entire process may take place in a few minutes, such as when a client is given a series of X-rays, or it may last through months of testing or treatment. (Purtilo, 1990)

In most cases, clients initiate the first medical encounter, but the purpose of the meeting may be different for the client than for the physician. While the client may seek the services of the doctor to get relief from pain or discomfort, the doctor on the other hand, may see the purpose of the medical encounter to reach an accurate diagnosis and /or prescribe appropriate treatment procedure.

There are a number of important features of the relationship between doctor and client including the client's trust and confidence in the physician and the autonomy of the client. Illnesses that lead people to seek help are more often than not, accompanied by anxiety, feelings of helplessness and disruption in the client's normal relationships with those around him. Illness can evoke fears of financial troubles or occupational difficulties; sometimes illness is provoked by such or similar stresses. The client can come to the doctor bearing not merely the symptoms of a particular illness but considerable worry about possible causes and effects. Mixed up with such worries is hope that something can be done and that not merely will health be restored, but so too will the client's ability to cope and control his life once more. The ability of the doctor to be aware of and cue into the client's anxiety suggests to the client that he is in the hands of a true professional. Merely for the doctor to acknowledge the possibility of anxiety on the client can help. Conversely, any suggestion of lack of time, impatience, lack of sympathy insensitivity to how the client is feeling at the outset of the interview can undermine the subsequent relationship in a grievous way.

The nature of the doctor/ client relationship varies. Szasz and Hollender have described three types: activity-passivity, guidance-cooperation and mutual participation. The degree of participation and the feeling of autonomy on the part of the client are the two main variables in these three types of relationship (Clare, 1991)

In the **activity/passivity** type of relationship, the doctor exploits all the authority and control inherent in his status while the patient experiences and wields no autonomy. The client does not actively participate in the treatment, but accepts what is decided. Such an arrangement is appropriate in emergency situations in which rapid decisions of a professional kind have to be made and implemented, but it is highly inappropriate when diagnosis interviewing, data gathering and treatment are involved. The activity/passivity model of interviewing involves the doctor asking all the questions and the client is answering them in a model that closely resembles legal cross-examination in a courtroom. It is an approach, which may be all very well when a doctor is struggling to establish a set of facts such as the doctor is trying to establish how a client is feeling.

In the **guidance-cooperation** type of doctor/client relationship, the doctor still wields considerable authority but the client experiences a greater degree of personal autonomy and is able to participate somewhat more actively. This approach, while more effective in putting the client at ease, still restricts the agenda of the discussion to what the doctor wants. The client's desire to please the doctor may still lead to a partial account of problems. For example, the doctor may focus on a particular set of symptoms and indicate to the client that he has all the time in the world to discuss these. However, while the client may feel that there is another symptoms altogether which worries him more, or which he feels is for some other reason more important, he, nonetheless, keeps it to himself because it does not appear to figure on the doctor's agenda for discussion. The client is indeed required to collaborate and actively participate in this relationship model but the terms of the relationship are still laid down by the doctor.

The **mutual participation** is usually the most desirable for the interview leading towards a diagnosis, for the management of chronic and disabling illnesses and for the resolution of anxiety and tension related to the interview itself. In this model, doctors and client are expected to behave as active participants and to exercise personal responsibility; and the clients are encouraged to feel some responsibility for the successful completion of the interview. The doctor has to acknowledge the reality of his professional status and authority if only to make explicit to the client that they are of very much less importance in the interview setting given the nature of the aims of the interview and its desired outcome.

Depending on the purpose of the interview, the circumstances in which it is carried out and factors relating to the client's problems, these three relationships will be variously exploited. It is one of the tasks of a physician to be able to establish a doctor/ client relationship or modify an existing one so that its characteristics are appropriate for the client to resolve conflicts and difficulties within it. In what ways do expectations affect the doctor/client relationship? Clare (1991) noted that:

> In general, patients expect doctors to be interested, compassionate, reassuring, sensitive and skilful. If patient are particularly distressed, they are exceptionally vulnerable and their expectations of care and compassion are the more intense. There is the expectation too that the culmination of the interview will bring some feeling of relief as well as the absence of discomfort or pain. Doctors should attend to such expectations and where it is feasible they should attempt to fulfil them. Where the doctor identifies unrealistic expectations (of, for example, a dramatic cure when what is being presented is a chronic, intractable problem), he should acknowledge the gap and encourage the client to examine the discrepancy between ideal and reality. Open and frank discussions about treatment and prognosis are usually helpful, but in most instances, can only be undertaken with confidence and safety if some degree of trust and confidence between doctor and client has already been established.

## The Consultation

In undertaking a clinical interview, there are a variety of tasks the doctor must attend to. According to Clare (1991), these include:

- *Having a rough plan of the interview:* It is useful if the doctor has a rough plan of the interview: in his mind, a plan that can be quickly modified in the light of what the client reveals.
- *Persuading the client to talk:* This requires that the doctor provides the time and the opportunity for even the most timid or suspicious client to begin to articulate the problem.
- *Controlling and guiding the client with encouragement and appropriate questioning:* Any tendency on the part of the client garrulousness, over-inclusiveness, obsessional reporting or circumstantialities should be gently curbed.
- *Recording the salient features of the interview:* Occasionally, it may be helpful to report verbatim what the client says, but usually, a summary is sufficient. However, the doctor needs to avoid seeming to pay more attention to the need to record the client's problems rather than to attend to them.
- *Arriving at a diagnosis:* Usually, the doctor has to come to some conclusion concerning what the client has told him. Insofar as there is uncertainty, it may be necessary to indicate this or at least to make clear that further information may be required by way of, for example, physician examination, laboratory tests, third-party interviews, access to other notes, etc.
- *Summarising and making decisions on treatment:* At the conclusion of the interview, the client expect a summary of the findings. In most instances, this will require not merely information about what is wrong, but what the prognosis is and what treatment is required. Some clients, however, do not want to know about the diagnosis and prognosis, while others, in contrast, will want as much information as possible. What the doctor needs to discover is the client's wishes in this regard, and it may be necessary for the doctor to seek this information on a number of occasions in the interview and not just once.

The discussion should be clear and straightforward. The significance of any findings should be clarified. If there are areas of uncertainty, it may be necessary to admit to these. It is important, however that client is not overloaded with information and the doctor should be very alert to any indications that the client is not attentive to or has misunderstood. Many clients consider it impolite or inappropriate to interrupt the doctor for clarification on what they did not understand. It can be helpful to ask the client to summarise what he has been told which quickly reveals the extent to which what has been said was understood.

*Eliciting the client's feelings:* Throughout the interview, the doctor should be sensitive to how the client is feeling. When a client does express feelings, the doctor should be quick to provide support. It is unwise to challenge a client's feeling save in the most extreme circumstances (e.g. when what is said appears to conflict with how the client appears or behaves). The doctor should resist the temptation to argue with client about feelings of anger, despair, resentment, rejection, etc, a temptation which can be very pressing if the doctor feels threatened, criticised or attacked by what the client is saying. Indicating empathy with revealed feelings suggests to the client that the doctor understands what is going on and such reassurance is important, particularly if the client has been anticipating rejection or bewilderment. Some clients are reluctant to reveal feelings lest they be ridiculed or dismissed. Indeed, one way of encouraging client to be more forthcoming is to acknowledge how difficult it can be to reveal feelings of anxiety of self-consciousness. Some of those clients who are most fearful or anxious find it particularly difficult to ask questions and may need help to relax first. Often, the less information somebody already has about a condition or treatment, the less he ask for.

## Problem Situation

The doctor/ client relationship tends to elicit attitudes and behaviour, which reflects previous relationships with figures in authority including other doctors, teachers or parents. The more sick, helpless and vulnerable the client feels, the more likely his behaviour will reflect these attitudes. For example, a client who has had an ambivalent and competitive relationship with his father may react to the doctor in the same way even though the doctor has done nothing to provoke such a reaction. Thus, the interaction between doctor and client can become highly charged with emotions and this in turn can seriously affect the behaviour of both doctor and client. Some of the common responses that cause problems for the doctor include silence, over-talkativeness, seductiveness, suspicion, anger and aggressive behaviour, and passive dependent behaviour.

### General Points

Most of the problems that surround the consultation can be eased if attention is paid to some basic points. The position adopted by the doctor *vis-à-vis* the client for example, is important. Face-to-face meetings across a table are often perceived as more competitive and confrontational than seating arrangements which have doctor and client sitting at right angles, perhaps across the corner of a table. Distance between doctor and client is also important. Too close suggests intrusion of body space and therefore threat while too distant suggests coolness and uninvolvement. There are often cultural differences in relation to body spaces and these can lead to misunderstanding.

Certain postures such as leaning forward from time to time, head nodding and maintaining a reasonable amount of eye-to-eye contact help the client sees his doctor as warm, empathic and involved. Conversely, if the doctor does not look interested, or maintains poor eye contact or maintains a formal and detached manner, client may find it difficult to discuss intimate matters or to relax and communicate freely and effectively. But sometimes too, intense eye contact can deter client from talking freely, and experience suggests that the doctor busying himself with some aspect of the physical examination can enable the client to talk about an embarrassing matter, such as sexual worry, etc. which would otherwise be difficult to express.

## FACILITATING EFFECTIVE COMMUNICATION

There are a number of factors which can affect the patterns of doctor/client communication. Of particular importance are the methods by which a doctor can facilitate effective communication. These help to elicit as accurately as possible in the limited time available the information needed to make a diagnosis and plan treatment while giving the client adequate opportunity to express his feelings. Whatever the nature of the verbal exchanges, the client's body language, which is likely to convey information of its own, must be carefully observed throughout.

## Vocabulary

The doctor should ask questions in clear, unambiguous language suitable to the client's age, education and cultural background. The information often gained during the introductory phase of the interview about the client's general background will be of assistance. Unsuitable language whether in vocabulary, accent or overformal style, can regrettably inhibit rather than facilitate dialogue. The vocabulary chosen should not include technical term or unfamiliar words. If the doctor senses that the client is hesitating for want of suitable vocabulary, he should attempt to include the needed non-technical words in his questions. This applies especially to enquiries about sexual function. When the doctor supplies in a comfortable, open way, suitable, simple but explicit words describing sexual functions, this does more to facilitate discussion than merely providing a vocabulary. (Myerscough, 1992).

The client can follow the purpose and direction of the doctor's enquiries more readily if the pattern of questions follows some logical grouping and sequence. Topics that the client may feel sensitive about should usually be introduced in the latter part of an interview when confidence and rapport have been established. Again, they should wherever possible, form part of a logical sequences of related enquiries.

## Ways of Facilitating Effective Communication

### *Non-verbal*

An unhurried manner is a basic and essential way of conveying the message 'I have time to listen'. While listening, the doctor can nod attentively (but nod off!). He should not be afraid to smile, since smiling is often best way of conveying reassurance, understanding, acceptance and warmth. If the client pauses, the doctor may lower his eyes for a moment without looking away and then look back at the client's face, signalling 'Go on'. At a certain point, it is helpful to discard pen and notes in an obvious way, and push them to one side, perhaps adding 'so tell me more about...' referring to a more sensitive topic that has not yet been ventilated adequately, and about which the doctor feels there is more to be said. If what seems a delicate question has to be posed, it can help to lean forward towards the client, underlining the intimacy and confidentiality of the conversation.

As the client talks, the doctor is not just a passive observer, but is 'actively' listening by using appropriate body language; hearing not only what the client says, but how he says it; noting the tone of his voice, his choice of word, expressions and gestures.

Appropriate use of touch can be of help to convey concern, reassurance and encouragement, particularly when dealing with the frail, the fearful or the depressed. A brief contact on the back of the hand or forearm (which is the least threatening areas) will sometimes be enough. The gentleness used during clinical touching will also convey a message.

***Speech***

A variety of simple and short responses from the doctor will encourage the client to continue speaking, especially if accompanied by a brief smile: 'Yes, I see', 'Go on', I understand' or sometimes 'I don't quite follow you', inviting the client to give a fuller account.

***Reflection***

Somewhat similarly, but more positively, the doctor can encourage the client to continue speaking by repeating, and so reflecting back to him, a phrase, idea or significant word from what the client has just said. By picking up a word from or expression in this way, the client is prompted to express himself further.

***Clarification***

This term is used to describe another ploy, which helps to make clear to the client what he is trying to put into words, and also allows the doctor to check on his own tentative deductions:

> You seem to be saying that, since the pains began, you not only gradually lose your appetite, but also lose interest in all kinds of everyday activities. Is that correct?

### *Summary*

It can also be very helpful, particularly when the history is long and complicated, to attempt at some point to summarise all or part of the client's account of things. This recapitulation must be done tentatively, getting the client to corroborate the more important details, otherwise, there is the danger that a compliant client may accept the doctor's version of the history, which could reflect more of the doctor's preconceived ideas than what actually happened.

### *Appropriate Use of Silence*

One of the anxieties of the inexperienced student or doctor is that he will dry up during the interview; or run out of questions, and an embarrassing silence will open up, creating discomfort and disrupting communication. In contrast, an easy interview often seems to flow along in sustained dialogue with barely a pause. The learner can avoid an undesirable hiatus of his own making by having in reserve one or two fill-in questions that cannot be answered very briefly (e.g. a question about the client's childhood or about other family members) but which have some loose relevance to the presenting symptoms. One of these questions can be thrown in when such a silence threatens. While the client is answering, the questioner can pick up the threads and poise himself for his next line of enquiry

## Obstacles to Effective Communication

Myerscough (1992) has identified four major obstacles to effective communication in hospital/clinical setting. The obstacles so identified are:

### (1) *The Problem of Time*

The time for an interview varies from doctor to doctor, and from day to day. The conduct of the interview is bound to be influenced by this constraint, but the doctor must not let the pressure of time affect his interviewing style in a way that inhibits open communication. In contemporary hospital practice, more rapid turnover in the wards, the growth of high-tech, high-dependency care and expanding day-case care have all progressively increased the pressure on staff. Doctors and nurses alike are often short of time to watch over, as well as monitor clients, and may be, at times, short of sleep. The quest for cost efficiency itself involves many obstacles to effective communication.

In general practice and in some busy hospital clinics, the average time available for a client may be only five to ten minutes, although a little more time is often allocated to "new" client. In a less pressured general medical clinic, thirty minutes or more might be available, and most psychiatrist doctors prefer to spend a full hour with a new client. In each of these settings, therefore, a different pace and style of interviewing has to be adopted.

Obviously, the shape of an interview depends largely on whether it is a first consultation or a renewal of contact in the courses of continuing care. For instance, in many general practice consultations, the doctor already knows much that he has learnt about the client in previous contacts. The doctor should try to appear unhurried and ready to listen, even when time is limited. Any evidence that he is short of time is likely to be spotted by the client who will then be less willing to open up. If the client enters the room to find the doctor hurriedly completing case notes or pathology forms, or dashing through a phone call; or if the doctor hustles the nurse or remain standing, jumps straight to the presenting complaint; the interview will be constricted by a sense of haste. It can be seen that 98 percent of clients in general practice and 70 percent in private hospital consultations took less than two minutes to describe their complaints. Even in hospital consultations, only one client in five needed four minutes or more (Myerscough).

Using selective questions, the skill and experience of the practitioner pay dividend, through his ability to formulate a logical sequence of enquiries that leads via the least number of diagnostic steps, towards a presumptive diagnosis. The learner needs to remind himself repeatedly that medical diagnosis is in very many instances a statement of probability, rather than the elucidation of an absolute truth. One could spend half a lifetime looking for certainty, but medical decisions are always constrained by time.

On occasion, an over-talkative client will begin to take an inordinate amount of time, embarking on a sequence of irrelevant items of gossip. The client may be a lonely character, for whom a visit to the doctor can provide a wonderful conversational outlet full of reminiscence, or he may be a born talker who turns every encounter into a self-centred monologue. The doctor, listening patiently, may detect features of obsession or anxiety, manipulative fiction, or the stale smell of alcohol.

In such encounter, the doctor has to draw his own lines, in a responsible way, between therapeutic listening and unproductive time-wasting. If he feels that the client's rambling loquacity is seriously wasting his time, he should attempt to maintain control of the dialogue without losing the client's confidence.

### (2) *The Problem of Pain, Suffering and Death*

Doctors need some protective insulation from the emotional distress that can be generated by the pain, suffering, death and bereavement encountered in the course of clinical work. They, therefore, need to develop an understanding of how these influences, and that of death in particular, affect communication. Although death is the one certainty in each of our futures, the common lot of all humanity, it is something which people are reluctant to contemplate or to discuss.

To detach themselves from the painful feelings associated with serious illness and death, doctors may elect, almost unconsciously, to avoid eliciting from their clients expression of any distressing feelings, and may be inclined, therefore, to adopt a rather distant and impersonal attitude in clinical work generally. Maguire (1989) described the following ploys, which doctors may use to distance themselves from their clients' feelings.

- Restricting the focus of discussion to non-emotive topics.
- Diverting the focus of discussion away from possibly emotive topics.
- Playing down the feelings as 'normal'.
- Blanketing the client with over-reassurance.
- Using leading questions and pre-empting the replies.
- Jollying the patient along, with platitudes and clichés.

Specifically, they can often find the utmost difficulty in speaking honestly with the client whose illness is likely to be mortal. In many instances, they may have recourse to evasion, silence, half-truths, or even deliberate deception. The assumptions that underlie these behaviours run as follows: People do not want to die, therefore, they do not want to know that they are dying. They could not tolerate being told that they are not dying, nor do they recognise that they are dying.

The consequences of this unwillingness to acknowledge the moment of truth that mortal illnesses almost inevitably bring are usually disastrous for the doctor/ client relationship. Confidence, trust and rapport are likely to melt away, and cannot subsequently be restored. The client's close relatives may be taken aside and given a true account of the client's condition, but made accomplices in the attempt to deceive. When they in turn later become clients, they already know how the pretence is staged. In this way, a doctor can in large measure destroy his ability to reassure those clients whose illnesses are not in fact serious, for his word is no longer regarded as trustworthy.

Death and suffering remains tragic enigmas of the human condition. But doctors have a special need to come to terms with these emotive experiences and not to allow their professional caring role to be diminished because they feel uncomfortable when confronted with the prospect of death. Specifically, doctors in training for clinical practice should make it their business to acquire the skill used in the care of the dying and the bereaved. To achieve this, they have to overcome resistances within themselves, while at the same time, learning more about the physical needs of the dying: the relief of intractable pain, vomiting dyspnoea, or other physical distress; the pattern of emotional reaction during terminal illness; and the most appropriate language to use when facing the insecurity of clients and the anxiety of relatives.

### (3) *The Problem of Sexuality*

One of the basic requirements in clinical settings is that the physical intimacy of clinical examination has to be professionalised, and so rendered safe for both clients and doctors. In effect, this means that clinical contacts have to be dissociated from sexual connotations or feelings, which, in other settings, might be evoked by nakedness and intimate touching. In consequence, the client can feel at ease and secure, and the doctor is not exposed to disturbing or intolerable feelings.

This neutralisation of sexual feelings and reactions is not something affecting only the doctor. Equally important is the client's perception of the correctness of the professional relationship, – how secure he or she feels. This is influenced by the client's cultural background. There is little teaching in medical schools about how to desexualise the nudity and intimate touching encountered in clinical work and the subject is rarely discussed. Perhaps the topic is thought too sensitive to be aired, and it is hoped that, by not giving the matter any consideration, it will assume less significance, so that clinical work will cease to have a sexual connotation.

Several features of the doctor's style and behaviour help to bring about this desexualisation: formal clothing (in hospital, often a white coat); a serious demeanour; formal correctness of address; and a detached manner, giving no indication of any affective response to the intimacy of clinical contact. These trappings of professionally 'correct' behaviour may still not provide enough protection for some doctors, who might feel over-conscious of their good name and of the need to avoid the faintest imputation of familiarity; or who may find it genuinely difficult to rid the clinical relationship of all sexual connotations. Such individuals may, perhaps unconsciously, find it necessary to exclude any thought or discussion of the client's sexuality from the clinical situation. But in a more general way, because of this wish not to be 'too personal', some doctors may therefore find it difficult to discuss the client's close relationships and feelings at all. As consequence, the client may be seen in a rather narrow, disturbed perspective which more or less ignores the social context of his ill health. The doctor's lack of insight can, at the worst, produce a situation in which his relationship with the client is not only desexualised, but also virtually dehumanised. It has become 'clinical' in the very worst sense of the word.

### (4) *The Problem of the Doctor's Anxieties*

Another group of factors that can inhibit effective communication between client and doctor are doctors' personal anxieties arising in the context of their professional work. It is not very difficult for a student to recognise and understand how a client's anxieties may influence the way he behaves. A similar mechanism can also affect doctors. Van Beukesom (1973) gave an excellent description of the influence of anxiety on doctor-client communication. Following his account, doctors' anxieties are liable to extend into the three main areas as explained below.

*Anxiety about Inadequacy or Failure*

When embarking on the practice of medicine, young doctors naturally feel rather insecure, if only because of their lack of experience. Confidence in one's professional skill and judgment grows gradually and at varying rates in different individuals, but some people compensate for the uncertainties of self-doubt and bolster a shaky confidence by adopting a rather pompous distant professional style. An authoritative, brusque manner can help to ensure that the doctor dominates the consultation, and make it likely that he is exposed to questioning that might reveal him not to be the clever, capable person he wishes to appear. As a consequence, he seems very unapproachable to the client, and the aura of infallible competence that he carefully maintains makes it much more difficult for patients to expose their own emotional vulnerability to him.

It is easy for doctors to labour under the false belief that clients expect them always to have answers to their problems and cure for their ills. Of course, most doctors aspire to help their clients, and can therefore be reluctant to have to admit 'I don't know' or 'there is nothing more I can do'. As van Beukeson put it, doctors who adopt an aura of infallibility readily rationalised and justify their behaviour with assertions that 'The doctor must become high-priest of modern times'. But doctors' professional wish not to fail their clients can unfortunately become a barrier to honesty, openness and, eventually, trust.

*Anxiety about Clients' Emotional Reactions*

Doctors can feel seriously inhibited from mentioning topics that clients might be 'touchy' about, including such varies subjects as taking more responsibility for an aging demented client, previous termination of pregnancy, and thoughts of suicide. Other questions that might need to be raised can be deeply resented and make the client quite angry. These are matters such as infidelity, possible child abuse, homosexuality, incest and the possibility that a skin rash might be factitious.

A student or less experienced doctor may not have learned the least upsetting ways of posing 'difficult' questions of this sort, but with or without this technical skill, may be desperately anxious not to evoke an angry scene. He may avoid this anxiety by never discussing 'personal' topics with clients.

Another emotional reaction from the client that a doctor may fight shy of experiencing it is the distress provoked by bad news. Doctors get considerable professional and personal satisfaction from being the bearers of good news (of cure, recovery, or a problem resolved), but there are inevitable occasions when they must act as the bearers of bad news likely to cause emotional distress, tears, bewilderment and grief. They might have to tell someone that they are permanently and seriously disabled following injury; tell a couple that their infertility is absolute; tell a pregnant woman that her unborn infant has a major malformation; and because he is the bearer of the news, the doctor may, quite wrongly, feel blameworthy, and shrink from the task, or tackle it very awkwardly (Buckman, 1984).

*Anxiety Relating to Unresolved Personal Problems*

An area of interpersonal conflict can create even more intense anxiety for a doctor if the difficulty in his client's life mirrors some unresolved problems within his own personal and family life, or some painful, distressing circumstances that he is trying to forget or keep out of his mind, or even to deny. There might, for example, be disharmony in his marriage; anxiety or conflict resulting from adolescents' children's experiments with sex, alcohol, or other drug; guilt about an extramarital affair; or an abortion. Sometimes, the doctors' personal encounters with illness, disability, or emotional distress can provide him with great insight into clients' problems, and reinforce his ability to respond empathically to client with similar misfortunes. If he gains the confidence to share his own experiences, thus self-disclosure can promote strong mutual understanding. But if the life has left him with tender emotional scars that have refused to heal, he may be professional harmstrung when a client presents him with a comparable problems (Myerscough, 1992).

The health care provider-client relationship can be improved if the following methods are incorporated into the service provided in our health institutions.

- Inculcate cultural practice of greeting
- Institute friendly tone of instructions in all interactions
- Ensure that clients understand all instructions
- Provide opportunity for questions.
- Show good response to encourage and reassure clients
- Give instruction(s) on what and or where next helpful
- Ensure that clients perception about his problem is addressed, and this implies some measure of satisfaction.

## References

Bennett, A. E. (1976). (ed). *Communication between Doctors and patients.* London: Oxford University Press.

Buckman, R .(1984). "Breaking Bad News". *British Medical Journal,* 288,597.

Clare, A. (1991). "Developing Communication and Interviewing Skills". In Corney, R.H (ed) *Developing Communication and Counselling Skills in Medicine.* London. Routledge.

Corney, R.H. (1991). (ed) *Developing Communication and Counselling Skills in Medicine.* London. Routledge.

Fishbein, M. (1976). "Persuasive Communication". In Bennett, A. E. (ed) *Communication between Doctors and Patients,* London. Oxford University Press.

Freeling, P. and Harris C.M. (1984). *The Doctor-Patient Relationship.* 3rd edition. Edinburgh. Longman Group Limited.

Fletcher, C.M. (1973). "Communication in Medicine," *Rock Carling Monograph*. London; Nuffield Provincial Hospital Trust.

Maguire, P. (1989). In *Psychological Management of the Physically Ill.* (Lacey & Burns (ed). P. 193-212 Church – Livingstone, Edinburgh.

Myerscough, P.R. (1992). *Talking with Patients: A Basic Clinical Skill.* 2nd edition. New York: Oxford University Press.

Purtilo, R.B. (1990). *Health Professional and Patient Interaction.* 4th edition. Philadelphia. Harcourt Brace Jovanovich, Inc.

Van Beukesom, J.A.H. (1973). "Anxiety Factors in Comprehensive Patient Care". *Excerpta Medical*: 26-31.

*Chapter 5*

# FORMULATION AND IMPLEMENTATION OF STRATEGIC MANAGEMENT IN HEALTH CARE ORGANISATIONS: AN INDUSTRIAL SOCIOLOGIST'S PERSPECTIVE

*Ogunbameru, O.A.*

**About the Contributor**

Dr Olakunle Ogunbameru is currently a Reader, and he teaches Industrial Sociology, Social Research and Social Gerontology at the Department of Sociology and Anthropology, Obafemi Awolowo University, Ile-Ife. He has published extensively numerous articles both in national and international journals. He has also written many books including his latest book, *Organisational Dynamics*.

## INTRODUCTION

In this chapter, the formulation and implementation of strategic management in health care organisations are broadly examined. The discussion starts with the conceptual clarification of certain basic concepts. Following this is lucid explanation on the formulation and implementation of strategic management with specific reference to health care organisations. Finally, the relevance of creating policies that empower as well as the relevance of leadership and culture to strategic management are adequately discussed.

## CONCEPTUAL CLARIFICATION

For a clear understanding of this chapter, the following five basic concepts are briefly defined: strategy, management, strategic management, organisation and health care organisation.

**Strategy:** A strategy is a company's game plan involving future-oriented plan for interacting with the competitive environment to achieve a company's objectives. It reflects a company's awareness of *how*, *when*, and *where* it should compete, against whom and for what purpose.

**Management:** Management refers to the process of achieving organisational goals by engaging in the four major functions of planning, organising, leading and controlling.

**Strategic Management:** For the purpose of this chapter, Pearce and Robinson's definition of strategic management is adopted. The duo define *strategic management* as "the set of decisions and actions that result in the formulation and implementation of plans designed to achieve a company's objectives". This is made up of nine critical tasks, namely:

1. Formulate the company's mission including broad statements about its purpose, philosophy, and goals.
2. Conduct an analysis that reflects the company's internal conditions and capabilities.
3. Assess the company's external environment, including both the competitive and general contextual factors.
4. Analyse the company's options by matching its resources with the external environment.
5. Identify the most desirable options by evaluating each option in light of the company's mission.
6. Select a set of long-term objectives and grand strategies that will achieve the most desirable options.
7. Develop annual objectives and short-term strategies that are compatible with the selected set of long-term objectives and grand strategies.

8. Implement the strategic choices by means of budgeted resource allocations in which the matching of tasks, people, structures, technologies and reward systems are emphasised.
9. Evaluate the success of the strategic process as an input for future decision-making.

**Organisation:** An organisation can easily be defined as a collection of people who with consciously-coordinated efforts pursue and contribute to the attainment of a common purpose.

**Health Care Organisation:** Health care organisation refers to the coming together of people for the provision of medical skills to benefit patients.

The subject of strategic management is the positioning of the firm in its broadest sense – its relationship with its customers, suppliers and competitors (Kuper and Kuper, 1999:846). Strategic management was first recognised as a subject in the early 1960s. It originated from the integrative management courses taught at the Harvard Business School, and in such works as Ansoff (1965) and Andrews (1980).

The health care organisation is usually represented by the hospital. A hospital can simply be defined as an institution for the treatment of the sick and the injured. It can also be used to refer to an institutional provider of general medical and surgical services. Hospitals must have physician staff, continuous medical and nursing cares to patients, and maintain inpatient facilities.

## CLASSIFICATION OF HOSPITALS

The classification of hospitals may be based on the following factors: ownership, length of stay and the nature of service offered. On ownership, one needs to consider whether it is owned by government (public hospital), or by a private individual, or by multinational bodies. With respect to length of stay, consideration is focused on the following: outpatients, inpatients, day care hospitals, and outpatients and inpatients hospitals combined. Classification of hospitals on the nature of service offered fall into the following categories:

**Obstetrics and Gynaecology Hospital:**Medical science outfit which deals with the care of pregnant women or the diseases and disorder of women, especially the organs of reproduction.

**Dental Hospital**: Its services have to do with the prevention, diagnosis and treatment of deformities, pathology and traumatic injuries of oral-facial complex.

**Neurology Hospital**: This sees to the study and treatment of the structure, function and diseases of the nervous system.

**Psychiatric Hospital** :It deals with the study and treatment of mental disorders.

**Orthopaedic Hospital:** It focuses on the treatment and cure of bodily deformities, especially in children.

Hospitals can also be classified on the levels of medical care. The three major classifications are primary, secondary and tertiary. **Primary** level refers to the medical care of a patient at the initial stage and place where the patient is present. **Secondary** level refers to the medical care of a patient by a physician acting as a consultant. The provider of primary medical care usually refers the patient to this level of care. **Tertiary** level refers to the medical care of patient in medical facilities, adequately staffed and equipped to administer comprehensive care.

## STRATEGIC MANAGEMENT AND HEALTH CARE ORGANISATION

Writers on strategic management commonly distinguish three phases of the process. First, the application of the internal and external environment within which the firm operates. Secondly, the choice of a strategy to match that environment, and finally, the implementation of the preferred strategy within the firm (Kuper and Kuper, 1999).

In addition to the management of the internal activities of a health care organisation, the modern executives must also respond to the challenges posed by the firm's immediate and remote external environments. The components of the immediate and remote external environments of an organisation are shown in figure 5.1 below.

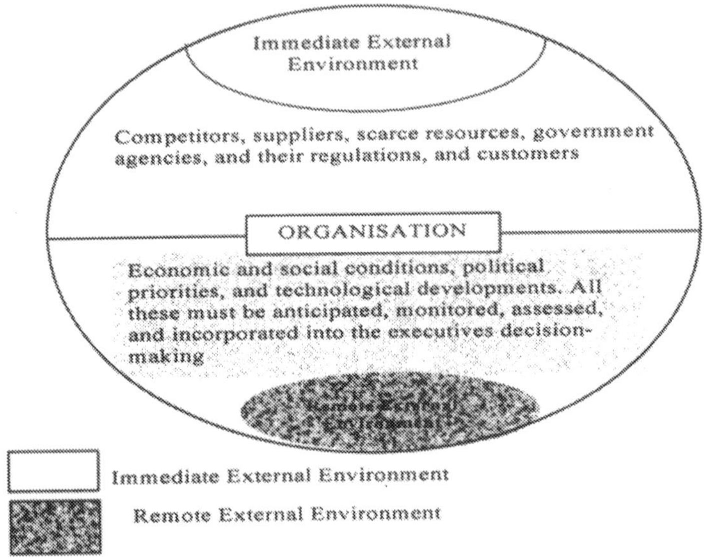


**Fig. 5.1: Immediate and Remote External Environments of an Organisation**

The key components of strategic management are: company mission, internal analysis, structural analysis and choice, long-term objectives, generic and grand strategies, functional restructuring, reengineering, and refocusing the organisation; and structural control and continuous improvement (see figure 5.2)

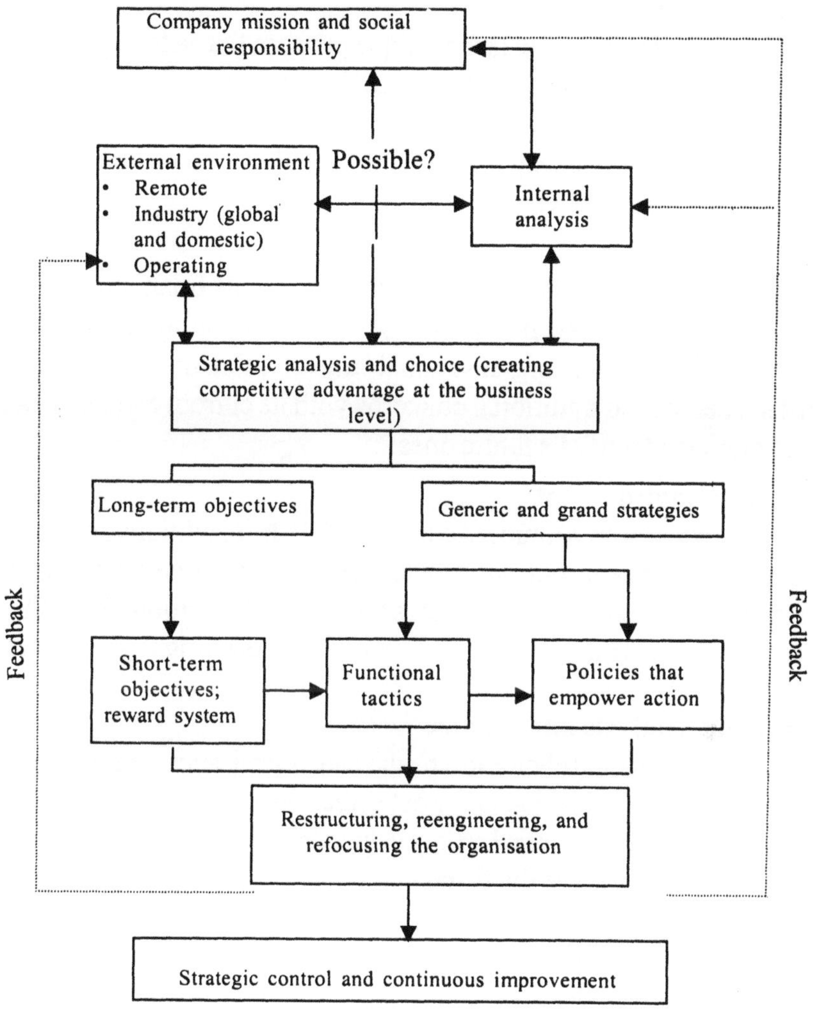


**Fig. 5.2: Strategic Management Model**

**Source**: Pearce, J.A. and R.B. Robinson, Jr. *Strategic Management: Formulation, Implementation, and Control*. Irwin McGraw-Hill, Boston, 2000:12.

**Company Mission**

The mission of a company is the unique purpose that sets it apart from other companies of its type and identifies the scope of its operations. The mission describes the company's product, market and technological areas of emphasis in a way that reflects the values and priorities of the strategic decision-makers.

**Internal Analysis**

A company analyses the quantity and quality of its financial, human, and physical resources. It also assesses the strengths and weaknesses of its management and organisational structure. Finally, it contrasts its past successes and traditional concerns with its current capabilities in an attempt to identify its future ones.

**External Environment**

A firm's external environment consists of all the conditions and forces that affect its strategic options and defines its competitive situation. The strategic management model shows the external environment as three interactive segments: the remote, industry and operating environments.

**Strategic Analysis and Choice**

Strategic analysis and choice in a health care organisation centres around identifying strategies that are most effective at building sustainable competitive advantage based on key value chain activities and capabilities – core competencies of the firm.

**Long-Term Objectives**

The results that an organisation seeks over a multi-year period are its *long-term objectives*. Such objectives typically involve some or all of the following areas: profitability, return on investment, competitive position, technological leadership, productivity, employee relations, public responsibility and employee development.

**Generic and Grand Strategies**

Many businesses including health care organisations explicitly and implicitly adopt one or more *generic strategies* characterising their competitive orientation in the marketplace. Low cost, differentiation, or focus strategies define the three fundamental options. Enlightened managers seek to create ways for their firms to possess both low cost and differentiation competitive advantages as part of their overall generic strategy. The chief executive of a health care organisation, for example, combines these capabilities with a comprehensive general plan of major actions through which the organisation intends to achieve its long-term objectives in a dynamic environment. Called the *grand strategy*, this statement of means indicates how the objectives are to be achieved. Although every grand strategy is, in fact, a unique package of long-term strategies, in which fourteen basic approaches can be identified, namely: concentration, market development, product development, innovation, horizontal integration, vertical integration, joint venture, strategic alliances, consortial, concentric diversification, conglomerate diversification, turnaround, diverstiture and liquidation.

**Action Plans and Short-Term Objectives**

Action plans translate generic and grand strategies into "action" by incorporating four elements. First, they identify specific functional *tactics* and *actions* to be undertaken in the succeeding week, month, or quarter as part of the business's effort to build competitive advantage. The second element is a clear timeframe for completion. Thirdly, action plans create accountability by identifying who is responsible for each "action" in the plan. Fourthly, each "action" in the action plans has one or more specific, immediate objectives that are identified as outcomes that action should generate.

**Functional Tactics**

*Functional tactics* are detailed statements of the "means" or activities that will be used to achieve short-term objectives and establish competitive advantage.

**Policies that Empower Action**

*Policies* are broad, precedent-setting decisions that guide or substitute for repetitive or time-sensitive managerial decision-making. Creating policies that guide and "pre-authorise" the thinking, decisions and actions of operating managers and their subordinates in implementing the business's strategy is essential for establishing and controlling the ongoing operating process of the firm in a manner consistent with the firm's strategic objectives. Policies often increase managerial effectiveness by standardising routine decisions and empowering or expanding the discretion of managers and subordinates in implementing business strategies.

## Restructuring, Reengineering and Refocusing the Organisation

*Downsizing, restructuring and reengineering* are terms that reflect the critical stage in strategy implementation wherein executives attempt to recast their organisation. The company's structure, leadership, culture, and reward systems may all be changed to ensure cost competitiveness and quality demanded by unique requirements of its strategies.

Simply put, *organisational downsizing* refers to a set of voluntary activities, undertaken on the part of the management of an organisation, designed to reduce costs (M. Warmer, 1999). It is an intentionally-instituted set of activities designed to improve organisational efficiency and performance which more often affect the costs, or technological costs of an organisation (O.A. Ogunbameru, 2003).

*Reengineering* is so popular in organisations today because of the changing global environment and organisation structures that have gotten too heavy. Reengineering involves radical redesign of work to combine fragmented tasks into streamlined processes that save time and money. In a simple form, reengineering is the fundamental rethinking and radical redesign of business processes to achieve dramatic improvements in critical, contemporary measures of performance, such as cost, quality, service and speed. In the words of T.H. Berry (1991):

> Reengineering means that management should start with a clean sheet of paper – rethinking and redesigning those processes by which the organisation creates value and does work, voiding itself of operations that have become antiquated in the computer age.

## Strategic Control and Continuous Improvement

*Strategic control* is concerned with tracking a strategy as it is being implemented, detecting problems or changes in its underlying premises and making necessary adjustments. In contrast to post-action control, strategic control seeks to guide action on behalf of the generic and grand strategies as they are taking place and when the end results are still several years away. The rapid accelerating change of the global marketplace of the last one decade has made continuous improvement another aspect of strategic control in many organisations. *Continuous improvement* will provide a way for managers of health care organisations to provide a form of strategic control that allows their organisations to respond more proactively and timely to rapid developments in hundreds of areas that influence business's success.

## STRATEGIC MANAGEMENT FORMULATION

Generally, *strategic formulation* guides executives in defining the kinds of business their firms are involve, the ends they seeks, and the means they will use to accomplish those ends. It should be noted that structural formulation combines a future-oriented perspective with concern for the firm's internal and external environments.

The strategy formulation process begins with definition of the company's mission. A company is expected to determine the basic goals and philosophies that will shape its structural posture. The fundamental purpose that sets a firm apart from other firms of its type and identifies the scope of its operation in produce and market terms is defined as the company mission. It embodies the business philosophy of the firm's principal product or service areas of the primary customer, and the needs the firm will attempt to satisfy. Simply put, it describes the firm's product, market and technological areas of emphasis and it does so in a way that reflects the values and priorities of the firm's strategic decision-makers.

A company's mission is designed to accomplish seven outcomes:

1. To ensure unanimity of purpose within the organisation,
2. To provide a basis for motivating the use of the organisation's resources,
3. To develop a basis, or standard, for allocating organisational resources,

4. To establish a general tone or organisational climate; for example, to suggest a businesslike operation,
5. To serve as a focal point for those who cannot do so from participating further in its activities,
6. To facilitate the translation of objectives and goals into a work structure involving the assignment of tasks to responsible elements within the organisation, and
7. To specify organisational purposes and the translation of these purposes into goals in such a way that cost, time and performance parameters can be assessed and controlled (King, W.R. and D.O. Cleland, 1978:24).

**The External Environment**

The external factors that influence a firm's choice of direction and action, and its organisational structure and internal processes, can be divided into three interrelated categories: factors in the *remote* environment, factors in the *economic* environment (concern the nature and direction of the economy in which a firm operates); *social* factors (beliefs, values, attitudes, opinions, and lifestyles of person in the firm's environment); and *political* factors. The direction and stability of political factors is a major consideration for managers on formulating parameters within which the firm operates. In addition to these are the technological and ecological factors.

*Technological* factors: To avoid obsolescence and promote innovation, a health care organisation must be aware of technological changes that might influence its performance. Creative technological adaptations can suggest possibilities for new products, for improvements in existing products, or in manufacturing and marketing techniques.

*Ecological* factors: *Ecology* refers to the relationships among human beings and other living things and the air, soil, and water that support them. Environmental legislation impacts corporate strategies worldwide. Thus, many companies fear the consequences of highly restrictive and costly environmental regulations.

Based on the factors enumerated above, modern executives now realise that business concerns including health care organisations can no longer ignore environmental factors. Every activity is linked to thousands of other transactions and their environmental impacts; therefore, corporate environmental responsibility must be taken seriously and environmental policy must be implemented to ensure a comprehensive organisational strategy.

**International Environment**

Factors used in assessing international environment are: economic, political, legal and cultural (see figure 5.3)

| **Economic Environment** | **Political System** |
|---|---|
| Level of economic development<br>Population<br>Gross national product<br>Per capita income<br><br>Literacy level<br>Social infrastructure<br>Natural resources<br><br>Climate<br>Membership in regional economic blocs (EU, NAFTA, LAFTA)<br>Monetary and fiscal policies<br>Wage and salary levels<br>Nature of competition<br>Currency convertibility<br>Inflation<br>Taxation system<br>Interest rates | Form of government<br>Political ideology<br>Stability of government<br>Strength of opposition parties and groups<br>Social unrest<br>Political strife and insurgency<br>Governmental attitude towards foreign firms<br>Foreign policy<br><br>**Cultural Environment**<br>Customs, norms, values, beliefs<br>Language<br>Attitudes<br>Motivations<br>Social institutions<br>Status symbols<br>Religious beliefs |

| |
|---|
| **Legal Environment**<br>Legal tradition<br>Effectiveness of legal system<br>Treaties with foreign nations<br>Patent trademark laws |

**Fig. 5.3: Factors Used to Assess the International Environment**
**Source:** Adapted from Pearce, J.A. and R.B. Robinson, Jr. *Strategic Management: Formulation, Implementation, and Control (7th ed.)*. McGraw-Hill, Irwin, 2000:84

## Industry Environment

The nature and degree of competition in an industry hinge on five forces (Porter, M.E. 1979:137-145). These are: the threat of new entrants, the bargaining power of customers, the bargaining power of suppliers, the threat of substitute products or services, and the jockeying among current contestants. To establish a strategic agenda for dealing with these contending forces and to grow in spite of them, a company must understand how they work in its industry and how they affect the company in its particular situation.

## How to Identify Competitors

In identifying their firm's current and potential competitors, executives consider several important variables including the following, among others:

1. *How do other firms define the scope of their market?* The more similar the definitions of firms, the more likely the firms will view each other as competitors.
2. *How similar are the benefits the customers derive from the products that other firms offer?* The more similar the benefits of products or services, the higher the level of substitutability between them. High substitutability levels force firm to compete fiercely for customers.
3. *How committed are other firms to the industry?* Although this question may appear to be far removed from the identification of

competitors, it is in fact one of the most important questions that competitive analysis must address, because it sheds on the long-term intentions and goals. To size up the commitment of potential competitors to the industry, reliable intelligence data are needed. Such data may be related to potential resource commitments (for example, planned facility expansions).

### Common Mistakes in Identifying Competitors

Identifying competitors is a milestone in the development of strategy. But it is a process laden with uncertainty and risk, a process in which executives sometimes make costly mistakes. Examples of these mistakes are:

1. Overemphasising current and known competitors while giving inadequate action to potential entrants.
2. Overemphasising large competitors while ignoring small competitors.
3. Overlooking potential international competitors.

All these must regularly guide the executives of health care organisations in the formulation of their strategies.

## STRATEGY IMPLEMENTATION

In this section, attempt is made to examine what is often referred to as the *action phase* of the strategic management process: implementation of the chosen strategy. To ensure success, the strategy of a health care organisation must be translated into carefully-implemented action. This means that:

1. The strategy must be translated into guidelines for the daily activities of the firm's members.
2. The strategy of the firm must become one, that is, the strategy must be reflected in the way the firm organises its activities and in the firm's values, beliefs, and tone.
3. In implementing the strategy, the firm's managers must direct and control actions or outcomes and adjust to change.

## How to Successfully Initiate Organisational Action

There are four known ways to successfully initiate organisational action. These are: creating clear short-term objectives and action plans, initiating specific functional tactics, communicating policies that empower people in the organisation, and designing effective rewards.

1. *Creating clear short-term objectives and action plans.* Generally speaking, short-term objectives help in the implementation strategy in three ways by:

   (a) "operationalising" long-term objectives,

   (b) raising issues and potential conflicts within an organisation which usually require co-ordination to avoid dysfunctional consequences.

   (c) identifying measurable outcomes of action plans or functional activities which can be used to make feedback correction and evaluation more relevant and acceptable.

It should however be noted, that short-term objectives are more consistent when they state *what* is to be accomplished, *when* it will be accomplished, and *how* its accomplishment will be measured.

2. *Initiating specific functional tactics. Functional tactics* translate business strategy into daily activities people need to execute. Simply put, *functional activities* refer to the key, routine activities that must be undertaken in each functional area – marketing, finance, production/operations, research and development, and human resource management in order to produce the business products and services. In short, they translate thought (grand strategy) into action designed to accomplish specific short-term objectives.
3. *Communicating policies that empower people in the organisation. Policies* refer to empowerment tools that simplify decision-making by empowering operating managers and their subordinates. Policies can empower the "doers" in a health care organisation by reducing the time required to decide and act.

Empowerment can be created in a health care organisation in the following ways: training, self-managed work groups, elimination of whole levels of management and aggressive use of automation. The central thrust of empowerment is the need to ensure that decision-making is consistent with the mission, strategy and tactics of the business – while at the same time allowing considerable latitude to operating personnel.

This can be done through the use of policies, that is, by designing directives to guide the thinking, decisions, and actions of managers and their subordinates in implementing a firm's strategy. Policies help to increase managerial effectiveness by standardising many routine decisions and clarifying the direction managers and subordinates can take in implementing functional tactics.

## Creating Policies that Empower

Pearce and Robinson (2000:380-381) identify eight different ways by which policies are designed to control decisions while defining allowable discretion within which operational personnel can execute business activities. Health care organisations can also use these ways. These are:

1. Policies establish indirect control over independent action by clearly stating how things are to be done *now*. By defining discretion, policies in effect, control decisions yet empower employees to conduct activities without direct intervention by top management.
2. Policies promote uniform handling of similar activities. This facilitates the coordination of work tasks and helps reduce friction arising from favouritism, discrimination, and the disparate handling of common functions – something that often hampers operating personnel.
3. Policies ensure quicker decisions by standardising answers to previously-answered questions that otherwise would recur and be pushed up the management hierarchy again and again – something that requires unnecessary levels of management between senior decision-makers and field personnel.
4. Policies institutionalise basic aspects of organisation behaviour. This minimises conflicting practices and establishes consistent patterns of action in attempts to make the strategy work – again, freeing operating personnel to act.

5. Policies reduce uncertainty in repetitive and day-to-day decision-making, thereby providing a necessary foundation for coordinated, efficient efforts and freeing operating personnel to act.
6. Policies counteract resistance to or rejection of chosen strategies by organisation members. When a major strategic change is undertaken, unambiguous operating policies clarify what is expected and facilitate acceptance, particularly when operating managers participate in policy development.
7. Policies offer predetermined answers to routine problems. This greatly expedites dealing with both ordinary and extraordinary problems – with the former, by referring to these answers; with the latter, by giving operating personnel more time to cope with them.
8. Policies afford managers a mechanism for avoiding hasty and ill-conceived decisions in changing operations. Prevailing policy can always be used as a reason for not yielding to emotion-based, expedient, or temporarily valid arguments for altering procedures and practices.

**Advantages of Written Policies**

Policies may be written and formal or unwritten and informal. *Informal or unwritten* policies are associated with a strategic need for competitive secrecy. However, *written,* or *formal* policies have the following advantages:

1. They require managers to think through the policy's meaning, content, and intended use.
2. They reduce misunderstanding.
3. They make equitable and consistent treatment of problems more likely.
4. They ensure unalterable transmission of policies.
5. They communicate the authorisation or sanction of policies more clearly.
6. They supply a convenient and authoritative reference.

7. They systematically enhance indirect control and organisation wide coordination of the key purposes of policies (Pearce and Robinson, 2000:382).

**Designing Effective Rewards**

One powerful part of getting things done in any organisation which health care organisations can also use is in the way its reward system rewards desired actions and results. Rewards that align managers and employees priorities with organisational objectives and shareholders values provide very effective direction in strategic implementation.

**Implementing Strategy through Leadership and Culture**

More often, people wrongly use leadership as a synonym for management. Kotter, J. (1990) a renowned leadership expert, who has this to say about the distinction between the two, has corrected this wrong impression:

> The leadership challenge is to galvanise commitment among people within an organisation as well as stakeholders outside the organisation to embrace change and implement strategies intended to position the organisation to do so.

A leader can galvanise commitment to embrace change through three interrelated activities:

1. *Clarifying strategic intent:* This refers to an articulation of a simple criterion or characterisation of what the company must become to establish and sustain global leadership.
2. *Building an organisation:* A leader spends a considerable time shaping and refining their organisational strategy and making it function effectively to accomplish strategic intent. A leader finds himself addressing such problems as he attempts to build or rebuild his organisation.
3. *Shaping organisation structure:* Leaders must know how the values and beliefs shared throughout their organisations shape how

the work of the organisation is done. In addition, when attempting to embrace accelerated change, reshaping their organisations' culture is an activity that occupies considerable time for leaders.

Leaders should be able to use reward systems, symbols and structure to shape the organisation's culture.

**Organisational Culture**

Pearce and Robinson (2000:419) define an organisational culture as "the set of important assumptions that members of an organisation share in common". Such culture is similar to an individual's personality that provides meaning, direction, and the basis for action. Just as personality influences the behaviour of an individual, the shared assumptions (beliefs and values) among members of staff of a firm influence opinions and actions within that firm.

Leaders can help to create distinct cultures through the following variety of ways:

- Emphasising key themes or dominant values. Insightful leaders nurture key themes or dominant values within their organisations that reinforce competitive advantages they seek to maintain or build.
- Encourage dissemination of stories and legends about core values. Companies with strong cultures are enthusiastic collectors and tellers of stories, anecdotes, and legends in support of basic beliefs. These stories help in developing an organisational culture, because organisation members identify strongly with them, and come to share the beliefs and values they support.

**Institutionalising Practices that Systematically Reinforce Desired Beliefs and Values**

Companies with strong cultures are clear on what their beliefs and values need to be and take the process of shaping those beliefs and values seriously. Such values help to undergird the strategies they employ.

The management of health care organisations should know that the stronger a company's culture and the more that culture is directed toward customers and markets, the less the company uses policy manuals, organisation charts, and detailed rules and procedures to enforce discipline and norms. This is because the guiding values inherent in the culture convey in crystal clear fashion are what everybody supposed to do in most situations.

## BENEFITS OF STRATEGIC MANAGEMENT

According to Pearce and Robinson (2000), the behavioural consequences of strategic management are similar to those of participative decision-making. In addition to the profitability of strategic plans are several benefits on the firm's welfare which include the following:

1. Strategy formulation activities enhance the firm's ability to prevent problems. Managers who encourage subordinates' attention to planning are aided in their monitoring and forecasting responsibilities by subordinates who are aware of the needs of strategic planning.
2. Group-based strategic decisions are likely to be drawn from the best available alternatives. The strategic management process results in better decisions because group interaction generates a greater variety of strategies, and; because forecasts based on the specialised perspectives of group members improve the screening of options.
3. The involvement of employees in strategy formulation improves their understanding of the productivity-reward relationship in every strategic plan and, thus, heightens their motivation.
4. Gaps and overlaps in activities among individuals and groups are reduced as participation in strategy formulation and clarify differences in roles.

## References

Andrews, K.R. (1980). *The Concept of Corporate Strategy* (Revised ed.) Homewood, Il.

Ansoff, H.I. (1965). 'The Firm of the Future', *Harvard Business Review*, 43(5).

Berry, T.H. (1991) *Managing the Total Quality Transition*. New York: McGraw-Hill.

King, W.R. and Cleland, D.I. (1978). *Strategic Planning and Policy*. 24. New York: Van Nostrand Reinhold.

Kotter, J.P. "What Leaders Really Do" *Harvard Business Review* 68, No. 3 (May – June 1990), P. 104.

Kuper, A. and J. Kuper (ed.) (1999). *The Social Science Encyclopedia*, (2nd ed.) London: Routledge.

Ogunbameru, O.A. (2004). *Organisational Dynamics*, Spectrum Books Ltd, Ibadan.

Pearce, J. and R. Robinson (2000). *Strategic Management: Formulation, Implementation and Control (7th ed.)* 2000.

Warmer, M. (ed), (1999). *International Encyclopedia of Business and Management*, Vol. 2, London and New York, Routledge.

## *Chapter 6*

# HEALTH FINANCING IN A DEVELOPING ECONOMY

*Oribabor, P. E.*

**About the Contributor**

Oribabor is a professor of Management. He is the Head of Department of Management and Accounting; and the Director, MBA Executive Programme, Obafemi Awolowo University, Ile-Ife. He is a specialist and consultant in Human Resource, Strategic Management and Industrial Relations; and a consultant to Federal Government of Nigeria, State Governments and World Bank. He has published numerous articles both in local and international journals and also authored and co-authored many books in the field of management.

## INTRODUCTION

Health care is a basic human need, but in most developing countries, like Nigeria, the prospect of achieving even minimal adequacy of health and health services remain a distant goal. The basic health needs of large number of people remain unmet and the pursuit of improved standards of health has become a primary concern over the years. In response to the myriad of problems besetting the health sector globally, member states of the World Health Organisation (WHO) in 1977 declared that the target of governments and WHO should be "the attainment by all citizens of the world by the year 2000 of a level of health that will permit them to lead a socially and economically productive life". This was further followed in 1978 at a conference in Alma-Ata in the former USSR, by a declaration that primary health care (PHC) was the key to attaining the target of "health for all".

The Nigerian government can be said to have embraced the main propositions of the above two concepts and accorded them a strategic place in the National Health Policy which was adopted in 1988. Apart from giving it a pivotal role, the health policy ensures that PHC services are to be supported by an efficient referral system and by appropriate ancillary services. It likewise ensures adequate provision of supportive information, education and communication system. The attainment of the objectives of the health policy, in line with WHO's strategy, will require not merely the enactment of a policy, but the cost-effective implementation of the health policy.

Arising from above framework, one may begin to raise a number of critical questions. What is the health status in Nigeria today? What care system is in place to meet the health care needs of the citizens? What measures – particularly funds – are available? What are the sources of the funds? Are the funds allocated to the health system adequate to support its programmes and objectives? In this chapter, attempt is made to address some of these issues, particularly funding.

## HEALTH STATUS IN NIGERIA

The health status in the country today is very alarming. The World Health Organization has recorded and placed Nigeria in the 187th position out of 191 countries in its 2000-2001 reports on Global Performance of Health System. It was also reported that this country is lagging far behind her neighbouring countries. This report brought furore to some if not to many. Issues on indicators used were then raised. However, Lucas (2001), opined that instead of criticising the indicators used, such as level of population, health distribution, level of responsiveness to emergency, fairness of financial contribution to health, and overall system attainment, it would be more useful to reflect on why Nigeria is doing so badly in comparison with other African countries that have fewer resources and are otherwise less developed.

Ransome-Kuti (1989) identified seven major defects of health services in Nigeria. These are inadequate coverage, inappropriate orientation, weak management, lack of community involvement, poor recordkeeping, inadequate funding and unreliable infrastructure, and poor logistic support. Considering these few observations among the myriads of factors known to be responsible for low health services in the country, the author would like to support the view that gross resource deficiency is merely always a symptom of the interplay between more complex problems.

## THE NIGERIAN HEALTH CARE SYSTEM

The national health policy published by the Federal Ministry of Health in 1988 has assigned the responsibility for health care to the three tiers of government, thus:

- The Local Government Authorities (LGA) have responsibility for the delivery of primary health care services.
- The State Governments operate secondary care hospitals, training of allied health professionals and supporting local government authorities in primary health care.
- The Federal Government is responsible for providing services that are national in scope, and these include:
    - Development of national health policy and procedure.
    - Coordination of health strategies.
    - Provision of technical support and training for implementation of State and Local Governments primary health care programmes.
    - Operation for tertiary care services and programmes for disease control.

At the State level, the Ministry of Health of each State of the federation has specific objectives and responsibilities in order to carry out the national health policy. The Hospital Management Board in each State supports and complements the health care services. In other words, modern health services in Nigeria today as witnessed by everybody, are provided by the Federal, State, and Local Governments. Also, we cannot deny the participation of non-governmental (for profit and not for profit) organisations (NGOs). These three tiers of governments operate through a network of primary, secondary, and tertiary level health facilities. The major responsibility of PHC rests with the LGAs with active support from the State Ministry of Health. At the secondary level, specialised services are provided to patients referred from the primary health care level, the tertiary health care provides highly specialised services to primary and secondary levels of the health care delivery services.

## FUNDING THE HEALTH CARE SYSTEM

Fund requirement to carry out and sustain the objectives and responsibilities of the three tiers of government for health care system in the country operating under established medical facilities is very evident and essential. The state of health sector financing has frequently been presented in the form of its most obvious problem. That is, pervasive underfunding and insufficiency of financial resources to provide pertinent services for those in need of health care.

The World Development Report on, "Better Health in Africa" (World Bank, 1993) noted that national spending in public services, including primary health care in developing countries, has decreased considerably. In 1990, the total health spending in the developing countries came to only US$170 billion compared to almost a US$1500 billion in the industrialised countries (World Bank, 1993).

In Nigeria, there was a drastic change in funds, which resulted from the major downturn in the world oil market. Foreign exchange earnings fell from US$24 billion in 1981 to only about US$6 billion in 1985. A Structural Adjustment Programme (SAP) was put in place in September 1986 with a view to removing several areas of administrative control and adopting a free market-oriented economy that would, among other things, encourage private enterprise and more efficient use of resources.

**Table 6.1: Federal Government Recurrent and Capital Expenditure (In million₦)**

| Year | Recurrent | | Capital | | Total |
|---|---|---|---|---|---|
| | Expenditure | % | Expenditure | % | |
| 1980 | 361.1 | 51.3 | 348.0 | 48.7 | 709.1 |
| 1981 | 234.0 | 48.3 | 250.8 | 51.7 | 484.8 |
| 1982 | 282.8 | 45.5 | 236.3 | 45.5 | 519.1 |
| 1983 | 211.5 | 54.4 | 200.3 | 48.6 | 411.8 |
| 1984 | 146.7 | 73.1 | 53.9 | 26.9 | 200.6 |
| 1985 | 167.7 | 74.9 | 56.2 | 25.1 | 223.9 |
| 1986 | 264.9 | 77.5 | 77.0 | 22.5 | 341.9 |
| 1987 | 143.8 | 70.6 | 59.9 | 29.4 | 203.7 |
| 1988 | 142.5 | 58.7 | 101.1 | 41.3 | 243.6 |
| 1989 | 119.8 | 72.2 | 46.2 | 27.8 | 166.0 |
| 1990 | 170.8 | 60.8 | 110.0 | 39.2 | 280.8 |
| 1991 | 186.8 | 80.2 | 46.4 | 19.8 | 223.2 |
| 1992 | 290.5 | 85.1 | 51.0 | 14.9 | 341.5 |
| 1993 | 309.4 | 90.6 | 32.1 | 09.4 | 341.5 |
| 1994 | 177.4 | 73.7 | 63.5 | 26.3 | 240.9 |
| 1995 | 162.7 | 71.7 | 63.5 | 28.3 | 226.2 |
| 1996 | 121.6 | 65.7 | 63.5 | 34.3 | 185.1 |
| 1997 | 162.4 | 64.2 | 90.4 | 35.8 | 252.5 |
| 1998 | 170.2 | 39.1 | 265.1 | 60.9 | 435.3 |
| 1999 | 261.1 | 54.4 | 221.8 | 45.7 | 482.9 |

**Source:** *Computed Data* from *CBN Annual Reports and Statement of Accounts, Statistics Bulletin*, Vol. 8, No. 2, December, 1977.

Funding for health in Nigeria has usually fallen below the minimum five percent of total budgetary allocation prescribed by the WHO. On the account of the Federal Government, Tables 6.1 and 6.2 show the recurrent and capital expenditures of the Federal Government, and the total health expenditure as percentage of Total Budget (TB) and Gross Domestic Product (GDP) from 1980 to 1997. In 1980, 2.5% of the TB was allocated to health sector with a total of ₦709.1 million. This was over 2.5 times the value of ₦280.8 million allocated in 1990. The allocation to the health sector dropped from ₦341.9 million in 1986 to ₦203.7 million instead of increasing. The allocation dropped to the lowest ebb in 1989 with a total of ₦166.0 million. The downward trend continued until 1999 with ₦482.9 million which was still low compared to what was allocated almost two decades ago in terms of per capita.

**Table 6.2: Total Health Expenditure as Percentage of Total Budget (TB) and Gross Domestic Product (GDP)**

| Year | % TB | % GDP |
|---|---|---|
| 1980 | 2.50 | 0.71 |
| 1981 | 3.86 | 0.82 |
| 1982 | 1.27 | 0.30 |
| 1983 | 2.21 | 0.45 |
| 1984 | 1.04 | 0.19 |
| 1985 | 1.51 | 0.31 |
| 1986 | 1.86 | 0.43 |
| 1987 | 0.56 | 0.11 |
| 1988 | 2.08 | 0.40 |
| 1989 | 1.94 | 0.35 |
| 1990 | 1.35 | 0.32 |
| 1991 | 1.16 | 0.24 |
| 1992 | 0.43 | 0.07 |
| 1993 | 1.10 | 0.37 |
| 1994 | 1.35 | 0.31 |
| 1995 | 1.68 | 0.23 |
| 1996 | 1.46 | 0.17 |
| 1997 | 1.77 | 0.32 |

**Source:** *CBN Statistical Bulletin* Vol. 8, No. 2, December, 1997.

This downward trend in the percentage of total health sector allocation of fund based on TB and GDP to a large extent is a reflection of the country's economy. The Nigeria economy has experienced stunted growth for the greater part of the period since independence. Even during the oil boom, Nigeria did not experience a positive growth rate. The first half of the 1980s was particularly bad, being characterised by negative rates of growth (Federal Ministry of Statistics, 1996). This negative growth rate indicated a depressed economic situation of the country partly caused by global economic recession; and partly by seemingly overdependence on oil proceeds and the perceived gross mismanagement of the country's economy.

**Table 6.3: Real Federal Government Expenditure (FGE, Gross Domestic Product (GDP), and Federally-Collected Revenue (FCR)**

| Year | GDP (in million ₦) | FGE (in million ₦) | FCR (in million₦) | Growth rate of FGE | Growth rate of GDP |
|---|---|---|---|---|---|
| 1970 | 1277.5 | 256.8 | 144.0 | - | - |
| 1971 | 1543.0 | 237.5 | 254.1 | -7.5 | 20.8 |
| 1972 | 1674.6 | 405.2 | 305.5 | 70.6 | 8.5 |
| 1973 | 1696.8 | 269.5 | 256.9 | -33.5 | 1.3 |
| 1974 | 1900.0 | 430.3 | 458.3 | 59.7 | 11.8 |
| 1975 | 1845.7 | 699.9 | 467.3 | 62.6 | -2.9 |
| 1976 | 2042.4 | 718.6 | 501.2 | 2.7 | 10.7 |
| 1977 | 2212.6 | 790.2 | 543.4 | 10.0 | 8.3 |
| 1978 | 2050.2 | 701.0 | 418.8 | -11.3 | -7.3 |
| 1979 | 2125.7 | 649.8 | 537.6 | -7.3 | 3.7 |
| 1980 | 2020.5 | 1034.7 | 665.2 | 59.2 | -4.9 |
| 1981 | 2030.0 | 849.6 | 487.2 | -17.9 | 0.5 |
| 1982 | 2027.8 | 602.7 | 461.3 | -29.1 | -0.1 |
| 1983 | 1936.5 | 388.9 | 352.6 | -35.8 | -4.5 |
| 1984 | 1817.4 | 333.9 | 319.7 | -13.7 | -6.2 |
| 1985 | 1987.8 | 407.4 | 403.5 | 22.0 | 9.4 |
| 1986 | 2052.3 | 471.2 | 345.6 | 15.7 | 3.4 |
| 1987 | 2039.0 | 412.3 | 473.2 | -12.5 | -0.6 |
| 1988 | 2719.9 | 519.7 | 516.8 | 26.1 | 33.4 |
| 1989 | 2409.4 | 439.7 | 512.3 | 15.4 | -11.4 |
| 1990 | 2606.4 | 602.7 | 852.5 | 37.1 | 8.2 |
| 1991 | 2729.7 | 560.9 | 850.8 | 6.9 | 4.7 |
| 1992 | 2810.9 | 474.4 | 973.7 | -15.4 | 2.9 |
| 1993 | 2874.6 | 731.2 | 794.9 | 54.1 | 2.3 |
| 1994 | 2913.0 | 459.6 | 674.8 | -37.1 | 1.3 |

***Source:*** *Federal Office of Statistics, (1995)*

The data in Table 6.3 show the direction of the real GDP, Federal Gross Expenditures (FGE), and Federal Collected Revenue (FCR). The fiscal balance was always in deficit throughout the two and a half decades. The real FGE could be observed to have a consistent rise between 1973 and 1980, while real FCR oscillated between ₦144 million and ₦665.2 million between 1970 and 1980 respectively. They both consistently decelerated between 1980 and 1984. A fluctuating trend could be observed from 1984 to 1995 for both the FCR and FGE. During this period, the national current account balance was mostly negative. The period of 1980 to 1983 recorded deficits of ₦19.489 billion and in 1994 deficit was registered as ₦48.581 billion (FOS, 1996). The economic deterioration could be the result of the depression in the crude oil earnings and the exchange rate depreciation

**Table 6.4a: Budget Percentage Allocation of the Social Service Sector in Osun State**

| Sector | 1995 ₦ | 1996 ₦ | 1997₦ | 1998₦ | 1999₦ |
|---|---|---|---|---|---|
| Education | 22.43 | 15.41 | 15.09 | 13.90 | 13.38 |
| Health | 4.27 | 2.85 | 2.27 | 2.21 | 3.69 |
| Information and Culture | 6.97 | 14.50 | 18.38 | 16.19 | 16.77 |
| Social Development, Youths and Sport | 2.08 | 1.31 | 1.04 | 0.81 | 1.38 |

**Source:** *Approved Budgets, 1995-1999 of Osun State, Nigeria.*

**Table 6.4b: Total Budgetary Allocation to Key Sectors**

| Sector | 1996 | | 1997 | |
|---|---|---|---|---|
| | Budget in billion(₦) | % of Total Budget(₦) | Budget in Billion(₦) | % of Total Budget(₦) |
| Defence | 15.500 | 10.90 | 17.445 | 11.95 |
| Police | 9.841 | 6.90 | 12.309 | 8.40 |
| Agriculture, Water Resources and Rural Development | 5.569 | 3.90 | 12.822 | 8.78 |
| Health | 4.838 | 3.40 | 7.343 | 5.02 |

| | | | | |
|---|---|---|---|---|
| Education | 15.350 | 10.81 | 16.840 | 11.53 |
| Infrastructure | 9.176 | 13.50 | 34.524 | 23.64 |
| Industry, Solid Minerals, Commerce & Tourism, and Steel | 2.196 | 2.05 | 12.430 | 8.51 |

**Source:** *Press Briefing on the 1997 Budget by the Honourable Minister of Finance, Osun State Approved Budget, January, 20, 1997.*

The data in Table 6.4a show the budgetary allocation of Osun State to key social service sectors of the State. Health was allocated 4.27% of the total budget as compared to 22.43% allocated to education sector and 6.97% to information and culture in 1995. The allocation given to the health sector showed a declining pattern from 1996 to 1998 in contrast to education, and information and culture sectors having an allocation of 18.38% and 15.09% respectively in 1997. As demonstrated by data in Table 6. 6.4b, the picture at the Federal level is similar to that at the State level. This inconsistency in the commitment to the health sector depicted in the government expenditure might have been responsible for the poor status of health in the Nigerian society that all citizens are witnessing if not experiencing.

**Table 6.5: Federal Ministry of Health Expenditures as Percentage of Total Federal Expenditures**

| Year | Recurrent | Capital | Total |
|---|---|---|---|
| 1986 | 3.6 | 1.4 | 2.4 |
| 1987 | 2.5 | 0.8 | 1.4 |
| 1988 | 2.4 | 1.2 | 2.0 |
| 1989 | 1.5 | 4.7 | 1.8 |
| 1990 | 2.1 | 3.1 | 2.4 |
| 1991 | 5.6 | 0.6 | 1.4 |
| 1992 | 2.8 | 1.2 | 1.1 |
| 1993 | 2.5 | 1.7 | 2.3 |

***Source:*** *Federal Office of Statistics (1996), Socioeconomic Profile of Nigeria.*

## ADEQUACY OF FUNDS IN HEALTH CARE

In the same vein, the data in Table 6.5 above demonstrate the neglect of the government in the health sector. This neglect is reflected in the tendency of the recurrent expenditure to dominate the capital expenditure. This became so evident in 1991 when the proportion of recurrent expenditure accounted for 90% of the total expenditure. The only exception was the period of 1989 and 1990, when ₦4.7 billion and ₦3.1 billion were allocated or spent for capital expenditure in contrast to ₦1.5 billion and ₦2.1 billion respectively. This data suggest that very limited fund was available for capital projects resulting in the collapse of health care infrastructure like buildings, equipment, and other physical facilities. Invariably, most of us are witnessing outdated machines, equipment, and even apparatuses due to lack of fund. This is to be expected when the data clearly illustrate that capital spending is, to some extent, a residual on what is left after the obligations of the recurrent budget have been met.

The point that needs to be stressed is that even in absolute terms, the yearly amount allocated is grossly insufficient to the projects and programmes of the sector. This situation is usually compounded by the inability of the sector to get yearly increases in budgetary allocation that keeps pace with inflationary rate. Thus, in real terms, what the health sector gets for its programmes has been on the decline over the years. Health managers not only have to contend with very meager financial allocation, but also do not know how much will be released and when. An intractable problem of health sector financing in Nigeria is the presence of both allocative and technical inefficiencies in the application of limited and scarce resources at the disposal of the sector.

**Table 6.6: Financial Statements (1996- June 2000 in million ₦)**

| Details of Revenue | 1996 | | 1997 | | 1998 | | 1999 | | June 2000 | |
|---|---|---|---|---|---|---|---|---|---|---|
| Federal Government subvention | 188.1 | | 244.2 | | 286.0 | | 366.0 | | 176.3 | |
| Internally Generated Revenue | 55.7 | 244.2 | 9.7 | 252.2 | 30.3 | 316.4 | 36.5 | 403.1 | 48.9 | 225.2 |
| Personnel and overhead cost | | 194.4<br>49.9 | | 246.9<br>5.1 | | 315.7<br>0.7 | | 448.4<br>-45.3 | | 267.8<br>-42.6 |
| Capital Receipt Transfer from personnel and overhead Capital Grant | 49.9<br>22.2 | 72.1 | 5.1<br>27.4 | 32.8 | 0.7<br>37.3 | 38.0 | -45.3<br>51.3 | 6.0 | -42.6<br>10.0 | -32.6 |
| Capital Expenditure Surplus/ Deficit | | 20.6<br>51.5 | | 19.2<br>13.6 | | 45.9<br>-7.9 | | 74.6<br>-68.6 | | 25.2<br>-57.8 |

**Source:** *Omosolo (2000) Unpublished Thesis: "Budgeting in Governmental Institutions", Ile-Ife.*

Additionally, taking into consideration the data in Table 6.6, you and I would be surprised with the increasing deficits over years. Aren't these data very alarming? In 1998, the deficit was ₦7.9 million and in 1999, it rose to ₦68.6 million. Would these figures mean adequate funds? The rising costs of personnel and overhead were inevitable over the years and the costs of capital projects too, knowing the significance of these in bringing about improved health services. Despite all efforts, Ransome-Kuti (1989) claimed that no more than 35% of the population had access to modern health care services. In spite of some improvements as evidenced by the increase in the number of health facilities, and the emphasis on primary health care, the health situation in Nigeria has not yet improved. Reports on health recorded that mortality rates are still high, and the major causes of morbidity have not changed in the recent past, which we all know that these issues are accounted for the low productivity level of the nation.

## WAY FORWARD

The information on the real level of Federal and State health expenditures suggests that there has been considerable fluctuation in the level of resources available to provide health services since the mid 1980s. The decline in resource availability did not reflect changes in government priorities, but rather, a decline in total government resources availability and per capital income that has accompanied falling oil revenues. Because the three tiers of government are completely dependent on the Federation Account (the principal source of government revenue) the quantity and quality of health services available to the population is extremely vulnerable to changes in world oil prices. This volatility of revenue therefore creates difficulties in planning at all levels of the health care systems. The overriding impact of financial constraints in the health sector is a decline in the quality and coverage of services provided.

Alternative revenue sources would have to be given serious consideration. Cost recovery for health services is currently widespread in many government health facilities. Revenues from such cost recovery schemes have the potential to stabilise the quantity and quality of services, provided that appropriate institutional mechanisms are put in place for their effective and efficient operation.

Implementation of a National Health Insurance Scheme is another viable option for financing health services. It is hoped that the Health Ministry has studied the issues involved in detail. The proposed programme has many positive features. In particular, the use of capitation scheme puts the burden for controlling costs on the primary health care physician.

The major question surrounding the programme is whether the capitation fee will be adequate to finance the care of the enrollees.

Given the data limitations in Nigeria, measures will be needed to either generate sufficient actuarial information before implementing the programme or to protect the capitated physicians from financial collapse if the initial rates set are too low.

**References.**

Central Bank of Nigeria, (1997). CBN Annual Reports and Statements of Accounts (1997), *Statistical Bulletin*, Vol. 8, No. 2, Lagos.

Federal Office of Statistics, (1996). Socio-Economic Profile of Nigeria, Statistical Information for the Nation, Lagos, Nigeria.

Lucas, A. (2001). "WHO 2000 Report and Nigeria", *The Guardian* Newspaper, August, Lagos, Nigeria.

Omoloso, M. (2000). "Budgeting in Governmental Institution", Unpublished thesis for Master in Business Administration, Obafemi Awolowo University, Ile-Ife.

Osun State of Nigeria, (1995). *Approved Budget for 1995*, Ibadan. TAA Printing and Publishing Co., , Nigeria.

Osun State of Nigeria, (1996). *Approved Budget for 1995,* TAA Printing and Publishing Co., Ibadan, Nigeria.

Osun State of Nigeria, (1997). *Approved Budget for 1995,* TAA Printing and Publishing Co., Ibadan, Nigeria.

Osun State of Nigeria, (1998). *Approved Budget for 1995*, TAA Printing and Publishing Co., Ibadan, Nigeria.

Osun State of Nigeria, (1999). *Approved Budget for 1995*, TAA Printing and Publishing Co., Ibadan, Nigeria.

Ransome-Kuti, O. (1989). "Historical Antecedent" in *Health Care and Health Care Services in Nigeria,* O. Erinosho (ed). Lagos, Nigeria.

World Bank, (1993). *Better Health in Africa*, Human Resources and Poverty Division, Africa Technical Department, Africa.

World Health Organization, (1977). "Improve our Health, Improve our World", *WHO Position Paper*, WHO, Geneva.

## *Chapter 7*

# HOSPITAL INFORMATION SYSTEM (*HIS*) MODEL IN A NIGERIAN UNIVERSITY TEACHING HOSPITAL

*Daini, O.A., Makanjuola, R.O.A. & Ojo, J.O.*

**About the Contributors**

Professor Makanjuola Roger holds B.Sc, MBBS (London), M.Phil, Ph.D (Edinburgh), MRC Psych., FMC Psych., FWACP Psych. He is currently Vice-Chancellor of Obafemi Awolowo University, Ile-Ife. For two terms, he was the Chief Medical Director (CMD), Obafemi Awolowo Teaching Hospitals Complex (O.A.U.TH.C.) He is a Consultant Psychiatrist of international repute.

Daini is a lecturer in the Department of Computer Science, Obafemi Awolowo University, Ile-Ife, Nigeria.

Ojo is a senior officer in Obafemi Awolowo University Teaching Hospital Complex, Ile-Ife, Nigeria.

## INTRODUCTION

In this chapter, the Hospital Information System of the Obafemi Awolowo University Teaching Hospitals Complex is hereby described. It is based on VA MUMPS/FileMan Technology and is operational on a 386-microcomputer system with four terminals. The system has proved reliable, easy to use and efficient. It is currently enhanced with the installation of an Electronic Mail facility and expansion work in the processing of morbidity and mortality data of an adjunct hospital is in progress.

## BASIC CONCEPTS

In 1988, the Obafemi Awolowo University Teaching Hospitals Complex (OAUTHC) decided to computerise the operations of its Medical Records and Accounting Department. The primary objective of a computerised medical records system is to provide health professionals in a Teaching/Specialist Hospital with timely delivery of both current and past relevant information which will aid in the medical decision-making process of health evaluation and medical treatment. However, it should operate at a reasonable cost.

(1) On the other hand, a computerised accounting system comprising procedures for payroll and advances, expenditure control and financial accounting, is a subset of a medical administration system which is synonymous with a computerised management Information System (MIS) for effective administration of a medical or health institution.

The first phase of the requirement was to establish a Hospital Information system (HIS) for a computerised medical records system. The primary objectives of the HIS were that the system should:

(a) provide for timely delivery of information in the form of:
   (i) Daily Bed Statistics;
   (ii) Appointment lists;
   (iii) Diagnostics and Operations Codes extracted from the Inpatients' Discharge Summaries filled by consultants;
   (iv) Statistics for the Ministry or Funding Agency;

(b) improve the quality of patients' care by providing access to all relevant patient data;

(c) aid in diagnosis and research, for example, find the Case Notes (records) of patients with a given diagnosis for resident doctors doing research (2, 3).

It was decided that the system could initially focus on the specialist in and outpatient activities of the main hospital in Ile-Ife, that is, Ife State Hospital (ISH) with future expansion to adjunct hospitals and health centres, and application expansion to include inventory control program for pharmacy and the VA outpatient scheduling package.

## HISTORY

At the same period OAUTHC was planning to computerise, the Computing Centre of University of Kuopio, Finland, established an experimental research project on health informatics in Africa and selected Obafemi Awolowo University (OAU) for a Visiting Research Fellow for the project with OAUTHC to be the resource centre. By 1989, a joint Nigerian-Finnish project involving OAUTCH, the Computer Science Department, OAU and the University of Kupio, Finland, was established to develop on a microcomputer, a low-cost multi-user system for the basic Medical Records functions or OAUTHC. It was based on VA MUMPS/FileMan technology, public-domain admission-Discharge Transfer application software from USA, to be developed on a standard microcomputer and modified to suit the Nigerian Medical Records environment.

The software development work took place at the Computer Science Department, OAU and thereafter, it was transported to OAUTHC for trial runs at the Medical Records Department. In 1990, OAUTHC purchased a 386-microcomputer system with other peripherals for the installation of the system and by 1991; it has become fully operational as the only MUMPS and VA software application installation in Nigeria. The system was enhanced in 1992 by the installation of an Electronic Mail (e-mail) facility between it and the computer system at the University of Kuopio, Finland.

## SYSTEM ARCHITECTURE

### Hardware

Initially, the HIS was developed on an Olivetti M280, a 286-microcomputer system with IMB storage and a hard disk storage capacity of 60MB. The attached peripherals were a printer, a terminal, a tape streamer, a voltage stabiliser to normalise fluctuations in electrical current and an Uninterrupted Power Supply (UPS) for transitional power supply during power failures. The microcomputer with its peripherals was brought from Finland for the project and because the equipment were suited to European conditions, we experienced some problems with their use in a Tropical African environment. In fact, the Olivetti M280 was the only one of its model in Nigeria and was difficult to maintain locally without documentation and spare parts specific to this model such that it had to be sent to Finland for repairs on two occasions.

In order to avoid the equipment maintenance and reliability problems, OAUTHC decided in 1990 to purchase a popular 386-microcomputer system with its peripherals from a reliable local computer vendor. The system comprised an IBM PS/2 Model 70 with 4MB storage, hard disk storage of 120MB and a tape streamer installed as an optional hardware feature. The peripherals were a printer, three terminals, a voltage stabiliser and a UPS. The *HIS* was installed on the microcomputer alone until the technical problems on the installation of the remote terminals were resolved through the use of current loop cables instead of local area network which was deemed to be too expensive and sensitive to environmental hazards. By January 1991, the four-user system became operational at the Medical Records Department and three locations around the hospital premises.

**Software**

A public-domain (free) applications package from the U.S. Department of Veterans Affairs (VA), based on the **MUMPS** programming language and VA tools, was used as a basis for the development of a basic Medical Records system. The VA Admission Discharge-Transfer package was compared with the requirements of Ife State Hospital (ISH), the major hospital unit to OAUTHC, and within a couple of weeks of programming by the Finnish Researcher it was adapted to reflect the existing manual practice (2). The data entry functions comprise patient registration, admissions, discharges and transfers, and discharge summaries. There are also the statistical and systems management functions. The most important outputs are the Daily Bed Status and the Monthly/annual return of Mobility and Mortality, according to the ICD-9 codes.

It is a four-user system which has been in daily operational use from the beginning of 1991. The system was enhanced in 1991 by the installation of an e-mail facility between it and the computer at the

Computing Center, University of Kuopio, Finland via a telephone line by a modem using the VA Mailman software application part of Kernel by the two computers. Since the computer at the University of Kuopio is connected to Internet global network, an opportunity of global computer electronic mail communication is provided OAUTHC via the computer at the University of Kuopio.

**Database**

The nucleus of the database is the patient identification and bio-data comprising patient's name, address, hospital unit number, X-Ray number, age, sex, marital status, name and address of next of kin, place of birth, occupation and religion. This represents the information contents on the inner cover of a patient's Case Note. The database contains the data records of ISH inpatients from January 1991 to date and there are over 100,000 Case Notes in the Archive to be converted into the system. The database is structured on the hard disk by the VA FileMan database management system which provides good end-user oriented facilities for ad hoc information retrieval and report generation. The VA FileMan also provides facilities for data protection in form of passwords, as well as access and verify codes. An online backup copy of the entire hard disk is made on tape streamer once a week. Three sets of backup tapes in form of grandfather-father-son approach are maintained for fast recovery of the entire database in case of technical failure.

**Infrastructure and Operations**

The Hospital Information System (*HIS*) is at present operated concurrently at the Medical Records Department and at the three terminals at the Consultant Out-Patient Department (COPD), Radiology Department and the statistics office respectively. Late at night, the system is set for e-mail message processing to/from the University of Kuopio, Finland. Data entry of nucleus database of new patient records is primarily from the system console at the Medical Records Department and from the COPD terminal. The others are usually for specialised information storage and retrieval, for example, processing patients' names, X-Ray numbers and Hospital Unit numbers at the Radiology

Department and statistical data at the statistics office, but they could also be used for full concurrent operation as at the system console. Patient records are updated at the system console in the Medical Records Department with the final diagnosis on discharge. Reports are produced regularly and on demand, for example, request for specific patients' case notes or epidemiological reports. Annual Morbidity and Mortality Statistical Reports required by the Federal Ministry of Health is readily available on the system.

**Organisation of Product Development**

The development of the *HIS* software of the joint project from an existing model was through on-site technical assistance by a Finnish researcher from the Computing Centre, University of Kuopio,, Finland. Within this period and trial runs at OAUTHC, a Nigerian research assistant was trained to provide a sustained technical support for the system. It should be noted that the Medical Records Staff at Ife State Hospital (ISH) participated in specifying the system and in experimenting with it. Therefore, they were highly motivated towards making their system work. Although a MUMPS group was established at the Computer Science Department, OAU, for long term support and further development, technical assistance through correspondence and supply of literature on technical issues continued to be offered by the University of Kuopio. The installation of an e-mail communication between OAUTHC and the Computing Centre, University of Kuopio makes such technical assistance highly productive. Since the present system covers the basic inpatient functions, areas for software expansion and hardware upgrade are under consideration. Processing of inpatient Case Notes from January 1991, of Wesley Guild Hospital, an adjunct hospital unit of OAUTHC, is also being considered.

**CONCLUSION**

The Joint Project is a pioneer experiment in introducing a low cost model of a basic structure of *HIS* for the Nigerian environment. In two years of operation, the model has proved to be cost-effective, productive and highly desirable. The cost-benefits and successes of the system have been publicised through a National Workshop on *Computers in Medicine and Health Care Management* held from June 17-19, 1992 at Ile-Ife and attended by participants from other Nigerian University Teaching Hospitals, Federal and State Ministries of Health/ parastatals and other Health Institutions. It is hoped that the model will be adopted for operation at other health institutions in due course.

## References

Collen, M.F., Brunt, E.E. and Davis, L.S. (2-5 March, 1976). "Problems of computerisation of Large Computer Medical Record System", *In Proc. Int. Symposium on Medical Data processing* by IRJA, eds. Laudet, M. Anderson, J. and Begon, F. Toulose; P.47-53.

Makanjuola, R.O.A., Daini, O.A., Soriyan; H.A. and Korpela, M. (19-22 Aug., 1991). "Low-cost Hospital Informatics in Africa: The Ile-Ife Experience, In *Proc. Medical Information Europe* 1991. eds. Adlassing, L.P., Grabner, G., Bengtsson, S. and Hanson R., Vienna, Austria. P.111-115.

Zimmerman, H. (2-5 March, 1976). "Introduction to processing of Patients Records", In *Proc. Int. Symposium on Medical Data Processing* by IRIA, eds. Laudet, M., Anderson, J. and Begon, Toulose, 976. P.449-460.

# *Chapter 8*

# PHARMACY INFORMATION NEEDS AND PRIORITIES

*Ilesanmi, L.A.*

**About the Contributor**

Dr Ilesanmi is the Director of Administration and Secretary to the Management Board of Obafemi Awolowo University Teaching Hospitals Complex, Ile-Ife. He is a British-trained professional Health Service Manager. He has M.Sc. (Management Studies), Scotland and Ph.D.(*Honoris Causa*),U.S.A. He is a Fellow of the Nigerian Institute of Health Service Administrators. Formerly a teacher and journalist, he has presented many scientific papers at different academic workshops and published many works both in local and international learned journals.

## INTRODUCTION

This chapter identifies hospital pharmacy information needs from the viewpoint of informatics as essentially relating to drug supply management and drug use control. It considers the use of computer capabilities as a necessary development for effective and efficient performance of pharmacy information functions in contemporary health care delivery system. Also, suggestions are made on the development of drug information service, the adoption of unit dose dispensing method and the training of staff hospital pharmacists to be computer literate as the three foremost priorities for the contemporary hospital pharmacy generally in Africa and particularly in Nigeria.

In this chapter, the focus is on hospital pharmacy in the context of health care delivery services with particular reference to Nigeria.

The pharmacy occupies a central position in the modern hospital system as its services extend to all the major hospital functions which are quality patient care, teaching/training, research, and community health promotion.

## PHARMACY INFORMATION NEEDS

Essentially the hospital pharmacy information needs can be examined under two broad headings which are:

### (1) Drug Supply Management Information

Drug supply management information for effective decisions on drug procurement and inventory activities is required for effective pharmacy input to health care delivery

In a health care system, while drugs alone cannot ensure good health care, without them, there can be no credible and effective health care delivery as more and more diseases are treated at some stage by chemotherapy. Indeed, it has been estimated that every hospital patient receives between two and three drug prescriptions on average each day he is in the hospital (1).

### *Drug Procurement Information*

To achieve pharmacy effectiveness, drug procurement must be planned and this involves various information and decisions including the following: (1) what to procure (2) how much to procure (3) when to procure (4) what source, and (5) terms of supply. Some of the above information and decisions are based on the particular hospital management policy with regards to the hospital formulary, patient service/satisfaction levels and costs, environment, and national drug policy.

Responding to the WHO Essential Drugs Policy; Nigeria and other African developing nations, had developed National Formulary and Essential Drugs List which form the basis for hospital purchases and prescriptions. The first Nigerian National Drug Formulary and Essential Drugs List containing some 204 drug items in generic nomenclature was published in 1986 (2). That list was updated in 1989 with the adoption of 409 essential drugs (3). The 1989 list included those drugs considered vital to the tertiary health institutions but which were not included in the 1986 list. Another update of the National Essential Drugs List was published in 1991 (4). The second revision of the National Drug Formulary as essential companion to the Essential Drugs List is already in progress.

***Drug Inventory Control Information***

As part of the functions of Drug Supply Management, drug inventory control plans for and ensures adequate availability of stocks with particular attention ,to cost and service. This function required information and data relating to each drug item approved to be available in the pharmacy. These include:

(1) Annual demand forecasts.
(2) Maximum-minimum stock levels.
(3) Lead times.
(4) Safety stock level.
(5) Reorder point discount.

To effectively fulfil its drug service to patients in a rapidly changing health environment most economically, the pharmacy required continuous calculations and updating of the above-mentioned data.

***The Use of Computer in Drug Supply Management***

To effectively perform the drug procurement and inventory control functions of the modern pharmacy, a great deal of data and information as outlined above has to be produced regularly and reliably. Computers are known to be widely used in developed countries in connection with drug procurement and stock records and updating them by posting transaction data.

Computer systems can provide a variety of reports and statistical analyses. In Nigeria, the Lagos State Government has decided to computerise its drug storage and distribution systems. The project which would computerise the operations of the state's control medical records and drug depots at Oshodi and estimated to cost ₦.5million is aimed at checking the "out-of-stock" (O/S) syndrome in the State's hospitals and dispensaries. The computer systems would install an alarm system that would ensure regular and adequate flow of drugs by setting and indicating the levels (reorder points) at which fresh stock should be ordered for each drug. Another advantage envisaged in the project is its ability to check frauds and irregularities as it would enable the stock and movements of drugs to be adequately monitored (5).

There are many available systems hardware and software for hospital service. These include Information Access Architecture Manufactured by HBO and Company (6), the MUMPS software which is relatively low-cost and successfully being used by the Obafemi Awolowo University Teaching Hospital Complex, Ile-Ife, Nigeria.

The point to emphasise is that, to promote effective hospital service in Africa in this modern era, computer capabilities should be employed to perform the massive and complex information work involved in the contemporary hospital pharmacy service.

## (2) Drug Use Control Information

While the real advances and effectiveness in medical treatment since the third of the century (1930s) can be attributed to spectacular progress in drug therapy, it has been estimated that, 958 of the drugs in use today were unheard of in 1950. On the other hand, medication errors, resulting from drug incompatibilities contribute to health hazards (7). Therefore, effective drug use control requires adequate knowledge of drug incompatibilities; and of drug information.

### *(i) Drug Incompatibility*

The term incompatibility refers to the impact of certain drugs combinations upon the condition of particular patient. Incompatibility may take five basic forms namely:

(1) sensitivity or allergy to a given drug or class of drugs;
(2) interference between a drug with some other prescribed or patent medication;

(3) interference between a drug and certain foods;
(4) contraindication of a drug in a specific clinical situation; and
(5) interference of a drug with certain laboratory or other diagnostic tests.

### *(ii) Drug Information*

Drug Information (D.I.) has been defined as "an essence of pharmacy practice whether community or hospital, whereby a registered pharmacist provides accurate and factual information on drugs to other health professionals". It is any objective scientifically derived and documented data on:

(1) identification of the drug;
(2) the pharmaceutical properties of the drug;
(3) characteristics of the drug;
(4) the therapeutic usefulness or relative merit of the drug compared with other drugs;
(5) brand and generic ranges of the drug;
(6) absorption, distribution, metabolism and excretion ;
(7) the contraindication of the drug ;
(8) the adverse effects of the drug when used alone or in combination with other drugs;
(9) the drug interaction of clinical relevance;
(10) dose or useful dosage range, the dosing intervals and the average duration of treatment;
(11) toxic effects of the drug and the treatment of poisoning when it occurs;
(12) the formulation of the drugs that are available;
(13) the status of the drug whether narcotic or non-narcotic prescription or non-prescription;
(14) storage condition for the drug ;
(15) dates of manufacture and expiry of the drug to indicate its efficacy or potency life;
(16) name and address of orders or prescriptions and patient record summaries from prime enable the pharmacist to audit the kind and

amount of drugs being given to the patient and monitor his drug therapy response.

Cases of errors in drug prescriptions and administration due to lack of auditing exercises by pharmacists abound in Nigerian hospitals. They remain unpublished for legal and public relations implications.

## THE USE OF COMPUTER IN DRUG THERAPY AUDIT

The increasing size and complexity of drug inventory coupled with massive drug information and growing concern about drug incompatibilities as well as concern for quality and effective care for the patient necessitate the screening of prescriptions for sensitivities or allergies, contraindications, or overdoses. This task which has become enormous in a contemporary hospital pharmacy cannot be effectively executed without some automation aids. Outpatients are processed each day by the contemporary medium-sized hospital as the case is with each unit of the OAUTHC, Ile-Ife, Nigeria, where in a typical day, a unit (Ife State Hospital) dispenses drugs to 340 in-and outpatients each receiving three to four drugs on average. There is simply no sufficient time to examine manually the medical record of each patient receiving a drug.

A computer system can perform this screening task with relative ease once a few ground rules are set and a database established. The data required are essentially of two kinds namely:

(1) Data on each drug in the formulary with usual or maximum doses, contraindications and possible drug interactions; and
(2) patient oriented drug data that include a record of what is being taken, likely allergic reactions; diagnosis and so forth.

It would be more effective and efficient if computerised pharmacy system is integrated with computer medical records system as both have much to offer as Nigeria is in the process of computerising its pharmacy having successfully done so with its medical records systems.

## PHARMACY PRIORITIES

There could be many different priorities for a hospital pharmacy depending on the pharmaceutical inventory it handles, the operational methods already installed and the level of performance desired. However, in most of the hospitals in the developing countries of Africa and with particular reference to the Obafemi Awolowo University Teaching Hospital Complex, Ile-Ife, Nigeria, priorities should be:

(1) Development of drug information service (DIS).
(2) Adoption of unit dose dispensing method.
(3) Training of hospital pharmacists to be computer literate.

### Drug Information Service (*DIS*) Development

Drug Information service involving giving advice on drug therapy has always been a part of pharmacy practice. However, the extent to which this role has been developed varies greatly especially in African health care system. Many factors could be responsible for this situation including medical profession's opposition or lack of support and past inadequate training of pharmacists in clinical pharmacy. With the introduction of clinical pharmacy in the curricula of contemporary pharmacy schools, the second inhibiting factor has been removed leaving essentially only the medical profession's lack of support. Once this service is reasonably developed, then it can be computerised.

### Adoption of Unit Dose Dispensing Method

The unit dose distribution system which sounds foreign to virtually all Nigerian Government Hospitals allows the pharmacy to dispense exact doses to the patient. The unit dose system as opposed to the traditional bulk dispensing system is individual patient-oriented. The advantages of unit dose method over the bulk distribution by the hospitals that have adopted include giving greater accuracy in drug preparation and greatly reducing the uncertainty of quality and inventory control.

Clearly, the pharmacist must have a great deal of information concerning both the drugs he dispenses as outlined under drug information, and of the patient for whom he is intended as contained in the patient record summaries if he is to discharge adequately the new responsibilities of clinical pharmacy.

A hospital that contemplates on utilising computerised pharmacy systems for the ordering, issue and recording administration of drugs and medications would need to adopt the unit dose system. In addition to other advantages when suitably programmed, computerised pharmacy systems are able to indicate to the prescriber any drug sensitivities of the patient that have already been discovered and recorded, contraindications for certain therapy, incompatibilities in drug therapy and when dosages depart from the norm [9].

## Training of Pharmacists to Be Computer Literate

The efficient use of computers in pharmacy functions will largely depend on the computer literacy level of the pharmacists. Therefore, it is necessary to train staff pharmacists of the hospital that desires to computerise its pharmacy in computer application. In OAUTHC, Ile-Ife, Nigeria, many members of staff who are Medical Records Officers were trained to operate its Medical Records Computerised System at installation. Similar approach could be adopted in the case of any hospital pharmacy in Africa which plans to computerise.

Furthermore, and as a long term proposal, computer application should be included in the medical, pharmacy and nursing training curricula in Nigeria.

## CONCLUSION

This chapter has necessarily been selective in the treatment of pharmacy needs and priorities from the perspective of informatics with particular reference to Nigeria.

## References

Colin Grant, (1973). *Hospital Management*, Churchill Livingston Edinburgh and London.

Essential Drug List – First Revision (1989). Federal Ministry of Health, Lagos.

Essential Drugs List – Second Revision (1991). Federal Ministry of Health, Lagos.

Hospital Management International, (1992). (International Hospital Federation). P.302.

Ms Uche Ochei, (1992). "Drug Information Service" – A lecture paper.

Nigerian National Drug Formulary and Essential Drugs List, (1986). Federal Ministry of Health.

Noah Abisogun (Dr.), Lagos State Commissioner for Health: report in *The Guardian* Newspaper, issue of 27 October, 1992. P.3.

Raymond D. Garrett, (1973). *Hospitals: A System Approach*, Auerbach Publishers Inc.

Rockwell Schultz, and Alton C. Johnson, (1976). *Management of Hospitals*; McGraw-Hill Book Co, A blackiston publication, N.Y.

## *Chapter 9*

# NATIONAL HEALTH INSURANCE SCHEME: THE NEED FOR OPTIMISATION AND MASS PARTICIPATION

*Irinoye, A.I.*

**About the Contributor**

Irinoye is a Medical Doctor in general practice at the Health Centre, Obafemi Awolowo University, Ile-Ife. His areas of interest are Health Education and Health Management.

## INTRODUCTION

The primary health care is the first point of contact with the patients. Referrals are made from this primary level to the secondary level and to the tertiary level. This is done to ensure that the tertiary level is not saddled with the responsibilities of secondary level and the secondary level is not saddled with the responsibilities of the primary level. However, the national health policy did not ensure the attainment of health for all by the year 2000, as anticipated.

Nigeria having adopted the target of health for all by the year 2000, and with this target still elusive by the year 2003, it is therefore important to examine funding and other critical factors from time to time. However:

> Health insurance offers a means of obtaining a substantial part of the funds for urban health services from employers and employees, both private and public so that taxes realised from contributions can be released for preventive and promotive action and for primary health care where coverage is now inadequate or absent (Hetherlington, 1975).

The concentration of health infrastructures and services in the cities to the neglect of rural dwellers has worsened the available "epileptic" health services to the poor, the aged, the very young, and the unemployed. This call for the search for an improved source of health funding that will increase the quality of life of all the citizenry irrespective of their status and where they live. This chapter which is based on a study carried out, assessed the current system of health funding, its deficiencies; and determines the suitability of national health insurance as an alternative system of health funding in Nigeria.

The objectives of this study are:

1. To examine the current system of funding Health Services;
2. To determine the deficiencies in the current system of funding health service; and
3. To assess the appropriateness of National Health Insurance Scheme as an alternative system of health funding.

The study is significant in a number of ways. First, while other reports on the subject matter are based on mere hearsays, gestures, and newspaper reports, the findings of the present study are based on empirical investigation. Secondly, the study will serve as a baseline study for further investigations. Finally, the findings will be of immense importance to the federal and state governments in the area of National Health Insurance Scheme as an alternative source of funding health care.

## THE STATE OF THE HEALTH CARE SERVICES

The health care services of Nigeria has evolved through a series of historical developments including a succession of policies and plans which had been introduced by previous administrations.

The health care services as currently organised show major defects which are widely recognised, thus:

a. The coverage is inadequate. It is estimated that no more than 35% of the population has access to modern health care services (FMOH 1988:4). Rural Communities and the urban poor are not well served.

b. The orientation of the services is inappropriate with a disproportionately high investment on curative services to the detriment of preventive services.

c. The management of the services often shows major weaknesses resulting in waste and inefficiency, as shown by the failure to meet targets and goals. With several different levels of governments, voluntary organisations and other agencies providing health care, the various inputs are poorly coordinated.

d. The involvement of the community is minimal at critical points in the decision-making process. Because the communities are not well-informed on matters affecting their health, they are often unable to make rational and informed choices.

e. The lack of basic health statistics is a major constraint at all stages of planning, monitoring and evaluation of health services.

f. The financial resources allocated to the health services, especially to some priority areas, are inadequate to permit them to function effectively.

g. The basic infrastructure and logistic supports are often defective owing to inadequate maintenance of buildings, medical equipment and vehicles; unreliable supply of water and electricity; and the poor management of drugs, vaccines and supplies system.

Whilst this list is an accurate summary of the broad range of defects in the health services, there are also encouraging cases in which dynamic health administrators, professional persons and lay members of the communities have successfully corrected these faults within their local areas. Such successful programmes provide useful models of what can be done with limited resources in spite of various constraints.

The best available estimates are obtained from a few centres where such data are collected, from sample surveys, from institutional records and from special studies as shown in Table 9.1 below:

**Table 9.1: Vital Health Statistics in Nigeria**

| | |
|---|---|
| Crude Death Rate: | 16 per 1000 population |
| Crude Birth Rate: | 50 per 1000 population |
| Childhood Mortality Rate: | 144 per 1000 children aged 1-4 years |
| Infant Mortality Rate: | 85 per 1000 live births |
| Life Expectancy at Birth: | 50 years. |

**Source:** *Nigeria Fertility Survey* 1981-82 World Demography Record.

## CURRENT TRENDS IN NIGERIA'S HEALTH CARE PROFILE

Nigeria, with a current estimated population of 99 million in 1991 is expected to double this in 23 years with an estimated population growth rate of 2.8 percent, (*World Development Report*, 1993). With the expected improvement in health care services, lower infant mortality rate and longer life expectancy, there is a trend toward more hospital care, need for social insurance, more facilities, increased management efficiencies and specialised care including nursing homes.

With increase in chronic diseases and deterioration of the extended family system, there is a general trend to greater demand for hospital care, new technologies and management techniques, new facilities and insurance to cover costs.

All these coupled with increasing health care costs necessitate the search for more efficiency, better technology and a major overhaul of the present methods of health care delivery in Nigeria.

***Social Insurance*** is now accepted internationally as applying to schemes, which provide benefits to individuals or their dependants *in* return for payment of contributions by those individuals, their employers, or both. In this case, the insurance principle is strictly adhered to. If a social insurance arrangement is made on a global (that is, national) level, it is called **National Insurance**. This is in line with the socialist ideology: from each according to his ability and to each according to his needs.

## THE DIFFERENT METHODS OF FINANCING HEALTH CARE

In Nigeria, the different methods of funding health care are:

1. Extending existing sources of finance.
2. Developing new sources of revenue.
3. Local community effort.
4. Foreign assistance.
5. Social security approach.

## THE NEED FOR A HEALTH INSURANCE SCHEME

A health insurance scheme is a necessary consequent upon:

i. The general poor state of the nation's health care services.
ii. The excessive dependence and pressure on government provided health facilities.
iii. Dwindling funding of health care in the face of rising cost.
iv. Poor integration of private health facilities in the nation's health care delivery system.

## WAYS OF MANAGING HEALTH CARE

Some ways of managing health care include:

i. *Reliance on assistance from other people especially relatives:* This may never come and if it does, it is inadequate or late.

ii. *Bearing the cost alone from personal savings:* This could endanger the life of the person as the fund may not be readily available.

iii. *Retaining the illness:* This means that the patient may go about with an illness undiagnosed either because they are unaware (lack of knowledge) or they cannot afford the cost of treatment – this is not advisable.

iv. *Self-medication*: This is very dangerous and only suppresses the disease for a more dangerous effect later.

v. *Prevention:* Illness can be prevented through personal hygiene, and good food, health maintenance, environmental sanitation, etc. Although prevention is better than cure, but unfortunately, not all mishaps can be avoided.

vi. *Protection which insurance provides:* This is a more practical and economically sound technique of managing health risks like most other risks. Insurance system is a highly developed form of providence even when not adequately arranged as where there is under-insurance, a reasonable cover is provided and the situation is reasonably controlled. By insurance arrangement, the small amount of contributions are pooled and are used to make good the individuals' incurred expenses within the approved agreed limit of benefit thus spreading their losses over a large group of people that contributed to the insurance.

The basic options for financing health care must be studied to see which one is the most adequate in any given country. There are more to health than just health care and these entails the prevention of communicable diseases, the reconstruction and modernisation of physical facilities and health manpower and its development which may make it unlikely for government to increase the budget for the continuous delivery of good quality health care.

## CLASSIFICATION OF NATIONAL HEALTH INSURANCE SCHEME (NHIS) PROGRAMMES

NHIS should be designed to cover the following segments of the society.

i. Formal Sector Social Health Insurance Programme

ii. Rural Community Social Health Insurance Programme

iii. Urban Self-employed Social Health Insurance Programme
iv. Children under Five years Social Health Insurance Programme
v. Permanently Disabled Persons Social Health Insurance Programme
vi. Prison Inmates Social Health Insurance Programme
vii. Geriatric Social Health Insurance Programme

**Advantages of National Health Insurance Scheme (NHIS)**

NHIS has the following advantages:

i. NHIS can assist Nigeria Indigenous Pharmaceutical Manufacturers Association (NIPMA) to meet the expected rise in demand for drugs. Employment will necessarily be created as idle capacity is utilised.
ii. NHIS contributes directly to the peoples' health care, the use of health facilities would improve, so also the general health of the people. There is improvement in the well-being of the society, and it will translate into higher productivity. It provides improved health status and life expectancy.
iii. NHIS will provide the 'free' health care services for workers to **enjoy**. Workers spend more than they are expected to contribute as NHIS subscription on their families' health on a monthly basis. NHIS provides basic health care for all citizens as a right and at affordable cost to individuals thus promoting household spending on health care. NHIS gives a more equitable access and higher quality basic services with the pooling of resources and spreading of risks in defined population.
iv. NHIS provides the opportunity for Nigeria to turn the health care industry over to the private sector. With the benefit of hindsight, that opportunity should have been embraced, but it was not. Today, privatisation is the *buzzword*, and the NHIS of today is another God-sent opportunity.
v. NHIS provides continuous source of health care to the unemployed and those who lost their jobs on account of ill health. These same set of people have opportunistic infections like tuberculosis, skin infections, skin cancer and diarrhoea.

vi. NHIS provides generation of additional funds for health care broadly.

vii. NHIS reduces the difficulties faced by government in developing and maintaining resources to provide health care through general taxation revenue.

**Disadvantages of NHIS**

The disadvantages of NHIS are:

i. The total health care expenditure may rise due to more people making use of NHIS but it is anticipated that the increase will reflect more equitable access to a high level of better funded basic services.

ii. NHIS contributions from new enterprises may be low and not worth cost of inspection at the early stage.

iii. NHIS may create the need for contributions to increase as the scheme develops and the insured population grows.

iv. NHIS contributors include all groups of employers some of whom may avoid payment of taxes that increase labour costs.

v. NHIS may cause more chronic health condition arising from increased life expectancy.

vi. NHIS promotes a rapid and steep rise in health care spending. It is indeed likely to begin as a response to the need for additional funds and not to immediately substitute for other financing sources if developed in low income countries.

vii. NHIS scheme being national should include the civil servants who account for a larger number of salaried workers in any country, but they and the Ministry of Finance may be the first to oppose contributions to the health scheme.

Health Insurance has been found to be feasible and is a very good approach to solving most of our health care financing problems. It has been practised in many developed and developing countries like Kenya in Africa. Why not in Nigeria?

## Impact of NHIS on the Developmental Process

The impacts of NHIS on the developmental process include:

(1) NHIS creates new and continuing allocations of resources that would not otherwise be available through public health budgets, whose share of general revenues has to be competed for among the demands from other government spending departments, probably on an annual, and thus, uncertain basis.

(2) NHIS stimulates and promotes the building up of hospitals, clinics, dispensaries and related facilities, which are not only valuable as treatment centres, but also offer health professionals and auxiliaries new and increasing opportunities for employment which is both socially useful and remunerative.

(3) NHIS thus supports increase in the number and skills of the available health manpower; indeed, emigration of doctors, which is of special concern in some developing countries, may well be curbed.

(4) NHIS erodes the commercial private health sector, and relieves the public health services of care for the persons covered by social security, so assisting these services to concentrate their attention more effectively on care in areas that are especially badly served and for sections of the community as yet excluded from social security protection, and on improved preventive activities, from which such services are irreplaceable.

(5) NHIS improves the health of the labour forces so protected, thus increasing the productivity needed for economic development and, more generally, contributes to raising living standards. In the words of the 1970 Joint ILO/WHO Committee, "each skilled worker represents a social investment (in his training, experience, etc.); therefore the maintenance of his health serves the good of the entire society".

(6) NHIS is general irrespective of political doctrine, and creates health awareness.

## METHOD OF INVESTIGATION

Data for this research was derived from secondary sources of information. The method of investigation employed in selecting any particular source of data depended mainly on the relevance and currency to the research topic. In order words, the type of data or information required to address the objectives of the study dictates the source.

## Secondary Data Sources

The secondary data sources for this study were obtained from books, articles, journals, newspapers, government bulletins and seminar reports. The data were sourced from the following institutions and libraries.

(1) Obafemi Awolowo University, Ile-Ife, Nigeria
(2) National Library, Lagos
(3) British Council Library, Ibadan
(4) Federal Ministry of Health, Abuja.

## Data Presentation, Analysis and Discussion

All the data obtained are related to countries where NHIS is practised and those practising other forms of financing health care. The data obtained were compared with what obtains in Nigeria based on some health parameters and other social indicators. These are statistical data that provide information about the quality of life in a country (see Table 9.2 below)

**Table 9.2: Infant Mortality Rate, Life Expectancy, and Adult Literacy Rate of Some Selected Countries in Most Recent Estimates**

| Country | Infant Mortality Rate 1989 (Percent) | Life Expectancy Rate 1989 (Years) | Adult Literacy Rate 1985 (Percent) |
|---|---|---|---|
| Malawi | 1.47 | 48 | 41 |
| Nigeria | 10.0 | 51 | 42 |
| Burkina Faso | 13.5 | 48 | 13 |
| India | 9.5 | 59 | 43 |
| China | 5.0 | 70 | 69 |
| Kenya | 6.8 | 59 | 59 |
| Indonesia | 6.4 p | 61 | 74 |
| Bolivia | 10.6 | 54 | 74 |

| | | | |
|---|---|---|---|
| Egypt | 6.8 | 60 | 44 |
| Ecuador | 6.1 | 66 | 82 |
| Mexico | 4.0 | 69 | 90 |
| Malaysia | 2.2 | 70 | 73 |
| Brazil | 5.9 | 66 | 78 |
| Korea, Rep. Of | 2.3 | 70 | - |
| Germany | 0.8 | 75 | 95 |
| United States | 1.0 | 76 | 95 |
| Japan | 0.4 | 79 | 95 |
| U.S.S.R | 24 | 70 | - |

**Source:** *WHO: The Developing World Toward a Better World*, (1978).

Table 9.2 shows health indicators like infant mortality rate, adult literacy rate and life expectancy of Nigeria compared to a few other nations both developed and developing. This table shows that Nigeria has a high infant mortality rate of 10 percent, which is just a little bit lower than that of Burkina Faso and Malawi that have 13.5 and 14.7 percent respectively. All these countries operate *pay as you receive treatment.* The developed countries like former USSR, USA, Japan, Germany where NHIS operate have infant mortality rates far lower than that of Nigeria, whereas countries like Malawi, Burkina Faso, India and Nigeria that operate pay as you receive treatment have comparatively low and poor health indices. Health indices are a measure of the level of health care of any community and it provides a basis for comparison. It is however observed that countries practising National Health Insurance Scheme have better health indices as shown in the table above.

The population of selected countries showing the average annual growth rate and the estimated population by the year 2025 was also obtained. (see Table 9.3. below)

**Table 9.3: Population Data of Some Selected Countries**

| Country | Average annual rate of population growth 1980-89 (Percent) | Population (1989) | Estimated Population (2025) |
|---|---|---|---|
| Malawi | 3.4 | 8,200,000 | 27,000,000 |
| Nigeria* | 3.5 | 113,800,000 | 298,000,000 |

| | | | |
|---|---|---|---|
| Burkina Faso | 2.6 | 8,800,000 | 23,000,000 |
| India | 2.1 | 832,500,000 | 1,350,000,000 |
| China | 1.4 | 1,113,900,000 | 1,597,000,000 |
| Kenya | 3.7 | 23,500,000 | 62,000,000 |
| Indonesia | 2.1 | 178,200,000 | 282,000,000 |
| Bolivia | 2.7 | 7,100,000 | 16,000,000 |
| Egypt | 2.5 | 51,000,000 | 86,000,000 |
| Ecuador | 2.7 | 10,300,000 | 19,000,000 |
| Mexico | 2.1 | 84,500,000 | 142,000,000 |
| Malaysia | 2.6 | 17,400,000 | 31,000,000 |
| Brazil | 2.2 | 147,400,000 | 236,000,000 |
| Korea, Rep. Of | 1.2 | 42,400,000 | 53,000,000 |
| Germany | 0.0 | 62,000,000 | 57,000,000 |
| United States | 1.0 | 248,800,000 | 309,000,000 |
| Japan | 0.6 | 123,100,000 | 131,000,000 |
| U.S.S.R. | 1.4 | 287,600,000 | 312,000,000 |
| * Estimated | | | |

**Source:** *WHO: The Developing World toward a Better World, (*1978).

Table 9.3 shows that Nigeria has the highest annual growth rate among the countries practising pay-as-you-receive treatment. A population growing at one percent a year like U.S.A. doubles in 70 years while a population growing at less than one percent a year like Japan will not double for more than seventy years whereas Nigeria with an annual growth rate of 3.5 percent will double in just thirty-six years.

This means that with a rapid population increase in Nigeria more resources including finance will be required to support the health of the teeming population. The search for a better health care system with community involvement, community participation and community empowerment is therefore imperative.

Data from the health infrastructure and expenditure in Nigeria was obtained *vis-à-vis* countries where NHIS is in operations as shown in Table 9.4.

**Table 9.4: Health Infrastructure and Expenditure in Nigeria, Great Britain and Sweden**

| Country | Population 1991 (m) | Doctor per 1000 Popul-ation 1982-92 | Nurse to Doctor or ratio 1988- 92 | Hospital beds per 1000 population 1985-90 | Total Health Expenditure (Official Exch. Rate dollars) | | Health Expenditure as a Percentage of GDP | | |
|---|---|---|---|---|---|---|---|---|---|
| | | | | | Millions 1990 | Per capita 1990 | Total 1990 | Public sector 1990 | Private sector 1990 |
| Nigeria | 99.0 | 0.15 | 6.0 | 1.4 | 90.6 | 9 | 3.7 | 1.2 | 1.6 |
| G.Britain | 57.6 | 1.40 | 2.0 | 6.3 | 59.6 | 1,039 | 6.1 | 5.2 | 0.9 |
| Sweden | 8.6 | 2.73 | 3.4 | 6.2 | 20.1 | 2,343 | 8.8 | 7.9 | 0.9 |

**Source:** World Bank. *World Development Report (1993)*

Table 9.4 compares Nigeria with Great Britain and Sweden where NHIS is practised. Nigeria has the highest population of 99 million as at 1991 with a ridiculously low doctor per 1000 population ratio of 0.15, nurse to doctor ratio of 6.0 and a total health expenditure as a percentage of Gross Domestic Product of 2.7 as shown in the Table 9.4 above.

The data on the Federal Government Actual Expenditure on Health (1983-1993) was also obtained as shown in Table 9.5.

**Table 9.5: Federal Government Actual Expenditure on Health (1983-1993)**

| Financial Year | Health Expenditure | Total Federal Government Expenditure | Percentage Share of Total |
|---|---|---|---|
| 1983 | 269.0 | 11,525.1 | 2.3 |
| 1984 | 210.9 | 11,686.6 | 1.8 |
| 1985 | 222.5 | 20,130.5 | 1.1 |
| 1986 | 377.2 | 15,934.5 | 2.4 |
| 1987 | 354.6 | 25,515.1 | 1.4 |

| | | | |
|---|---|---|---|
| 1988 | 496.8 | 25,220.5 | 2.0 |
| 1989 | 501.7 | 28,444.1 | 1.8 |
| 1990 | 904.9 | 36,943.3 | 2.5 |
| 1991 | 1,087.9 | 75,453.9 | 1.4 |
| 1992 | 1,050.1 | 46,035.9 | 2.3 |
| 1993 | 2,682.9 | 114,600.5 | 2.3 |

**Source:** Federal Ministry of Health, *Nigeria Health Profile (1992-1993) p.76*

Table 9.5 shows the Federal Government Actual Expenditure on health from (1983-1993). The highest health percentage share of total expenditure was in 1990 with 2.5 percent, while in 1983 and 1993, both have 2.3 percent. In 1985, it was 1.1 percent, yet WHO stipulates that at least 5 percent of any country's budget should go to the health sector.

**Table 9.6: Basic Issues in National Health Insurance Scheme; Consumers and Providers Views**

| Basic Issue in NHIS | Consumers | | | | Providers | | | |
|---|---|---|---|---|---|---|---|---|
| | Yes | | No | | Yes | | No | |
| | NOR | % | NOR | % | NOR | % | NOR | % |
| 1. Coverage Preference: Universal | 136 | 88 | 19 | 12 | 28 | 62 | 17 | 38 |
| 2. What should be covered? Preference; Both Preventive and Curative Care | 93 | 60 | 62 | 40 | 43 | 96 | 2 | 4 |
| 3. Should Patients share in costs? | 17 | 11 | 138 | 89 | 38 | 84 | 7 | 16 |
| 4. The Plan should be financed through General Tax Revenue | 150 | 97 | 5 | 3 | 40 | 89 | 5 | 11 |
| 5. Providers should pay through accredited Health Care Institutions | 96 | 62 | 59 | 38 | 21 | 47 | 24 | 53 |

NOR - Number of Respondents

**Source:** Aregbeyen (1997), National Health Insurance Scheme in Nigeria.

Table 9.6 shows health consumers and health care providers views on some basic issues concerning NHIS as conducted in a field survey done by Aregbeyen in 1995. Here, about 88 percent of health care consumers and 62 percent of health providers interviewed believed that a NHIS with a universal coverage is preferable.

Figure 9.1 below shows the infant mortality rates in 1985 and 1991 in underdeveloped, developing and developed countries. There is a decline in the rate in 1991 compared to 1985 in all countries, this can be explained by the introduction of free immunisation for children in the subsequent years.

There was a striking difference between developed and developing countries in the share of gross national product allocated to health (3.3% and 0.9% respectively in 1991).

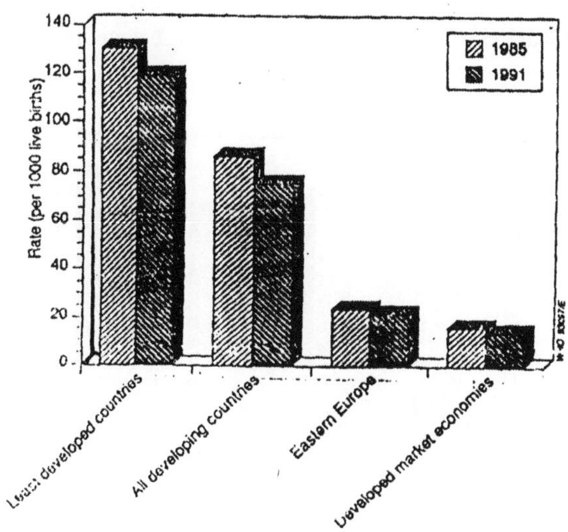


**Fig.9.1: Infant Mortality Rates 1985 and 1991**

Figure 9.1 and 9.2 buttress this point. As immunisation becomes free, available and accessible, this leveller made every child to have it, thereby increasing their survival rate and good health.

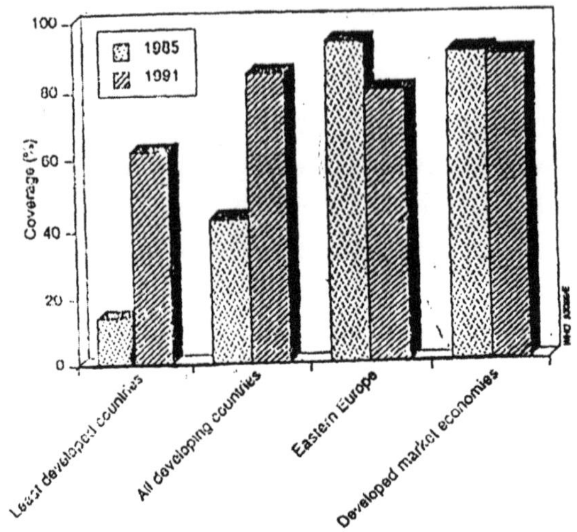


**Fig.9.2: Immunisation of Infants: Coverage by DPT vaccine, 1985 and 1991**
***Source:*** *World Health Forum*

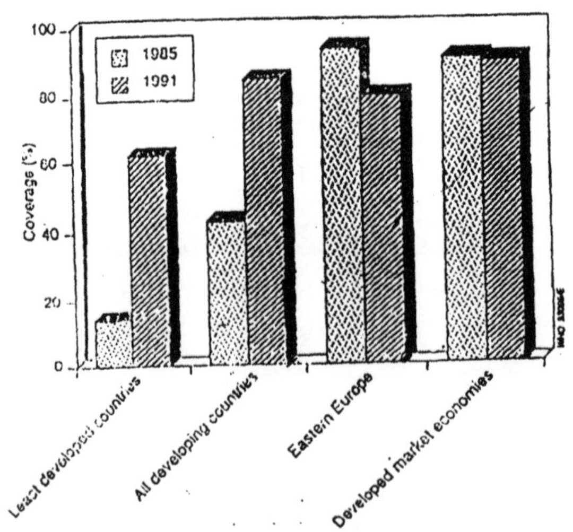


**Fig.9.3: Immunisation of Infants: Coverage by Poliomyelitis Vaccines, 1985 and 1991**
***Source:*** *World Health Forum*

## CONCLUSION

From this study, the following conclusions can be made. Social insurance arrangement is *compulsory* and is often designed to provide a *minimum economic security* for large groups of persons, particularly those in the lower economic classes. It concerns itself with the unfavourable losses (income and costs) resulting from the perils of accidental injury, sickness, old age, unemployment, and the premature death of the family wage earner. The compulsion element in a social insurance arrangement is predicated upon the experience that some persons cannot or will not voluntarily purchase insurance, and the obligation of the government derives from the duty to protect the general welfare of its citizens. Compulsory membership mitigates adverse selection against the insurers. Social insurance is designed to provide an answer to dependency problems of society.

Fragmentary information indicated that many countries had started to review and reform the organisation of health care systems including their financing with various modified forms of NHIS. This to a large extent has addressed the imbalance and inequity in the health service provision. It has also ensured adequate integration of human resources into the health systems and technologies sufficiently applied to the process of health development.

NHIS has helped to increase production in countries where it operates in that, it breaks the vicious cycle of poverty. This poverty is the bane of developing countries. The circle can be depicted by a flow chart:

Low production→ Low saving →Low investment in capital→Poor health→Low consumption→Low production.

This vicious circle has an upward moving spiral ever widening arcs that can only be broken by NHIS. This is the only way to ensure that subscribers pool resources together for increased productivity, progress and growth of the society. NHIS is both a landmark and a watershed in the annals of the health care system of the Nigerian nation.

The right time to start implementing NHIS is now, the good health care for the poor must not wait for tomorrow that may never come. If NHIS is to be effective both economically and socially, the people have to accept an increase in their contributions toward financing health care services.

## RECOMMENDATIONS

It is recommended that Nigeria should undertake periodic surveys of financing and resource allocation to the health sector to monitor and evaluate the efficiency and effectiveness of any policy.

Nigeria should establish designated centres for information/data collection on all available data on health ranging from financing, distribution, utilisation of health care to health parameters and technology and such information should be freely accessible to everybody.

The outcome of empirical studies on the subject matter has shown that countries practising NHIS have better health care services, therefore Nigeria cannot be an exception if she is to achieve good health for all at whatever year.

## References

Aregbeyen, J.B.O. (1997). *National Health Insurance Scheme in Nigeria: Benefits, Costs & Consequences*, Ibadan, NISER. Monography Series No. 2.

Centre for Insurance Research, (1998). Proceedings of the National Health Insurance Seminar, Emanco Print Holding, Nigeria.

Federal Ministry of Health, (1985). *Report of the Special Committee on National Health Care Financing,* Lagos. FMOH.

Federal Ministry of Health, (1988). *Policy and Strategy to Achieve Health for All Nigerians* Lagos: FMOH.

Federal Ministry of Health, (1992-1993). *Nigerian Health Profile*, Lagos: FMOH.

Hetherlington, Robert W. *et al*, (1975). *Health Insurance Plans: Promise and Performance*. New York, Wiley.

Nigeria Fertility Survey. (1981-82). *World Demography Record.*

WHO 1978. "The Developing World, Towards a Better World".

WHO 1986. "Funding Health for all: Is Insurance the Answer" *World Health* Forum, Geneva: WHO.

World Bank 1990. *World Development Report* 1990. New York: Oxford University Press.

World Bank 1993. *World Development Report* 1993: *Investing in Health*. New York: Oxford University Press.

World Health Organization. (1987). "Health Care – Who Pays" *World Health Forum.* Geneva: WHO.

## *Chapter 10*

# HEALTH MANAGEMENT: MARKETING PERSPECTIVE

*Egbuwalo, M.O.*

**About the Contributor**

M.O. Egbuwalo holds Ph.D in Agricultural Economics. He has taught both at the secondary and tertiary levels. He joined the Code of Conduct Bureau and rose to the rank of Director in 2001, a position he is occupying till date. He has served the bureau both at the state and national levels. He has published many articles in learned journals and authored four other books. A member of the Institute of Chartered Accountants of Nigeria (ICAN). Dr Egbuwalo is genuinely interested and actively involved in research works.

## INTRODUCTION

The relationship between economic growth and health has long been of interest to social and medical scientists (Diop *et al*, 1991). Psacharopoulos (1995) believed that productiyity and length of potential working lives are directly affected by health and nutrition. Nutritional deficiencies in childhood can affect adult height (which is a good indicator of) productivity, morbidity and mortality.

For most people in developing countries, loss of working time because of ill health means loss of income. Even then, every individual cherishes good health; apart from the fact that ill-health has a negative impact on the Gross Domestic Product (GDP) of every nation. This is because the impact of man-hours, or man-days lost through ill-health could be substantial when translated into output. Economic growth could be promoted by good health and reduction in mortality. As adult mortality falls (because of improved health status) and life expectancy increases, people are more inclined to invest in education and training. These investments, together with lower adult and child mortality are associated with lower fertility and higher rates of economic growth (Psachoropoulos, (1984, 1994); World Bank (1993 (a), 1995 (a,b) ); Becker, (1995).

Studies revealed that fertility choices have great bearing in the relationship between economic growth and human capital investments (Becker, 1995). Families choosing to have fewer children are able to invest more in the health, nutrition, education, and training of each. Low fertility, small family size, and large investments in human capital are associated with higher incomes and a faster-growing economy (Chernichovshy, 1979). Better health and lower mortality reinforce these decisions, which lead to a virtuous cycle of prosperity and release individuals and nations from their former trap of poverty, characterised by low investments in human capital, low incomes, high fertility, and low growth. In addition, rapid population growth can destroy the potential for growth of national economies and living standards.

The foregoing underscores the need for optimal management of health care organisations and making conscious efforts to market health care/medical services to the citizenry.

This chapter has attempted a definition of the concept of optimal management. It has also explained the concepts of health care organisations and marketing.

The demand and supply analyses of the medical market have been made with graphical illustrations without going into the derivation of the demand and supply schedules/curves. Elasticities of demand for medical services have also been analysed.

The chapter goes on to discuss the marketing of physical products and services with a view to bring into a focus the differences between them. The marketing strategies for health care or medical services have also been addressed.

## THE CONCEPT OF OPTIMAL MANAGEMENT

Management has been defined in various ways by various scholars. Prasad and Bannerjee (1997) define management as the manner in which a given task is executed and supervised. It also means accomplishing a task within limited resources available and the skill in the manipulation of the resources. Management is "getting things done through people by effective utilisation of resources, time and environment". Environment includes government policies, legal frameworks, economic and social factors, competition, etc.

"Optimal management" could be conceptualised as the effective utilisation of resources to obtain the best results in an environment within a timeframe.

Optimal management of health care organisations or industry or hospitals is the effective management of human, financial, material and time resources to effectively deliver health care services to the consumers of medical services in an environment. It is the most efficient level of service delivery by the organisation, from which consumers derive maximum satisfaction.

## THE CONCEPT OF HEALTH/HEALTH CARE

Health is a somewhat nebulous condition that is difficult to define, and never in a state of perfection. It might be helpful to define health, good or bad, in measurable terms and interpretation with respect to the ability of the individual at the time of measurement to function in a normal manner with respect to the likelihood of imminent disease. Thus, health has been defined as "a state of complete physical, mental, social and economic well-being, and not merely the absence of disease or infirmity". This definition has also been interpreted as "the ability to lead a socially and economically productive life" (Anyanwu, 1997).

Health care implies "the provision of conditions for normal, mental and physical development" and the functioning of the human being individually or in a group. It includes health protection measures, promotion of health, prevention of sickness, curative and protective medicine in all its ramifications.

In Nigeria, health care is a shared responsibility among the Federal,

State and Local Governments. The Local Governments are supposed to take care of the primary level (emphasising preventive medicare - health clinics, dispensaries, etc), while the State Governments are responsible for the secondary level (emphasising curative medicare/ first referral - general hospitals, etc). On the other hand, the Federal Government is in charge of the tertiary level of health care (emphasising referral medicare) to which teaching and specialist hospitals belong.

However, there are private individuals that operate private hospitals and providing some or all these categories of medical services. Health care services include all health sector services whose primary intention (regardless of effect) is to improve health. Thus, activities like health promotion and prevention of diseases, diagnosis, treatment and care, and rehabilitation relative to illness, disability or injury are included (Lee and Mills; 1983).

## HEALTH CARE SERVICES: DEMAND AND SUPPLY ANALYSES

The derivation of the demand curve for medical services requires the establishment of the relationship between the quantity of medical services and utility. The stock of health can be treated as a durable good that generates utility and is subject to the law of diminishing marginal utility. This means that each incremental improvement in health generates successively smaller additions to total utility. It should be noted that medical services are inputs in the production of health because a person consumes medical services for the express purpose of maintaining, restoring, or improving health.

To Santerre and Neun (1996), the demand for medical care is a "derived demand" and it depends on the demand for health and the extent to which medical care influences the production of health. The law of diminishing marginal productivity causes the marginal improvement of health brought about by each additional unit of medical care or service consumed to decrease.

From the foregoing discussion, it follows that medical care indirectly provides utility. Medical care helps to produce health, which in turn generates utility. Consequently, utility can be specified as a function of the quantity of medical care.

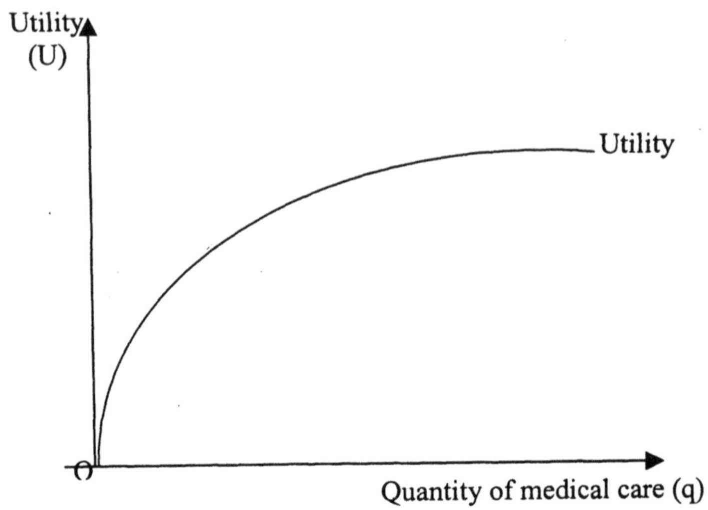


**Fig. 10.I: The Relationship between Utility and Medical Care**
**Source:** Santerre, R. E.*et al* (1996) Health Economics: Theories, Insights and Industry Studies.

In Fig. 10.I, utility is specified on the vertical axis while the quantity of health care services/medical care (q) is measured on the horizontal axis. The shape of the total utility curve indicates that utility increases at a decreasing rate with respect to medical care or that medical care or health care services are subject to diminishing marginal utility.

Marginal utility decreases because:

(a) each successive unit of medical care generates a smaller improvement in health than the previous unit (due to the law of diminishing marginal productivity) and

(b) Each increase in health, in turn, generates a smaller increase in utility (due to the law of diminishing marginal utility).

**Utility - Maximising Rule**

Given market prices at a point in time, consumers must decide which combination of goods and services, including medical care, to purchase with their fixed incomes. Each consumer chooses the bundle of goods and services that maximises utility. Consumers' utility is maximised when the marginal utility gained from the last Naira spent on each product is equal across all goods and services purchased, and if all prices are known, income is spent over the period in question and all products are subject to the law of diminishing marginal utility. This is the utility - maximising rule, which states that total utility reaches its peak when the consumer receives the maximum "bang for the buck" in terms of marginal utility per naira of income from each and every good.

Santerre and Neun (1996), Koutsoyiannis (2000), have shown that this rule can be mathematically stated as

$$MUq / Pq = MUz / Pz \quad \ldots\ldots\ldots\ldots\ldots\ldots(1)$$

Where MUq represents the marginal utility received from the last unit of medical care purchased, q, and MUz equals the marginal utility received from the last unit of all other goods, z . The latter goods are often referred to as composite goods.

The downward-sloping nature of the demand curve for a particular medical service such as physician services is based on the equilibrium condition specified in equation (1), with the assumption that:

(a) the prices of all other goods and consumer's income remain constant, and
(b) initially the consumer is purchasing the optimal mix of physician services and all other goods.

The downward-sloping demand curve for the physician's services reflects the inverse relationship between the quantity demanded and the price of the physician's services, all other things being equal.

But of course, the demand for health care is also influenced by other economic and non-economic factors or variables. Santerre and Neun (1996) states that unlike price, which causes a movement along the same demand curve, other factors influence the quantity demanded by altering the position of the demand curve. Such other variables include:

(i) real income of the consumer

(ii) prices of other goods (medical care) that are complementary
(iii) prices of substitutes (medical care)
(iv) time cost
(v) availability of health insurance scheme
(vi) taste and preference of the health care services demander (consumer)
(vii) marital status of the health care service demander (consumer)
(viii) age of the medical care demander (consumer)
(ix) level of education of the medical service demander (consumer)
(x) environmental factors (stock of health)
(xi) quality of medical service.

The supply of health care services in Nigeria can be divided into two segments; viz Private Hospitals and Government Hospitals. Essentially, the provision (supply) of health care or medical services is done by both the private and the public sector of the economy. The private sector health care services providers are the private hospitals or health care organisations, while government hospitals constitute the public sector providers (suppliers). All the health care organisations operate in a perfectly competitive health care/medical services market, as it is with most industries manufacturing physical products.

Koutsoyiannis (2000), Henderson and Quandt (2000), opined that a perfectly competitive market is characterised by:
(i) free entry into and exit from the market
(ii) perfect knowledge of the market by participants
(iii) free mobility of factors of production
(iv) product/service homogeneity
(v) every participant in the market is a price-taker, so that every economic agent in the market is so small that it cannot exert a perceptible influence on price.

As the demand for and the supply of tangible goods can be explained with the classical framework of the demand and supply curves, so also the demand for and the supply of health care services can be explained with the same tool. It should be noted that the production and consumption of medical services are synchronised, as it is with other service industries. Therefore, their demand and supply schedules may not lend themselves to easy tabulation.

The range of other service industries include accountancy, advertising, airlines, banks, barbers, hairdressing, car hire, computer services, dry cleaners, hotels, insurance, law, theatre artists, universities/polytechnics/monotechnics, etc.

The demand and supply analyses of health care services in Nigeria can be explained with the aid of Fig. 10.2a and 10.2b.

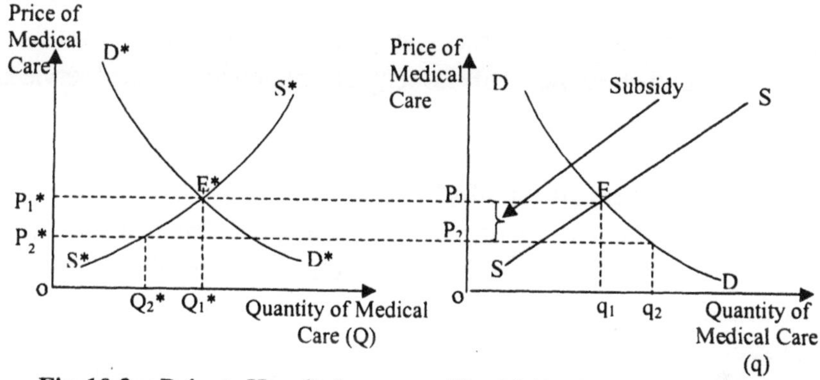


**Fig. 10.2a: Private Hospitals** **Fig. 10.2b: Government Hospitals**

**Source**: Santerre, R. E. *et al* (1996) Health Economics: Theories, Insights and Industry Studies.

Fig 10.2a depicts a situation whereby the equilibrium is achieved at point E* between the demand for and the supply of health care services in a private hospital. At price $OP_1*$, $OQ_1*$ number of patients benefit from the health care services provided by private hospitals. Alternatively, $OQ_1*$ represents the quantity of health care services sold at the unit price $OP_1*$. Correspondingly, at price $OP_1$, in Fig. 10.2b, $Oq_1$, number of patients benefit from the health care services provided by government hospitals. The corresponding prices and quantities are the same in both Fig 10.2a and Fig 10.2b.

The provision of health care services is one of the social responsibilities of government. Because of this, government does not allow market forces to determine the prices to be paid for health care services in government hospitals, hence the government subsidises the cost of providing health care services, so that more people could benefit from such services. As a result of the subsidy, represented by the gap $P_1P_2$ in Fig 10.2b, consumers pay lower prices for health care services than the market determined price of $OP_1$* or $OP_1$ in both figures. Consumers now pay price $OP_2$ in Fig 10.2b, while the number of beneficiaries of the health care services increases from $Oq_1$ to $Oq_2$. Point E, Fig 10.2b is the equilibrium point between the demand curve DD and supply curve SS. With subsidy, health care services are apparently cheaper in government hospitals than in private hospitals.

At this point, the concept of elasticity of demand for medical services will be considered.

## Elasticity of Demand for Medical Services

The commonest elasticity of demand is the Own-Price Elasticity of Demand. This measures the extent to which consumers alter or change their consumption of a product or service when its own price changes. It is usually calculated with the formula:

$$E_D = \%\Delta Q_D / \%?P \qquad (2)$$

Where ED denotes the price elasticity of demand, $\%\Delta Q_D$ represents the percentage change in quantity demanded of the product or service, and $\%\Delta P$ stands for percentage change in price. $E_D$ is a simple ratio that equals the percentage change in quantity demanded divided by the percentage change in price. Because elasticity is specified as a ratio of two percentages, it is scale free. This makes it a lot easier to compare elasticities across different goods.

The value of $E_D$ is negative. This reflects the inverse relationship between price and quantity demanded. In economics, the normal practice is to take the absolute value of the price elasticity of demand measure or $|E_D|$, and ignore the negative sign.

If the price elasticity of demand is greater than unity in absolute terms $|E_D|>1$), the demand for the product or service is referred to as price elastic. In mathematical terms, $|E_D| > 1$ if the absolute value of the percentage change in price is smaller than the absolute value of the change in the quantity demanded, or $|\%\Delta P| < \%| Q_D|$.

The price elasticity of demand is referred as inelastic if $/E_D/ < 1$, but greater than zero. In this case, $|\%| P| > |\%| Q_D$ ç, or the percentage change in price is greater than the percentage change in quantity demanded of medical services in absolute terms.

If $|E_D|$ happens to equal one(1) because $|\%\Delta P|$ equals $|\%\Delta Q_D|$, the price elasticity of demand is equal to unity or unit elastic. This implies that one percentage decrease in the price of the product or service leads to one percentage increase in the quantity demanded.

A demand curve that is vertical is said to be perfectly inelastic because no change occurs in the quantity demanded when the price changes: In mathematical terms, $E_D$ equals zero because $\%\Delta Q_D$ equals zero. At the other extreme, if the demand curve is horizontal, it is referred to as being perfectly elastic and $|E_D|$ equals infinity ($\infty$). Any change in price leads to an infinite change in the quantity demanded.

| Verbal Description | Perfectly Inelastic | Inelastic | Unitary | Elastic | Perfectly Elastic |
|---|---|---|---|---|---|
| Mathematical Representation | $\|ED\| = 0$ $\%\Delta Q_D = 0$ | $\%\Delta\|$ $Q_D\| < \|\%\Delta P\|$ | $O < \|E_D\| < 1$ $\|\%\Delta Q_D\| =$ $\|\%\Delta P\|$ | $1 < /E_D\| < \infty$ $\|\%\Delta Q_D\| >$ $\|\%\Delta P\|$ | $1 < /E_D\| < \infty$ $\%\Delta P = O$ |

Graphical Representation

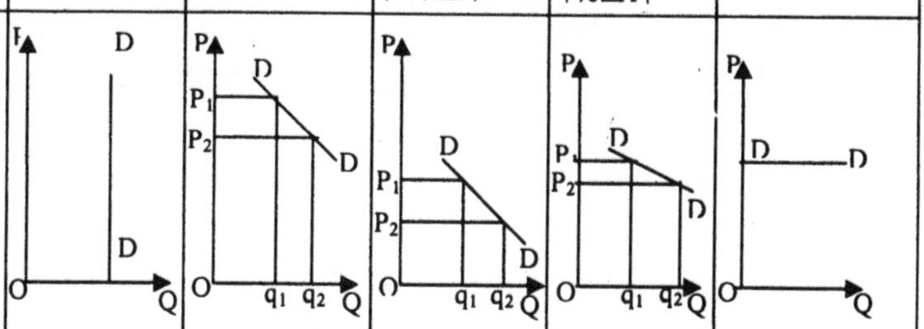


Fig.10.3. | Fig.10.3b | Fig.10.3c | Fig.10.3d | Fig.10.3e

**Fig. 10.3: Summary of Own-Price Elasticity of Demand**
**Source:** Santerre, R. E.*et al* (1996) Health Economics: Theories, Insights and Industry Studies.

The availability of substitutes is another determinant of price elasticity. Various types of medical services may serve as substitutes for one another. As a result, the quantity demanded of any medical service is likely to be much more sensitive to price changes when the alternative means of acquiring medical care are available. The demand for a medical service should become more price elastic as the number of substitutes expand. One implication is that the demand for an individual medical service or an individual medical care provider is likely to be more elastic than the overall demand for medical care.
The own-price elasticity can be used to predict what happens to total health expenditures if price increases or decreases. Total revenues (or total expenditures, from the consumer's perspective) equal price times quantity. In mathematical notation:

$$TR = PQ_D \quad \ldots\ldots(3)$$

Where TR stands for total revenue. Demand theory tells us that as the price of a product increases, the quantity demanded decreases, or that P and $Q_D$ move in opposite directions. Whether total revenue increases or decreases, the price changes is dictated by the elasticity of demand. Consider an increase in the price of physician services where demand is inelastic. This means that $\%\Delta| Q_D| < |\%\Delta P|$ or that the percentage increase in price is larger than the percentage decrease in quantity demanded in absolute terms. This means that total revenue must increase with a higher price.

If demand happens to be elastic, the opposite occurs: quantity demanded falls faster than price increases, as a result, total revenue decreases. No change occurs in total revenue when demand is unitary because the increase in price is matched by the same percentage decrease in quantity demanded. The implications of a price decrease on total revenue could also be explained when demand is elastic, inelastic, and unitary.

Elasticity of demand has implications for the marketing of medical services. Therefore, a good knowledge of it will assist medical practitioners in charging prices or marketing of their services.

## THE CONCEPT OF MARKETING

The production of goods and services are not complete until the goods or services produced get into the hands of the final consumers. This understanding makes marketing very relevant in any human society.

Marketing practitioners and scholars have defined marketing in many ways which include the following:

(i) The Chartered Institute of Marketing in the United Kingdom defined marketing as "the management of process which identifies, anticipates and supplies customers requirements efficiently and profitably".

(ii) The American Marketing Association defined marketing as "the integrated analysis, planning and control of product, price, promotion, and distribution, to create exchanges and satisfy consumer and organisational needs".

(iii) Runyon (1982) defined marketing "as the performance of business activities that direct the flow of goods and services from producer to consumers".

(iv) Kotler (1997) stated that marketing is "a human activity directed at satisfying needs and wants through exchange processes".

(v) In this chapter, marketing is conceived as "human efforts that direct the flow of goods and services from the producers to the consumers at a price, place and time".

Marketing as an activity is not new. It has been practised in rudimentary fashion by traders thousands years ago. But in advanced industrial countries where specialisation of production, labour and managerial talents is widely adopted, marketing has acquired significance as a distinctive area of management activity and responsibility. Marketing as a separate, identifiable function of management has evolved from the business philosophy which recognises the importance of the customer to the success of the business. Management must recognise the fact that "the customer is king" and must therefore be treated with reverence.

Chisnall (1975) viewed that, for a business organisation to achieve its objectives, be it profit-oriented commercial company marketing consumer, industrial produces or public services utility, optimal planning, control and management of resource utilisation are very vital.

## The Marketing Mix

The marketing of products (goods or services) requires the use of marketing mix or strategies. These are the four controllable variables or elements that marketers use in influencing buyer's response. These four elements are commonly referred to as the 4P's (Cannon, 1998; Olowo, 2001). The four P's are product, price, promotion and place.

### *Product

A product is simply a good or service or an idea which satisfies human needs. A good is a tangible entity, while a service is intangible. Service results from the application of human or mechanical efforts directed to people or objects. In his own view, Olowo (2001) believed that ideas are concepts, issues, philosophies or even images that help in understanding and solving problem.

Cannon (1998), is of the opinion that a product can be sub-divided into quality levels, special features, styling, branding, product range or mix, service backup, warranty, durability and packaging. The product mix of these features can vary enormously. A firm might invest heavily in quality control and first-rate materials to ensure a top quality, durable product, which would keep its service and quality costs down. Another company might provide an array of products each with a different combination of these elements, for example, a low-quality product backed by a high service element in combination with a masthead, high-quality product.

### *Price

Price is the mechanism of exchange between firm and customer. It incorporates level(s), credit (terms and sources), discounts, margins, resources, financial services (for example, advice), allowances or trade-ins and strategy and tactics. As in the case of products, considerable scope exists for establishing a different sub-mix of price elements. One firm might have a high premium price but offers generous credit terms, while another might have a far low price but give virtually no credit. The mix can vary between levels of the market. The retailer might be encouraged through high discount to buy low and sell high to end-users.

***Promotion**

Promotion encompasses the two broad areas of advertising (including below-the-line) and personal selling: advertising comprises main media/ display, main media/classified, and below-the-line; merchandising comprises promotional support for the retailer; personal selling comprises salesman's special discounts; and publicity comprises press and public relations.

Promotion consists of all activities used by producers to inform and persuade buyers to buy a product or service.

***Place**

Place or distribution is an element of the marketing mix. It involves the process by which a company makes its product or service available and accessible to customers at a profit. Distribution is, therefore, an important element of the four (4P's). It ensures that the right quantity of goods is placed at the right place for the right customers and at the right time. The activities of distribution or place include transportation, inventory management, warehousing, materials handling, factory location, stocks, freight, insurance, etc.

## Marketing of Services

A service is any activity or benefit that one party can offer to another that is essentially intangible and does not result in the ownership of anything, but must be able to provide want satisfaction.

Cannon (1998) defined services as those separately identifiable, essentially intangible activities which provide want satisfaction, and which are not necessarily tied to the sale of a product or another service. To produce a service may or may not require the use of tangible goods. However, when such use is required, there is no transfer of the title (permanent ownership) to these tangible goods. Human and/or mechanical efforts directed at people are used to produce services.

Take for example, the teacher using his/her efforts to provide education (service) directed at students who are the customers. Legal advice from a lawyer is a service using human efforts. The transportation of people or objects from one place to another involves the use of both human and mechanical efforts. A good number of services such as haircut, health care, car repairs, landscaping, etc, involve both human and mechanical efforts.

### *Characteristics of Services*

Services possess some characteristic features which make them differ from physical products. These differences are found in the characteristics of services. These are:

#### **Intangibility*

By this, we mean that a service cannot be touched, tasted, seen, smelled or a part taken to be examined before purchase. This is not to say that some services do not involve physical goods. Equipment rental service has physical components. One thing is clear about a service: the buyer of a service is not sure of what he/she is paying for and very often, has difficulty in comparing offers. The pricing of some services is usually difficult because they are difficult to evaluate before consumption. This is the reason why the consumers of some services like medicare, education, do not know in advance the actual amount they will pay before delivery.

#### **Inseparability*

This means that the production and consumption of services cannot be separated. In other words, as services are produced, the consumption also take place at the same time. So the production and consumption are synchronised. It is not possible to buy a service and take it home, store and consume it at a later date. The production of some services like hairdressing/barbing of hair, medical services involve the participation of the buyer in the production of the services.

**Heterogeneity*

Unlike products, services are not usually standardised. For example, a product like Lux Soap is standardised. A tablet of Lux Soap in Nigeria is of the same size and quality throughout the country. But in the case of a service, like hairdressing or hair barbing, there is no way to ensure that it is the same service that is offered throughout the industry in a country. Such services vary from one producer to another; there is no uniformity or standardisation or homogeneity of services.

However, services could be designed around the specific requirements of the individual customer. For example, an insurance company will quote for each person a policy based on their specific industry, goods, prospects, even location although using a fixed formula.

**Perishability*

Due to the fact that production and consumption are simultaneously carried out, services are regarded as perishable in a sense. By this, Olowo (2001), it is meant that any unused capacity now cannot be reserved for the next period. For example, an unused seat in a commercial vehicle represents a loss of revenue to the owner for ever, since the unused seat cannot be stocked or held over. So also are hotel rooms that are left vacant for one or more nights cannot be added to the following night's capacity.

In this sense, the unused capacity is regarded as perishable.

**Lack of Ownership*

In a service industry, access to or use of a facility does not mean that the customer obtains ownership of it. The hotel room, car, telephone or computer service is only hired for a period, and ultimately ownership revert back to the firm offering the service.

**Customer Contact*

By this, we mean the interaction between the service provider and the service buyer in the course of delivering the service. For the service buyer to be satisfied, the service provider becomes very important. A satisfied service provider or employee leads to satisfied service buyers or customers. As a result, service companies should endeavour to carefully select their employees and train them very well for the job. Similarly, service providers or employees can be motivated by both monetary and non-monetary incentives.

## Marketing Strategies for Health Care Services

Like the product or goods firms, the health care firms (organisations) in Nigeria are also operating in a competitive environment. For them to keep afloat, they need to adopt potent marketing strategies for their services. Private hospitals are in business to make profits, while government hospitals are in business to provide health care services to the people and not necessarily to make profits. But they need to justify their existence by providing excellent services to the people.

Since services differ from tangible goods, they require more than the 4P's (product, price, place and promotion) for their marketing to be successful. Promotion entails advertisement which is not allowed in the medical profession. The advertisement of hospitals and their services is regarded as unethical and it is therefore prohibited.

However, advertisement in the medical profession could be done by Government or Non-Governmental Organisations (NGO's) to create awareness for the public about the prevalence of a particular deadly disease like the Human Immunodeficiency Virus/Acquired Immune Deficiency Syndrome (HIV/AIDS), malaria, and so on; and to create awareness about the availability of the therapy and / or prevention.

In addition to the 4P's, the marketing strategies for health care organisations should focus on both the internal marketing as well as interactive marketing.

## Internal Marketing Strategies

This refers to effective training and motivation of employees that normally have contact with customers and generally all the supporting staff so that they can work as a team. A successful health care organisation starts with taking good care of those who take care of patients.

In order to get the best from the staff of an organisation, the staff need to be motivated. By motivation, we mean inducement or encouragement given to individual or group of people to make them perform willingly and perform optimally in a given circumstance (Armstrong, 1999). Motivating strategies or factors aim at creating a working environment and to develop policies and practices that will provide for optimal levels of performance from employees. Such strategies could either be: (a) monetary and (b) non-monetary rewards or incentives.

### (a) *Monetary Incentive*

Monetary incentive can provide positive motivation in the right circumstance, not only because people need and want money but also because it serves as a highly tangible means of recognition. But badly designed and managed pay system can de-motivate. In other words, the reward should be clearly related to efforts or level or responsibility and people should not receive less money than they deserve compared with their counterparts in the same job and environment.

Emphasis on financial reward seems greater among the jobless who will accept any wage just to make ends meet. Later on, they have other demands that have little to do with their earnings. There are people who leave higher paying jobs for lower paying jobs in a more conducive environment.

Employees draw a line between "good money" which is adequate reward for a day's work with sufficient time for rest and enjoyment of the earning and the "big money windfall" which could be realised only at the expense of good health, enjoyment of leisure and social engagements. Increases in wages, therefore, may fail to motivate workers to put in more hours if they prefer good functional social amenities, infrastructures and leisure to the "big money"

### (b) *Non-Monetary Incentive*

Non-monetary incentives that can motivate workers in an organisation to put in their best include:

(i) *Recognition*: Workers in an organisation need to be given recognition by management as a morale booster. Treatment as a human being rather than as a robot, and credit for accomplishment go a long way to boost workers' ego and give a feeling of pride and a sense of belonging or achievement.

(ii) *Valuing Employees:* Motivation and commitment are likely to be enhanced if employees feel that they are valued by management. This means investing in their success, trusting and empowering them, giving them the opportunity to be involved in matters with which they are concerned, keeping them fully in the picture, treating them fairly and like human beings rather than "resources' to be exploited in the interest of management; and providing them with rewards (financial and non-financial) that demonstrates the extent to which they are valued.

(iii) *Behavioural Commitment*: This means that individuals will direct their efforts to achieving organisational and job objectives. It can be engendered by getting people involved in setting objectives, giving people more responsibilities to manage their own jobs as individuals or as teams (empowerment) and providing for rewards to be clearly related to success in achieving agreed goals.

(iv) *Employee Development:* For the optimal management of any organisation, staff development is highly essential. Self-development and self-managed learning are the best forms of development. Employees should be giving the opportunity for self-development through training and re-training.

(v) *Fairness and Justice:* The fundamental human rights of the people should not be subordinated to egocentricity of the people in position of leadership. Human beings cherish fair treatment and adequate reward for meritorious service with judicious degree of punishment for infraction as and when due. Leaders must not only be fair, but must be seen to be fair.

**Interactive Marketing Strategies**

Interactive marketing means interaction between buyers and sellers during service encounter. The quality of a service provided depends very much on the service deliverer and the quality of delivery. For example, the customer judges the quality of surgery, not only on the success of the operation, but also on his/her encounter with the doctor and the other relevant medical staff. Good human relations (customer-friendly) are highly essential, even after the administration of treatment to patients.

Modern management theory requires that on the part of the leadership, in addition to the foregoing, probity, accountability, transparency, hard work, commitment to duties, patriotism need to be called into play so as to achieve optimal management of a health care organisation; be it private or public.

From the foregoing scenario of marketing strategies, it becomes clear that the marketing mix has gone beyond the four (4Ps). In addition to the conventional 4Ps (Product, Price, Place, and Promotion) we now have people, processes and physical evidence. These three additional variables are sometimes, referred to as the "soft elements" of the marketing mix and they are regarded as being relevant to the internal, rather than the external aspects of the organisation, although they are all relevant to the customer.

*** People**

This aspect covers the training and motivation of the people involved in the marketing effort. This people are directly involved in the marketing of the prescription products. In a large health care organisation, this aspect may be the pharmaceutical department of the hospital.

*** Processes**

The marketing mix should be seen as a "tool box" which contains the controllable variables used by the marketers to satisfy customer needs. This element refers to the systems used in the organisation which contribute to the marketing effort. The customer comes in contact with the organisation in many ways; making enquiries, making a purchase, seeking advice on delivery dates, receiving invoices and statements, and after sales. If the marketer can influence or modify the organisational processes in such a way that they become customer-friendly, it will add to the overall marketing effort.

**** Physical Evidence***

This aspect refers to what the customer "sees" surrounding the purchase of a service or a product. The term covers the physical appearance and ambience that collectively imprint on the customer's mind. This could be the quality of information leaflets referred to as "detail aids" in the case of drugs given to patients or other products that have information leaflets to guide the customer or the user on how to use the product.

These additional three marketing mix have now been recognised in the intellectual world and by the marketing practitioners as equally important to all types of marketing activities as the conventional 4Ps are (Adetola, 2001). Therefore, we now talk of the 7Ps as our marketing mix.

## CONCLUSION

As it has been pointed out earlier in this chapter, the provision of medical services is one of the social responsibilities of government to the people. Therefore, the determination of the prices to be paid for medical services should not be left for market forces, even though most sectors of the world economy have been deregulated. In this way, most citizens of the world would be able to have access to qualitative medical care at affordable costs.

## References

Adetola, T. (2001). "Innovative Marketing in a Highly Regulated Environment: A Case Study of Marketing Prescription Drugs in Glaxosmithkline Nigeria Plc". Unpublished MBA Project, Department of Management and Accounting, Obafemi Awolowo University, Ile-Ife, Nigeria.

Anyanwu, J. C. *et al* (1997). *The Structure of the Nigerian Economy* (1960-1997) Onitsha: Joanee Educational Publishers Ltd., Nigeria.

Armstrong, M. (1999). *A Handbook of Human Resource Management Practice*. London: Kogan Page Ltd.

Becker, G.S. (1995). Human Capital and Poverty Alleviation: Human Resources Development and Operations Policy (HRD) Working Papers, World Bank, Washington D.C., March 1995.

Cannon, T. (1998). *Marketing: Principles and Practice*. New York:Cassell Publishers Ltd.

Chernichovshy, D. (1979). "Personal Savings and Family Size and Composition: The unresolved Issues" in *International Union for the Scientific Study of Population, Economic and Demographic Change: Issues for the 1980s*. Helsinki 1979, Vol. 1, Liege, Belgium.

Chisnall, P. M. (1995). *Marketing: A Behavioural Analysis*. McGraw-Hill Book Coy Ltd, U.K

Diop, F., Hill, K. and Sirageldin, I. (1991). *Economic Crisis, Structural Adjustment and Health in Africa*. World Bank Working Papers (NPS) 166, World Bank, Washington D. C.

Englewood Cliffs: Prentice Hall. U.K.

Henderson, N.V. (2000). *Henderson County Health 2000 Report*. www.plfo.org/Reports Presentation/Henderson Health 200 htm.

Kotter, P. (1997). *Marketing Management: Analysis, Planning and Control*.

Koutsoyiannis, D. (2000). *et al. Journal of Public Health Medicine*. www.ucl.ac.uk/stats/research/catalogue/2000 Pub.html.

Lee, K. and Mills, A. (eds) (1983). *The Economics of Health in Developing Countries*. OUP, Oxford.

"Mass Returns to Investment in Education: A Global Update" World Development Papers, (Sept. 1994).

Olowo, T. (2001). *Basic Marketing*: Oluwatimilehin Press Ltd., Ilorin, Nigeria.

Prasad, L. and Bannerjee, A. M. (1997). *Management of Human* Resources. Sterling Publishers Private Ltd, New Delhi.

Psacharopoulos, G. (1984). "The Contribution of Education to Economic Growth: international Comparisons" in Kendrick J. W. (ed) *International Comparisons of Productivity and Causes of Slowdown* Ballinger, Cambridge.

Runyon, K. E. (1982). *The Practice of Marketing* Merrill Publishing Coy, Columbus, Ohio.

Santerre, R. E. and Neun, S. P. (1996). 'Health Economics: Theories, Insights and Industry Studies". Richard D. Irwin, *Times Mirror* Higher Education Group Inc. Coy. U.S.A.

World Bank (1993a). *World Development Report: Investing in Health*. World Bank Washington D. C.

(1993b). "Human Resources in Latin America and the Caribbean: Priorities and Action", World Bank America and Caribbean Region Washington D. C.

(1995a). *Priorities and Strategies for Education: A World Bank Review*, World Bank, Washington D. C.(1995b); *Investing in People: The World Bank in Action*. World Bank, Washington D.C.

# *Chapter 11*

# FACTORS OF HEALTH HUMAN CAPITAL ACCUMULATION IN NIGERIA

*Adebayo, A.A. & Oladeji, S. I.*

**About the Contributors**

Dr Abayomi Adebayo is currently, a senior lecturer in Economics in Obafemi Awolowo University, Ile-Ife. On different occasions, he has won many awards locally and internationally. He also co-authored several books currently been used in most Nigerian universities and has published several articles in local, national and international learned journals. He is a member of Osun State Manpower Board, Osogbo. He is an assessor in Economics and Qualitative Analysis of the Institute of Chartered Accountants of Nigeria (ICAN) from 1992 till date.

Oladeji is currently a Professor of Economics in Obafemi Awolowo University, Ile-Ife. He has authored and co-authored several books and has published several papers both in local and international journals. He is a chief examiner/ supervisor at the Institute of Chartered Accountants of Nigeria (ICAN), Chartered Institute of Bankers (CIBN), and the Chartered Institute of Stock-brokers. He is a consultant and resource person to the National Manpower Board, National Centre for Economic Management and Administration (NCEMA) and National Centre for Technology Management (NACETEM).

## INTRODUCTION

The pivotal role that human capital accumulation plays in the process of economic growth is increasingly being recognised by researchers and policy-makers (Laroche, 1998). An assessment by the World Bank (1995) shows that human capital account for close to 64 percent of the wealth in about 192 advanced countries, while physical and natural capital account for 16 percent and 20 percent respectively. Besides, recent empirical studies of economic growth suggest that higher stock of human capital can allow less developed country (LDC) to converge more rapidly to the income levels of a developed country through increase absorption of international technologies and capacity of imitation (Laroche, 1998). Thus, human capital can be of immense economic benefit, especially to LDCs, if the stock is well-developed through investment in nutrition, health and education.

Despite the recognition of the prime role of human capital, Laroche (1998) argues that neither economic accounts nor endogenous growth models capture fully the specific elements of human capital. To be precise, education and health are two critical aspects of human capital formation. However, in terms of studies and practical policy actions, emphases appear stronger on educational dimension of human capital than health and other health impairing environmental problems. African Development Report (1998) recognised that less research has been done on returns to health and nutrition than on the returns to education. The report noted that greater longevity; reduced suffering and absence of disability are very central and fundamental to success and contribution of people in anything. As regards policy actions, granted that there have been positive health changes over the years, high rates of disease and premature mortality are still prevalent in Africa, and especially in Nigeria where millions are been afflicted. Still prime among the causes of health affliction are malaria, respiratory infections, diarrhoea diseases, childhood diseases, parasitic diseases, HIV/AIDS, sexually transmitted diseases, tuberculosis, leprosy and injuries. Thus, in Nigeria, there is no wondering when the following demographic statistics are considered: the infant mortality rate is still 105 per 1000 live births and the under five mortality is put at 178 per 1000 live births. While the CBN estimates suggest that life expectancy at birth is 54 years, WHO's estimate puts it at 48.2 years of female and 46.8 years for males. Better control of these diseases would allow increase human capital contribution to economic development through increased productivity and longevity. Besides, improved health carries positive effect on return to investment in education because of longer life expectancy. However, generally, inadequate actions and provisions for better health are concentrated in curative dimension. In addition, an enabling environment for good health is being impeded by more deep-seated problems.

According to Monekosso (1994), poor health causes pain and suffering, reduces human energies, and makes millions of Africans less able to cope with life, let alone enjoy it. Besides, poor health shackles human capitals, reduces returns to learning, impedes entrepreneurial activities, and old back growth of gross national product (GNP). In essence, health human capital is a fundamental asset and the economic consequences are immense when not adequately attended to.

Besides, Feachem *et al.* (1992) shows that too many adults still die relatively young in Africa. The study indicated that 38 percent of the fifteen year olds do not see their sixtieth birthdays. In essence, development in the area of health is weak and in most African countries, particularly in Nigeria, the nature of health challenges remains poorly understood and appreciated. Also, while policies in both curative and preventive sub-sectors appears fair; lack of commitment at level of implementation remains a serious obstacle.

Therefore, this chapter examines the investment in health and other macro-environment factors, critical to health human capital accumulation and its benefits in social and economic development. This is done, using descriptive analytical method on secondary data that are available. This attempt is pertinent in many sub-Saharan Africa, especially Nigeria, where human resource is poorly developed. The poor development of human resources is reflected from the result of many studies. For instance, Odusola (1998) shows that the relationship between human capital investment and economic growth in Nigeria is weak, confirming that the nation's growth motivating wealth is still largely in natural resources.

Furthermore, in the context of globalisation and rapid technological changes, there has arisen a strong drive from resource-based towards knowledge-based economies. To catch up with this development, human capital has become one of the leading public policy themes. In essence, given the policy relevance of human capital in the emerging knowledge-based economies, it is essential that all critical elements of human capital be properly understood and captured in policy formulation and implementation.

## CONCEPTUAL CLARIFICATION

The concept of human capital is complex and multifaceted. In economics, human capital is used to capture the stock of all physical, intellectual, skill and psychological capacities of people (Laroche, 1998). It represents the aggregation of investments in activities, such as education, health, on-the-job training and migration that enhance individual's productivity in the labour market {see Todaro and Smith, 2003; Behrman and Taubman, 1982; and Laroche, 1998}. In this sense, when investment is made towards improving health and educational status, a stream of higher returns in term of income and health status as quality of life is expected.

As captured by African Development Report (1998), education and health in the context of their effects on human capital are interconnected. Going by studies such as Strauss and Thomas (1995), Schultz (1995) and Hobcroft (1993), expenditure on education may affect health and parental education and it has implications for children health. Health expenditure and improvement in health that it may generate affect rate of knowledge acquisition and value of education. Also, household income and improved nutrition have implications for education and health. Thus, many aspects of human capital are interrelated in a complex manner that could cause over evaluation of the contribution of any of them to human productivity and development. In the context of this relationship, therefore, development policy needs not just focus on income and education but also simultaneously on health to address the stubborn problem of poverty ( Todaro and Smith, 2003:P366).

With regards to health, according to *Mosby Medical Encyclopedia* (1992; P 360), it is a state of physical, mental and social well-being and the absence of disease and other abnormal condition. Economists see this state of well-being and freedom from diseases as a type of capital inherent in the person who possesses it. In an economy, this state of good health is basic to human welfare and fundamental to economic progress. And to individual, going by Grossman (1972), the flow of services produced from the stock of health "capital" is consumed continuously over an individual's lifetime.

On the determinant of health status, Santerre and Neun (1996), state that the initial stock of health and the rate of depreciation vary across individuals and depend on the individual's age, physical make-up, lifestyle, environmental factors, and the amount of medical care consumed. To World Bank (1995), the health of household members is affected by the nutritional value of food intake, the safety of drinking water, habitual self-care practices, purchase and use of pharmaceuticals, visit to traditional healers and local providers of modern health care.

In addition, as reported by Santerre and Neun, another variable found to contribute to health is marital status. Married adults appear to experience better health than their single counterparts, if other factors are held constant. The study shows that the existence of a spouse augments the production of health within the home and that the marital relationship may exercise positive effect on health, by altering preferences for risky behaviour. Thus generally, a state of good health is influenced by variety of factors, including the quality and amount of medical care consumed. However, socioeconomic status, lifestyle and environmental factors appear to play a much greater role in the production of good health.

On returns to health capital, less research has been done, perhaps because of the non-monetary aspects of these returns. Thus, African Development Bank (1998) observed that economists have generally only included, education and post school years of experience in estimating wage functions in many low-income labour markets.

Consequently, the report indicates the likelihood that the returns to education are overstated because health, nutrition; status and mobility are not simultaneously considered.

## ANALYTICAL FRAMEWORK

The model presented in this section is incorporated to provide analytical structure for the analysis of the factors affecting human health capital level and accumulation in the context of LDCs and particularly in the Nigerian economy. The aim is to sensitise policy-makers to many factors that affect health but which are not usually directly situated within consideration for health status of citizenry.

The analysis of health status in economics is within the framework of production theory .To economist, good health is an output, which involves a production process. To attain a state of good health, which is fundamental to any meaningful economic activity, individuals, given their natural health composition use medical inputs and other factors, such as lifestyle. The relationship between medical inputs and output can be captured in what economists call a production function. The function is just a mathematical expression of how the level of output depends on the quantity of various inputs.

The function, in the context of level of health can take the form of

H= f {Edt, MDC, Lfs, SES, EV}
H: Level of health at a point in time.
Edt: Endowment
MDC: Medical care/ Health care system
Lfs: Lifestyle
SES: Socioeconomic status
EV: Environmental factors

In respect of the level of health (H) of people, from national perspective, it can be measured by health statistics, such as the infant mortality rate, the under five mortality, and the life expectancy at birth.

Endowment (Edt) refers to the natural health composition of individual. Each person is endowed with a given stock of health at birth or at the beginning of a period such as a year. The depreciation or augmentation of this stock with age depends on many factors already identified in the literature review. Worthy of note is that, there is a critical minimum level of individual stock of health below which death occurs

(Santerre and Neun, 1996: P. 21).

Medical care (MDC) at micro level refers to the quantity of medical services and care consumed by individuals. It also incorporates the quality of services offered which are reflected by the nature of equipment and technologies of service provision. In addition to these, are the quality of medical consumables such as quality of drugs and other material inputs. At the macro level, other issues involved in medical care are access to the services and the cost to people. The availability of health services that treat the sick and rehabilitate the impaired is important to health of people in an economy. As stated by Kyellsterom, Koplan and Rothenberg (1992), many deaths occurring in developing countries could be avoided with appropriate treatment. Adding that the dramatic improvement in maternal health that occur with development cannot but be connected with improved prenatal and obstetric care and other factors like reduction in fertility rates. Thus, the existence of sophisticated and comprehensive medical care facilities that are accessible, influence human health and consequently, national productivity.

Lifestyles (Lfs) of people affect household consumption choices and determine variables such as diet and exercise. Besides, it affects compliant with medical instruction and prescription.

Socioeconomic status (SES) reflects the impact of social and economic factors. Among the indicators of social economics status of people are: educational attainment, nature of occupation, income, family background, nature of property ownership and wealth. The social economic status of every member of a population in any society determines the privilege, power and prestige available to them (Hobbs and Blanks, 1975). Thus, there is no gainsaying that the nature of health seeking behaviour exhibited by people and quality of health services that they can enjoy has associations with the social economic status.

As regards environment (EV), this composes of a vector of factors including air and water quality, hygiene, sanitation, nature of drainage and garbage disposal, and how congested or crowded living conditions are. Besides, it also includes noise level and any side effect associated with the intensity of industrial activities in an economy. As industrial activities increase and cities grow, the resulting urbanisation comes with overcrowding slums, air, water and noise pollution that have serious negative implication on health of people. Based on the analytical framework above, an empirical evaluation of the factors already identified is provided in the subsequent section.

## CRITICAL FACTORS IN HEALTH HUMAN CAPITAL ACCUMULATION IN NIGERIA

Nationally, the macro human health status indicators are the infant mortality rate, the under five mortality, the general life expectancy at birth and signals from Human Developing Index (HDI) which is a composite of standard of living, longevity and literacy rate. The level of these statistics in any country is determined by many direct and indirect factors. These determinants include the quality of health care system, which is dictated by health policy and public expenditure on health. The socioeconomic status of people, which can be analysed at macro level with income per capita, and the general lifestyle of people. Besides, is the physical environmental condition, covering air, water, hygiene, sanitation etc.

### Health Care System

A health care system consists of the organisational arrangements and processes through which a society makes choices concerning the production, consumption and distribution of health care services. This system takes responsibility for how to provide appropriate health care services for all people within the country and address all challenges of diseases and sicknesses, including motor accident experiences. The nature of the health care system and how comprehensive its services are, affects human health within an economy. Therefore, the condition and characteristics of the Nigeria's health care system are analysed with respect to size, quality of services provided, cost-funding and policy response to the sector condition.

### Size and Quality

The health care system in Nigeria, based on available Federal Office of Statistics' data (presented on Table 11.1) includes about 13964 hospitals of different types as at 1991.

**Table 11.1: Health Establishment in Nigeria (1987-1991)**

| Establishments | 1987 | 1988 | 1989 | 1990 | 1991 |
|---|---|---|---|---|---|
| General Hospitals | 763 | 897 | 897 | 897 | 897 |
| Pediatrics | - | - | - | - | 1 |
| Maternity | 3090 | 3172 | 3172 | 3331 | 3349 |
| Infectious Diseases | 30 | 47 | 47 | 48 | 48 |
| Neuro-Psychiatrics | 13 | 16 | 16 | 15 | 16 |
| Orthopaedic | 3 | 3 | 3 | 4 | 3 |
| Tuberculosis | - | - | - | - | 12 |
| Ophthalmic | - | - | - | - | 10 |
| Medical Health Centres | - | - | - | - | 985 |
| Prison Hospital | - | - | - | - | 4 |
| Leprosarium | - | - | - | - | 43 |
| Dispensaries | - | - | - | - | 8405 |
| Teaching Hospitals | 14 | 14 | 14 | 14 | 14 |
| Armed Forces Medical Services | - | - | - | - | 177 |
| Others | 8700 | 9405 | 9405 | 9649 | 9649 |
| **Total** | **12,613** | **13,518** | **13,518** | **13,958** | **13,964** |

***Source**: FOS, Annual Abstract of Statistics. 1999.*

Specifically worthy of note are Teaching Hospitals (14), General Hospitals (897), Maternity (3349), Medical Health Centres (985) and Dispensaries (8,405). Others are special hospitals dealing with special cases such as psychiatrics, orthopeadic, leprosarium, ophthalmic and tuberculosis. Note that the number of hospital may not give clear indication of the proportion of the population serviced, except the information is complemented with the hospitals' size in terms of bed spaces. The total bed spaces available to all Nigerians based on the Annual Abstract of Statistics (presented on Table 11.2) is 106,453.

**Table 11.2: Hospital Beds by Type of Hospital (1990)**

| Type of Hospital | Number of Beds | Proportion |
|---|---|---|
| General Hospital | 56,688 | 53% |
| Maternity | 20,370 | 19% |
| Infectious Diseases | 1,200 | 1.1% |
| Orthopaedic | 733 | 0.007% |
| Psychiatric | 2,791 | 2.6% |
| Teaching | 7,130 | 6.7% |
| Others | 18,034 | 16.9% |
| **Total** | **106,453** | **100%** |

**Source:** *FOS, Annual Abstract of Statistics, 1999*

If the contribution of each type of hospital to human health care service is considered, general hospital appear to have a wider coverage in Nigeria than all other type of hospitals put together. For instance, as at 1990, Nigeria had 897 general hospitals with 56,688 bed spaces (Table 11.2). This figure comparatively implies that the general hospitals provide 53 percent of all the available bed spaces in all hospitals in Nigeria. It is important to recognise that, in term of ownership, general hospitals are owned and managed by state governments. This, in essence, is a reflection of the comparatively higher contribution to health care service in terms of the number of people who can be housed for treatment.

Also, quantitatively 7,267 health establishments are traceable to local government councils in Nigeria. This figure constitutes about 52 percent of all the health establishments. While in term of size, these hospitals may be individually small but their wide distribution across local towns and villages is considered very important for management of human health at the grassroots of the economy. It is important to point out that access to health tends to be highly unequal across administrative districts and between rural and urban areas. Among the states in Nigeria, the number of health facilities ranges from one per 200 people in Lagos State to one per 129,000 in Benue State. Three-fourth of Nigeria's public and private health facilities are located in urban areas, which contain only about 35 per cent of the population (World Bank, 1994).

Beyond the health care establishments and bed spaces is the quality of services offered. In the literature, this is measured by the nature of medical equipment and technologies in use for provision of medical services. When such equipment and technologies are current and advanced, and practitioners could effectively handle them, quite significant value is added to quality of health care services. The number and quality of health personnel, who work in these hospitals and how their services are managed, directly influence the quality of health service delivery. Also, the incidence of diseases as to whether they are declining or increasing and the prevailing life-expectancy over years, show the standard of the general health services, especially it reveals whether there is improvement or not. Other factor relevant to quality is the adequacy of the number of medical practitioners, dentists, physiotherapists, and nurses and midwifery.

Within the structure of the Nigerian health care system, the Federal Office of Statistics (FOS) data's list of health personnel shows that the country has about 21,739 physicians, 1,335 dentists, 80,186 registered nurses, 62,386 registered midwives, 14,145 special type of nurses (that is, Grade II midwives, community midwives, psychiatric, public health nurses and anaesthetics ), 620 radiographers, 4,118 laboratory technologists and about 701 physiotherapists as at 1993 (Table 11.3).

**Table 11.3: Type of Health Personnel in Nigeria (1984-1993)**

| Year | Medical Practitioners | Dentists | Registered Nurses | Reg. Midwives | Other Nurses | Radio-graphers | Lab. Tech. | Physio-.therapist |
|---|---|---|---|---|---|---|---|---|
| 1989 | 17954 | 1087 | 64503 | 52379 | 12773 | 570 | 3,052 | 685 |
| 1990 | 19126 | 1150 | 67764 | 55151 | 13127 | 585 | 3,206 | 701 |
| 1991 | 20210 | 1197 | 71712 | 58036 | 13433 | 600 | 3,499 | n.a. |
| 1992 | 21325 | 1295 | 75980 | 60227 | 13747 | 620 | 3,782 | n.a. |
| 1993 | 21739 | 1335 | 80186 | 62386 | 14184 | 620 | 4,118 | n.a. |

***Source***: *FOS, Annual Abstract of Statistics. 1999.*

If the number of all hospitals is compared to the number of medical practitioners, less than two physicians will be obtained per hospital. Noting that the professional medical personnel are disproportionately distributed to Teaching Hospitals and other major hospitals, urban-based hospitals are relatively better stocked with different kinds of medical practitioners, which are far above the average obtained. By implication, other local public hospitals, which are close to 65 per cent of all the existing hospitals, may not have physicians to manage health cases. In essence, the adequacy of the number of physicians is a thing of concern. To be specific, most local government owned hospitals in local town and villages in Nigeria serving close to 70 percent of the population are manned by personnel that are less than the grade of a registered nurse. Thus, even when the health services are offered free, the quality of the services is critically low, because those who have inadequate knowledge of the cases offer the services. By implication, this affects the overall infant mortality rate, the under five mortality and the life expectancy figure in Nigeria. It is also important to note that as at 1990 when the population of Nigeria was around 100 million, the total number of nurses of all kinds and grades was about 156,756. This shows that Nigeria has a ratio of about one nurse to 600 persons. This is considered quite low in term of adequacy.

## Cost of Health Care Service

In line with the structural adjustment programme (SAP) philosophy, which was introduced in 1986 and has continued to affect the style of management of every sector in Nigeria, incremental privatisation in the delivery of social services was a component of the health services delivery. Incremental privatisation has to do with delivery of public sector services in a way that recognises the role of the users in paying fees to assess the public services so that the cost of providing such services can be recovered. Cost recovery in health refers to a system whereby government recovers in part or whole, the cost of funding health through users-fee charges. Consequently, fees were introduced for various health services among which were: consultation, drugs and medical consumables. This was introduced on the premise that it will lead to improve delivery of health care services, supplement government expenditure on health and make drugs and other consumables constantly available in the health care centres.

Assessment of the introduction of users' fee charges on health delivery services in Ghana, Uganda and Nigeria appeared to show that the policy is being pursued beyond reasonable expectation. In the case of Nigeria, Centre for African Settlement Studies and Development (CASSAD) indicates in 2003 that fees were introduced for various health services among which were: consultation, drugs and medical consumables.

Consequently, irrespective of the condition of patients (that whether emergencies or outpatients) health facilities had to demand fee from users for any service to be performed or consumables to be used to obtain attention. Due to high rate of poverty, the development reduced pattern of utilisation of the PHC, General Hospital and Teaching Hospital. It, however, substantially increase the patronage of Private Hospital, Mission Clinics, NGO's health care centre and traditional healer which are less equipped for proper management of health problems.

**Funding of Health**

Health care is classified under social and community service in Nigeria Federal Budget. The Central Bank Statistical Bulletin (2001) shows that allocation to this class in the budget has been unpredictable. Between 1990 and 2001, budgetary allocation to this class fluctuated between 2.2 per cent and 12.2 per cent in 2001

Health expenditure is one of the critical determinants of human health capital accumulation in any economy. This is because expenditure on health directly affects quantity and quality of different type of hospitals that are available to provide health care services. Besides, national government is responsible for overall health policy and strategic planning for health and it is expected that national government is also supposed to be the major source of health financing and health expenditures. In reality, as shown in Table 11.4c, the allocation to health as a share of the Federal Government total capital and recurrent expenditures is quite low and varies widely from 1998 to 2002. Specifically, in some year it was as low as 1.4% and 2% of the capital and recurrent expenditure respectively.

**Table 11.4a: Federal Government Recurrent Expenditure (₦ Million, 1998-2002)**

| Sector | 1998 | 1999 | 2000 | 2001 | 2002 |
|---|---|---|---|---|---|
| Administration | 54,673.5 | 97,224.1 | 121,299.1 | 180,819.0 | 331,736.0 |
| Economic Services | 11,862.1 | 20,481.2 | 29,816.3 | 53,011.1 | 65,910.9 |
| Social & Community Services | 22,777.6 | 37,748.3 | 58,802.4 | 79,634.4 | 189,431.6 |
| Education | 14,034.8 | 23,047.2 | 39,034.0 | 39,884.6 | 100,240.2 |
| Health | 5,333.6 | 8,793.2 | 11,579.6 | 24,523.5 | 50,563.2 |
| Others | 3,409.2 | 5,907.9 | 8188.8 | 15,226.3 | 38,628.2 |
| Transfer | 88,784.6 | 294,238.8 | 251,690.7 | 265,873.6 | 109,699.3 |
| **Total** | **200,875.4** | **487440.7** | **520410.9** | **658972.5** | **886209.4** |

***Source:*** *Central Bank of Nigeria, Annual Report & Statement of Account, 2002*

**Table 11.4b: Federal Government Capital Expenditure (₦Million, 1998- 2002)**

| Sector | 1998 | 1999 | 2000 | 2001 | 2002 |
|---|---|---|---|---|---|
| Administration | 35,270.4 | 42,737.2 | 53,279.5 | 49,254.9 | 73,577.4 |
| Economic Services | 200,861.9 | 323,580.8 | 111,508.6 | 259,757.8 | 215,333.4 |
| Social and Community Services | 23,365.6 | 17,253.5 | 27,965.2 | 53,336.0 | 32,467.3 |
| Education | 10,579.3 | 8,516.6 | 10,529.2 | 19,860.0 | 9,215.0 |
| Health | 8,307.2 | 7,386.8 | 8,865.6 | 20,128.0 | 12,608.0 |
| Others | 4,479.1 | 1,350.1 | 8,570.4 | 13,345.0 | 10,644.3 |
| Transfer | 49,517.7 | 114,456.1 | 46,697.6 | 76,347.8 | 00 |
| **Total** | **332381.2** | **515281.1** | **267416.1** | **492029.5** | **353845.4** |

***Source:*** *Central Bank of Nigeria, Annual Report & Statement of Account, 2002*

As pointed out by World Bank (1994: P. 146), it is hard to explain why some African governments have committed less to health than others. The study noted that most African governments appear to be able to make substantial improvement in health expenditures given their substantially huge allocation to defence. Allocation to defence appears to be about three times of what is allocated to health. Also, in Nigeria allocation to administration appears to be above 30% of the whole expenditures on yearly basis.

**Table 11.4c: Share of Health in Federal Government Expenditure (1998- 2002)**

| Year | Capital Expenditure % | Recurrent Expenditure % |
|---|---|---|
| 1998 | 2.6% | 3.0% |
| 1999 | 1.4% | 2.0% |
| 2000 | 3.7% | 2.5% |
| 2001 | 4.5% | 4.2% |
| 2002 | 3.9% | 7.2% |

***Source:*** *Obtained from Table 11.4b and 11.4b*

## Policy Response to the Condition of Health Care Delivery

In attempt to improve the condition of the health care system, the Federal Government increased budgetary allocation to the sector by 1.3 percent between 2001 and 2002. Also, grants of about ₦457.0 million were given to some Federal University Teaching Hospitals and Federal Medical Centres. The grants were released for special projects, including the building and upgrading of facilities (CBN, 2002. P 55)

Besides, since 2002, immunisation against polio and other childhood killer diseases was intensified. To create enabling environment for appropriate qualitative health service delivery, the National Agency for Food, Drugs and Control (NAFDAC) has intensified its surveillance efforts aimed at ridding the country of fake, expired and substandard drugs/products.

Also, the National Health Insurance Scheme (NHIS) took off in March, 2002 as one of the government efforts aimed at improving health care delivery in Nigeria. It's implementation in Nigeria covers various health services, including outpatient care, provision of prescribed drugs and maternity care for up to four live births for every insured person. The scheme's coverage, also extend to routine immunisation and hospital care in a standard hospital during a stated duration of stay for physical or mental disorders.

## Health Seeking Behaviour and Lifestyle

Most health and disease states are influenced by individual behaviour and lifestyle. Lifestyle affects individual preferences and therefore refers to individual choice and diet, physical activity, use of alcohol, drugs and sensitivity to health risks and injuries. Behaviour and lifestyle of people also influence practice of basic hygiene, spread of diseases, planned versus unplanned pregnancy and the use of contraceptives.

In the African countries and in Nigeria in particular, literacy rate is still low. Low level of literacy has implication for the nature of people's lifestyle and behaviour. Illiterates are generally associated with lifestyle that exposes them to great health risk.

**Table 11.5: Literacy Rate In Nigeria**

| **Adult Literacy** | % |
|---|---|
| National | 48.9 |
| Female | 40.7 |
| Male | 58.0 |
| Net Primary School Attendance Rate | % |
| National | 55.1 |
| Female | 52.9 |
| Male | 57.2 |
| Gross Primary School Enrolment | % |
| National | 80.7 |
| Female | 77.3 |
| Male | 84.0 |

***Source:****FOS, UNICEF & UNSN (2001)*

As reflected in Table 11.5, literacy rate in Nigeria is about 48 per cent. This implies that more than half of the population is illiterates. In reference to gender, literacy rate for female (40%) is below the national rate. This is important because, mothers education has been found to be positively associated with lower risk of premature death, and with better child anthropometrics status. A survey reported by African Development Bank (1998: P 123) shows that educated parents, especially mothers, are better in recognising medical problems in their children. Besides, when literacy rate is low, the positive effect of any information directed at influencing the behaviour of people is usually low.

Also connected with the low literacy rate is the pervasiveness of poverty that is currently affecting close to 60 percent of the population. Nigeria is one of the low-income countries of the world with low saving and productivity. The income level of people affects the quality of health service that they can afford. Poverty among higher proportion of the population in Nigeria then appear connected with the existence of large number of quack doctors and unlicensed but well-patronised local hospitals.

By implication, the high rate of re-occurrence of some sicknesses and loss of lives from minor illness and injuries are not unconnected with bad management of health condition by the many substandard health service-providing outlets. The issue is that all these have serious negative implication for labour, productivity and health human capital stock in an economy if not confronted with appropriate policy programmes.

**Environmental Factor**

The environment poses serious threat to health through poor hygiene and sanitation, poor supply of potable water, poor drainage and garbage disposal and overcrowding. According to Bauld (1998), an estimate of 40 percent reduction in the disease burden associated with poor potable water supply, sanitation and hygiene and a 15 percent reduction in diseases associated with indoor pollution and overcrowding can be achieved through proper environmental protection and sanitation programme.

In contemporary Nigeria, in spite of the existence of institutions such as Federal Environmental Protection Agency (FEPA) and State Environmental Protection Agencies (SEPA); and National Policy on the environment, most Nigerian cities lack coordinated and consistent environmental sanitation culture or structure. Besides, government at all levels often give higher priority to social activities such as sports, festivals, and other ceremonial-oriented expenditures rather than these human resource preserving investment in transforming environmental condition.

Casual observation of condition in most urban areas in Nigeria will show that, not so much concern or understanding is demonstrated on the need for potable water, good drainage system and well-structured process of garbage collection.

Consequently, the stock of human health and human growth process suffer serious impairment as a result of high incidence and prevalence of many diseases associated with negative impact of poor environmental condition in Nigeria. Going by annual abstract of statistics (1999), currently, among the ten leading causes of admission to hospitals in Nigeria are parasitic and infectious diseases. In essence, policy-makers need to realise that where there is poor sanitation and hygiene, prevalence of overcrowding and indoor pollution, the human growth process and development are negatively affected, if not completely terminated by death resulting from infection.

In addition, impairment to human health caused by environmental pollution has implication for frequency of hospital visit and consequent expenditure on health at government and individual levels. It would appear that at least a third of all hospital expenditures could be avoided if more cost-effective strategies than remedial care were used to reduce the incidence of infectious and parasitic diseases. Among such health preserving strategies are vector control, environmental protection measures, and construction of household sanitation facilities.

## SUMMARY

Factors that determine health human capital accumulation in Nigeria were descriptively analysed using some secondary data collected from the Federal Office of Statistics (FOS) and the Central Bank of Nigeria (CBN). Analysis of the size of Nigeria's health care system showed that the country has 13,964 hospitals of different type and sizes. The size in term of bed spaces is 106,453 bed spaces, implying that if the population of Nigeria is 110 million, the bed space ratio to the population will be one bed to about one thousand people. With respect to type of hospital, it appears that general hospitals have a wider coverage accounting for about 53 percent of the existing total bed spaces.

The quality of health services offered was examined using the number of qualified medical practitioners and other health personnel such as dentists, physiotherapists, nurses and midwives. The study shows that

Nigeria has 21,739 physicians as at 1990 when the population was not less than 100 million. A comparative analysis of the number of physician with the number of hospitals shows that less than two physician is obtained per hospital on the average. On this, the study observes that given the disproportionate distribution of physician in favour of urban centres, local public hospitals which are close to 65 percent of all the existing hospitals may not have had qualified physicians.

On the cost of health care services, the study's findings show that a user's fee charge are in operation. It was introduced to recover cost in attempt to supplement government expenditure on health. An analysis of government fundings of health care services shows that health is classified with social and community services. It was observed that between 1990 and 2001, budgetary allocation fluctuated between 2.2 per cent and 12.2 per cent. In specific case of the health sector component, expenditure allocation was found to be as low as 1.4 per cent and 2 per cent of the total capital and recurrent expenditure respectively. In this study, it is suggested that government can substantially improve on the expenditures on health, given the substantial allocation to other comparatively less important sector.

Other important influences on health human capital that were analysed in this chapter are health seeking behaviour and environmental factors. The discourse associated high illiteracy level with the crude lifestyle of people that exposes them to health risk. This is further supported with the high poverty rate affecting the quality of health services that more than half of the population can afford. On the environmental factor, it is observed that investment in environmental transformation is an health preserving preventive measure. However, the study argued that most urban centres in Nigeria are still shockingly dirty and lack coordinated and consistent environmental sanitation culture and structure. Therefore, generally, emphasis on health care appears more of curative nature rather than preventive.

## CONCLUSION

Human capital has always been central to economic development. And as the understanding of the importance of human capital is growing, the appreciation of the fundamentality of the health human capital component of the general human capital is crucial in Nigeria and all developing countries in general. This is because, large proportion of attainable productivity is being lost to workers' illness, invalidity and premature death in these economies. If the need to address health problems is realised and accepted, a comprehensive approach to transforming health human capital must take cognisance of the following:

First is the need to improve the quantity and quality of health establishments, health care personnel, pharmaceuticals and consequently, budgetary allocations. However, it must be recognised that how these inputs are planned, allocated, organised and managed can determine whether the services are cost-effective and can make the difference between sustainable and unsustainable outcomes.

Secondly, it is equally important to make more efficient use of public funds by allocating them from expensive and relatively cost-ineffective tertiary care to cost-effective preventive and primary care services. Thus, more attention should be comparatively given to preventive care services.

Thirdly, if Nigeria health care system is to devote greater attention to preventive and primary care, the recovery of cost then becomes very important for sustainability. While the users' fee, as a measure of cost recovery currently operated in Nigeria is welcome, it is important that the charges be modest to ensure affordability to large proportion of Nigerian. To be specific, the fee structured public hospitals should be made to reflect the fact that most clients are poor.

Fourthly, to improve health seeking behaviour and influence the lifestyle of people, intensive effort is required in the area of providing more health information to the public and to health care providers in Nigeria. This hopefully will produce behavioural changes in the long run.

Lastly, Nigeria is currently overdue for a practical implementation of sustainable intersectoral interventions at the community level, particularly in the area of access to safe water, sanitation, nutrition and family planning service.

## References

African Development Bank (ADB), (1998). African Development Report.

Central Bank of Nigeria (2002). *Annual Report and Statement of Account*, 2002.

Federal Office of Statistics (1999). Annual Abstract of Statistics. FOS, Abuja

Feachem, R. G. A., Phillips, M.A. and Bulatao, R. A. (1992). "Introducing Adult Health" in Feachean, R. G. A *et al* (eds.) *The Health of Adult in Developing World*. World Bank.

Grossman, Michael, (1972). "On the concept of Health Capital and the Demand for Health" *Journal of Political Economy* 80 (March - April) P. 223 - 55

Hobcroft, (1993). "Women's Education, Child Welfare and Child Survival: A Review of Evidences" *Health Transition Review*, Vol.3, No. 2.

Hobbs, D.A. and Blank, S.J. (1975). *Sociology and Human Experience*, John Waley Incorporation.

Kjellstrom, T., Koplan, J.P. and Rothenbery, R . B. (1992). "Current and Future Determinants of Adult Ill-Health" in Feachem, R. G. A. *et al* (eds); *The Health of Adults in the Developing World*. World Bank.

Mireille, Laroche, (1998). *On the concept and Dimensions of Human Capital in a Knowledge-based Economy Context*. Mimeo, University of Ottawa.

Monekosso, G.L. (1994). "Foreword" *Better Health in Africa: Experience and Lessons Learned.* World Bank Washington D.C.

Mosby, C. V. (1992). *Mosby Medical Encyclopedia.* New York City.

Santerre, R. E. and Neun, S. P. (1996). *Health Economics Times Mirror* Higher Education Group.

Schultz, T. P. (1995). "Human Capital and Development" In G. H. Peters, *et al.*, eds. *Agricultural Competitiveness*, Aldershot, England: Dartmouth Pub. Co.

Strauss, J. and Thomas, D. (1995). "Human Resources: Empirical modelling of Household and family Decisions" in J. R. Behrman and T. N. Srinivasan, eds., *Handbook of Development Economics, Vol. IIIA*, Chap. 34, Amsterdam: North-Holland Pub. Co.

Todaro, P. M. and Smith, S.C. (2003). *Economic Development.* Person Education, Asia.

United Nations System In Nigeria (2001). *Country Assessment* UN.

World Bank, (1995). *Monitoring Environmental Progress* Washington D.C.

# Chapter 12

# PATIENT THERAPY AND DRUG CONTROL IN HEALTH CARE ORGANISATIONS

*Afolabi, M.O.*

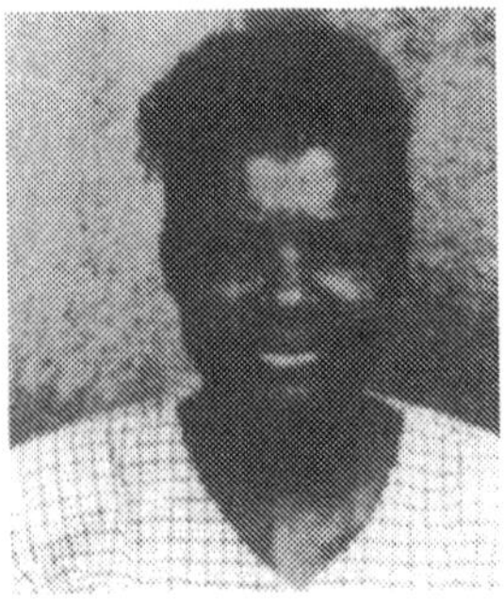

**About the Contributor**
Mrs Margaret Olubunmi Afolabi holds B.Pharm(Hons) Benin, M.Sc. (Pharmaceutics), M.B.A. and M.Phil.(Business Admin.) from Obafemi Awolowo University, Ile-Ife. Currently on her Ph.D. programme, she is a senior lecturer in the Department of Clinical Pharmacy and Pharmacy Administration, Obafemi Awolowo University, Ile-Ife.

## INTRODUCTION

Pharmacists play a crucial role in the medication use process. Specifically, the pharmacists review and evaluate all prescriptions or medication orders before dispensing or administration. They are expected to control the distribution of every dose dispensed or administered to individual patient. Pharmacists contribute to positive medication outcomes by assuring that each patient receives safe, appropriate and effective drug therapy through the provision of pharmaceutical care. Pharmaceutical care is the responsible provision of drug therapy for the purpose of achieving defined therapeutic outcomes that improve a patient's quality of life while minimising patient risk (Hepler and Strand, 1990). The provision of pharmaceutical care extends the pharmacists responsibility beyond the delivery of drug products to include the outcomes of drug therapy. Pharmacists are drug use experts and they have the ultimate responsibility for the control of medication distribution even in cases of emerging pharmacy automation.

Drug utilisation studies or drug monitoring programmes are control strategies designed to enhance the standards of medical treatment at all levels of health care delivery system. When drug usage data from such studies are programmed with other patient data, they provide the medical staff with a true profile of local drug practices for any period or point in time. Usually, the analysis would reflect and suggest changes for the future. This monitoring program upgrades the quality of patient care. In addition, it has a special significance in large hospitals where the young physician develops his initial prescribing habits. Tertiary health institutions, in particular, must maintain leadership in the rational selection and use of drugs. A well-coordinated program of drug monitoring would give detailed information on the various aspects of drug selection, drug utilisation and even drug performance.

Such profiles depict the local character of drug usage and provide the basis of reports to responsible members of the medical staff or to an appropriate hospital committee where they will be interpreted, evaluated and used to substantiate a recommendation to improve the drug use situation, if the facts so indicate. In this regard, the pharmacist can help the medical staff to discover a drug related problem in the hospital. Patient outcome and quality of life are improved by enhancing the standards of medical treatment in the health care organisation. Setting standards and assessing the quality of patient care through performance review should be integrated as an ongoing process in health care systems. (Patterson, 1986).

## DRUG UTILISATION STUDIES (DUS)

Pharmacists become involved with drug control in health care organisations in two areas, and these are drug utilisation studies conducted jointly with the medical staff, and peer review type activities related to the other aspects of pharmaceutical service (e.g drug distribution and control). To some extent, other professional groups such as nurses also do participate in both aspects of the studies. The most pressing need for pharmacists' participation in quality assurance framework is in the area of drug utilisation studies. Management of drug distribution in the hospital is the duty of the pharmacists and drug utilisation studies serve as a valuable tool for the optimisation of drug therapy and drug use.

The World Health Organisation regional office for Europe in Copenhagen (Denmark) fostered an interest in DUS initially. This international organisation published an early work on drug utilisation review (DUR) in 1968, which led to an Oslo (Norway) meeting in 1969 and to subsequent formation of the Drug Utilisation Research Group (DURG), in which scientists from many different nations participated.

Drug utilisation studies (DUS) may be defined as "the marketing, distribution, prescription and use of drugs in a society, with special emphasis on the resulting medical, social and economic consequences". The studies involve socioeconomic evaluation of drug use and these embrace two main aspects, which include the process and effects of drug utilisation along the drug distribution chain. DUS can provide valuable information on both the harmful and beneficial effects of drugs and the cost implications. The outcomes of the studies may be used to discover problematic areas and also to establish possible measures or interventions to solve the likely problems.

Drug therapy forms the pivot of orthodox medicine and as such, the use must be adequately monitored for appropriateness, rationality and improved patient outcomes. Spitzer (1991) pointed out that:

> If drugs are prescribed and used properly, it can be plausibly postulated that they improve health with all the attendant economic benefits and reduced expenditures on physician and hospital services

Certain medical injuries may be due to inappropriate drug use through selection, prescribing and administration errors. Some of these errors are preventable, if detected early enough. For instance, a medication error is preventable but it may cause or lead to inappropriate therapy or patient harm if it goes undetected in the drug chain. On the other hand, DUS may facilitate an early detection of some unavoidable adverse drug effects to allow for immediate follow-up actions such as patient education, supportive care treatment or even withdrawal of the drug concerned.

Drug utilisation studies include all the activities designed to monitor the drug use process in the society. Drug utilisation review (DUR) and drug utilisation evaluation (DUE) are subsets of drug utilisation studies (DUS) and they form part of the quality assurance activities designed to monitor drug use in health institutions. They are used as important tools in ensuring rational and cost-effective use of drugs with the aim of shortening patient stay in hospitals and returning the patient back to the community (Talley, 1994).

Many researchers have seen DUS simply as a procedure for quantifying drug usage within the facility or ascertaining patterns of prescribing. Brodie and Smith (1977) viewed this procedure as "an authorised, structured and continuing program that reviews, analyses and interprets patterns of drug usage in a given health care delivery system against predetermined standards." This definition lacks the provider follow-up phase, that is, an educational correctional component. However, if we view DUS as a combined pharmacy-medicine audit process, this cooperation must be there for it to meet the requirements for a patient care audit.

DUS is a quality assurance program for drug therapy and should conform to the principles of quality assurance as shown later. This programme is unique in the hospital review system since the use of drugs is part of an interprofessional interface at which the legal and professional responsibilities for patient care are equally shared. Both the physician and the pharmacist are obligated to see that patients receive the proper choice of drug in the correct dose for the proper length of time. However, the pharmacist will be involved specifically in developing (and revising) criteria and standards for drug use, maintaining, organising and analysing drug use data; and participating in educational programs involving drugs, that is, pharmacists should be involved in all phases of the DUS system.

## Types of Drug Utilisation Studies (DUS)

Stolar (1978) gave the operational definitions of DUS and the functional characteristics as shown in Fig. 12.1. These studies can be of 2 types - quantitative and qualitative studies.

## *Quantitative DUS*

Quantitative DUS are concerned with quantifying various facets of drug use within a health care system, area or group. They involve the collection, organisation and display of estimates, measurements, or amounts of drug use. The results of these activities usually take the form of absolute or relative quantitative data describing the use of drugs within specified timeframes and drugs, patient and/or prescriber categories. Quantitative DUS have been used in the following cases:

(1) to ascertain the quantities of drugs consumed in a specific period and in a specific geographical area;
(2) to investigate the development of drug utilisation over a period of time;
(3) to compare drug consumption in different geographical areas;
(4) to identify possible over or underutilisation of drugs;
(5) to estimate the utilisation according to such variables as age, sex, social class etc.;
(6) to estimate the prevalence of particular illnesses based on the consumption of drugs utilised in their treatment; and
(7) to investigate different prescribing practices.

Quantitative DUS yield specific information such as this; "17% of the prescription written for our clinic patients in the past year were for benzodiazepine drugs". These data are often used for making purchasing decisions or other financial activities (for example, drug budget planning) provided such information has been collected in a valid manner. This is a rational use of such studies. However, the DUS may be a guide to action in respect of the quantity or appropriateness of the drug use base, that is, it may have been that the drug under study is being grossly misused or overused thus, making it necessary to have some control over its use. This may be applicable in extreme situations of obvious misuse. Data from a quantitative drug use review should generally be considered suggestive and not conclusive with respect to quality of drug use. Quantitative DUS may or may not be an ongoing activity and they may be initiated by the pharmacy department.

### *Qualitative DUS*

These are multidisciplinary operations, which collect, organise, analyse and report information on the rationality of the drug use base. They are generally one-time examinations of narrowly-defined areas of drug use, usually specific drugs or sometimes a specific disease or diagnosis. The crucial operating difference between these studies and quantitative DUS is that they include the concept of **criteria**. Criteria are predetermined elements against which aspects of the quality, medical necessity and appropriateness of medical care (for example drug use) may be compared. By using these criteria, qualitative DUS provides a solid foundation upon which judgments concerning the appropriateness (or otherwise) of the drug use base may be constructed. Drug use criteria may be based upon such items as daily dose, duration of treatment, indications for use and utilisation of fixed drug combinations. In a study by Baksaas (1981), specific problems and drugs were defined as the focus of the DUS. Intervention criteria developed and used in this study included drug-drug interactions, therapeutic duplications and high daily dose for some classes of drugs which include angiotensin converting enzyme (ACE) inhibitors, calcium channel blockers, cardiac glycosides and benzodiazepines. Others include antidepressants, antipsychotics, anti-histamine (H2 receptor antagonists) and nonsteroidal anti-inflammatory drugs (NSAIDS). Refills for relevant drugs were also screened by the quantitative studies.

These DUS criteria are tools by which the quantity of drug use is measured, and may be developed through a joint effort of the pharmacy and medical staffs. For instance, a drug specific review of care was conducted in a 600 bed teaching hospital and the pharmacy audit involved a review of warfarin usage (Keys *et al*, 1976). The audit criteria selected include drug daily dosage (DDD), daily prothrombin time (DPT), mortality rate, bleeding secondary to overdose and bleeding secondary to concurrent drug therapy which is a form of drug-drug interaction. Subsequent audit analysis resulted in recommendations by the Pharmacy Audit Committee (PAC) to the relevant departments of the hospital for necessary actions.

The pharmacy department was alerted on the need to evaluate the present control system for its drug distribution. The PAC felt there was a need to re-emphasise the monitoring of prothrombin times as a therapeutic endpoint and the committee emphasised the need to develop warfarin dosage and monitoring protocol. This review further underscored the importance of developing educational programs on current methods of administering a drug and on how to monitor its therapeutic outcome and complications.

In another study by Wareham and Deliganis (1976), DUS was carried out to investigate the rationality of fluid/electrolyte therapy at a 200 bed, non-profit community hospital. The findings revealed that the application of a simplistic **protocol** may not be appropriate for total determination of therapy in some instances, as actual therapy may differ strikingly from protocol therapy. The reason being that such protocol by necessity ignores many parameters unique to individual patients and to individual disease states (for examples, patients' peculiar clinical condition, other drug therapy (such as diuretics, steroids, etc, oral supplementation of nutrients or electrolytes, variations in solutions actually received versus rational therapy, etc). The multiple factors leading to fluid/electrolyte therapy should be recognised when considering the concept of ideal therapy or drug protocol. The study presented a case where approximations and variables inherent in a therapy would impose severe limitations upon utilisation studies.

Both quantitative and qualitative DUS may be combined into a single effort to yield information about patterns and amounts of drug use as well as its quality. Drug utilisation activities as identified above have only limited impacts on the ways in which drugs are used, the reasons may be both conceptual and practical for reasons stated below:

(i) DUS are usually non-routine, ongoing efforts, but rather, one-time projects (with respect to a given topic) and any possible impact are quickly lost.

(ii) The studies provide for only minimal feedback to the involved practitioner and they may not even include any follow-up phase (that is, subsequent replication of the study) to ascertain if any changes in drug use have occurred.

(iii) DUS are not usually an integral part of the overall patient care review system.

On the other hand, DUS may also be designed as an authorised, structured ongoing system for improving the quality of drug use within a health care organisation. This may involve an evaluation using predetermined standards and initiating efforts to correct patterns of drug use, which are not consistent with these standards, and it also includes a mechanism for measuring the effectiveness of these corrective actions. From this description, it becomes obvious that DUS is a method of assuring the quality of drug use. The primary focus is not limited to the collection, analysis or reporting of quantitative and qualitative information on how drugs are used but the system includes criteria by which quality drug use is defined, measured and ultimately achieved. The pharmacy audit carried out by Keys *et al* (1976) may be viewed as an example of this program.

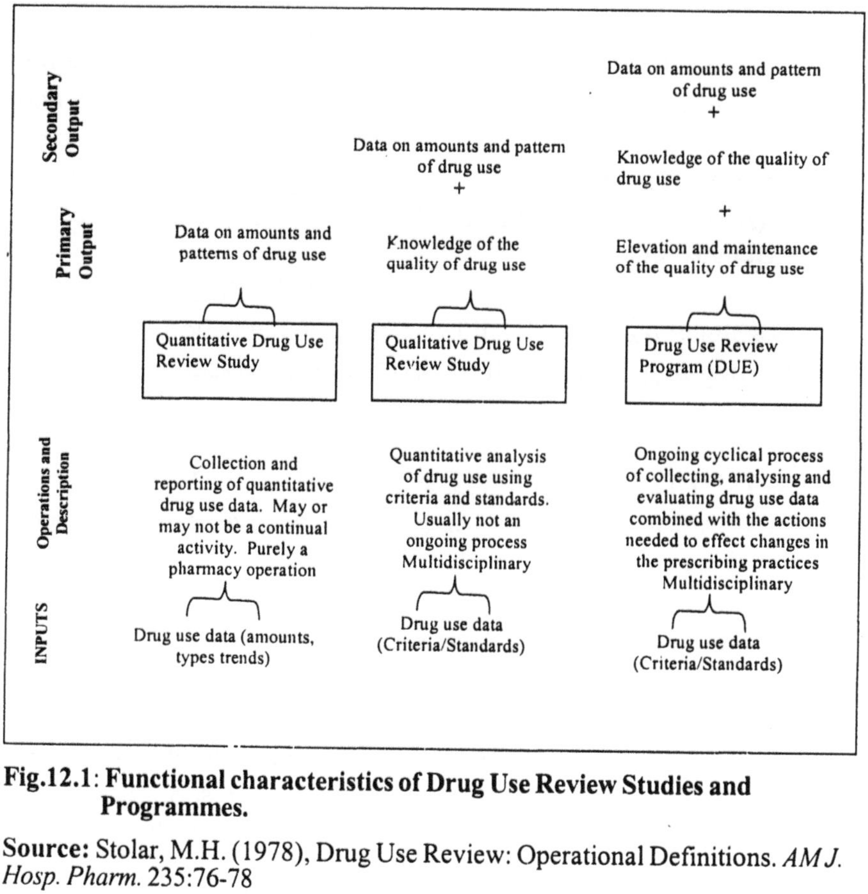


**Fig.12.1: Functional characteristics of Drug Use Review Studies and Programmes.**

**Source:** Stolar, M.H. (1978), Drug Use Review: Operational Definitions. *AM J. Hosp. Pharm.* 235:76-78

Fig. 12.1 summarises the various kinds of drug utilisation activities. The raw materials needed to operate each of the activities are shown as "inputs". The basic operations of each type of study are listed in the "processes" section while the "outputs" area of the scheme illustrates the main objective or product of the system and any subordinate products it yields.

In view of the functional characteristics of DUS as shown in Fig. 12.1, the following points become obvious.

(1) DUR programs or DUE contain the basic elements of qualitative DUR studies, which in turn are based on the simpler quantitative DUR study structure. DUE are qualitative studies which has incorporated the necessary corrective/educational, prescriber feedback and re-evaluation components.

(2) The results of quantitative DUR studies may provide some indication of potential problems in the quality of drug use, and may be therefore, the reason for initiating a qualitative DUR study of the "problem" area. If deficiencies in quality are uncovered, a DUE, which includes the problem area, should be conducted (or expanded to include it).

(3) Drug Use Review Programs (or DUE) should be instituted in hospitals and related facilities. Other DUS will be supportive to the ongoing DUE or will serve other purposes such as financial inventory management or research.

## DRUG UTILISATION REVIEW METHODOLOGY

Drug Utilisation studies may use a retrospective, prospective or concurrent review methodology.

### Retrospective Drug Utilisation Review (RDUR)

'Retrospective drug utilisation review is an authorised, structured and continuing program that reviews, analyses and interprets patterns of drug use (after the drug use has occurred) in relation to predetermined criteria and attempts to reduce inappropriate drug prescribing' (Stolar, 1978). This review gathers information and detects problems in the patient population after they might have occurred.

A retrospective study is carried out after the service has been rendered. However, the accuracy of this approach is dependent on the maintenance of adequate and up-to-date written records. This retrospective approach is the most common study type and it is also the most feasible and adaptable method, particularly in community hospitals. RDUR may be implemented by sending educational feedback letters to targeted physicians and pharmacists with a view to effect lasting and broad improvements in prescription quality that extend beyond the particular drug, patient or set of patients concerned. RDUR occurs over long periods of time and the intervention may not reach the physician until months after the events that precipitated them. Despite these limitations, findings from published evaluations suggest that RDUR letter or report interventions are effective in changing the prescription pattern.

The retrospective studies used for health problem detection are the main base to define objective, administrative and educational interventions with the aim of modifying and improving drug utilisation patterns in accordance with previously established criteria.

**Prospective Drug Utilisation Review (PDUR)**

Prospective drug utilisation studies anticipate and avoid problems that might occur in a particular patient prior to consumption of the drug. This review begins at the point of collection before a potentially inappropriate prescription is dispensed. Pharmacists initiate this study, reviewing prescriptions at the point of collection for potential problems and intervening with prescribers, other pharmacists or recipients as appropriate.

This type of approach may incorporate a review of the drug order before it is entered into the dispensing process. It is the most logical and effective type of review since, theoretically, substandard care is eliminated before it can be initiated and hence, the resultant deleterious effects of irrational drug use are avoided. Ideally, if prospective review is given to all drug orders, improper drug use will not likely occur. Prospective drug utilisation studies can be viewed from another angle, for instance, the routine process of examining incoming new drug orders for correctness and appropriateness is a very rudimentary prospective review using implicit criteria to screen the orders. A true prospective program becomes obvious when the criteria become explicit and well-written out with appropriate provider education and follow-up assessment procedures included. Complete information about patients' prescriptions is central to the success of PDUR and as such, an ideal situation will use On-line PDUR (OPDUR). This is a computerised screening system that incorporates information from virtually all the pharmacies used by the patient and in an hospital setting. The system also supplies medication history of the patient to appropriate users.

### Concurrent Drug Utilisation Review (CDUR)

The study of drug use becomes concurrent if the review is done at the same time the service is performed. The clinical function of reviewing the patient's chart and drug profile during hospitalisation to determine if any changes in the drug regimen are in order is a primitive, though incomplete form of concurrent study. However, these functions could also be developed into a formalised concurrent drug utilisation review program.

## CRITERIA DEVELOPMENT FOR DRUG UTILISATION STUDIES

Criteria are predetermined elements against which aspects of the quality of a medical service may be compared. They may be established as a means of attaching value judgments to usage data and they represent what their developers think ought to be the ideal or optimum. Professionals rely on their expertise and on professional literature in the development of relevant criteria for drug utilisation studies. These elements are differentiated from norms, which are numerical or statistical measures of usual observed performance. Norms describe medical practice as it is, but not necessarily as it should be. Realising the enormous potentials of drug utilisation studies in the promotion of rational drug therapy, international agencies like the World Health Organisation (WHO) and International Network for Rational Utilisation of Drug

(INRUD) came up with standard drug use indicators and data collection methods. The drug use indicators were developed as measures of performance in three general areas related to rational drug use (WHO, 1993). These three areas include prescribing practices by health providers, patient care assessment and indicators to measure availability of facility - specific factors which support rational drug use. These measures of performance can then be compared with relevant standard criteria in the health system.

## CONCEPTUAL FRAMEWORK FOR QUALITY ASSURANCE PROGRAMMES

A quality assurance programme constitutes a philosophical framework within which an audit or any review programme may be viewed. Basically, quality assurance (QA) involves a decision on what is to be done, doing it, measuring how well it was done, correcting the deficiencies if necessary and ensuring that future services or product will be acceptable. This procedure is applicable to any human endeavour which may be product-based or service-based and it is equally applicable to drug distribution, surgical operations or some other forms of patient care procedures. The quality assurance programme involves a prior decision on an acceptable level of quality against which to evaluate the existing service or product. In case of any short fall to the minimum standard, targeted educational or correctional activity may then be instituted to eliminate the deficiencies in future services or products.

A quality assurance programme is a structured formal procedure for applying the concepts of quality assurance to any activity and it is equally applicable to health care services. This programme is normally a continuous but cyclical process and five distinct components may be identified as follows:

(1) A definition of what constitutes acceptable service (or product) specified in form of written criteria and standards.
(2) An assessment phase utilising the written standards to determine product or service acceptability.

(3) An educational correctional phase designed to eliminate whatever deficiencies were uncovered in the assessment phase.
(4) A subsequent reassessment to determine if the educational - correctional actions have been successful and
(5) Periodic review of the set(s) of quality standards for necessary detection or modification based on new knowledge and resource.

This quality assessment procedure may be done retrospectively, concurrently or prospectively and each form may use structured, process or outcome types of norms, criteria and standards. Criteria are predetermined elements against which aspects of the quality of a service may be compared. Standards are expressions of the range of acceptable deviation from their respective criterion or norm. Norms are numerical measures of usual observed performance.

In an effective quality assessment programme, the set criteria must be explicit, that is they must be written before the assessment is performed and in such a manner that all judges using them to evaluate a given data set would obtain the same results.

Criteria can also be implicit but in this case they are unstructured and judgmentally determined by the individual evaluator. Such criteria may be time dependent and they also vary with individual evaluator. However, implicit criteria are neither reliable nor reproducible. Criteria may also be characterised as screening criteria or in-depth criteria. Screening criteria represent the few critical elements of a service whose absence upon review indicates that a more detailed look at the service in question is warranted. Further details are then done using in-depth criteria. In-depth criteria are generally many in number and they cover various aspects of the service under review. Screening criteria often involve outcomes while in-depth criteria usually focus on process. The screening approach may be used if a large number of items (such as patient charts) are to be reviewed.

Structures are the facilities, equipment, administrative organisation and personnel characteristics involved in providing the services and products being reviewed. Processes are the procedures and activities, which utilise these structures, while outcomes are the net results, impacts or end products of the structures and processes. A quality assessment programme thus uses structural, process or outcome standards (or combinations of the three) in its assessment activities.

The assessment of a service quality may be concurrent, prospective or retrospective based on the time the service under review is performed. A concurrent study is an assessment done at the same time the service is performed whereas a prospective analysis is done after the intent to perform the service has been given, but prior to its actual delivery. A quality assessment becomes retrospective if it is carried out after the service has been rendered. Conceptually, process review may be performed prospectively or concurrently but usually, it is carried out retrospectively. Normally, the retrospective approach requires the maintenance of adequate and accurate written records but these may or may not accurately reflect the services rendered. The success of a retrospective process review may be dependent upon the quality of record keeping.

An outcome review is, necessarily done retrospectively. Decisions to base a quality assurance program on outcome may be determined by the time lag between the process and the respective outcome. If the time lag is short, outcomes may be used as the basis for immediately adjusting the appropriate process. For instance, a lowering of blood sugar level (outcome) may be part of a feedback loop for adjusting the dose of an anti-diabetic drug (process). If on the other hand, the time lag is great (for example, years), outcome assessment will not be a feasible way of affecting the quality of performance or product within a reasonable time.

Quality assessment programmes may be done on individual situations or products but they must be evaluated, based on the overall pattern of performance. Individual cases are important only insofar as they contribute to the total system performance. Certain other considerations are also important in the assessment of service quality but a quality assessment programme may not capture some of these. Examples of such intangibles are attitudes, empathy and concern for one's patients.

## Quality Assurance Activities in a Health Care Organisation

The full range of quality assurance activities directly related to patient care in a hospital is shown in Fig. 12.2. These activities may be broadly classified into two which are "facility utilisation review" and patient care audits".

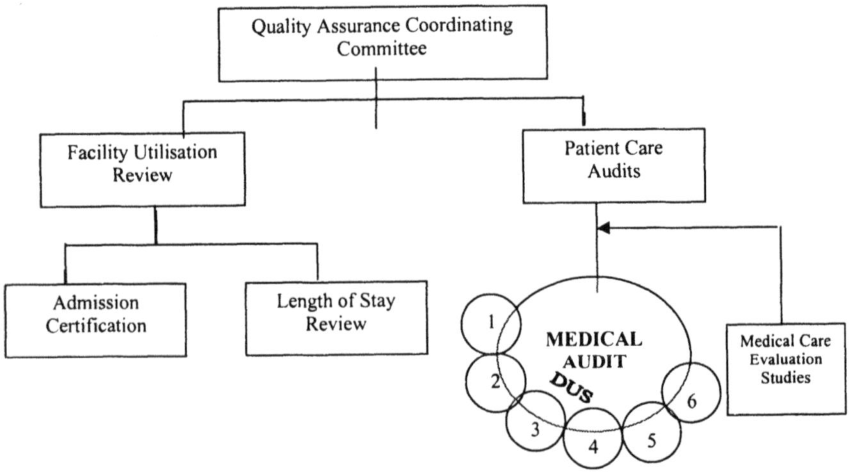


1. Occupational Therapy Audit
2. Dietary Audit
3. Pharmacy Audit
4. Nursing Audit
5. Medical Records Audit
6. Physical Therapy Audit

**Fig. 12.2: Conceptual Framework for Drug Usage Review, Medical Audit and Other Patient Care Review Procedures.**

***Source:*** Adapted from Stolar, M.H, (1978). Drug Use Review: Operational Definitions *AM J. Hosp. Pharm. 235:76-78*

### Facility Utilisation Review

This is quality assessment for the use of the health Care facility. It involves setting of criteria and standards and then a review or assessment phase, using a set of screening criteria or standards. In-depth criteria may be used for those cases not meeting the screen and subsequently a follow-up correctional phase with the provider (that is, physician). The facility utilisation review essentially deals with patient admission certification and length of hospital stay. The admission and the rationale for certification examines the patient's admission based on medically determined criteria while the length of stay review seeks to justify the patient's continued hospitalisation. The length of stay review is a concurrent analysis, which uses the length of stay norms to determine expected number of days for the specific diagnosis.

### Patient Care Audits

Patient care audits oversee the observance of standards for the professional services of all health care provider groups in the hospitals. The various system audits overlap, reflecting a merge in the professional responsibilities of the groups at various points. Such interlocking audits stem from health care provider groups such as occupational therapy, dietary, pharmacy, nursing, medical records, physical therapy and medical laboratory. However, each of the audits has an interface, with the medical audit. At such an interface, the respective provider groups have joint responsibilities for quality management whereas the open spaces represent those areas of each profession's services for which they have sole responsibility. For instance, in the patient care audit circles (Fig.12.2), the area of the pharmacy audit which interface between the two circles is the area involving drug utilisation studies. This area involves joint responsibilities between the physicians and the pharmacists to develop appropriate quality management procedures.

The bulk of hospital quality assessment activities fall into the category of 'Patient Care Audit' (PCA). PCA is used here as an umbrella term, which covers the quality assessment, and programmes for the professional services of all health care provider groups in the hospital.

It can be seen from Fig. 12.2 that, theoretically, these quality assessment systems overlap, reflecting the fact that the professional responsibilities of nurses, pharmacists, physicians, dieticians, etc, merge together at various points in a rather complex manner. However, it can be observed that each system has an interface with the physician, which includes some type of shared or delegated responsibility. In practice, conflicts do arise between the various professions in respect of when and where to keep, share or delegate the responsibility for a given aspect of health care. Many practitioners keep/share or delegate their responsibilities. Opportunities exist for the physician and the selection of the proper option may or may not be clear cut or mutually agreeable to the professionals involved. A peculiar situation in this regard is the selection and proper use of drugs, which may pose conflict between the physicians and the pharmacists. The legal liabilities and responsibilities of both professions are quite similar in this regard.

The actual relationship of the patient care audit circles is complex since each department or unit may have more than the maximum of three interfaces, which can be pictured in the diagram. Each system may even interact with services on the opposite side of the medical audit circle. The important implication of the interface in Fig.12.2 is involvement of two or more provider groups in patient care. Quality assessment programmes (or parts thereof) covering these areas must be jointly developed and administered, that is, there must be joint responsibilities and quality assessment procedures between the professionals concerned. However, the open spaces represent those areas of each professional services for which they have sole responsibility and quality assessment for these areas would involve peer review. The concept of peer review is also referred to as 'ancillary services review. It is the evaluation of one's performance by colleagues using standards developed by others of equal qualifications, for examples, education, training and experience.

Audit is defined as the evaluation of the quality of patient care based on explicit and measurable outcome criteria that can be applied to significant numbers of patient records for the purpose of documenting and improving provider input and overall quality care. If the evaluation indicates some unjustified departures from criteria established by the hospital Medical Advisory Committee (MAC) corrective measures are necessary. These measures may include continuing medical educational programs, organisational policy and procedural changes, direct intervention and/or limitation of privileges. MAC monitors the effectiveness of these corrective measures in an ongoing process and provides constant feedback into the system. This feedback provides the basis for improved patient care. A hospital will normally have a group of interlocking audits as shown in Fig. 12.2 and these make up the patient care audit program with each discipline focusing on appropriate outcome.

Medical audit oversees the observance of standards for medical treatment in clinical settings. The study of prescribing pattern is an aspect of medical audit designed to monitor, evaluate or even suggest modifications in prescribing practices of medical practitioners in a bid to make medical care rational and cost-effective. Prescription audit also forms part of drug utilisation studies (WHO, 1979). Medical care evaluation (MCE) study is a short-term patient care audit. It is a quality assessment program, which focuses on a narrowly-defined topic and it uses a retrospective methodology. It involves just one revolution of the quality assessment wheel.

### *Pharmacy Ancillary Service Review*

In Figure 12.2, the patient care audit circles have both the interface areas and the open spaces. The interface of the pharmacy and medical audit circles represents the drug utilisation studies, which involve joint responsibilities with the physicians. The open space of the pharmacy audit circle represents the peer review or pharmacy ancillary services section where only the pharmacists have sole responsibilities for the review and quality management. These services are primarily drug distribution and control of drug information, clinical pharmacy, continuing education and other pharmacy functions. Every pharmacy should develop an ongoing quality management programme for its services to assist an effective system monitoring.

The evaluation programme should be based on carefully-defined outcome criteria where possible. This will involve identification of detailed pharmacy functions and for each of these, sets of outcome criteria and standards should be developed. The criteria are designed to be used for departmental self-assessment and they form part of a total pharmacy system quality management effort. The outcome and process criteria may or may not directly involve a patient, depending upon the specific functions under review. Stolar (1978) gave examples of some outcome criteria and these include statements such as: "patients can state purpose of all medications identifying each by name"; "patients can state dosage and dosage schedule for each medication" and "mean waiting time for prescriptions does not exceed twenty minutes".

## CONCEPTUAL MODEL FOR DRUG UTILISATION STUDIES

DUS is a review and a quality assurance mechanism. Brodie and Smith Jr. (1977) identified that a conceptual model for this review could be based on five utilisation review principles featuring various structural components. The components of the model consist of an authority to carry out the study, an analysis of the operational and demographic characteristics of the delivery system and the population served, respectively and the existing profile of drug usage. Other aspects of the model include standards of appropriateness and a scheme of evaluation to measure the impact of drug usage review

### 1. Authority for DUS

DUS may be carried out in a health care organisation as a free-standing activity or it may be integrated with an existing hospital utilisation review programme. On the other hand, the hospital pharmacy and therapeutics committee may initiate the request for an evaluation study. Health care researchers may even attempt such studies for experimental purposes or comparative studies among similar institutions. The granting of authority can assure recognition of the study, continuity of support and availability of resources for the review programme. Whichever is the case, the authority for the study must be obtained in a hospital. Such an authority may be derived from the administrator's office or the medical staff or even from both.

**2. Demographic and Operational Characteristics**

It is necessary to have information relating to the hospital's pattern of organisation, services provided, operational statistics, patient population and the extent of staffing by categories of medical, nursing and pharmacy personnel. This information will provide denominator data such as the relative number of inpatient, outpatient, clinic visits and patient days especially when epidemiological studies of drug usage are performed. This component of the model is necessary because of the need for data and information that may be required in interpreting the existing pattern of drug usage or changes that take place in that pattern.

**3. The Existing Drug Use Profile**

This section of the DUS quantifies drug usage and corresponding costs for a given period of time. The drugs are classified according to individual drugs and groups of drugs. However, it is better to develop the profiles of a select number of key drugs in details. This selective approach focuses on drugs according to the cost and rate of usage. Drugs with potentials for inappropriate use and likely potentials for adverse reactions are also noted particularly. Drug usage may be related to the quantity prescribed or dispensed but this profile provides a less accurate accounting than expressing the usage as the number of units or doses of drugs administered.

**4. Standards of Appropriateness and Review of Drug Usage**

Hospitals with an existing facility utilisation review programme may have a DUS integrated with specifications on the review process. However, for a free standing review activity, four requisites must be fulfilled in order to achieve a viable review mechanism, and these are enumerated as follows:

(a) A knowledge of the existing patterns of drug usage,
(b) A set of in-house standards of appropriateness of use against which the existing patterns will be matched,
(c) A mechanism for identifying suspected drug misuse,

(d) A mechanism for evaluating suspected drug misuse.

In this section of the model, the most critical issue is the appropriateness of a drug for a diagnosis or other medical condition. This raises the question of "drugs of choice", the resolution of which depends largely on the disposition of the medical staff and the restrictive nature of the hospital drug formulary, if in existence. In some cases, drugs of choice may be agreed upon for specified conditions and this information may be stored in the computer system. When such a drug is prescribed and entered into the computer, it will be accepted if compatible with the disease profile. However, if the drug is rejected as inappropriate, a manual review may be necessary. This simply refers to consultation with the prescriber, chart audit or a review of other pertinent documents.

Standards are desirable in the use of a drug or drug combinations for a given diagnosis or medical condition. However, such a standard will apply to a limited number of key drugs. Setting standards in drug usage may serve as a means of identifying or obviating potential drug reactions or to monitor drugs with potentials for an abuse, misuse or those with high toxicity indices. As shown in Fig. 12.2, DUS is a joint responsibility of both the medical and pharmacy staffs. Standards for drug use in a hospital must therefore be shared by the staff and by the pharmacy and therapeutics committee if in active existence. DUS will fail in its goal of improving quality of patient care if standards are not established.

With appropriate set standards for evaluating drug usage level, the need for remedial programmes becomes obvious in problem areas. Such remedy programmes may take the form of continuing education for physicians, pharmacists or nurses as the case may be. Usually the setting of standards and whatever remedial programs are matters of local decisions and responsibilities; and as such, the design of DUS must be tailored to the local need.

## 5. Scheme of Evaluation

The evaluation component of the DUS model should provide information about the program goals, effectiveness and costs. This information must be obtained in an organised and systematic fashion. DUS should impact on patient care, drug costs, changes in drug usage patterns, effectiveness and acceptance. The various impacts may be determined using such organised information. The scheme of evaluation should be concerned with changes in various aspects of the drug use process such as drug consumption, cost of drugs and cost of patient care, frequency of adverse drug reactions and misusage of specific drugs. Also, pertinent to the evaluation is an assessment of the attitudes of hospital personnel and those of patients towards the DUS. In summary, the evaluation should address two major issues, which are: first, the impact of the study on both costs and rates of drug usage, and secondly, the cost of the utilisation studies weighted against the benefits accrued.

The conceptual framework identified above was based on the definition of DUS given by Brodie and Smith (1976),which described the programme as "an authorised, structured and continuing program that reviews, analyses, and interprets patterns (rates and costs) of drug usage in a given health care delivery system against predetermined standards". However, the educational component of the model could only be fulfilled in an organised health care delivery setting such as a hospital, skilled nursing facility or clinic. This conceptual model may be adapted to any hospital setting as indicated, subject to slight modifications. However, an institution should develop a programme that best serves its own needs and interests within the broad structural framework provided. A useful model should provide a broad structural framework that embodies the underlying principles of DUS, thus, providing the necessary flexibility for individual hospital.

## SIGNIFICANCE OF DRUG UTILISATION STUDIES (DUS)

Drug utilisation studies serve to improve prescribing practices and to reduce the frequency of preventable adverse drug outcomes. The results of DUS may be elaborated to discover the economic repercussions of inappropriate prescribing and to quantify the cost-effectiveness of various therapeutic interventions.

DUS provide tools and incentives for improved drug use and this may be achieved through the actions of pharmacists or the DUS committee directed toward prescribers, other pharmacists and the recipients. Armed with relevant information from these studies, pharmacists become better equipped for resolving prescribing or compliance problems. Prescription problems may include drug-drug interactions or therapeutic duplications. Expectedly, the prescriber is the key to any successful DUS intervention, even when the immediate problem seems to stem from patient non-compliance. The studies serve as necessary inputs to the design of programs to change prescriber behaviour. Such intervention methods can be loosely categorised into three which are educational interventions including individual or group feedback and clinical pharmacy programs; incentive-based interventions and administrative restrictions and regulations. A single, effective method of modifying prescriber behaviour does not exist but rather, the intervention methods may overlap. For instance, educational intervention methods may overlap with administrative restrictions and regulations. In addition, the choice of interventions may be affected by the clinical settings, prescribers and goals of the health care organisation.

Similarly, drug utilisation studies may be used for a review of prescription order information to assist in minimising potential drug related problems. Some of these problems would include inappropriate drug for intended use, drug overuse, drug underuse and unclear labelling information to the patient. Other problems that may be examined include duplication of an active prescription on file, potential drug-drug interactions and possible drug-laboratory test interference

This programme is not confined solely to a review of the prescriber's drug usage habits, but it also entails the pharmacist dispensing and patient use of drugs. In fact, Knapp *et al.* (1977) described the twin goals of drug usage review as the encouragement of optimal drug use and the provision of high quality drug therapy in an economic manner. The first goal has implications for the strong educational component, which exists with these studies while the second reflects the desire to assure the quality and efficiency of health care. The studies could also function as a screening device to separate those prescription orders which for some reasons might fall outside the established criteria. However, prescription orders, which fail a screen, are not necessarily incorrect but these may need to be examined further to ascertain whether or not a problem really exists. DUS in a hospital should improve the level of patient care with reduced cost of care and it is expected to improve the management and use of hospital resources. This program should clarify the drug component of patient care and better integrate pharmaceutical services with other hospital services. The design should improve the fact-finding capacity that can help to identify and solve hospital problems.

In summary, DUS seek to improve the quality of patient care through the prescription of appropriate drugs in conditions for which their use, based on sound medical judgment, is indicated and at a minimal cost consistent with an acceptable quality of care.

## APPLICATION OF DRUG UTILISATION STUDIES

### (1) Morbidity Data from Drug

DUS can be used to estimate the prevalence of an illness in a specific area based on consumption data for the drug(s) used to treat the disease state. These studies can also be used to compare the prevalence of an illness in different areas or to investigate different prescribing practices.

### (2) Estimates of Cost of Treatment

The unit of measurement of DUS is the cost of treatment per day. This is defined as the sale price to the public of the defined daily dose (DDD) of a specific drug. When used along with other appropriate database, DUS may permit approximate calculation of the cost of the drugs used to treat a particular illness.

### (3) Problems in Drug Use

The most important objective of DUS is to identify patterns of drug consumption, such as geographical differences in usage, overuse, misuse, underuse, incorrect use, different prescribing practices and groups of patients exhibiting high levels of therapeutic non-compliance. Comparisons of geographical differences in drug consumption and their relationship with morbidity data can be used to identify medical problems such as inappropriate prescriptions and its economic consequences.

### (4) Therapeutic Compliance

DUS may be used to estimate the extent of patient compliance to particular drug items. Patient non-compliance has important and economic consequences, which include a reduction in the theoretical effectiveness of a drug, prolongation of illness from lack of drug effect, unnecessary prescriptions and appearance of antibiotic resistance. Improving compliance in diabetic patients may result in a lower number of ketoacidosis.

### (5) Adverse Drug Reactions (ADR)

DUS can be used to estimate the incidence of adverse reactions associated with a drug, provided that a good drug surveillance system is available. ADR may also be estimated from a link of prescription records and morbidity data.

### (6) Effectiveness of Drugs Used

DUS can be used to evaluate both the overall quality and volume of drugs consumed in a geographical area.

### (7) Comparative Drug Study

DUS may be used to obtain information about which drugs are most commonly used for a specific indication. In most cases, the commonly used alternative is known without the need for a study but DUS can be useful when there is doubt.

### (8) Research on New Drugs

DUS can provide information about the drugs or drug groups having highest consumption and the appropriateness of this consumption. The therapeutic values of the drugs and areas for improvement in prescribing can allow comparison of the resources invested in different drugs according to their economic and clinical values. Such data can assist those interested in the development of new drugs, maximising the benefit of resources invested in drug research.

## EVALUATION OF DRUG UTILISATION STUDIES (DUS)

It may be necessary to evaluate DUS in order to see how far the studies were effective in the improvement of drug use and in reducing the negative consequences of drug misuse. Such negative consequences may be measured in terms of adverse clinical events and health service utilisation. The evaluation further serves to determine the cost of achieving these improvements *vis-à-vis* other policies and programs designed to achieve the same ends. Drug utilisation review evaluation may be designed to bring out descriptive information about the drug use pattern in a health care organisation or as a test for the aggregate effects of the studies on various relevant criteria. It may also be used to analyse the effects of clinical outcomes in the health system. The various components of such a review are described as follows:

### (i) Descriptive Contextual Information

This is a discussion of the problems encountered in the DUS and it includes analyses of attitudes and perceptions of pharmacists and prescribers toward DUS. Based on this survey, baseline comparisons may be made of prescription drug utilisation and problems among the reviewed institutions.

### (ii) Test of Aggregate Demonstration Effects

Statistical models may be used to test for the aggregate effects of DUS on such criteria as:

(a) the volume and costs of prescription drug utilisation
(b) the frequency of drug problems encountered
(c) the volume and costs of drug utilisation associated with diagnoses less than optimal prescribing, emergency room visits and physician office visits.

### (iii) Focused Tests of DUS Effects

The evaluation may conduct epidemiological analyses of the effects of DUS on adverse clinical outcomes, in the context of specific prescribing problems. For instance, by reducing the frequency of over-utilisation of benzodiazepines, the DUS may have effected a decrease in falls which is an associated clinical outcome. With focused studies, modelling and choice of covariates are then tailored to each clinical problem. Examples of focused studies include the extent of gastro-intestinal (GI) bleeding with the use of nonsteroidal anti-inflammatory drugs (NSAIDS), benzodiazepines and falls and the specific clinical outcomes associated with the use of cardiac drugs, beta-agonist inhalers and antidepressants.

## CONCLUSION

A number of challenges may emerge with the design , procedure and application of drug utilisation studies. Such challenges become evident when the study design meets the realities of limited resources in the organisation, institutional rigidities and protocols along with some other unforeseen events. However, with the continual and increasing emphasis on patient care evaluation procedures; it is imperative that pharmacists understand the principles and importance of quality assurance and drug use review. Drugs play a central part in patient care and hospital pharmacists will play a pivotal role in initiating and operating effective systems for assuring the quality of drug use. Deliberate efforts will therefore be necessary to address the challenges of a proper review programme. Utilisation of these studies in relevant situations will lead to a more efficient use of drugs which in turn will result in improved economic and social performance.

### References

Ahern, F,M., Heller, D. and Miles, T. "Impact of Prospective Drug Use Review on Health Outcomes".

Baksaas, I, and Lunde, P.K.M. (1981). Drug Utilisation: Pharmacokinetics in the Community. *Trend in Pharmacological Sciences* 2:5-7.

Baksaas, I. (1984). "Patterns in Drug Utilisation: National and Intern. Aspects - Anti-hypertensive Drugs". *Acta Medica Scandinavica* 683:59-66.

Bergman, U., Boman, G. and Wiholm, B.E. (1978). Epidemiology of Adverse Reactions to "Phenformin and Metformin". *British Medical Journal* 2:464-466, 1978.

Braybrook, S., Thomas, J.,Wilson, P.S., Haynes, W., Jarvis, I. and Conaty, D. "Pharmacist-led Hypertension Drug Use Review". *Int. Journ. Pharm.* Pract. 10 (suppl.): R20.

Brodie, D.C. and Smith, W. E. (Jr.), (March 1976). "A Conceptual Model for Drug Utilisation Review". *Hospitals* 50:143 - 149.

Brodie, D.C. (1977). "Drug Utilisation Review/Planning". *Hospitals* 46:103, 106-112.

Brodie, D.C., Smith, W. E. (Jr.) and Hlynka, J. N. (1977). "Model for Drug Usage Review in a Hospital." *Am. J. Hosp. Pharm.* 34:251-254.

Brudon, P., Rainhorn, J. and Reich, M.R. "Indicators for Monitoring National Drug Policies: A Practical Manual" WHO/EDM/PAR/99.3

Erwin, W.G. (1991). "The Definition of Drug Utilisation Review: Statement of Issues".*Clin. Pharmacology and Therapeutics* 16: 596-599.

Kanakambal, S., Murugesh, N. and Shanthi, M. (2001). "Drug Prescribing Pattern in a Tertiary Care Teaching Hospital in Madurai" (Tamilnadu). *Indian Journ. of Pharmac.*33:223.

Keys, P.W., Giudici, R.A., Hirsch, D. R. and Gonzales, S.M (Jan 1976). Pharmacy Audit: Aid to Continuing Education *Am. J. Hosp. Pharm.* 33: 52 - 55.

Knapp, D.A., Knapp, D.E., Brandon, B.M, *et. al* "Drug Use Review - A Manual System *Am.J Pharm. Ass* NS13:417 - 421.

Lee, D. and Bergman, U. (1989). "Studies of Drug Utilisation: in Storm" (ed.) *Pharmaco-epidemiology* P. 259-274, NY.

Sacristan, J.A. and Soto, J., (1984)."Drug Utilisation Studies as Tools in Health Economics" *Pharmaco-economics* 5:299-312.

Spitzer, W.O.(1991). "Drugs as Determinants of Health and Disease in the Population: An Orientation to the Bridge of Phamacoepidemiology". *Journ. of Clin. Epidem.* 44: 823-830.

Stolar, M.H., (1978). "Drug Use Review: Operational Definitions "*Am J. Hosp Pharm.* 35:76-78.

Talley, C.R. (May 1, 1994). "Protocol Medicine". *Am J. Hosp. Pharm.* 51:1171.

W.H.O. (1990). The Selection of Essential Drugs. Progress Report (A43/10) by the Director General, 43rd Health Assembly.

W.H.O./DAP/93.1 (1993). "How to Investigate Drug Use in Health Facilities: Selected Drug Use Indicators". Action Programme on Essential Drugs.

Wareham, D.U. and Deliganis, S.G. (June 1976). "Rational Fluid and Electrolyte Therapy Utilisation Review". *Drug Intelligence and Clinical Pharm.* 10:339-345.

Westerholm, B; Agenas, I, Dahlstrom, M. and Nordenstam, I. (1984) "Relationship between Drug Utilisation and Morbidity Patterns. *Acta Medica Scandinavica* 683: 95-97.

Westerholm, B. (1983). "Drug Utilisation Studies a Valuable Tool for the Optimisation of Drug Therapy and Drug Control". *Journ. of Soc. and Admin. Pharm.* 1:1-8.

# *Chapter 13*

# STRESS AND STRESS MANAGEMENT

*Ogunlade, J.O.*

**About the Contributor**
Ogunlade is a physician in the Department of Medicine, Obafemi Awolowo University Teaching Hospitals Complex (O.A.U.TH.C.), Ile-Ife. Osun State, Nigeria.

## INTRODUCTION

Stress is an essential stimulus for survival and active productivity. Excess stress is counterproductive and can consume its bearer at the unguarded moment. One of the essential but often neglected elements of optimal management of an institution is stress management. Apart from managing the institution technically, an administrator must learn how to recognise and manage stress and provide opportunity for the training of his employees on how to cope with the stress of life.

The successes of health care organisations depend not only on the facilities available in the institution but also on the skills of its manpower and the ability of the health administrator to coordinate his staff for optimal productivity without conflict. If a stressed individual cannot manage himself, how much more of an institution. Let us consider a case of a medical doctor of a big hospital who lost his best employee in a ghastly motor accident. He was shocked when he received the news.

He gave his best to ensure assistance before and after the burial of the worker. Although, this big shock stressed the doctor but the work of the hospital must continue.

Patients continued to visit the hospital for the treatment of their ailments. Transactions within the hospital could not be suspended. The medical director was slow to adjust. He found it difficult to replace the lost fellow on time.

The alarm of stress signed in when he discovered the piling up of work supposed to be done by the deceased fellow. Hence, he continued to do the work himself. As the director, he tried to complete the backlog of work, he was limited by twenty-four hours a day and ability. He became frustrated and suffered. He realised that he was losing energy and that his production level waned. "What a tragedy?" He often lamented.

He needed to do something to survive but he did not know what to do on time. He became overwhelmed by the irreparable loss of his best employee. He wanted to complete most of the office works himself, but realistically, it was impossible. Fears of failure gripped him as such; he lost some degree of concentration. Hence, the director often made some subtle but administratively significant management error and omissions.

As the situation continued, he became burnout, thinking of afflictions by the enemies. He picked up fight with his wife at home because she accused him of staying back excessively in office. "Darling, you need to pay attention to your family too. All is not work. Neither is office the ultimate". His wife often stressed. The medical director became stress-out and experienced fatigue instead of being relieved by night sleep and sleeping drugs. At the office, he often became nervous, irritable, tensed and displayed anger at the slightest provocations.

To cope, he started to drink alcohol and even contemplated smoking. However, as a public figure, he thought that smoking would be shameful. Being a medical doctor, he realised that he needed the assistance of a physician. Who would he consult? He knew that an administrative psychiatrist better handles such a case. "We don't have such in this hospital." He muttered to himself. Anyway if he received treatment from the psychiatrists, people would be of the opinion that he was having mental problems. Hence, he refused to consult any physician.

Within a short time, he became anxious. As the situation worsened, he became depressed and lacked motivation necessary to find pleasures in his activities.

His inadequacies and errors gradually backfired and manifested almost in every section of the hospital management. Patients complained of decrease efficiency in the hospital. Observers commented as situation degenerated. Some faithful members of staff of the hospital even went spiritual, as they perceived the imminent collapse of the reputable hospital.

The previous good deeds of the medical director were forgotten. It was as if all was against him. He was accused of mismanagement. Some even suggested to him to resign without delay.

On realising the real state of things both in the hospital and at home, he felt bad and overwhelmed. "This is too much for me to bear". He commented pessimistically. On one Monday morning, while his children had gone to school and his wife gone to work, he came back home and committed suicide. Such is the havoc that stress and abnormal response to stress can cause.

It is clear that:

> Excess stress is a consuming fire, and it is more beneficial but less stressful to stress that escaping the dangers of stress requires every wise person to learn how to recognise and manage the stress of life before the body is stressed beyond the limit of its ability.

Hence, the need to consider the topic in more details. What is stress? What are stressors? How do we recognise stress? Then, how do we manage stress without been stressed? These and more will be considered in simple terms in this chapter.

## WHAT IS STRESS?

Stress can be defined as the body's non-specific response to any demand placed on it whether pleasant or not. Stress also refers to a complex pattern of emotional states, physiological reactions, and related thoughts occurring in response to external demands (stressors). Such demands are called stressors and could be from within or without. Institutional organisations undergo stress too, for example, banks. Stressors include work, peer pressure, family demands, societal expectations, loss of relative, fellow co-worker, too big plans, ambitions, interpersonal conflicts, accidents, errors and omissions, demands during joyful situations such as marriages, promotions, etc. Strain refers to the effects of the stress, primarily to deviations from normal states or performance resulting from exposure to stressful events.

Some regarded stress as only being negative and counterproductive. This may not always be true. Stress is not only a negative phenomenon, at certain level, it could be positive for optimal performance and achievement of a specific goal. However, excess stress is certainly consuming. An individual with little or no stress has neither stimulation nor challenge and may not be able to achieve much. However, with moderate stress, an individual is challenged, motivated, and he devises solution to problems, hence the resultant optimal output. Excess stress inhibits output, an individual becomes overwhelmed and could not cope with demand, hence the decline in output.

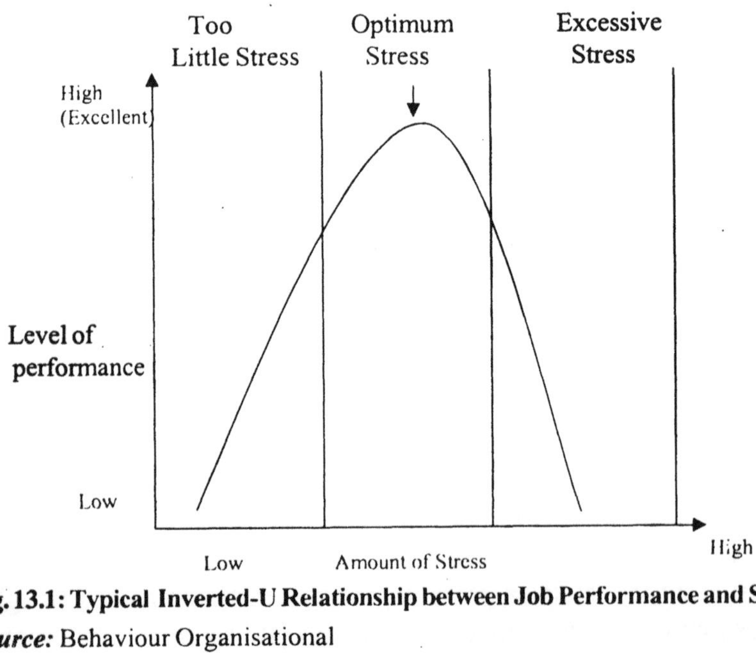


**Fig. 13.1: Typical Inverted-U Relationship between Job Performance and Stress**

***Source:*** Behaviour Organisational

**Table 13.1. Causes of Stress**

| | | | |
|---|---|---|---|
| **Intrapersonal*** Individualistic expectations of self. | *Lack of self organisation. | *Need to be in control. | *Inability to set limits. |
| Inability to manage time effectively. | *Feelings of inadequacy.<br>*Under or overestimating abilities. | *Inability to delegate responsibility. | *Financial concerns. |
| **Interpersonal** | | *Lack of respect from others. | |
| *Being required to fulfil others expectations. | *Lack of autonomy at work. | *Being taken for granted. | |
| *Demands for perfection from family, superiors. | *Dealing with aggressive or manipulative people. | *Not being involved in decision-making. | |
| **Organisational** *Poor professional communication systems. | *Lack of clarity and agreement about the values and goals of the organisation. | *Lack of positive and/or critical feedback to employees.<br>*Inadequate staffing levels for the job at hand. | *Lack of team and organisational identities.<br>*Highly competitive structures. |
| *Extremes of management styles.<br>*Working with an inexperienced staff. | *Lack of consideration for the individual within the organisation. | | |

| **Community** | **Cultural** | **National** | **International** |
|---|---|---|---|
| Inadequate local services.<br><br>*Noise pollution.<br><br>*Traffic congestion.<br><br>*Lack of space.<br><br>*Lack of sense of community.<br><br>*High crime rates. | *Racial, religious and sexual prejudice and discrimination.<br><br>*Rigid expectations of certain types of behaviour from people according to their gender, class or status irrespective of their individual differences and expectations. | *Government * policies affecting defence, the economy, unemployment, public services, taxation and rates.<br><br>*Civil unrest.<br><br>*National disasters.<br><br>*War and the threat of war. | Difficulties in understanding different values, politics and cultures.<br><br>*War and disasters in other countries.<br><br>*Environmental damage affecting large parts of the entire planet. |
| **Universal**<br>*The experience of being vulnerable. | | *The transitions that must be as you grow older. | *The comparative insignificance of the individual human being within the universe. |

| | | | |
|---|---|---|---|
| *Accepting the frailty of the human body. | *Having to sacrifice some individuality to function in a group, partnership or team. | *Spiritual ambiguities. | *The inevitability of death. |

***Source:*** *Management and Organisational Behaviour*

**Table 13.2. Organisational Factors Contributing to Stress**

| Organisational Design Variables | Interpersonal Variables | Career Variables |
|---|---|---|
| Physical work environment (noise, heat or cold, long working hours, dangerous job conditions, shift work, repetitive work). | Leadership style. Lack of group cohesion. Lack of participation. | Occupational level. Entry. Mid-career. |
| Incentive system. | | |
| Role pressures (role conflict and ambiguity). | Responsibility for people. | Retirement. |
| Work overload and underload (qualitative and quantitative) | | Demotion. Stagnation. Obsolescence. |

***Source:*** *Management and Organisational Behaviour*

## Work-related Causes of Stress

As anyone who has ever held a job well knows, work settings are often highly stressful environments. Yet, they vary greatly in this respect. Some jobs and organisations expose individuals to high levels of stress while others involve much lower levels of stress. Many factors account for these differences and they include:

***Occupational Demands:*** Some jobs are more stressful than others. What exactly makes some jobs more stressful than others? Apparently, several factors. Jobs become increasingly stressful to the extent that they require (1) making decisions, (2) constant monitoring of devices or materials, (3) unpleasant physical working conditions, (4) repeated exchange of information with others, and (5) performing unstructured rather than structured roles or tasks.

***Conflict between Work and Non-work:*** This is stress from competing demands, for example, full-time working women juggling with family demands.

***Role Conflict:*** incompatible demands made on an individual by different groups or persons.

***Role Ambiguity:*** This is stress from uncertainty. Even if individuals or organisations are able to avoid the stress with role conflict, they may still encounter source of job-related stress in role ambiguity. This occurs when an individual or organisation experience uncertainty about what actions to take to fulfil a job. Most people dislike uncertainty and find it quite stressful, but it is difficult to avoid.

***Overload and Underload:*** This is doing too much or too little *Quantitative overload* is a situation in which individuals are required to do more work than they can actually accomplish in a given period of time. While quantitative underload is a situation in which individuals have so little to do that they spend much of their time doing nothing.
*Qualitative overload* is the belief among employees that they lack the skills or abilities needed to perform their jobs. While qualitative underload is the lack of mental stimulation that accompanies many routine and repetitive jobs.

***Responsibility for Others: A Heavy Burden***
Research findings indicate that in general, people who are responsible for others – who must motivate them, reward or punish them, communicate with them – experience higher levels of stress than those who handle other organisational functions. Such people are more likely

to report feelings of tension and anxiety, and are actually more likely to show overt symptoms of stress such as ulcers or hypertension.

***Lack of Social Support***: The cost of isolation is severe. When confronted with stressful situations, we are much better when we have a network of friends and associates to whom we can turn to for support and counsel.

***Sexual Harassment:*** This is a pervasive problem in work settings. Sexual harassment can be defined as unwanted contact or communication of a sexual nature. No sex is immune to harrassment.

***Unpleasant Physical Working Conditions:*** Most work settings are relatively safe and comfortable due to legislation aimed at protecting the health and well-being of the employees. There are however a host of variations to this.

***Stressful Life Events***: Unpleasant eventualities like the death of a loved one, accident, stock market crash, burglary, etc, can cause unquantifiable levels of stress. The daily hassles of life also cause a lot of stress.

**Table 13.4: Stressful Life Events**

| Event | Relative stressfulness |
|---|---|
| Death of a spouse | 100 |
| Divorce | 73 |
| Marital separation | 65 |
| Jail term | 63 |
| Death of a close family member | 63 |
| Personal injury or illness | 53 |
| Marriage | 50 |
| Fired from a job | 47 |
| Retirement | 45 |
| Pregnancy | 40 |
| Death of a close friend | 37 |
| Son or daughter leaving home | 29 |
| Trouble with in-laws | 28 |
| Trouble with boss | 23 |
| Change in residence | 20 |

| | |
|---|---|
| Vacation | 13 |
| Christmas | 12 |
| Minor violations of the law | 11 |

**Source:** *Management and Organisational Behaviour*

***Total Life Stress:*** It is useful to adopt a broad approach in which work - related and personal causes of stress are combined into the construct of total negative life stress suggested by the fact that total stress is a better predictor of negative organisational outcomes.

**Table 13.3: Primary Causes of Stress at Work: A *Wall Street Journal* Survey.**

| Factor | Percentage Response |
|---|---|
| Not doing the kind of work I want | 34 |
| Coping with current job | 30 |
| Working too hard | 28 |
| Colleagues at work | 21 |
| A difficult boss | 18 |

***Source:*** *Stephen P. Robbins (1998) Organisation Behaviour (8th. edition).*

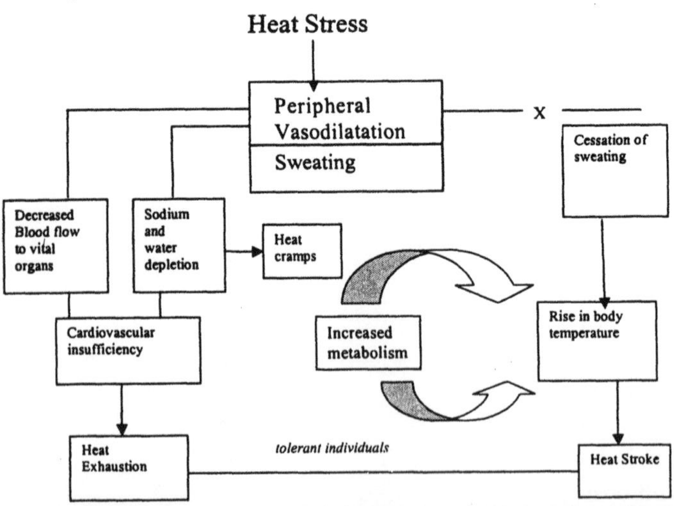


**Fig.13.2: The responses to heat stress that may lead to the production of heat disorders as classified by WHO**

**Table 13.5: The Most Stressful Jobs**

| Rank Score | Job | Stress score | Rank score | Job | Stress score |
|---|---|---|---|---|---|
| 1. | U.S.president | 176.6 | 47. | Auto salesperson | 56.3 |
| 2. | Firefighter | 110.9 | 50. | College Professor | 54.2 |
| 3. | Senior executive | 108.6 | 60. | School principal | 51.7 |
| 6. | Surgeon | 99.5 | 103. | Market research analyst | 42.1 |
| 10. | Air-traffic controller | 83.1 | 104. | Personnel recruiter | 41.8 |
| 12. | Public-relations executive | 78.5 | 113. | Hospital administrator | 39.6 |
| 16. | Advertising account executive | 74.6 | 119. | Economist | 38.7 |
| 17. | Real estate agent | 73.1 | 122. | Mechanical engineer | 38.3 |
| 20. | Stockbroker | 71.7 | 124. | Chiropractor | 37.9 |
| 22. | Pilot | 66.9 | 132. | Technical writer | 36.5 |
| 25. | Architect | 64.3 | 149. | Retail salesperson | 34.9 |
| 31. | Lawyer | 68 | 173. | Accountant | 31.1 |
| 33. | General physician | 64 | 193. | Purchasing agent | 28.9 |
| 35. | Insurance agent | 63.3 | 229. | Broadcast technician | 24.2 |
| 42. | Advertising salesperson | 59.9 | 245. | Actuary | 20.2 |

**Source:** *Stephen P. Robbins (1998) Organisation Behaviour 8th Edition.*

## Experience of Work Stress

Whether or not, an individual experiences of work stress is determined by a number of factors, including:

a. Individual's perception of the situation – which influences how stress is experienced.
b. Past experience – which influences familiarity with the stressors.
c. Relationship between stress and task performance – an optimum level of stress may exist in some job situations.
d. Interpersonal relationship among workers – the presence or absence of others may influence how stress is experienced.
e. Individual differences – personality features may explain differences in susceptibility and coping ability. In fact, individual characteristic

is a vital mediating variable in the stressor - consequence relationship.

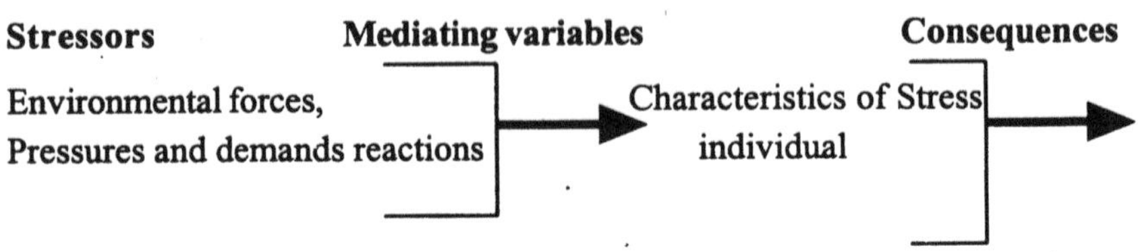


**Fig. 13.3: Model of Individual Stress**
***Source:*** Organisational Behaviour

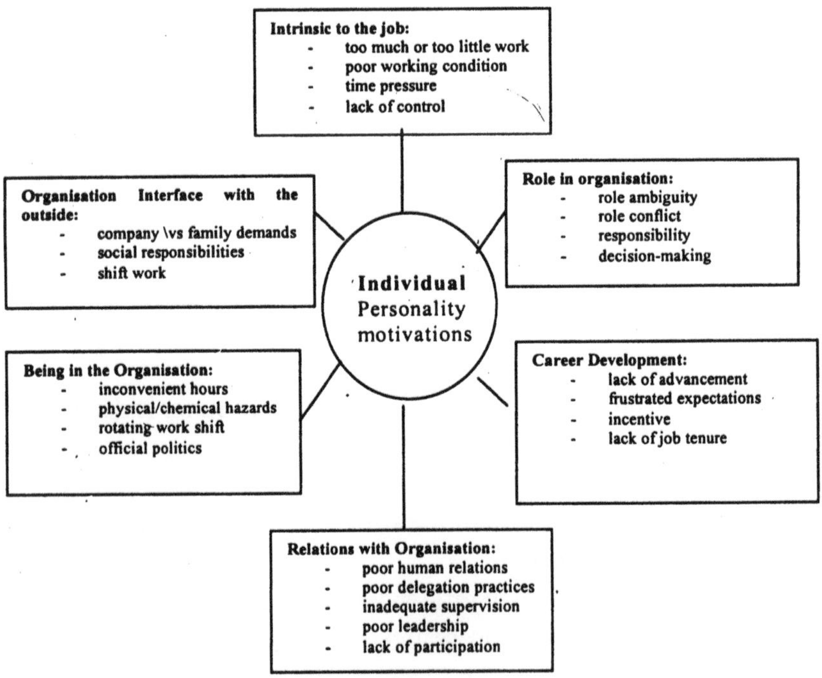


**Fig. 13.4: Sources of Work Stress**
***Source:*** Organisational Behaviour

## INDIVIDUAL DIFFERENCES IN REACTION TO STRESS.

Each individual reacts differently to differing levels of stress. The different trait inherent in each individual dictates the specific reaction to a particular stressor. These traits reflect in behavioural patterns – some people can accommodate job enrichment and job enlargement simultaneously while this assignment may be self-destructive to others.

There is a strong link between stress and personal health. There are life-threatening ailments such as heart diseases, stroke, diabetes, ulcers, headaches, cancer, etc. Extreme stress often leads to depression, which is reduced inner will. It may also precipitate degenerative diseases and infectious diseases that are caused by bacteria, viruses and fungi.

**Table 13.6: Individual Symptoms of Stress (Schuler 1980)**

| | |
|---|---|
| 1. **Physiological** | |
| Short term: | Heart rate and respiration increase, headache |
| Long term: | Ulcer, blood pressure, heart attack |
| Non-specific: | Adrenalin, noradrenalin, thymus deduction, lymph deduction, gastric acid production, ACTH hormone production. |
| 2. **Psychological Responses (affective and cognitive)** | |
| Fright or withdrawal: | Inability to organise self |
| Apathy or resignation: | Inner confusion about duties or roles |
| Boredom: | Dissatisfaction |
| Regression: | High intolerance for ambiguity |
| Fixation: | Inability to deal well with new or strange situation |
| Projection: | Tendency to begin vacillating in decision-making |
| Fantasy: | Tendency to become distraught with trifles |
| Expression of boredom: | Inattentiveness, loss of power to concentrate with much of everything, forgetfulness, irritability and procrastination |

| | |
|---|---|
| Feelings of persecution: | Tendency to misjudge people; uncertainty about whom to trust, guilt-level feelings of unexplainable dissatisfaction |

3. ***Behavioural***

A. *Individual consequences*

Loss of appetite
Sudden, noticeable loss or gain of weight
Sudden change of appearance: decline/improvement in dress
Sudden change of complexion (sallow, reddened, acne)
Sudden change of hair style and length
Difficult breathing
Sudden change of smoking habits
Sudden change in the use of alcohol

B. *Organisational consequences*

Low performance-quality/quantity
Low job involvement
Loss of responsibility
Lack of concern for organisation
Lack of concern for colleagues
Loss of creativity
Absenteeism
Voluntary turnover
Accident proneness.

***Source:*** *Organisational Behaviour*

**Burnout**

This is a syndrome resulting from prolonged exposure to stress, consisting of physical, emotional, and mental exhaustion plus feelings of a lack of personal accomplishment. Its major components is when people are exposed to high level of stress over prolonged periods of time, they may experience burnout. This syndrome involves physical, mental, and attitudinal exhaustion, plus feelings of low personal accomplishment. The traits described here have been found to influence the extent to which individuals are susceptible to the harmful effects of stress. Burnout can be reversed if ongoing stress is reduced, if burnout victims can add support from workmates, friends, and relations; and if they cultivate the habit of developing hobbies, such people can escape from the dead-end trap of burnout.

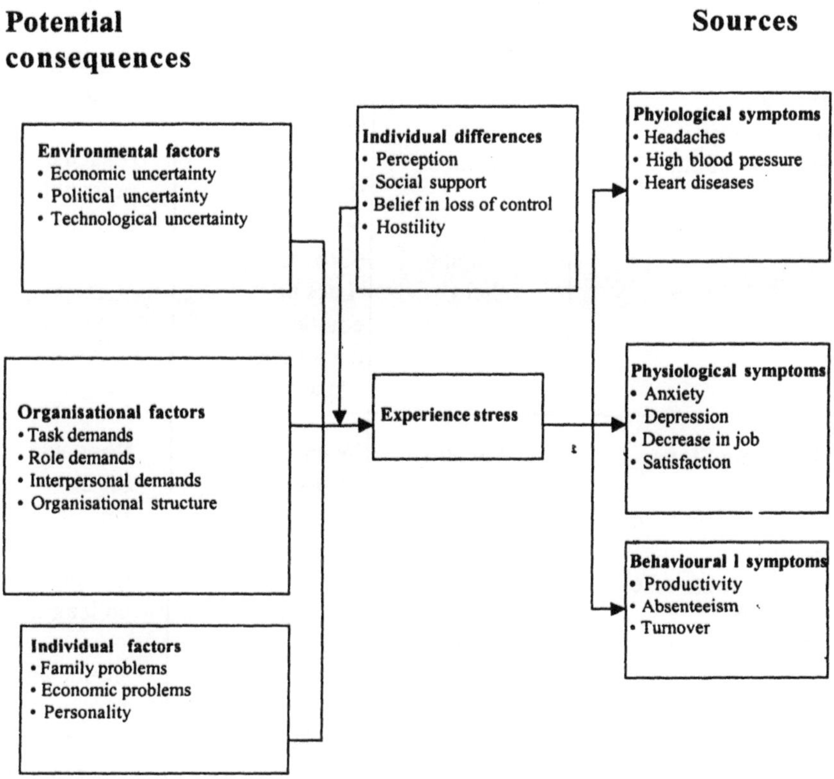


**Fig.13.5: A Model of Stress**
***Source:*** Organisation Behaviour

**Table 13.7: The Burnout Scale.**

| Stage 1 | Stage 2 | Stage 3 | Stage 4 |
|---|---|---|---|
| •Lots of energy and enthusiasm.<br>•Overconscientious.<br>•Overworked.<br>•Feelings of uncertainty<br>•Doubts about coping. | •Short-lived bouts of irritation.<br>•Tiredness and anxiety.<br>•Feelings of Stagnation.<br>•Blaming others. | General discomfort.<br>•Increase anger or resentment.<br>•Lowering of self-esteem.<br>•Growing guilt<br>•Lack of emotional commitment<br>•Apathy. | •Withdrawal<br>•Illness.<br>•Feelings of failure.<br>•Extreme personal distress. |
| **Warning Signs**<br>•Too busy to take holidays.<br>•Reluctant to take days off.<br>•Bringing work home.<br>•Too little time with partner/family.<br>•Frustrated with results.<br>•Unable to refuse more work. | **Warning Signs**<br>•Complaints about the quality of other people's work.<br>•Unable to cope with commitments.<br>•Working long hours.<br>•Unable to manage time effectively.<br>•Too many social or work commitments. | **Warning Signs**<br>•Lack of enjoyment of life.<br>•Extreme exhaustion.<br>•Reduce commitment to work.<br>•Reduced commitment at home. | **Danger Signs**<br>•Increasing absenteeism.<br>•Avoiding colleagues.<br>•Reluctance to communicate.<br>•Increasing isolation. |

**Source:** *Organisation Behaviour*

## HOW TO RECOGNISE STRESS

Recognition of stress is not stressful. It requires an individual to understand himself in order to detect the manifestations of stress.

Stress could present itself in three stages; namely:

1. The Alarm stage
2. The Resistance stage
3. The exhaustion stage.

### 1. The Alarm Stage

At this stage, stress manifests by warning signs. Upon exposure to stressors or stressful situation, the person becomes aware of the excess demands on him, or his inability to meet a demand such as excess workload. Within, the individual lacks peace of mind, have headache and feels uncomfortable. If the stressful situation is not controlled, it becomes overwhelming. For instance, in the case of the Medical Director illustrated above, he finds it difficult to replace the deceased fellow. The alarm of stress came in when he could not complete the office work and he became disturbed and uncomfortable.

### 2. Resistance stage

This usually follows the alarm stage and manifests as frustrations, loss of energy and decrease in productivity but the individual is still coping. At this stage, even other people could observe that the individual is passing through stressful situation.

### 3. Exhaustion stage

This is the final stage. The individual coping mechanisms breakdown. The affected individual becomes anxious and depressed and often develops easy fatiguability and insomnia (inability to have adequate sleep). He becomes pessimistic. More often than not, at this stage, depending on the genetic predisposition, an individual may develop stress-related health disorders such as depression and its complications such as suicide. On the other hand, an individual may develop hypertension and its complications such as stroke. Both diseases act to take the individual off the stress. Such is the case of the Medical Director illustrated above. Therefore, an uncontrolled stress will control its bearer to the point of elimination.

## HOW TO MANAGE STRESS

Optimal management of health care organisations requires that the health care workers should strategically optimise or maximise their potentials to ensure optimum output of the health care organisation (that is, efficient and effective health care delivery). A tensed up health care worker cannot deliver at optimal level. Moreover, a tensed up institution can collapse without appreciable output.

Health care organisation like any other organisation, almost always undergoes a series of disturbances, following which there would be a re-establishment of its equilibrium. The disturbances may arise either from internal or external stressors arising from daily transactions in a bid to maintain an efficient and standard health care delivery.

The administrators of the health care organisations should be familiar and sensitive to the needs and problems of such institution. They should understand themselves and identify negative stressors among health care workers and between sections of the organisation while unifying the workers to express their problems. They should challenge workers to be sensitive to their work while improving communication between workers and management. However, for effective management of stress, the following strategies are beneficial.

### 1. Recognise the Stress

Everyone is susceptible to stress irrespective of age, sex, status, religion, and experiences. It is imperative that an individual should be able to detect subtle but early manifestations of stress. Upon recognition of stress in one's life or institution, an individual should develop positive mental attitude towards the situation while strengthening his inner capacity to overcome the situation no matter its form, manifestations, cause and course. Thereafter, having taken the stressful situation as a challenge, then the situation must be met by appropriate positive response. As such, individuals should device a solution to the problem.

Such solution may consist of some actions or inactions and may be passive or active.

**2. Develop self-understanding**

An individual in an institution either as ordinary staff or as an administrator should, apart from understanding himself, also study and understand his/her job, expectations, environment and even the co-workers. Failure to do this may lead to conflict of interests with resultant effect as stress upon the individual. We should understand that, as an individual could be stressed to the point of breakdown, so also the facilities in an institution could be stressed to the point of collapse.

**3. Plan**

Good plan accompanied by properly organised set of actions leads to optimum output without appreciable stress. He who fails to plan has planned to fail. Planning is a good strategy to meet the various demands of life. Without appropriate planning in an institution or by an individual, various non-goal specific demands will arise even to jeopardise the legitimate goal-directed projects.

It is an indisputable fact that time is equally universally available to mankind, for everyone has twenty-four hours in a day, no more no less. We are limited by time. It then becomes imperative to plan the time and on time and execute such project or action at appropriate time. In life, there should be time to work and time for relaxation. Moreover, in order to make effective use of time to achieve a desirable goal, we must plan for each day, each month and each year while operating on the long-term plan. Planning includes budgeting and devices of strategy to achieve optimal output.

When stress surfaces, relax first, study the situation, take it as a challenge and strengthen the inner mind to overcome, then, device solution plan and go ahead to execute thc plan at the appropriate time. However, this requires wisdom.

**4. Solve Problem of Succession.**

Many people find it difficult to change or accept a change. Stress usually accompanies a change. Stress is always generated within a system whenever there is turnover of executives. Even before the change, anxiety usually develops in anticipating the new administrators, while ruminating on the departed leader. As the new leader attained the position, a period follows in which the staff begins to study the new leader while comparing him with the old. A phase is reached when tension usually arise as the new leader roll out his plans and implements new policies. The strains of change, the challenges and the fear of the new policies demand for adjustment on the part of the staff and even within the organisation. Change is a continuum and inevitable part of life. Hence, the stress generated by change is expected and should be catered for by the executives and the staff.

**5. Acquire Training**

For efficient management of health care institution, there is need for in-service training of the administrators in administration and management of interpersonal conflict and stress. Physicians head most health care organisations. However, being a physician does not automatically transform an individual into a good administrator. Hence, the need for special training for such leaders.

Administrative training should include, not only specific instructions on budgeting, law, public relations and fund-raising, but also crisis management, confrontations, critical attacks and interpersonal conflicts among the staff without being overwhelmed.

**6. Control Stress**

This section intimates us with various tit-bits of controlling stress. Most of the points here are directed towards invigorating individuals to cope with and control stress. Control of stress could be viewed in three major areas; namely: control of the environment, bodily control and mental control.

**a. *Control the Environment***

i. Keep your environment clean and organised.
ii. Avoid choky environment, try to live and work in space, which is reasonably large.

iii. Avoid noisy surroundings.
iv. Create a good working environment.
v. Try to enjoy nature. Beautify your environment with flowers.
vi. Save free time for hobbies, relaxation and recreation.
vii Dedicate enough time for your family.
viii As much as it depends on you, try to live and work peaceably with everyone.
x On interpersonal relation, always listen first.
xi Avoid aggressive argument.
xii Learn how to resolve conflict without conflict.

**b. *Mental Control of Stress***

i. Think positively and maintain positive mental attitude.
ii. Take a stressful condition as a challenge.
iii. Plan your time and activities. Take advantage of time without becoming a slave to your plans or to the plans of others.
iv. Worry less, accept your mistakes and turn your mistakes and trials to challenges. Devise means of solving problems of life without frustration.
v. Choose to be assertive. Assertiveness involves expression of one's feelings in a sincere, spontaneous and open manner without hurting other people.
vi. Share your wealth, talents and resources with others without a feeling of regret.
vii. Take time to relax. Relaxation relieves stress and provides appropriate milieu to solve problems.

**c. *Bodily Control***

i. Be master over your body especially the mouth and tongue.
ii. Eat plenty of fruits and vegetables.
iii. Take a balanced diet.
iv. Drink a lot of water.
v. Reduce intake of fat and cholesterol.
vi. Reduce intake of salt and sugar.
vii. Avoid smoking. Many people smoke to relieve stress. This is

effective on a short term but on a long-term could be counterproductive.

viii. Reduce intake of alcohol.
ix. Reduce intake of processed foods.
x. Avoid all types of stimulants.
xi. Have regular moderate isotonic exercises. This includes brisk walking, jogging, running, bicycling, games and sports. However, take advice from a physician before commencing an exercise programme.
xii. Reduce weight if overweight.
xiii. Learn to consult a physician before coping mechanism breakdown.

**Organisation-Based Strategies for Managing Stress**

Organisations too take steps to reduce the level of stress experienced by their employees. Several organisation-based or organisation-initiated tactics can be highly effective in this regard. These are:

(1) ***Family-supportive practice***: This helps to reduce the stress of work-family conflicts or obligations for example, establishing day care centres at workplace, on-site care for sick children, flexible work schedules, and supervisor support like switching schedules to accommodate family responsibilities.

(2) ***Stress Management Programs***: Organisations have employed systematic efforts designed to help employees reduce and/or prevent stress. This include life insurance policy for its employees, retirement planning schemes, employee assistant programs (EAPs) such as providing employees with assistance in solving various problems (for example, housing, furniture, car, career planning, legal and financial problems). Others are provision of luncheon vouchers, reduced communication tariffs, employing ergonomics in the job design, monitoring job rotation, regular retreat sessions etc.

**Stress Management Unit**

Every health care organisation should have a unit for managing stress. In such unit, a physician preferably a psychiatrist, will be able to assist the members of staff in a long way to cope with stress and control the stress of life. Stress unit will provide counselling, organise seminars and workshops to educate people on stress and coping strategies.

**References**

Adam Kuper and Jessica Kuper, (1996). *The Social Science Encyclopedia,* 2nd edition.

Adams, .J. (1989). *Stress : A New Positive Approach.* Newton Abbol:

Atkinson, J.M. (1988). *Coping with Stress at Work.* Thorsons Publishing Press.

Fontana, D.(1989). *Managing Stress*, Leicester/London: British Society/Routledge Ltd.

Kathryn M. Bartol, (1994). *Management* 2nd edition. P.614-679.

Laurie J. Mullins, (1996). *Management and Organisational Behaviour.* 4th edition

Lucas, A.O., and Gilles, H.M. (1990). *A New Short Textbook of Preventive Medicine for the Tropics*, the Bath Press, Avon, Great Britain.

Melgosa, J. (2001). "Less Stress" Editorial Safeliz.

Mills, J.W.(1982). *Coping with Stress: A Guide to Living.* New York: John Wiley and Sons Inc.

Ogunlade, O. (2003). *The Silent Killer.* Akure: Success Communications.

Ogunlade, O.(2002). *War Against Hypertension*. Akure: Success Communications. P.115-116, 200-204, 524-529, 582.

Stephen P. Robbins, (1998). *Organisation Behaviour* 8th. Edition. P.625-626, 654-663.

# *Chapter 14*

# OLDER ADULTS AND GERONTOLOGICAL NURSING

*Fajemilehin, B.R.*

**About the Contributor**
Bolu Fajemilehin is a Clinical Nurse Specialist (Elderly Health) and an Associate Professor in Nursing Science, Department of Nursing Science, College of Health Sciences, Obafemi Awolowo University, Ile-Ife. Osun State, Nigeria. He has published extensively many articles both in national and international journals.

## INTRODUCTION

### Demographic Factors

Persons who are of the age of sixty years and above nearly comprise 3.4 percent of 1963, 4 percent of 1980, and 5.2 percent of 1991 census figures, and it is expected to be greater than this in the subsequent years (FOS, 1963; NPB, 1988; NPC, 1994). Future predictions are that the elderly will continue to grow numerically at a more rapid rate than the population as a whole. Even, dramatic is the growth of elderly person who live alone between 1991 and 2000. The number has increased from 5.2 percent to about 6 percent of the population. In less than five years from now, the number of the elderly growing beyond sixty years of age may be very close to about 15 percent of the total population (Fajemilehin, 2001).

Life expectancy is the average number of years that a person can be expected to live. It was Siegel (1982) who said that the increase of man's lifespan by eighteen years in a period of fifty years was more revolutionary and had more profound medical, economic and socio-cultural implications than such things as atomic energy, air transport and modern communications (Population R. Bureau, 1999).

The main factors responsible for most of these increases in life expectancy have been the declining birthrate, reduction of infant and childhood mortality as well as control of infection through advances in medical technology in mid-span, coupled with decreased mortality among the middle-aged and elderly population (Bamigboye, 1999).

The elderly population is increasing more rapidly than the total population, and this, combined with the reduction in working hours, has produced considerable changes in society. And because more people are living longer, health professionals will be expected to help the geratic patient make these added years healthy and productive.

The older adult referred to as "senior citizens" represents a social paradox in that, having laboured long and had to achieve an extended span of life, the society seems unwilling to provide much satisfaction for those at the top end of the span of life; being unable to meet most of their needs. It is a supreme irony that this very society which values long life also tends to regard the aged as problems and liabilities.

But if the older adults are a liability to the society, it must also be recognised that advanced age too is often a liability to the individuals. In terms of health when compared with younger age groups, the older adults have the higher prevalence of illness, visit the physicians more, spend more time in the hospital, endure more days of restricted activities due to illness, have less money with which to purchase health care and prone to chronic illness. Hence, the goals of this contributions are to:

(i) ensure healthy agent through adequate health-promotion, health-preventive, nutritional and rehabilitative approaches,
(ii) keep the elderly patients functioning through proper management of chronic illnesses, which are rarely curable and seem to be the

**Elderly As Destitute in Ile-Ife**

**Homevisit to an Oldie**

inevitable companion of advancing age, and

(iii) ensure social reorganisation or reformation of the traditional family system and promote healthy family support and coordination through a cultural readjustment to state of change.

However, for the comprehension of this chapter, certain terms need to be defined and the older adults grouped.

- ***Geriatrics:*** This is the study of old-age which includes the physiology, pathology diagnosis and management of the disease of the older adults.
- ***Gerontology***: It is the study of the aging process and includes the biological, psychological, and sociological sciences.
- ***Gerontological Nursing:*** It is the field of nursing that specialises in the care of the elderly.
- ***Aging***: It is a set of social characteristics and complex process of biological, psychosocial, cultural, and experiential changes. And according to Bortz (1990), aging is a self-fulfilling prophecy, and only the individual can decide the kind of person he or she will become.
- ***Ageing:*** Simply means the process of growing old beginning from conception to death.

### *Grouping of the Older Adults*

- 60-69 - Young Elderly
- 70-79 - Middle Elderly
- $80^{+}$ - Elderly proper or Senior Citizen.

## THE OLDER ADULTS IN THE TRADITIONAL NIGERIA SOCIETY

In the traditional Nigerian society, the elderly persons were far from frustration of poverty, deprivation, malnutrition, neglect and/or isolation. The society was based on descent and kinship ties amidst the native culture of traditional farming system which further enhanced group solidarity and reverence for the old people (Oyeneye, 1989; Fajemilehin & Ademola, 2000). The bond between children and parent was very strong thereby enhancing their involvement in the marriage processes of their children and ensuring security in old age. It was the cultural imperative for children to support and respect the older adults. The elderly could move freely among members of the extended family and be assured of the best of cares. The social relationship and structure of the extended family were such that promoted closeness among members, thus, reducing the problems of isolation and loneliness among the aged subgroups (Oyeneye, 1989).

The aged enjoyed a privileged position in the society and were accorded high status because of their knowledge and wisdom. They were respected for their knowledge of the laws and traditions of the society. The elderly were allowed to take major decisions concerning the governance of the society. The younger members of the society all along look up or sought advice from the older ones on important matters.

Within the extended family, the elderly played very important roles which placed them in unique positions. They knew the family history and preserved the family customs and ancestral values. They were responsible for the transmission of the society's customs and skills to the younger generations as well as settle dispute and ensure proper conduct among the family members. In addition, the elderly persons controlled family lands and other properties and ensure that family members had access to them when needed.

The elderly were always in charge of ritual duties attached to ancestral shrine where the spirits of the departed were evoked from time to time, an aspect which agrees with that of Fagunwa (1949) in his *Igbo Olodumare*, who posited that, the elderly were not only political heads but also personalities in charge of spiritual needs.

The general concept and situations that were revealed in the olden days and the level of care and support enjoyed by the older adults made people to aspiring to the old age. Even when such older adults had no surviving children, they were still very sure of necessary care and support from the other members of the extended family. The uniqueness and importance of culture to people, made old age a symbol of wisdom and rallying point of respect cherished by Yorubas.

## CURRENT REALITIES

The state of the nation's economy and quality of life for over two decades has been that of uneasy confusion to the general population and regret to the elderly for being very old to witness the absolute downturn from the joyful old age orientation to utter neglect (Fajemilehin & Ademola, 2000). Though Nigeria is a country richly blessed with both human and natural resources, yet, these endowments have not placed her at the rightful position in the comity of nations, due to several factors such as political instability, bad leadership and high level of mismanagement coupled with misplaced priorities.

Of importance, also were the processes of modernisation, influence of Western education, urbanisation and the introduction of local government administrative reforms which have underhinged the position of the elderly persons as traditionally defined in the Nigerian society. The process of the new reforms not only made the elderly persons powerless but completely left out of the decision-making structure in the society. The resultant effect of the various reformations progressively weakened the extended family system and traditions to the extent that the old established tradition that one should care for his elderly wards becomes greatly disregarded.

Today, there are situations in which children decidedly abandoned their aged parents. Some parents have lost contact with their children and cannot even ascertain whether their children are alive or dead. In some cases, the state of neglect is not intentional but a product of economic problem.

The situation of the retirees also had no positive reference, with regard to the inadequacies and irregularities in the payments of retirement benefits as found on pages of our newspapers, such as "The Pension reforms, pensioners' cry over labour loss"; "Obasanjo brought Taylor to eat free food while we are left to die - Blind Pensioner", (*Nigerian Tribune*, 7 September 2002, *Nigerian Tribune,* 19 January 2004; *Nigerian Tribune,* 23 January 2004).

## CHANGES IN BODY SYSTEMS AND FUNCTIONAL STATUS OF THE ELDERLY PERSONS

In Table 14.1 below, changes in the body system and functional status of the elderly persons are indicated, viz. age related changes, nursing assessment (Subjective and objective findings), and health promotion strategies.

**Table 14.1: Changes in the Body System and Functional Status of the Elderly Persons.**

| Age Related Changes | Nursing Assessment (Subjective and Objective Findings) | Health Promotion Strategies |
|---|---|---|
| ***Cardiovascular System***<br>•Decreased cardiac output; diminished ability to respond to stress: heart-rate and stroke volume do not increase with maximum demand.<br>•Slower heart recovery rate. Increased blood pressure. | •Complaints of fatigue with increased activity.<br>•Increased heart-rate recovery time.<br>•Normal BP < 140/90mm Hg. | Exercise regularly; pace activity; avoid smoking; eat a low fat; low salt diet; participate in stress reduction activities; check blood pressure regularly; medication compliance, weight control. |
| ***Respiratory System***<br>Increase in residual lung volume; decrease in vital capacity;decreased gas exchange and diffusing capacity; decreased cough efficiency. | Fatigue and breathlessness with sustained activity; impaired healing of tissues due to decrease oxygenation; difficulty in coughing up secretions. | Exercise regularly, avoid smoking; take adequate fluid to liquify secretions; receive yearly influenza immunisation; avoid exposure to upper respiratory tract infections. |
| ***Integumentary System***<br>Decreased protection against trauma and sun exposure; | Skin appears thin and wrinkled;complaints of injuries; bruises; | Avoid solar exposure (clothing, sunscreen, stay in doors); dress |

| | | |
|---|---|---|
| decreased protection against temperature extremes; diminished secretion of natural oils and perspiration. | and sunburn; complaints of intolerance to heat; bone fracture is prominent; dry skin. | appropriately for temperature; maintain a safe indoor temperature; sower preferable to tubbath; lubricate skin. |
| ***Reproductive System***<br>*Female*: Vaginal narrowing and decreased elasticity; decreased vaginal secretions.<br>*Male*: Decreased size of penis and testes.<br>*Male & Female*: Slower sexual response. | *Female:* Painful intercourse; vaginal bleeding following intercourse;vaginal itching and irritation; delayed orgasm.<br>*Male*: Delayed erection and achievement of orgasm. | May require vaginal estrogen replacement; GYN/urology follow-up; use a lubricant before intercourse. |
| ***Musculoskeletal System***<br>Loss of bone density; loss of muscle strength and size; degenerated joint cartilage. | Height loss; prone to fractures; kyphosis; complaints of back pain; loss of strength, flexibility and endurance; joint pain. | Exercise regularly; eat high-calcium diet; limit phosphorus intake; take hormones; and calcium supplement as prescribed. |
| ***Genitourinary System***<br>*Male*: Benign prostatic hyperplasia. | Urinary retention; irritative voiding symptoms including frequency, feeling of incomplete bladder emptying, multiple night-time voidings. | Seek referral to urological specialist; have ready access to toilet; wear easily manipulated clothing; drink adequate fluids; avoid bladder irritants (e.g.caffeinnated beverages; alcohol, artificial sweeteners); pelvic floor muscle exercises, preferable learn via biofeedback. Consider urologic workup. |

| | | |
|---|---|---|
| *Female:* Relaxed perineal muscles, detrusor instability (urge incontinence) urethral dysfunction (Stress urinary incont- inence) | Urgency/frequency syndrome, decreased "warning time", bathroom mapping. Drops of urine loss with cough, laugh, position change. | |
| ***Gastrointestinal System*** Decreased salivation; difficulty in swallowing food; delayed esophageal and gastric emptying; reduced gastro-intestinal mortility | Complaints of dry mouth, complaint of fullness, heart burn, and indigestion; constipation, flatulence,and abdominal discomfort | Use ice chips, mouthwash; brush, floss, and massage gums daily; receive regular dental care; eat small, frequent meals; sit up and avoid heavy activity after eating; limit antacids; eat a high fiber, low fat diet; limit laxatives; toilet regularly; drink adequately fluid. |
| ***Nervous System*** Reduced in nerve conduction; increased confusion with physical illness and loss of environmental cues; reduce cerebral circulation (becomes faint, loses balance). | Slower to respond and react; learning takes longer;becomes confused with hospital admission;faintness; frequent falls. | Pace teaching; with hospitalisation, encourage visitors; enhance sensory stimulation; with sudden confusion, look for cause; encourage slow rising from a resting position. |
| ***Special Senses*** *Vision*: Diminished ability to focus on close objects; inability to tolerate glare; difficult adjusting to changes of light intensity; | Holds objects far away from face; complaints of glare; poor night vision; and confuses colours. | Wear eye glasses, use sun-glasses outdoors; avoid abrupt changes from dark to light; use adequate indoor lighting with area lights and night lights; use large printed |

| | | |
|---|---|---|
| decreased ability to distinguish colours. | | books; use magnifier for reading; avoid night driving; use constrasting colours for colour coding; avoid glare of shinning surfaces and direct sunlight. |
| *Hearing*: Decreased ability to hear high frequency sound. | Gives inappropriate responses; asks people to repeat words; strains forward to hear. | Recommend a hearing examination; reduce background noise; face person; enunciate clearly; speak with a low-pitched voice; use non-verbal cues. |
| *Tastes and Smells*: Decreased ability to taste and smell. | Uses excessive sugar and salts. | Encourage use of lemon mint, spices and useful herbs. |
| ***Absorption*** Reduced gastric acid; increased pH (less acid). Reduced GI mortility; prolonged gastric emptying. | Rate of drug absorption – possibly delayed. Extent of drug absorption – not affected. | |
| ***Distribution*** Decreased albumin sites. | Serious alterations in drug binding to plasma proteins (the unbound drug gives the pharmacologic response); highly protein-bound drugs have fewer binding sites, leading to increased effect and accelerated metabolism and excretion. | *Selected highly proteins binding drugs*: Oral anticoagulants (warfarin), Oral hypoglycemic agents (sulfonylureas); Barbiturates Calcium channel blockers, frusemide (Lasix) Non-steroidal anti-inflammatory drugs (NSAIDs) Sulfonamides, quinidine, phenytoin (dilantin). |

| | | |
|---|---|---|
| Reduced cardiac output; Impaired peripheral blood flow; Increased percentage of body fat; | Decreased perfusion of many bodily organs. Decreased perfusion. Proportion of body fats increases with age and thus gives the body an increased ability to store fat-soluble drugs; this causes drug accumulation, prolonged storage, and delayed excretion. | *Selected fats soluble drugs*: Barbiturates, diazepam (Valium), lidocaine, Phenothiazines (antipsychotics). |
| Decreased lean body mass. | Decreased body volume allows higher peak levels of drugs. | Ethanol Morphine. |
| ***Metabolism*** Decreased cardiac output and decreased perfusion of the liver. | Decreased metabolism and delay of breakdown of drugs, resulting in prolonged duration of actions, accumulation, and drug toxicity. | All drugs metabolised by the liver. |
| ***Excretion*** Decreased renal-blood flow; loss of functioning nephrons; decreased renal efficiency. | Decreased rates of elimination and increased duration of action. Danger of accumulation and drug toxicity. | *Selected drugs with prolonged action*: Aminoglycoside antibiotics, cimetidine (Tagmet) chlorpropamide (Diabinese) digoxin, lithium, procainamide. |

## IMPLICATIONS FOR NEEDS AND SERVICES

Human services requirements will escalate to meet the myriad needs of older people. Needs will be thè determinant for care. Older people have the same needs as people of all age groups. The ageing process alters their roles and functions. The struggle for adaptation and survival is hence heightened. Ageing individuals sustain multiple losses. It means that developmental tasks of old age, more specifically, imply adjustment to losses. They include adjusting to decreasing physical strength and health, confinement and reduced income, death of spouse, establishing explicit affiliation with one's age group, meeting social and civil obligations and establishing satisfactory living arrangements.

How the individual adjust to these age-related changes is a product of the person's previous patterns of coping acquired throughout his or her lifetime, and success in period of culmination and also that of contraction.

## THE SOCIAL IMPACT OF AGEING: SOME MAJOR ISSUES

### (1) Social and Economic Measures

Many aspects of the social environment are believed to influence health and mortality and potentially account for the observed associations between marital status and health. These factors include characteristics of the social networks (such as the type of individuals included in the network and the closeness and frequency of ties); the nature of the support (both positive and negative) received from members of the network; and the extent of social control resulting from networked members (Gore, 1990; Restrepo and Rozental, 1994; Fajemilehin, Jinadu, Ojo & Feyisetan, 1996).

Numerous studies have shown that lower socioeconomic status (SES) is associated with poor health and elevated mortality risks. Gore(1990), in his detailed review of literature, reported that a variety of SES indicators (including education, income, wealth or permanent income and occupational status) have been linked to health or mortality. Although, Gore(1990) concluded that each of those variables probably exerts an independent influence on mortality, the relationship among them remains fuzzy. Another relevant issue is the extent to which economic factors associated with health, and middle-age are also associated with health status among the elderly.

Atchley (1981) and Schultz(1988) observed that financial security largely determines the range of alternatives people have in adjusting to aging. Older people with adequate financial resources can afford to travel, go shopping, entertain friends, seek the best health care, and keep a presentable wardrobe in their households, own their own cars, and have financial assets to supplement their retirement incomes. It is difficult to determine the financial needs of older people in general, because the older population varies considerably (Gore,1990). Atchley(1982), estimated that in order to maintain the same level of living following retirement, older people must have a retirement income that replaces about 75 percent of their pre-retirement income.

Gore (1990) and Atchley (1982) identified that income for older people comes primarily from earnings, assets and social security. Compounding the problem is the fact that many older people will be relying on fixed or semi-fixed sources. Bixby, Schultz and Atchley analysis of cues and issues around the elderly established and identified that, effect of inflation has been disastrous on them and their fixed in-elastic income. Fajemilehin *et al* (1996) also observed that inadequate income will continue to be a problem for the future generations of the aged who are today's workers. There is a lack of available accurate information on which to base informed decisions regarding planning for income adequacy in retirement, and hold certain unrealistic expectations about sources and amount of potential additional income in retirement.

**(2) Association between Socio-Demographic Studies and Health**

Substantial body of research has demonstrated different associations between marital status and health for both men and women (Gore, 1990; Gliksman, Lazarus and Leader, 1995; Fajemilehin *et al,* 1996). Studies have detected large variations in the social environment by gender (Urberson, 1987; Antonocci and Akiyama, 1987; and Bowling, 1991). Previous research have also discovered variations in economic status by gender (Oni, 1996; Siegel, 1982, UN, 1985). Recently, new studies (Fajemilehin, 2000, Fajemilehin 2001) suggested that in the social and economic environment may have different effects on the health status of elderly men and women. Fajemilehin, (2000) asserted that, in contrast to this, the social environment and economic status of married persons appear to be considerably better than those of their unmarried counterparts.

## (3) The Cultural Issues

The interaction between biological and social realities is essential to the analysis of issues related to aging since social, psychological and biological factors are inseparable aspect of the whole aging process.

Aging, being the last stage of biological life, is when physical deterioration inevitably develops, ending with death. But aging is also the last stage of individual social life, the end result of an individual's personal and collective social experience (Restrepo and Rozental, 1994). To study common old age as a biological issue is an abstraction, for human beings are cultural beings who never live, or age, in a natural state; hence, our aging processes are determined – and determine – the societies in which we live (Restrepo and Rozental, 1994).

According to Restrepo and Rozental (1994), aging is, therefore, a complex cultural issue. Cultures explain human life and allowing societies to organise their living. Within the basic biological commonalities and peculiarities, human beings are different because of cultural differences. Culture determines biological aspect of human beings by either setting limits or offering opportunities. Likewise, human biology sets limits to individual and collective cultural development. The interaction and interrelatedness of the cultural-biological aspects of human being is such that it is difficult or almost impossible to comprehend or study them separately.

It is within different cultures and in different ways that aging occurs, and has occurred throughout history, in fact, within the same societies, aging has been profoundly different at each stage of history.

In order to comprehend aging issues within cultures, it is imperative to recognise those basic values upon which any given culture stand. We, therefore, need to replace myths and stereotypes – including our negative image of the old (Fajemilehin and Ademola, 2000) – with an understanding of the cultural and socioeconomic factors involved (Janing, 1991).

### (4) Social Gerontology Perspective

The discipline of social gerontology has gone beyond the study of aging as a biological and psychological individual issue to address the aging process through the interactions between individuals and society (Restrepo and Rozental, 1994; Townsend, 1981; Olson, 1982; Estes, Swan, and Gerard, 1982; Marshall, 1989; and Estes, 1989).

Social structures determine, to a great degree, the real possibilities and opinions that individuals and social groups encounter in life (Adams, 1990); the situation of the elderly develops from their ongoing relationship with society (Olson, 1982); the political economy of aging studies, and the power relationship and resources allocation; with their determinant and impact on the aging process (Estes, 1988). Its basic premise is that social structures must be understood and changed by transforming social relationship in order to overcome the structure dependency of the elderly.

On the other hand, individuals, although limited by such social structures, are capable of changing them. Moral economics grounded on the use value, views economic structure as social creations and individuals both as shaped and shaping social structure (Guadagnoli, Cleary and Mcnell, 1995; Davis and Rowland, 1991, in "Old and Poor: Policy Challenges in 1990s". *Journal of Aging and Social Policy*: 37-39).

The individual's response to structural constraints defines the field of social psychology of the elderly persons. Therefore, the process of aging is a consequence of how polity, economy and society shape and condition experiences, treatment and health of older people. It is likely that class disparities rather than age are what determine the overall living conditions of the aged. Gender, marital status and race are other important determinants (United Nations, 1994). Social structure supported by market economy, are based on collectively shared assumption that define social relationship and resources allocation. The values on which these assumptions are grounded define a collective acceptance (conscious or not of what is due to the old in each society).

The social impact of aging is an issue in as much as it affects the market dynamics, driven by exchange values. The elderly find themselves at a disadvantage at exchange value-based societies that tends to dehumanise social processes by focusing on economic, rationality and the pragmatism of profits. Within these societies, individuals are valued in terms of their market potentials – their purchasing power and economically productive labour capacities.

Exchange value-oriented societies may either tend to ignore issues and needs related to the elderly or to generate incentives to incorporate them into the market, developing them as producers and consumers.

The exchange value market approach has so far failed to provide well-being to the elderly since it does not develop available concept of common social interest or link between individuals with their context.

Issues of the aged are generally not addressed by most individuals during their life course, but are left to those primarily concerned. This process tends to alienate individuals from understanding, becoming involved, and planning beyond their immediate circumstances. Such alienation promotes segmentation to the life course and competition for resources, as well as a distorted, prejudice view of the aged, thereby severing generations and social groups in need of each other.

Use-value economics would strive to develop public interest such that:

> As a negotiated role structure to which people adhere, even though it may run counter to their own immediately-desired satisfactions, since it improves overall opportunities of obtaining satisfaction.

Citizens are seen not as passive recipient or consumers of public policy, but as active moral agents (Larson, 1974).

Major social impact of aging societies identified by Restrepo and Rozental (1994) include:

(i) ***Impact of Social Organisation***
Basically, this is referred to the challenge aging population pose to societies organised under a global market economic system, by the degree to which most of the elderly can enter market dynamics for their own benefits. Their political and social visibility, place in the society, the resources available to them and their overall living conditions are mostly determined by these social dynamics which today tends to,marginalise this population particularly in developing countries where resources are limited and competition for them is tougher;

(ii) ***Impact of Class, Marital Status, Gender and Race Issues***
Most elderly come from, and willingly belong to lower socioeconomic classes, most are either widows or widowers and women, and many are from ethnic minorities in conditions of disadvantage in Western countries. The implications of this fact are manifold, but lead to greater dependency on social support, increased demand for service and more health, social risks and poor quality of life;

(iii) ***Impact of Social Relationship***
As the number and proportion of elderly persons increase, our perceptions and views of them as well as our relationship with them will inevitably undergo profound changes. The effect of the growing presence (needs and demands) of aging population enhances the challenges posed to insufficiently prepared societies facing rapid changes such as: the role of the government, urbanisation, family structure and women's role. As a result, tension and conflicts developed between social actors and the elderly themselves in divers scenarios.

(iv) ***Political Issues and their Impact Worldwide***
This should be critically examined.

**(5) Life Events and Stress in Aging Population**

The large and growing literature on life events stress and their correlates in aging population provides a useful point of departure for the study of role change or loss (Holmes and Rahe, 1967; George, 1980). This perspective emphasises both the cooping behaviour occasioned by life events rather than events pulse and the multivariate factors which mediate the adaptive or maladaptive outcomes which follows life events. Strokes and Maddox (1967) observed that if a life event activates cooping behaviour in the interest of adaptation, descriptions of adaptation to the event would necessarily take into account time since the event.

Life events do not occur in a vacuum. George(1980) posited that the impact of life events as the change or loss of central social roles is conditioned by a number of factors, including the salience of an event for an individual, the cooping skills and resources which can be mobilised, and the social support system which can be activated. Gore(1990) reported that the perceived deprivation associated with work loss has been shown to be associated with decrease life satisfaction generally, and satisfaction with retirement, specifically. Atchley (1981) found that the importance of work appears to be a measure of the salience of work and personal satisfaction associated with work. Hence, differences in the salience of work can be expected to affect the adaptation to change or in losses of major life roles accompanying aging process which have received considerable attention from social scientists.

According to Holmes and Rahe (1967), social psychologists' interest have focused particularly on the relationship between the resumed stress of life events and outcomes such as illness or a decrease sense of psychological well-being. Social gerontologists have focused their attention on the correlate of the role losses which commonly accompany the aging process. George(1980) generally stressed the centrality of the work role and suggested that, in any society and at any rate, occupation is a primary claim to social status; that work has a moral as well as a purely utilitarian meaning; and that occupation along with familiar involvement is a major source of adult identity. Streib and Schenider (1971) suggested multivariate framework as a necessary approach to the analysis of adaptation to retirement. George(1980) from their own observations suggested longitudinal study since methodologically adequate research on social processes requires longitudinal data. Therefore, multivariate analysis techniques with the general linear model seem best suited to problems of change scores which have been appropriately criticised by several authors such as Buchanan(1984) and Cowgill and Holmes(1972).

Backett and Davidson(1995) observed that health is a basic resources for social role enactment, retiring from work and particularly necessary for cooping with role change or loss implied by retirement.

Streib and Schneider (1971) observed that indications of maladaptation and dissatisfaction among retired persons might be better explained by poor health than the events of retirement. They further observed that the presence of social support in the form of friends and kinsmen is known to be related to adaptation in retirement. According to Uhlenberg, Cooney and Boyd(1990), Berkowiltz(1987) and Blazer (1982) departures from the married state, that is, becoming widowed or divorced is a stress provoking crisis that may result in higher risks of morbidity and mortality. The ability to perform routine daily tasks is an important aspect of quality of life. In general, this ability declines with age. (Rogers and Belanger, 1992).

However, decline and death were more prevalent in men 80 years of age and older and among the elderly with a pre-existing disability (Mor, Wilcox, Rakowski and Hiris, 1994). Mor *et al.* (1994) posited that illness and perceived health are robust predictors of all future outcomes states even moreso than age and nearly as much as function.

**(6) Elderly Abuse and Its Socioeconomic Implications**

According to Felton, Parsons and Bartoces(1997), many frail, dependent elderly persons within the community are receiving support and care from their families. Intentions may be good, but strains of relationship may develop over time. Research into family violence began in the 1960s with child abuse. Studies of marital conflict followed in the late 1970s. In this decade, a great deal of attention has been focused upon elderly abuse. George(1980); Gore(1990); and Felton *et al*, (1997) defined elderly abuse as an act or omission (non-accidental, causing harm) against an elderly involving two or more persons or their adult caring children.

Hays(1984) identified four specific areas of elderly's abuse. These are isolation of rights, materials abuse, physical abuse and psychological abuse. Murray, in *WHO*(1996) explained violation of rights as a broad category that encompasses denial of the basic right of the aged persons as enumerated by the 1961 and 1971 United House Conference on Aging.

Hays(1984) stressed that material abuse include theft or misuse of money or property by children visiting elderly persons and/or caring family members. Families may rely on the resource or other subsidies received for the older person's care. Any attempt to object to material and economic abuse may subject the elderly to further abuse, physically or psychologically. Therefore, money may serve as a motive for caring or keeping the older person in the family home even when institutionalisation is advisable.

The older person who is no longer capable of managing financial affairs may be at disadvantage by those caring for him. Money saved to provide for retirement needs may be used by the family for other purposes, sometimes with the result of depriving the aged persons of basic needs.

Hays (1984) expressed that physical abuse includes withholding personal care, medical care, or food. A sort of benign neglect is most prevalent. This occurs in families in which children are frustrated by their own inability to give proper care to the aged relatives, particularly in household in which both husband and wife must work. Fajemilehin (2000) identified neglect as the most common form of physical abuse among family of disabled elderly persons. Hays(1984) documented that aged persons were oversedated by relatives or tied while the caring children go shopping and simple motive also contribute to physical abuse. Anderson (1979) also found that aged parents were battered to control their behaviour or merely to vent unchecked frustration.

Psychological abuses according to Hays (1984) include verbal assault and threats, provocation or fear instillation, and isolation of the older persons either physically or emotionally. In their frustration with providing care for the aged, care givers may exhibit overt or covert hostility towards the older persons. Fear may be provoked when family members, who are aware of their power over the aged use subtle or obvious pressures and threats to force the elderly to conform. And because the elderly are aware of their dependency, they may conform because they are afraid that their basic needs will not be met (Gore, 1990). Gore(1990) identified a change in the role of the elderly in relation to their adult offspring as the main cause of the aged abuse. Gore(1990) concluded that a role reversal occurs when the aged parents have adult offspring into parental roles, expecting them to supply needs, guard status and/or make decisions.

### (7) Measures of Well-Being and Social Aspects of Aging Population

Population is aging worldwide (Skeet, 1991). The problems of this older population are not purely medical and their disorders are rarely curable; rather they require continuing care to facilitate their independence and personal well-being in the least restrictive feasible setting. The world assembly of aging agreed to use 60 years and above to identify persons in the population segment called the "third age". The assembly stressed that many stereotypes about aging should be eliminated, especially that of the aging myth. During a period in which the world is affected by a severe economic crisis, perception about aging and the manner in which the elderly are conceived must be changed.

According to WHO(1996), aging tends to be accompanied by social laws as well as personal decline. Couples become widow; children may be scattered and may themselves be growing infirm; and friends, siblings and relatives may die. People retire from the labour force, which often entails, both a drop in income and a reduced ability to maintain financial status in the face of inflation. The illnesses of later life are more likely to be chronic rather than acute and to be multiple rather than single. Hospital stays when they occur, tend to last longer than it is in the case of younger people. Some age-related conditions, such as decline in vision and hearing, manifest themselves in obvious ways. Changes in mental functioning, sometimes subtle, also occur. While it is neither serious nor markedly disabling for most people, the progressive deterioration in cognitive function than afflictions in minority of older adults severely destruct personal and family life.

Since such losses and declines rarely occur in isolation, the assessment of people in later life need to take into account both the individual and the settings in which the person live.

In dealing with this issue, it is necessary to pay attention to the critical conditions of certain vulnerable group, of which the elderly are a part, when designing policies to improve their economic situation (World

Bank,1994.) Nevertheless, policies are affected by world recession; for many countries' economic and social plans are not only threatened but collapsed. Faced with an increasingly complicated situations, government policies may result in the reduction of social welfare services (where available) and policy cancellation in new ones. These will probably have deplorable consequence of affecting the poor and less favoured group, among them, many elderly persons.

United Nations Organization (1988) observed that defining the elderly as persons of 60 years and over, they cannot be considered as a social problem or a problem group if not for the social structures and attitudes in posing the age definition as vulnerable or marginal. A consequence of this marginality has been the growth of programmes for groups of the elderly.

**The Age of Aging and Socio-Cultural and Economic Changes: The Implications for Nursing**

In Nigeria, situation of the elderly has changed from what it used to be in term of care and support, not only because more people are growing old, but because the concept of the informed structure of care and support through extended family system has since and for long, changed. In the olden days, the concept of polygamy and having many children provided a lot of social, moral, economic and psychological well-being and support satisfaction among elderly individuals; a cultural position which made the elderly to be more dependent on their women and children. Today, rising demands for formal education for all, and increased need for economic earning have made it more acceptable for women to work. At the same time, because of rural-urban migration, urbanisation, and the reduced importance of agricultural land, male children now feel less concerned and responsible for looking after their elderly parents in returns for the family assets which are no longer there. Furthermore, most adult children of today are very much unemployed, hence, economically unable to care for themselves as individuals not to talk of taking care of any associated elderly needs and responsibilities.

Based on the change in the situation of the subgroup, a large percentage of acute hospital beds are occupied by elderly patients, many of whom remain in the hospital sometime after their acute conditions had passed because their own situations did not allow for discharge and adequate follow-up care, moreso, when there is no other formal structure of care put in place in the community, and even, old people's home is a very unacceptable concept to our culture because it is alien. Frequently, information on available community services is lacking.

Older persons, even those who are in relatively good health, exhibit increasing frailty and a reduced tolerance for stress at a time of life when they often experience multiple losses and without familial care and support. The nursing professionals have much to offer elderly people. Health can be maintained and disability prevented or at least postponed, if nursing response with a broad range of health and social services to strengthen the coping ability of the elderly and all their care givers.

It is indeed a prime responsibility of nursing to promote the development or enhancement of self-reliance in the elderly individuals, based on recognition of his/her capabilities. The elderly must be encouraged to preserve or build their capacity for self-care through attentive guidance and intervention. Nursing should enable elderly people to optimise their physical, social and psychological functions as our culture permit during changes in their state of health.

### *Physical and Social Supports*

The development of many chronic conditions among elderly is associated with personal behaviour patterns many of which are amenable to change. While the elderly persons may have had years of self-imposed risks from an unhealthy lifestyle, it is never too late to change and improve behaviours. Nursing can respond with health promotion activities (see Tables 14.1), which if made available, may alter these lifestyle patterns, reinforce the positive health behaviour pattern and thus, the course of old age.

Underreporting of symptoms by older people who may erroneously attribute their problems to normal aging rather than disease, can hamper them from securing available treatments (Skeet, 1991). To assist these elderly individuals, nurses need to have the opportunity to provide health education and health monitoring to aid in early case-finding, prevention of disability, and health maintenance.

The nutritional status of old people in many countries today, specifically the developing ones, is a cause of concern. Studies to identify the nutritional needs of the elderly persons have been initiated by individual scholars, organisations and agencies. But effort should be made in these several countries to identify the elderly person's dietary problems, assess and refer appropriately through empowered community health nurses to available social services for such. Charitable organisations and churches should not relent in their efforts to see to the health of the ageing population through their frequent supply of needs and other needs to the subgroups.

High level of migration of young people from rural to urban areas to seek employment is being experienced by so many countries. In Nigeria, there has been a mass drift of the youths from rural to urban areas in search of economic comfort through city employment. All efforts by the subgroup to make life easy had turned to prove abortive. These trends have compounded the problems of the elderly having many of the older people without the usual traditional familial support system. Even in places where the traditional family structure still prevails, the economic situation often necessitates that all adults of working age seek employment outside the home environment, resulting in many elderly people either living alone, being left alone for long period or being admitted to health care institutions after found wanting in the environment for lack of familial attention.

Boredom and loneliness can result when an elderly person is left to his or her own resources for a long time with no planned activities. Nurses can help combat this social isolation by encouraging and facilitating visits to friends, family members, social exchanges, and actively participating in traditional events and activities as culturally defined. Ensuring and enabling the elderly to participate in these activities will take time and effort, but the results will be rewarding to both the patients and the nurses.

Another important contribution that can be made by community health nurses is the assessment of an elderly persons' potential for work and assistance in placement that is, in a community project.

While families remain the only hope for informal structure and important providers of services for their aged members, independent income from an elderly person is conducive to the continuation of their family ties and enables the poor to continue to care for their elderly relatives. An independent income also strengthened the position of the elder in the home and socially useful employment gives a boost to not only economic status, but morale.

To help relieve the strain on young women (Skeet, 1991) and others who must care for the two most vulnerable groups of people - the very young and the very old - some communities (for example, in Protein Energy Malnutrition (PEM) ) have established day care centres or formed organisation for mutual assistance. In Nigeria, allowing the elders to continue in various positions with the performance of all those culturally-defined roles in addition to the above, will achieve the loss of socio-psychological readjustment for them. The establishment of elderly day care centres will go a long way to assist nurses to be able to achieve health nutrition, and social assessments by the elderly and also to act as resource persons for their families.

### *Psychological Support*

The elderly feel threatened in many ways: physically (they sense their power and strength dwindling), psychologically (they are aware of being neglected to a lower status in the society) and emotionally (they suffer loneliness and insecurity). Often, these problems are exacerbated by the attitudes of others around them. Clinical experiences have shown that the nurse can assuage many of the above threats if well-prepared educationally. However, in order to promote a feeling of usefulness and wholeness in elderly people, the nurses (and other closed to them, that is, the social support network) must view them as capable, and useful human beings.

Caring for the elderly requires that a professional nurse should try to understand how elderly patients/persons feel in order to anticipate needs and intervene accordingly. Empathic understanding is a quality essential to the effective planning of activities suited to the age subgroups needs and capability. In addition, caring for them requires a constant and loving concern on the part of the nurse, demonstrated through congruence of attitudes and words. Genuine regard can raise the morale of an elder and motivate him or her to perform activities that enhance feelings of self-worth. Hence, nurses must take care to convey to the elderly persons the belief that they are able to function in certain tasks, that their company is valuable, and that their opinions are respected. Elderly persons are sensitive and may suffer hurt-feelings in silence.

The observant and compassionate nurse will notice that something is wrong, and encourage the individual to talk, and should show understanding about the situation. Contact with nature - through plants or a pet-should continue to be encouraged, since it can be very helpful in providing an emotional outlet for older people, especially those who live alone.

To assist the elderly with promising self-care, the nurse must not only recognise existing needs but anticipates future ones and provide guidance that allow the elderly person to participate in meeting them. The keys to enable the nursing professionals to effectively cope with the challenge of caring for the elderly, lie in research to improve understanding of aging and identify appropriate care responses and specialize training that equips nurses with the knowledge provided by such as research.

Health professionals who have received little or no training in the care of the elderly, do not find working with them rewarding (Fajemilehin, 2000). However, these same deficits have provided stimulus for innovations in the nursing practice, including the emergence of a nursing speciality, the development of the nurse practitioners role and the design of nursing care system for problems specific to the older population in the developed countries. While countries like Sweden, and Japan continue to empower families so as to enforce the continuity of reformed care to the aged subgroups by the various family members, the concept of familial care and support through traditional extended family system has become so weakened to the level of concern but with no recognition at the policy level in Nigeria.

Ensuring effective 'person-centred' care with older people is a complex issue for nurses and is fraught with difficulty. Lawler (1991) highlighted the reasons why there is a need for nurses to examine carefully the way they work with older people. 'Basically, nurses have an incredible amount of power (over patients). Most of them do not realise that they are very powerful people. You get somebody into the hospital; it does not matter who is he, and all of a sudden he is subservient. No matter who is he, it is the way you treat him that matter. You bring him into hospital, strip him of his clothes, put him in pyjamas and in bed; and tell him what to do and he obeys!'

For older people, the need for nurses not to exercise power over their care decisions is essential. This is because of the limitations to autonomy which inhibits their ability to 'speak for themselves' (McCormack, 1998). However, throughout the development of health and social care services, there is evidence of older people receiving care services that fail to meet their individual needs or to reflect the kind of choices they will make for themselves.

The health, social care and nursing services offered to older people today are influenced not only by issues such as societal perceptions but also by the way in which these services are deployed. It has been argued (Agich, 1993) that many of the traditional perceptions about nursing older people do not derive from other people themselves, and are not intrinsic to nursing them. Aspects such as chronic underfunding, inferior care environment, inadequate equipment, low staffing levels, lack of educational preparation, lack of continuous professional development, low priority given to the service and the general perception of older patients as inferior in some ways have profoundly influenced the way in which many, including health and social care professionals, think about nursing older people.

## (8) The Developed Countries Historical Contents

It is well known that services for older people originated in the workhouse. The speciality of 'geriatrics' as it was once termed, began in the 1930s under the leadership of Dr Marjorie Warren. She substituted her philosophy of 'old age is not a disease' for the previously existing *infirmary decubitis* and pioneered assessment, diagnosis and rehabilitation; and for the first time, acute and curative aspect of care for older people began to develop.

The development of nursing with older people needs to be considered alongside that of geriatric medicine (Baker, 1978; Evers, 1981 and 1986). Doctors working with older people were considered inferior in status and skills, particularly as cure was the highly-valued ultimate goal of the medical model. Older people do not fit easily into the standard medical paradigm (Latimer, 1997). A single diagnosis is rarely possible as disease manifestations are likely to be multiple and complicated by the effects of the aging process. Added to this, are the social situation, social networks and an ageist society, and one begins to see why working with older people is the challenge that it is. The 'quick cure' of one disease with no consideration of motivation, home circumstances, and abilities is not possible.

Historically, nursing was very much an evolving profession and influenced by many of the attitudes in medicine. The first major study of nursing older people was undertaken in 1962 by Northon and Eston-Smith (1975). They highlighted ritualised practice based on routine rather than needs. The research after this first study (Baker, 1978; Evers, 1981 and 1986; Wells, 1980), followed the theme of what was termed 'routinised geriatric care'. This was the care which many nurses first witnessed as students.

What are often not highlighted in these studies of nursing are the systematic disadvantages that nurses and the older people had to cope with during this time. This, of course, cannot excuse poor nursing practice, but it does help to explain and understand it. A parallel could be drawn with an individual or families systematically disadvantaged in society by inadequate finance, substandard education, impoverished and unsuitable housing and supports provided by unskilled, untrained and disinterested personnel. Traditionally, nursing has been regarded as one of the professional group that engaged in a series of practice and behaviours which focused on rituals and control. The history of nursing does not allow us to deny our past and we continue to learn from that past in order to create a future.

Nursing older people has now largely cast off the shackles of its legacy and has overcome the majority of the challenges presented by this. Through overcoming these challenges, it has become one of the most pioneering, courageous and innovative areas of practice. Nurses have had to fight for the recognition of their skills and what they have to offer to the lives and health of older people. As a consequence, there is a growing band of nurses working with older people who have developed superb assertion skills and are very able to confront ageist, discriminatory practice in the workplace. These nurses have had to be open to the realities and challenges of practice, flexible and responsive to needs, and creative in finding new ways of working to develop practice and services within their working environment. Therefore, what has been the drive for this? One answer lies in the drive to prevent the past from becoming the future. Nurses choosing to work with older people have consistently challenged prevailing attitudes and behaviours resulting in greater clarity about the nature of expert practice in gerontological nursing.

The key attributes of an expert nurse as defined by Manley and McCormack (1997) derived from the work of Benner (1984) and Benner *et al* (1996), that are illustrated through this example are:

1. ***Holistic Practice and Holistic Knowledge***: Synthesise different types of knowledge about Joan and different ways of knowing her in order to work holistically with her.
2. ***Saliency:*** See the most pertinent issues in the situation and the most appropriate ways of responding to them.
3. ***Knowing the Patient*:** Know her as a person and her typical pattern of responses in order to make a skilled judgement about the most appropriate response.
4. ***Moral Agency***: Show a concern for responding to Joan as a person, respecting her dignity, protecting her personhood in times of vulnerability, helping her feel safe, providing comfort and maintaining integrity in the relationship with her

5. ***Skilled Know-how:*** Let your performance be fluid, seamless

and highly proficient. Actions reflect atonement to the situation which is shaped by Joan's responses, and does not rely on conscious deliberation.

The factors which enable this expert practice to be sustained and, if present, would have prevented the final outcome for Joan, according to (Manley and McCormack 1997) are:

1. The ability to reflect on the effectiveness of practice.
2. Authority in land accountability.
3. Therapeutic interpersonal relationships with team members and patients.
4. A practice environment that enables a person-centred approach to the organisation of care services.

Expert practice in gerontological nursing is dependent on nurses seeing their role as an enabler of health, based on individual life choices and potentials. From such a basis, outcomes from nursing can be demonstrated and the Royal College of Nursing's (RCN's) current work on the 'assessment of older people's need for nursing' clearly demonstrates this (RCN 1997). Nurses need to be able to define and measure their contributions to the overall well-being of patients. This is especially challenging with older people because, in health care, one usually measures outcomes in terms of a 'health gain' (French 1995).

Clearly, nurses working with older people know that this is often not the priority and as a result, nursing and patient outcomes can be hard to identify and articulate, which in turn impacts on the way nursing is perceived, leading us to consider the educational preparation of nurses for the future.

## CONCLUSION

The importance of skilled, expert caring nursing practice can never be underestimated in the care of older people, because as Weinberg (1978) said:

> Each person has his own unique life, his own memories, hopes, expectations, habits, and biases. Each has had a responsibility

> in the management of his own life.... Each has found support, reinforcement, guidance, and correction from loving and perceptive others; and each has suffered at the hands of others.

Older people should not 'suffer' because of the care they receive from nurses. Humanistic nursing tries to give the patient as many opportunities as possible to exercise freedom of choice, express opinions, make decisions, talk while the nurse really listens and express his or her authentic self (McCormack, 1998). The development of expert gerontological nurses through frameworks of lifelong learning will enable such practice to happen and prevent a return to routinised, ritualistic and institutionalised practices (McCormack, 1999; Fajemilehin, 2001).

## References

Agich, G. (1993). *Autonomy and Long-term Care*. Oxford University Press, Oxford.

Atchley, R.C. (1981). *The Social Forces in Later Life: An Introduction to Social Gerontology*. Belmont: Wadsworth Publishing Company Inc.

Atchley, R.C. and Szinovacz, (1982). "The Process of Retirement Comprising Women and Men". *In Women's Retirement. Policy implications of Recent Research*. Beverly Hills, C.A: Sage

Baikeh, K.C. and Davidson, C. (1995). Life course and Lifestyle. The Social and Cultural Creation of Health Behaviours. *Social Science and Medicine* 40(5) 629-638.

Baker, D. E. (1978). *Attitudes of Nurses to the Care of the Elderly*. Unpublished Ph.D Thesis, University of Manchester.

Bamigboye, E. A, (1999). "Ageing Population and Population Growth". A Paper presented at the *Recreational Conference on Healthy Ageing* held on the 24 June at the University of Ibadan, Nigeria.

Benner, P. (1984). *From Novice to Expert: Excellence and Power in Clinical Nursing.*

Benner, P. *et al* (1996). *Expertise in Nursing Practice: Caring, Clinical Judgement and* Ethics. New York, NY, Springer.

Berkewitz, E.D. (1987). *Social Security After Fifty: Success and Failures*. New York: Greenwood.

Blazer, D.G. (1982). *Depression in Later Life*. St. Louis: Mosby.

Buchanan; R.J. (1984). "Medicaid: Family Responsibility and Long Term Care". *Journal of Long Term Care Administration.* 12(3),19-25.

Cowgill, D.O. and Holmes, L. (1972) *Aging and Modernisation*. New York: Appleton-Century-Crofts.

Davis, K. and Rowland, D. (1991). "Old and Poor: Policy Challenges in the 1990s". *Journal of Aging and Social Policy* 2:37-39.

Editorial Comment . "The Pension Reform". *Nigerian Tribune*, 19 January 2004. P.10

Edward, D. and Olawale, R.. "Pensioners' Cry Over Labour Loss". *Nigerian Tribune*, 23 January 2004. P.15.

Edward, D.. "Hell Has No Fury Than Angry Pensioners". *Nigerian Tribune*, 23 January 2004. P.17 & 19.

Estes, C. (1989). "Aging Health and Social Policy: Crises and Crossroads". *Journal of Aging and Social Policy*, 1(1-2):17-31.

Estes, C., Swan, E. and Gerard, K. (1983). *Political Economy, Health and Aging*. Boston: Little, Brown.

Evers, H. (1981). Tender loving care? - patients and nurses in geriatric wards.

Evers, H. (1986). "Care of the elderly sick in the UK". In Redfern, S.J (ed.) *Nursing Elderly People.* London, Churchill Livingstone.

Fagunwa, D.O. (1949). *Igbo Olodumare*, London: Thomas Nelson.

Fajemilehin, B.R. (2000). "Old Age in a Changing Society: Elderly Experiences of Care Giving in Osun State, Nigeria". *African Journal of Nursing and Midwifery,* South Africa, 2(1), May. P.23-27.

Fajemilehin, B.R. (2001). "Familial Expectation and Social Support for the Elderly in Yoruba Communities of Southwestern Nigeria". *Journal of Social Sciences*, India, 5(1): P.31-37.

Fajemilehin, B.R. (2000). "Health Behaviour of Patterns of the Elderly in Ife/Ijesa zone of Osun State, Nigeria", Unpublished Ph.D. Thesis, Department of Sociology and Anthropology, Obafemi Awolowo University, Ile-Jfe, Nigeria.

Fajemilehin, B.R. and Ade-Ademola. (2000). "Cultural Concepts and Healthy Aging Among Elderly Nigerians". *Castalia*, 3(1). P. 79-88.

Fajemilehin, B.R., Jinadu, M.K., Ojo A.A. and Feyisetan, B. (1996). "Social Supports Received by Elderly Persons in Ile-Ife, Nigeria. *Medical Practitioner*, Vol. 31, Nos. 5/6 May/June, 78-82.

Felton, G.H.; Parson, M.A. and Bartoles, M.G.(1970). "Demographic Factors: International Effects on Health-Promoting behaviour and Health Related Factors". *Public Health Nursing*, 14, 361-367.

French, B. (1995). The role of outcomes in the measurement of nursing.

George, L., Montere, C.A.(1980). "Role Transmissions in Later Life: A Social Stress Perspective". Brooks/Cole.

Gliksman, M.D., Lazarus, R., Wilson, A. and Leader, S.R.(1995)."Social Support, Marital Status and Living Arrangement Correlates of Cardiovascular Disease Risk Factors in the Elder". *Journal of Social Science and Medicine*. 40(6), 811-814.

Gore, M. S., Kane, R.L., Grimley, J.E. and MacFadyen, D.(1990). "Social Factors Affecting the Health of the Elderly". *Improving the Health of Older People: A Worldview*. New York: Oxford University Press. 107-123.

Guadagnoli, E., Cleary, P.D. and Mcnell, B.J.(1995) "The Influence of Socioeconomic Status on Change in Health Status after Hospitalisation". *Journal of Social Science and Medicine*. 40(10), 1399-1406.

Hays, J.A.(1984). "Aging and Family Resources: Availability and Proximity of Kin". *The Gerontologist*, 24: 149-153.

Holmes, F.H. and Rahe, R.H.(1967). "The Social Readjustment Rating Scale". *Journal of Psychosomatic Research*, 11; 213-218. In Copp, L.A. (ed.) *Care of the Ageing*. London, Churchill Livingstone.

Larson, L.E.(1974). "System and Subsystem Perception of Family Roles". *Journal of Marriage and the Family*. 36, 123-138.

Latima, J. (1997). "Figuring identities: older people, medicine and time". In Jamieson, A. *et al* (eds.) *Critical Approaches to Ageing and Later Life.* Buckingham: Open University Press.

Lawler, J. (1991). *Behind the Screens: Nursing Somology and the Problem of the Body.* London: Churchill, Livingstone.

Manley, K., McCormack, B. (1997). *Exploring Expert Practice. Distance learning Module.* MSc. Jn Nursing. London, Royal College of Nursing Institute.

McCormack, B. (1998). *An Exploration of the Theoretical Framework*

McCormack, B. (1999). "The Contribution of Expert to Gerontological Nursing". *Nursing Standard,* March 10, 113(25), 42-45.

Mor, V., Wilcox, V., Rakoski, W. and Hiris, J.(1994). Functional Transitions among the elderly: Patterns, Predictors and Related Hospital use. *American Journal of Public Health Vol. 84*, no 8, 1994; 1274 – 1280.

Norton, D. and Exton Smith, N. (1975). *An Investigation of Geriatric Nursing Problems in Hospital.* Second edition. London, Churchill Livingston. *Nurse Researcher.* 2,4,5-13.*Nursing Practice.* Menlo Park C.A, Addison-Wesley.

Olson, L.K. (1982). *The Political Economy of Aging.* New York: Columbia University Press.

Oni, J.B. (1996). "Qualitative exploration of intra household variations in treatment of child illness in polygamous Yoruba Families: the use of local expressions". *Health Transition Review Vol. 6* (1) April, 57 - 69.

Oyeneye, O.Y. (1989). "The Aged and Social Justice in Nigeria". The Conference Proceedings of the Nigerian Anthropological and Sociological Association. 86-195.

Population Beyond Six Billion, 54(10:March)

Population Reference Bureau (1994). World.

Restrepo, H.E. and Rozental, M. (1994). "The social support of aging population: Some major issues." *Social Science Medicine*, 39 (9): 1323-1338.

Rogers, R.G., Rogers, A. and Bellanger, A. (1992). "Disability-free life among the Elderly in the United States". *Journal of Aging Health, Vol. 4*, 19 - 42.

Royal College of Nursing (1997). What *a Difference a Nurse Makes -a* 15 report on *the benefits of expert nursing to the clinical outcomes of nursing older people.* London, RCN.

Schultz, J.H. and Dover, M.A. (1988). *The Economics of Aging* (4th ed.), Auburn House.

Siegel, J.S. (1982). "Demograghic Aspects of Health of the Elderly to the year 2000 and beyond". *WHO/ AGE*/182-3, Geneva.

Skeet, M. (1991). "The Age of Aging: Implications for Nursing". *Bulletin of the Pan American Health Organization,* 25(4):274-380.

Stokes, J.P.(1985). "The Relation of Social Network and Individual differences variables to Loneliness". *Journal of Personality and Social Psychology*.. 48, 981-990.

Streila, G.F. and Schneider, C.J.(1971). *Retirement in American Society: Impact and Process*. New York: Cornel University Press.

Uhlenberg, P., Looney, T. and Boyd, R. (1990). "Divorce for Women after Midlife". *Journal of Gerontology*. 45(1) S3-S11.

"Underpinning the Autonomy of Older People in Hospital and its Relationship to Professional Nursing Practice". Unpublished D.Phil. Thesis, Department of Educational Studies, University of Oxford.

United Nations. 1994. World Population Prospect, New York.

Wells, T.J. (1980). *Problems in Geriatric Nursing Care.* Edinburgh, Churchill Livingstone.

WHO. (1996). "Women, Aging and Health: Achieving Health Across the Span", *WHO/HPR/AHE/HPD/96.1.*

World Bank. (1994). "Better Health in Africa: Experience and Lessons Learned" (1-44). Washington, D.C.: *World Bank Publication.*

# Chapter 15

# RECREATION IN MEDICAL MANAGEMENT

*Adeyanju, S.A. & Olorunsola, H. K.*

**About the Contributors**

Adeyanju is a Professor of Physical Education. His research areas are Motor Control Learning, Exercise Physiology and Fitness and Wellness Education. He has taught and carried out many research work in the university setting for several years and has published many works in reputable national and international journals. He is currently a senior lecturer in Obafemi Awolowo University, Ile-Ife, Nigeria.

Henry Kofoworola Olorunsola holds B.Sc.,M.A. and Ph.D degrees in Physical and Health Education with specialisation in Administration, Recreation and Coaching. He has handled many sports activities such as Basketball, Badminton, Squash and Handball. He is currently a lecturer in Obafemi Awolowo University, Ile-Ife, Nigeria.

## INTRODUCTION

Recreation and Medical Management are two broad areas of endeavour which seems to have little or nothing to do with each other. While recreation is regarded as a worthwhile socially-acceptable leisure experience that provides immediate and inherent satisfaction to the individual who voluntarily participates in the activity, medical management, on the other hand, covers the control and making decisions regarding persons suffering from various types of illness in attempts to relief pain, speed up recovery and return individuals to normal health. Recreation in the traditional sense subsumes strong and healthy participants which automatically excludes people under medical management. This is not the case as innumerable recreational activities constitute a form of promotion of health in that exercise generally may assist in the prevention of illness and be consistent with generally-recognised medical principles conducive and beneficial to the soundness of body and mind. (American Therapeutic Recreation Association, 2002). In this chapter, the involvement of recreation in Medical Management will be discussed. However, the following areas will be briefly covered and they are:

- Concept of recreation.
- General values of recreation.
- Definition of therapeutic recreation.
- Purpose and Objectives of therapeutic recreation.
- Scope of therapeutic recreation.
- Therapeutic recreation programme.
- Specific uses of therapeutic recreation.

## CONCEPT OF RECREATION

The term "recreation' was derived from the Latin word *recreare* which means to restore, refresh or build a new. It also refers to some form of action which are essential to recreating or revitalising the individual (Hall, 1966). Carlson *et al.* (1970) also describe recreation as any enjoyable leisure experience in which the participant voluntarily engage and from which he receives immediate satisfaction. In its traditional sense, recreation was seen as a period of light and restful activity, voluntarily chosen and which restores one for heavy obligatory activity or work (Kaplan, 1960). The contemporary view of recreation emerged as a result of changing dynamics in the workplace where time and energy saving devices are employed. This has created a situation where more time become available for leisure activities. Modern society is less demanding physically thus many people become more fully engaged both physically and mentally in their recreation activities than work. For some other groups, the idea that recreation is primarily intended to restore one for work has no meaning since they have no work but certainly need recreation to make their life meaningful. The aged and children belong to this group (Kraus 1971).

## CHARACTERISTICS OF RECREATION

There are several views and definitions of recreation by notable authorities and professional groups. There are common areas of agreement. It is generally accepted that the motivating factors for recreation may not be the same for any two people and they vary from time to time for the same individual. Furthermore, the motivating factors may not be evident to even the participants. As varied as the motivating factors, so are the interests which include all subject areas and activities from which worthwhile values can be derived.

Other characteristics of recreation include the following:

- The choice of the recreation activity is voluntary.
- Recreation occurs during leisure time.
- Recreation provides enjoyment and satisfaction.
- Recreation involves activity not idleness.
- Recreation provides a refreshing change of pace.
- Recreation should be wholesome and constructive.
- Recreation should be socially acceptable.
- Recreation should contribute positively to the physical, social, mental and or moral welfare of the participants.

## VALUES OF RECREATION

Recreational pursuit confers some beneficial outcomes on the individual. For a person to derive positive values from participation in recreation, the acquisition of fundamental skills is very important without which such pursuit loses most of its potential value. An individual who is skilful in an activity is more likely to find the time and a place to use his skills (Richman, 1992). The more general benefits of recreational activity pursuits according to Heaton and Thorestenson (1978) include the following:

**Fellowship**

Loneliness is a common problem and recreational pursuit can be used as a means of reducing loneliness and provide opportunity for participants to fellowship with one another through meaningful involvement.

**Sense of Achievement**

Opportunities are provided in recreation to attain success even if that success is trivial to others, it is vital for emotional well-being of many.

**Physical Well-being**

Lack of physical involvement often result in atrophy and hypokinetic diseases. An awakening sense of self can come through activities and participation in sports and games which can promote improved co-ordination, strength, endurance and other fitness attributes.

**Use of Mental Power**

By encouraging the use of mental powers in activities such as scrabble, puzzles and the like, boredom can be eliminated and interest stimulated in new activities. Studies have provided evidence of significant rehabilitation which takes place when mental powers are challenged.

**Emotional Experience**

Individuals who are ill are often forced into a life that is passive. The only positive emotional experience which the sick and handicapped persons have, comes from fun-filled activities that are challenging, exciting and charged with enthusiasm. Recreation provides just that type of experience.

## CONCEPT OF THERAPEUTIC RECREATION

From ancient times, recreation was conducted and engaged in as an endeavour which had diverse inherent benefits for health and well-being. Evidence of this abounds in the ancient civilisations of China, Greece, and Egypt to mention a few. In more recent times in the cultures of Asia, Central Europe, North America and in Africa, the place of recreation in preventive and curative health has gained prominence.

In the United States of America, the expansion of State participation in the area of recreation was a striking post-Second World War trend. The need to provide rehabilitation for the ill and the handicapped informed this development. The institution of recreation programme in the hospital setting was advanced significantly particularly by Armed Forces hospitals, Veterans hospitals, State Neuropsychiatric hospitals and Children's hospitals.

Therapeutic recreation, according to Weiskopt (1975), is a specialised field within the recreation profession and it generally refers to the specific use of recreational activities in the care, treatment and rehabilitation of ill, handicapped and aged persons with a goal directed programme. Similarly, Corbin (1970) explained that therapeutic recreation makes use of play media to provide the mentally and/or physically ill with satisfactory interests and outlets in conjunction with other therapeutic means on hand. The therapy is suitable for all age groups and it is used as adjunctive therapy to promote general well-being and develop social skills as therapy progresses. The National Therapeutic Recreation Association of America views therapeutic recreation as:

> A special service within the broad area of recreation services for purposive intervention in some physical, emotional and/ or social behaviour to bring about a desirable change in that behaviour and to promote the growth and development of the individual.

From the definitions of therapeutic recreation presented above, the philosophy, purpose and values are apparent. The philosophy of therapeutic recreation and by extension, recreation therapist is that, recreation is a form of treatment in overcoming a dysfunction and also that all people regardless of their limitations have a right to participate in the recreation pursuit of their choice. Thus, the focus of recreation therapist is not only on improving patients' skills but also on adding fun and quality to their lives and ensures that they have opportunities for fun and recreation after discharge from hospital (Tense, 1992)

**Therapeutic Recreation Objectives.**

Arnheim (1977) provides some specific objectives of therapeutic recreation which include the following:

- instill morale in the ill and handicapped persons
- encourage the formation of proper habits and attitudes
- channel aggressive drives into constructive outlets
- encourage desire to overcome physical or mental barriers, and
- stimulate new or dormant interests and talents.

Therapeutic recreation service is provided in several major health setting among which are:

- Hospitals such as Veterans Administration in the U.S.A, the military, tertiary medical facilities, state and specialised private hospitals.
- Centres for physical medicine and rehabilitation.
- Special Schools for various disabilities such as schools for the deaf, blind and handicapped.
- Home for the Aged persons.
- Nursing Homes.

**Therapeutic Recreation Programme**

The recreation activities provided for in the programme of those who are ill or disabled are not different from the normal individual since such activities must be planned in terms of the patient's interests, needs and capabilities. His leisure experiences should be related to the treatment aims which vary with the illness, disability and the patient. It is important for patients to experience success with their activities and gain confidence as well as a sense of comfort. Furthermore, individualised treatment plan which is based on assessment which identifies patient's leisure interests and needs should be geared toward skill development and adapting previous leisure activities to enhance the patient's leisure lifestyles after discharge (Richman, 1992).

Some categories of activities that can be included in therapeutic recreation programme/ services are:

- Social activities
- Entertainment

- Sports and active games
- Hobbies
- Arts and crafts
- Drama/ performance art
- Outdoor activities
- Special events
- Excursion

The involvement of mentally or physically ill persons in recreation activities can provide them with tremendous emotional and social lift. Thus, by making patients happier and more co-operative will support other treatment measures and lead toward a speedy recovery ( Corbin 1970).

**Specific Uses of Therapeutic Recreation**

Therapeutic recreation services have been employed in the treatment of a number of disabilities in different countries. To provide evidences which are replete in the literature, three projects utilised as adjutants to the treatment of three disabilities will be highlighted. All the projects were carried out in the United States of America.

**1a. *Recreation Therapy Interventions with Person with Psychiatric Disabilities***

This project was carried out by the Centre for Recreation and Disability Studies. Mental health disability is one of the areas which employed recreation therapy early in the 20th century. The benefits of activities for psychiatric patients have been frequently cited. Numerous studies showed that positive health outcomes accrue from regular participation in structured physical, social and recreational activities for people with mental health disabilities. The outcomes reported by the project included:

- Decrease in manifestation of stress and depression.
- Significant decreases in depressive and stress-related symptoms such as tension, negative thinking, sleep disturbances, impaired concentration and subjective stress and anxiety.

- Improvement in social interaction skills which includes significant increased assertiveness and social interaction skills and significant increased communication and co-operative skills.

### 1b. *Reintegration through Recreation (RTR)*

This project was for a special group of psychiatric patients. The aim of the project was to enhance the quality of life for persons with severe and persistent mental illness by providing transitional therapeutic recreation services that enable recently hospitalised or other individuals already living in the community attain independent functioning in their home community. The outcome of RTR project indicated that recreation is a powerful rehabilitation tool that promotes independent functioning, community inclusion and provides opportunity for personal skill development and mastery. The project concluded that satisfying and successful recreation experiences can promote social integration, enhance employment, improve physical and mental health, help alleviate the effect of disabilities, bolster self-confidence and make significant contributions to self-determination friendship and social supports.

### II. *Physical Medicine and Rehabilitation*

This is an area of health care which provides recreation therapy services. It assists those who have lost physical capacities by maximising their leisure functioning and ideally return them to the community setting. It was observed that individuals suffering from physical capacity losses have been involved in a very active lifestyle prior to onset of disabilities. Such individual must learn how to cope with his loss as well as try to get well enough to return to the community. Patients in this category have many needs that are brought about as a result of their disabilities. The needs include physical, cognitive, social interaction skills as well as psychological adjustment and coping leisure functioning. After assessing the patients and developing goals and treatment plan, patients were encouraged to participate in some form of recreation activity and treatment. The outcome showed enhanced strength and endurance, interaction with others and better awareness of leisure and community resources.

### III. *Outcomes Of Recreation Therapy Interactions for Persons with Developmental Disabilities*

This project address development in physical, cognitive, social and behavioural domains with the objective of enhancing age appropriate and autonomous community functioning as appropriate to individuals interest needs and potential. Structured skills education, integrated experiences and coaching for reintegration were instituted. Outcomes of the intervention showed improvement in the physical functioning such as improvement in perceptual motor skill, balance, agility and athletic skills. Improvement in cognitive functioning as evidenced by increased attention span, problem-solving and decision-making skills. Improvement in communication and social skills also occurred. There were increased skills in conversation, assertion, cooperation and competition.

Reduction in non-adaptive or inappropriate behaviour was reported. Participation in structured physical and social activities especially those encouraging choice and control demonstrate significant decreases in self-stimulating or self-abusive or other non-adaptive or inappropriate behaviour. Enhancement of friendship and social support network were reported (American Therapeutic Recreation Association, 2002).

In summary, from the presentation in this discussion, there is growing support from the literature on the effectiveness of recreation therapy intervention in producing desired health outcomes. Recreation therapy is effective in alleviating primary symptoms of illness or disability, as well as in promoting and enhancing ongoing health maintenance, independent functioning and overall quality of life (American Therapeutic Recreation Association, 2002). Recreation therapy interventions result in positive health outcomes in psychological, attitudinal and lifestyle domains. The need to adopt and incorporate therapeutic recreation as adjuncts to all medical management in our medical facilities is long overdue.

**References**

American Therapeutic Recreation (2002). *Recreation Therapy: A Summary of Health Outcomes* Asburn. V.A.

Arnheim, D.D., Auxter, D. and Crowe, W.C. (1977). *Principle and Methods of Adapted Physical Education and Recreation*. St. Louis. The C.V. Mosby Company, 3rd edition.

Carlson, R.E., Deppe, T.R. and Maclean, J.R. (1970). *Recreation in American Life.* Belmont, Calf. Wadsworth.

Corbin, H.D. (1970). *Recreation Leadership.* Engleroad Cliffs. N.J. Prentice – Hall Inc. P.261.

Hall, J.T. (1966). *School Recreation: Its Organisation, Supervision and Administration.* W.M.C. Brown Company Publishers. Oubuque, Iowa.

Heaton, I.C., and C.T. Thoresthenson (1978). *Planning for Social Recreation.* Boston. Houghton Mifflin Company.

Kaplan, M. (1960). *Leisure in American: A Social Inquiry.* New York: John Wiley. P. 19

Kraus, R. (1971). *Recreation and Leisure in Modern Society* Corporation P. 260-61.

Richman, V. (1992). "Children Live the Challenge of Rehabilitation". *Illinois Parks and Recreation* No 27, March / April.

Tense, M. (1992). "The Role of the Recreation Therapist". *Illinois Parks and Recreation* . No 26, March / April.

Weiskopf, D.C. (1975). *A Guide to Recreation and Leisure.* Boston Allyn and Bacon Inc.

# *Chapter 16*

# SECURITY ISSUES IN HEALTH INSTITUTIONS

*Rotimi, A.*

**About the Contributor**

Adewale Rotimi is a senior lecturer in the Department of Sociology and Anthropology at the Obafemi Awolowo University, Ile-Ife. He has his B.A. from Texas Wesleyan University, Fort Worth, Texas, M.A. in Criminology from Sam Houston State University, Huntsville, Texas and Ph.D in Sociology from the University of North Texas, Denton, Texas, USA.

A former correctioner officer and researcher with Texas Department of Corrections, USA, Dr Rotimi has also worked with the Nigerian Prisons Services and has published many articles in both local and international journals.

## INTRODUCTION

Security, according to *Websters New Collegiate Dictionary*, is defined as a condition or state in which a person or place is free from danger. In other words, it is a situation which is considered not only safe from danger but also free from the threat of it. The major concern of any society therefore, is how to protect its citizens from those conditions or situations that may pose a threat to security of lives and property.

However, there are many conditions which may constitute dangers to the security of any society. They include poverty, inequality, adverse political conditions, extreme climatic changes, conditions that threaten a persons' occupation, etc.

Once an organisation is established, it is the responsibility of its leadership or management team to ensure the safety of lives and properties of the members. It is thus a significant role of the management to ensure security. This will create the atmosphere needed to work together, using the resources available to achieve the goals of the organisation. Security matters are therefore of immense concern to the management of such an organisation. As a human organisation, concern for security to life overrides but does not underrate the protection to property of all and sundry within the establishment.

Security in essence, means absence of violence, or threat to peace and prevalence of cordial interpersonal and industrial relationship. In fact, managing security is cheaper than quenching violence and chaos. There is need for effective networking of security system. This system has to be so effective and encompassing to prevent or solve all problems emanating from staff groups (unions), individuals, ecological/ environmental situations, and the communities resident within the organisation precinct. The security system should also be able to cope with security of internal and external matters relating to the organisation. It should also operate in conjunction with the local command of the Police force, the State Security Services unit and the national security system. Hence, keeping an organisation secure against internal and external disruptive forces (theft, vandalism, accidents and terrorism) is a gigantic task that must be done if the establishment is to run smoothly.

Perhaps, the greatest threat to the security of any society is poverty or inequitable distribution of resources. Poverty may be aggravated by unemployment, low income, and lack of credit facilities to start a business and so on. Common observation reveals that criminals are usually recruited from poverty-stricken populace. In Nigeria, where the extended family is fast crumbling, poverty has become more evident with the demise of social safety nets. Inequality in income and social amenities is a great threat to security. In Nigeria for example, there seems to be only two distinct social classes, the rich and the poor. From the lower classes, violent youth gangs, armed robbers are usually recruited.

Another factor which may pose a security threat to the society concerns health-related problems. In Africa, for example, the HIV/AIDS scourge has ravaged many societies, greatly depleting the working population. It has also created a feeling of insecurity between spouses and between men and women in the general population.

Political insecurity arises mainly from violence which may occur between rival political groups. In recent times, political assassinations seem to have become a way of life. The assassinations of the late Kudirat Abiola, Chief Alfred Rewane, Chief Bola Ige, Harry Marshall and others have created a sense of insecurity among members of the political class in Nigeria.

The security of the environment might also be threatened by deforestation, bush burning, erosion, dumping of toxic wastes into streams, lakes and seas.

Lack of adequate food supply may also pose a security threat. Besides, it may lead to malnutrition which may, in turn lower the body's immunity system, thereby, leaving people to the mercy of diseases.

Economic programmes of the government can also affect the security of the citizens for example, lack of adequate programmes to combat poverty, sudden change in the prices of commodities, most especially, petroleum products, low wages, non-payment of pensions and gratuities and so on, all pose serious security threats.

Also, national security can be threatened by high rate of unemployment, invasion from foreign countries, porous borders, etc.

In this chapter, having defined security and examined those factors that may affect the security of a nation, we will now turn attention to the state of security in Nigeria. Since health institutions are located within the Nigerian society, the state of security in those institutions may be a reflection of the security conditions observable in the general Nigerian society.

## STATE OF SECURITY IN NIGERIA

Although a detailed discussion of the state of security in Nigeria is beyond the scope of this discourse but a panoramic view of the security situation in Nigeria will throw more light on the security issues that are also encountered in the health institution in the country.

The security of life and property ranks high in the hierarchy of human needs. According to the Editorial Opinion of *Daily Times* of 11 August 1988, Page10, "Man needs personal security to improve himself to the limits of his ability and contribute his best to society. Perhaps, this is why, today, the problem of security is of such great concern to an average Nigerian" (Awe, 2000).

For the past three decades, the problem of insecurity has been of major concern to Nigerians. As far back as 1978, Akinrinsola, had observed that the streets of Lagos, Kano, Ondo and Calabar, just to mention a few, which, fifteen years earlier, one could walk through in the dead of the night, confident, that one would reach home a mile away without being attacked by armed robbers, were no longer safe.

The *West Africa* magazine of 8 September 1986 had observed that insecurity of life was exacerbated by the activities of armed robbers who had grown in number and in boldness that they even gave prior notices of their intention to attack their potential victims. By mid-1979s, police foot and motorised patrols had been abolished. Successive military administrations also ensured that the police was demoralised, underequipped and underfunded, and this inadvertently paved the way for criminals to operate almost unchecked and uncurbed.

Under the Abacha regime (1993 – 1998), the gradual emasculation of the police was completed. This led to an exponential rise in the crime rate. Armed robbery, ritual killing, murder, assassinations etc became a way of life (Ojeme 2000). There was a general breakdown of law and order. The crime wary citizens had thought that the nascent democracy would usher in a respite from insecurity hitherto unleashed by criminals. Unfortunately, Dickson (2003) has observed that life in Nigeria has never been known to be so short and brutish the way it has been for the past four years of democratic rule.

Newspaper reports indicate that, even, the police to whom the security of the citizens have been entrusted are felled daily by the superior firepower of armed robbers. This has created a 'siege' mentality in which every residential building now assumes the look of a mini-prison. High perimeter walls, topped with sharp metal spikes surround the buildings, doors are made of iron and windows are fortified and burglary-proofed with hard metals that crisis-cross them.

The observations made above confirm the speculation that the nation is at the brink of anarchy through both civil strife and the activities of armed criminals (Onyibe 2000:14). Despite the allocation of more funds to the police and the additional recruitment of 400,000 more police personnel, the security situation in the country is yet to improve. Some events which have recently been reported in the major newspapers in the country seem to have further confirmed the feeling of insecurity throughout the country.

In the *Nigerian Tribune* of 3 March 2003, it was reported that, earlier on Tuesday 25 February 2003, the governors of Enugu and Ebonyi States and some party members were travelling on the Enugu-Port Harcourt Expressway. Suddenly, some gunmen, lurking at Ishiagu junction rained a hail of bullets on the convoy. Similarly, Oyewole (2003) reported that, following the assassination of Marshal Harry, the National Vice Chairman of the All Nigeria People's Party (ANPP), more prominent Nigerians, including the former vice president under the former military president, Gen. Ibrahim Babangida (rtd) were on list. Oladeji (2004) reports that Ahmed Pategi, the Kwara State Chairman of the Peoples Democratic Party (PDP) was killed in August 2002. Also, in October 2003, a peoples Democratic Party chieftain and a former vice-chancellor of the University of Nigeria, Nsukka, Professor Chimen Ikoku was killed in October 2003.

Also, one Dele Arojo, a Peoples Democratic Party gubernatorial candidate for Ogun State was shot dead in October, 2003. With time, the situation seems to have worsened. Oladeji (2004) reports that the south-south National Vice Chairman of the ruling People's Democratic Party, Kala Amunasowi Kala Dikibo was murdered on 7 February 2004. Oladeji has also observed that, fear now grips many politicians.

It has also been reported by Oladipo *et al* (2004) that the chairman of the Kogi State Independence Electoral Commission, Chief Phillip Kayode Olorunnipa was shot dead in the morning of 6 March 2004 in his home in Lokoja and the Police has arrested a former gubernatorial candidate of the People's Democratic Party in Kogi State, Dr Steven Olorunfemi and two others in connection with the killing. Oladipo *et al* have also reported that President Obasanjo who has expressed concerns over the spate of assassinations in the country has summoned the security chiefs to a meeting in Abuja. Also, the *Nigerian Tribune* of 4 February 2003; reported an explosion which wrecked the Prudent Bank building at Idumagbo Street, in Lagos Island. Many bodies were later discovered buried in the wreckage. Some four men were suspected to have carried out the bombing of the building.

In the same newspaper mentioned above, Segun (2003) reported that in the Warri communal clashes, some policemen were killed while over 200 houses were burnt. Mukwusi (2003) also narrated the carnage which attended the Warri communal clashes. Also, in *The Daily Sun* newspaper of 31 August 2003 it was reported that the convoy in which the Niger State Governor, Alhaji Kure was travelling was attacked while he was travelling from Minna to Abuja. In the incident, the Governor's *aide-de camp* was killed. A few weeks earlier, it was also reported that the car belonging to the Ekiti State Governor, Mr Ayo Fayose was attacked and riddled with bullets in Lagos. Fortunately, the governor was not in the car when it was attacked.

It was also reported in the newspaper mentioned above, that, in Lagos, robbers killed and maimed innocent citizens at will. Usually, when distress calls are made to the police, they are ignored. However, the police sometimes "answer" these distress calls by arriving at the scene of crime after the bandits must have left. As observed by *The Daily Sun* newspaper of 31 August 2003, the men of the underworld have almost overwhelmed the entire security in the country. Added to the activities of the men of the underworld are religious riots, cultism and other criminal acts which put the entire security system in the country in great stress.

## SECURITY IN HEALTH INSTITUTIONS IN NIGERIA

For the purpose of this topic, a health institution will be defined as a health organisation which occupies a sizeable portion of land space and in which many health related activities and programmes take place. Specific examples are Teaching Hospital Complexes, Schools of Nursing, Schools of Health Technology, General Hospitals etc.

The problem of security which is very pervasive generally in the Nigerian society has also spread to health institutions resulting in feelings of physical and psychological insecurity. Hitherto, health institutions had been regarded as "sacred" areas where the incident of armed robberies would be deemed inconceivable. Some events of the past years have however proved the above feeling very questionable. For example, in the *Weekend Sketch* of 11 January 1997, a screaming headline appeared. It reads, "Robbers who posed as patients told UCH nurses, doctors to 'kiss' the floor". In the report, robbers who disguised as patients entered the casualty department of the University College Hospital (UCH), Ibadan at 3.00am and ordered nurses and doctors to lie face down while they forced other employees to release the cash box to them. Such incident has also been reported at Abeokuta and Lagos. *The Daily Sun* newspaper of 31 August 2003, also reported that doctors and patients were injured when some armed bandits invaded a General Hospital.

Apart from the armed bandits who often invade some health institutions and thereby constitute a security problem, there are other elements and activities within the health institutions which may threaten security. These may include, examination malpractices which may involve nursing, medical, dental and other students. Nurses and other workers may extort money from students and patients. Cashiers and other workers who handle money may misappropriate funds. Drug theft may occur among workers who work in the pharmacy section, and those in the kitchen and cafeteria may pilfer food items. There have been occasions when baby thefts were reported in some hospitals. Fire outbreak may also occur which would put the lives of both patients and employees in danger.

There are other factors which may directly or indirectly pose security threats to any health institution. They include, poor remuneration which may lead to exodus of staff; trade dispute between management and staff which may results in strike and endangers the lives of patients; members of staff with former criminal records may be employed by mistake and workers may lack the expertise to properly handle fire-prone equipment. There may be faulty equipments and appliances. To mitigate some of the problems outlined above, a typical health institution usually has a security department.

## SECURITY DEPARTMENT

To properly address the issue of security in a typical health institution, the writer has visited a few health institutions, both in Nigeria and the United States of America. Some time was specifically spent in studying the security department of the Obafemi Awolowo University Teaching Complex at Ile-Ife, Ọ̀sun State, Nigeria.

At the Obafemi Awolowo University Teaching Hospital Complex, the security department which has a separate building is manned by the Chief Security Officer who is a retired military officer. This seems typical of most security departments in many health and other institutions across the country.

The security department is divided into two major sections: administrative and field sections. The administrative section comprises of investigation and intelligence subsections. The field section comprises mainly of patrol officers. The field section is further divided into three zones. The first zone is the gate areas which lead into and outside the health institution. Another zone comprises of major buildings (wards, pharmacy, doctors offices etc). Yet another zone comprises of the nurses hostels, medical students hostels, and the doctors residence. Most beats are manned by patrolmen and women who do not bear arms. Night watchmen are employed to complement the activities of the patrolmen. The night watchmen carry arms. All their activities are co-ordinated to ensure an efficient security system. The data on the security department mentioned above would have been richer but for the fact that the Chief Security Officer interviewed declined to give specific information on the strength of the department in terms of the number of security men and women, number of cases of staff arrested for drug stealing and sale etc. Also, the number of cases prosecuted was not given to the writer.

**Responsibilities of Security Officers**

For a very efficient and effective security operation in any health institution, security officers must be conscious of the immense responsibilities which are reposed on them. All these must be repeatedly emphasised during seminars and workshops which must be regular features of security outfits. Their major responsibility is to effectively secure life and property. They must monitor the movements of people entering and leaving the facility, this must include conducting searches on incoming and outgoing vehicles. Various beats must be kept. Detailed daily report must be given to the Chief Security Officer. Security men and women must politely give necessary information to visitors.

**Some Preventive Measures**

For an effective security operation in any health institution, some preventive measures must be instituted. They are listed below:

1. There must be proper lighting of all parts of the institution.
2. Fire-fighting equipment must be well-serviced and maintained.
3. Fences must be properly kept and maintained.
4. There must be an efficient communication system within the institution and between the institution and the outside.
5. There must be proper screening of visitors.
6. There must be constant change in the deployment of security personnel to various beats. This is very important, especially for those posted to nurses hostels and doctors quarters.
7. No person must remove any property from the institution without proper clearance from the security department.
8. There must be proper stocktaking of equipment and other properties.
9. Bushes must be regularly cut and wastes properly disposed of.

## CONCLUSION

The issue of security in the nation has become a major concern. This concern is felt in so many institutions including health institutions. Within the health institutions, administrators must contend with the occasional invasion by armed bandits, baby stealers and others. However, many factors seem to militate against efficient administration. These include poor funding which may result in the use of obsolete equipment. Also, poor remuneration has resulted in brain drain where doctors and nurses have migrated to Europe, America and the Middle East in search of greener pasture. Security of life has been threatened by fake drugs, lack of water, stealing and diversion of drugs. In many health institutions, student hotels are built in isolated places with overgrown weeds being observed between the main hospital and nurses hostels. Occasionally, this has exposed the students to attack by rapists and other criminals. In some institutions, perimeter fences have broken down, thereby creating easy access for criminals who invade hospitals. For an effective security of life and property within the health institutions, efforts must be made to frequently examine all physical facilities of the institution.

## RECOMMENDATION

Today, the greatest threat to the security of health institutions is lack of adequate funds. Stakeholders to these health facilities must ensure that adequate funds are provided for necessary equipment and personnel. To ensure effective security within the institutions, there must be effective patrol by security men and women. There must be proper lighting, special attention must be paid to nurses hostels, medical students hostels and doctors quarters and other vulnerable places. Regular workshops must be conducted to ensure that workers are advanced in fire drills, patient evacuation techniques etc. Security personnel must be well-trained in observation skills, proper operation of fire-fighting equipment and effective searching and frisking skills.

Finally, members of staff should be made to realise that stealing or pilfering of drugs (essential drugs) is a crime to humanity. Besides, they and their families' members can be victims of non-availability of drugs after the drugs must have been stolen. Since no human being is totally immuned from falling sick, there are occasions that may warrant the use of the drugs, even for those who steal the drugs.

## References

Akinrinsola, Fola "Finding solution to rising violence in our society". *The Punch.* 8 March 1978. P. 9.

Awe, John. "Insecurity, bane of IT investment-expert" *Nigerian Tribune* 19 October 2000. P. 19.

Dickson, Edward. " Banks in distress: How politicians caused it all". *Nigerian Tribune.* 15 April 2003. P. 15, 17

Mukwuzi, Michael. "War without end: the oil city of Warri lives up to the billing as Nigeria's Middle East". *The News* 1 Sept. 2003. P.125

Oladeji, Bayo. "Fear grips politicians over surge in political assassinations" *Saturday Tribune*, 15 February 2004. P. 3.

Oladipo, Dotun., Layi Adeloye and Yusuf Alli . "Kogi electoral boss killed", *The Punch*, 8 March 2004. P. 4.

Ojeme, Sunday. "Security eludes the people". *The Comet,* 31 December 2000 P. 22.

Onyibe, Magnus. "Deregulating Nigerian Security System" *This Day.* 15 January 2002 Vol. 7 No. 2457. P. 14.

Oyewole, Dare. "Political assassination: Four more on hit list" *The Monitor* 10 March 2003. P. 1, 2.

Segun, James. "Policemen killed, 200 houses burnt in Warri again, Delta government imposes curfew". *Nigerian Tribune* 4 Feb. 2003. P.1.

"The collapse of security" *The Sun* 31 August 2003. P. 2.

"The attack on Enugu, Ebonyi Governors" Tribune Editorial. *Nigerian Tribune* 3 March 2003. P.10.

"We saw, mystery men before the blast- Residents. 7 more bodies recovered, bomb experts at the blast venue ..." *Nigerian Tribune* 4 Feb. 2003. P.1

"Robbers pose as patients, UCH Nurses, doctors ordered to kiss the floor" *Weekend Sketch* 11 Jan.1997. P. 1, 5.

"Rising tide of violence". *Daily Times* Opinion, 11 August 1988. P.10.

"Nigeria a feeling of insecurity" *West Africa* 8 September 1986. P. 59

*Websters New Collegiate Dictionary* (1977) Springfield: Massachusetts G. and C. Merrian Co.

# *Chapter 17*

# LEGAL ASPECTS OF HEALTH CARE ORGANISATIONS

*Orifowomo, O. A.*

**About the Contributor**
Mr Orifowomo Odunola Akinwale is a lecturer and Acting Head, Department of Jurisprudence and Private Law, Obafemi Awolowo university, Ile-Ife. His areas of interest include Law of Taxation, Labour Law and Law of Banking and Negotiable Instruments. He has a number of articles published in academic journals.

## INTRODUCTION

The ultimate goal of every health care organisation is to create a seamless delivery system. This quest becomes more pressing, considering the fact that the facilities of many of these organisations are notoriously fragmented. By repute, health care organisation is an instantaneous, curative environment; for the sick or injured people who need immediate medical attention.

Strange enough, doctors and nurses sometimes feel that hospitals want them to do more with the few resources and that the tools they have to do their jobs are now increasingly antiquated but that they don't have time to learn yet another new computer system, is an incidence of advancement in technology and communications system. On the other hand, patients view hospitals as foreign, threatening and impersonal, controlling, undignified, invading, painful, confusing, isolating and lonely. Clearly, health care delivery does not appear to be working well for either the providers or the patients[1].

Each of these sounds awful, but are they not the perceptions of the ordinary patient, whether inpatient or outpatient? When the hospital or its prevailing environment is brought up as a subject among the people, immediately they become subdued and cowed, with not a few offering prayers of deliverance, divine assistance and visitation for the hapless patient.

This chapter examines some of the legal aspects of health care delivery system, including the relations between the parties involved, with its attendant consequences both in normal and crisis/default times, the rights and duties of the parties, and other related issues.

## DEFINITION OF TERMS

**Optimal:** Optimal is defined as the most favourable or advantageous; or best. It is a word derived from the Latin word *optimus*. On the other hand, "best" is defined as superlative of "good", surpassing all others in quality; most excellent, derivative of Middle and Old English, best.[2] In other words, the dictionary considers the two words to be synonymous, having different etymological roots – one from Latin and one from English.[3]

**Delivery:** Delivery is the act of delivering or distributing something[4].

**Organisation:** Organisation is a group of people who work together.[5]

---

[1] Severns Mike, *"Technology Infrastructure: Tomorrow's Healthcare Delivery"*, http://www.expresshealthcaremgmt.com/cgi-bin/print/MasterPFP.cgi?doc=

[2] Morris W. *The American Heritage Dictionary of the English Language*, Boston, Houghton Mifflin Company, 1979

[3] Lanken Paul, *"Optimal Care for Patients Dying in the ICU"*, International Consensus Conference in Intensive Care Medicine "Challenges in End-of-Life care in the ICU" Brussels, 24-25 April 2003, http://www.esicm.org/consensus/Lanken%20text.htm

[4] http://www.thefreedictionary.com.organization

[5] http://selfknowledge.com/57493.htm

**Management:** Management is the act or art of managing; the manner of treating, directing, carrying on, or using, for a purpose; conduct, administration, guidance; control. It also means the judicious use of means to accomplish an end; skillful treatment.[6]

**Health Care Delivery System**

Three major components make up the health care delivery system. These are facilities, practitioners and entities.

Some common types of facilities are:

- Hospitals
- Ambulatory Surgery Centres: These perform minor surgeries in an approved facility other than a hospital.
- Skilled Nursing Facilities: Medicare-approved facility offering 24 hours nursing care to non-acute patients.
- Home Health Agencies: Nursing care provided in the patient's home.
- Freestanding Substance Abuse Facilities: They provide inpatients care for substance abuse patients.
- Hospice: Provide care for terminally ill patients.
- End-stage Renal Disease Centres: Provide care for patients with ESRD (End-stage Renal Disease).

Hospitals may provide different levels of care which include:

- Acute care for critically ill patients: Tertiary care is a designation given to hospitals that provide medical education and handle complex care. However, primary care is provided by most hospitals.
- Sub acute care for patients requiring hospitalisation, but not in a life-threatening condition.
- Swing-bed care for patients requiring skilled nursing when no skilled facility bed is available.

---

[6] *"Healthcare Delivery System"*, http://www.wellmark.com/e_business/provider/Online_Training/A-HealthcareDelivery.ppt

Practitioners are of two categories namely:
- Physicians
- Allieds or Extenders.

Physicians include:
- Medical Doctors (MD).
- Doctors of Osteopathic Medicine (DO).
- Pediatrists (DPM).
- Optometrists (OD).
- Chiropractors (DC).

All of these are addressed as **"Doctor".**

Extenders or allied providers are:
- Physician Assistants (PA)
- Nurse Practitioners (ARNPs)
- Certified Registered Nurse Anaesthetists (CRNAs)
- Therapists: Physical (PT), Occupational (OT), and Speech (ST).

Professions included in entities are:
- Home Infusion Therapy
- Orthotics and Prosthetics
- Home Medical Equipment Suppliers or Durable Medical Suppliers
- Freestanding MRI
- Freestanding Radiology
- Independent Laboratory
- Ambulance.

## RELEVANT CONSTITUTIONAL PROVISIONS

Section 1 (1) of the Constitution provides that the Constitution is supreme and its provisions shall have binding force on all authorities and persons throughout the Federal Republic of Nigeria.[7] Section 13 of the Constitution further provides that, it shall be the duty and responsibility of all organs of government, and of all authorities and persons, exercising legislative, executive or judicial powers, to conform to, observe and apply the provisions of this Chapter (that is, Chapter II) of this Constitution.

In specific terms, section 17 (3) (d)[8] then provides that the State (meaning the Nigerian State or Government, at all levels) shall direct its policy towards ensuring that there are adequate medical and health facilities for all persons.[9] In other words, the organic document of the land, prescribes that government shall make adequate provisions for the establishment, maintenance and sustenance of a medical/health structure, for its citizenry and other residents, alike. This presupposes a viable and vibrant health care delivery system, via recognised and approved health care organisations. In our own view, the imperative terms of this prescription, is in no wise whittled down by the provisions of section 6 (6) (c)[10], ousting the jurisdiction of courts in matters specified in Chapter II of the Constitution. The overall effect of this provision is to make matters in Chapter II non-justiciable.

## ESTABLISHMENTS OF HEALTH CARE INSTITUTIONS/ ORGANISATIONS[11]

### Hospitals

The hospital is an institution equipped and staffed to provide medical, surgical and sometimes, psychiatric care for the sick and injured.[12] Usually, hospitals managed by State governments are referred to as State Hospitals, while those managed by the Federal government are referred to as General Hospitals.

### Teaching Hospitals

Teaching Hospitals are established as affiliates of Universities, whether owned by the State or Federal Governments. They are established for

---

7 See Constitution of the Federal Republic of Nigeria 1999 (hereinafter referred to as "the Constitution").

8 1999 Constitution

9 *Ibid.*

10 *Ibid.*

11 See generally, Yakubu, J. A. *Medical Law in Nigeria*, 1st ed., 2002, Demyaxs Press Limited, pp. 68 - 70

12 *New* Lexicon *Webster's Dictionary of the English Language*, Deluxe Encyclopedic Edition, 1987, p. 468

providing such facilities for the training of medical and other students as are usually provided by teaching hospitals of internationally high repute.[13] The general law regulating the activities of Teaching Hospitals in Nigeria, is the University Teaching Hospitals (Reconstruction of Boards, etc.) Act.[14]

### Dispensaries

Sometimes, dispensaries are established in the rural areas where standard hospitals are not available. They give out medical prescriptions and advice and take up minor treatment at little or no cost.

### Maternity Centres

There are also maternity centres, which augment the efforts of hospitals. They provide needed medical care for women during periods of pregnancy and childbirth.

### Rural Health Clinics

Rural health clinics are established in the rural areas to take up the responsibility of both the dispensaries and maternity centres. Physicians visit these health clinics on regular basis to treat cases that cannot be taken care of by the nurses, midwives and other health officials.

## PARTIES IN HEALTH CARE DELIVERY SYSTEM

Parties involved in the health care delivery system largely fall into three categories:

***Employer***: The employer can be the government, be it at the Federal, State or Local government levels, depending on the establishing authority.

***Employee***: The employees would either fall within the category of Physicians, generally called Doctors, or Allied Practitioners or Extenders, on the other hand.

---

[13] See, for example, University of Nigeria Teaching Hospital Management Board Act, Cap. 460, section 1 (1) thereof

[14] Cap.463

***Patient***: The patient can be inpatient or outpatient, who would have presented himself for one kind of medicare or the other.

**The Employer**

The Constitution enables government, at all levels, to take every step deemed necessary, to ensure that there are adequate medical and health facilities for all persons.[15] In similar terms, the local government councils in each state are charged with the function, among others, of the provision and maintenance of health services.[16] Arising from this, each level of government is empowered to set up appropriate health units and organisations, within its jurisdiction, and employ suitable personnel to staff them. This effort can take any of the forms of hospitals, dispensaries, maternity centres, and so on.

**The Employee**

Different laws and regulations apply to the practice of the different categories of employees in the health organisations. Primarily, we have the Medical and Dental Practitioners Act.[17] This Act establishes the Medical and Dental Council of Nigeria, (The Council)[18] charged with the responsibility, among others, for determining the standards of knowledge and skill to be attained by persons seeking to become members of the medical or dental profession ("doctors").[19] Under the Act, the Registrar of the Council maintains a register of all persons who are entitled to be registered as medical practitioners or dental surgeons. Only those duly registered are entitled to practice, as such.[20] The Medical and Dental Practitioners Disciplinary Tribunal handle matters of discipline in the profession.[21]

---

[15] See section 17 (3) (d) of the Constitution

[16] See section 7 (5) and paragraph 2 (c) of the Constitution.

[17] Cap. 221, Laws of the Federation of Nigeria, 1990 (LFN)

[18] *Ibid.* section 1 thereof

[19] Section 2 thereof

[20] See sections 6 – 8 and 17 & 18 thereof

[21] Sections 15 – 17 thereof; see also *Olaye v. Chairman, Medical and Dental Practitioners Disciplinary Tribunal* (1997) 5 NWLR (Pt. 506) 550; *Denloye v. Medical and Dental Practitioners Disciplinary Committee* (1968) 1 All NLR 306

The Nursing and Midwifery Act[22] regulates, in terms similar to the Medical and Dental Practitioners Act, the nursing and midwifery profession, through the Nursing and Midwifery Council of Nigeria.[23] Only those who are duly registered may practice as nurses and midwives.[24]

The Medical Rehabilitation Therapists (Registration, etc.) Act[25] regulates the activities of physiotherapists.[26] Only those who have been duly registered in the register kept under the Act can practice as physiotherapists, chiropractors, occupational therapists, osteopaths and speech therapists.[27]

### Patients

In general terms, patients could be either inpatients or outpatients. Of course, the inpatients require closer attention by the physician. In fact, inpatients must be seen as often as possible inconsistent with good patient care. The doctor seeing the patient must write adequate notes in the case note every time he sees the patient. It is also required that the doctor should communicate regularly with the patient or his relation, as he may deem appropriate.[28]

## RELATIONS BETWEEN THE PARTIES

### Employer and Employee Relationship

There exists a contractual relationship between the employer and the employee. It is expected that the terms of the contract between the two parties must have been mutually agreed upon and adequately spelt out in writing. The essentials of such a contract must be contained in the

[22] Cap. 332, LFN
[23] Section 1 thereof
[24] See sections 6 – 11 and 20 of the Act
[25] Cap. 222, LFN
[26] See section 1 thereof
[27] See sections 1, 7 – 10 of the Act
[28] See Rules of Professional Conduct for Medical and Dental Practitioners in Nigeria, issued by the Medical and Dental Council of Nigeria

letter of appointment issued by the employer to the employee.[29] In such cases, the relationship is governed by the express terms of the contract.[30] Otherwise, resort is add to implied terms. Terms may be implied into the agreement between the parties either based on usage or custom, statute, or the Common law. Aside from the express terms, other terms may be incorporated into the agreement by reference to some other documents, such as the provisions of a collective agreement, handbook, and so on.[31]

The contract could have laid down, formal rules and procedures, such as those governing discipline and dismissal, as well as terms and conditions of employment.[32] These may include wages, salaries, bonuses, hours of work, nature of duties, holidays, overtime, sick pay, pension schemes, and so on.

Usually, rules of common law are applicable to the relationship between the parties. The common law imposed certain duties on the employee. These include:

(i) Duty of Obedience[33] ;
(ii) Duty of Care[34] ;
(iii) Duty to be ready and willing to work[35] ;
(iv) Duty to take care of employer's property[36] ;
(v) Duty of Fidelity/Good Faith[37] ,

The duties of the employer, at common law include: (i) Duty to pay wages/remuneration[38] ; (ii) Duty to provide work[39] ; (iii) Duty to

---

29 See section 7 Labour Act Cap. 198 LFN

30 See *Morohunfola v. Kwara State college of Technology* (1990) 4 NWLR (Pt. 145) 506

31 See *Ajayi v. Texaco Nigeria Limited* (1987) 3 NWLR (Pt. 62) 577

32 See *Ilodibia v. Nigerian Cement Company Limited* (1997) 7 NWLR (Pt. 512) 174

33 See *Pepper v. Webb* (1969) 2 All ER 216; *Turner v. Mason* (1845) 13 M. & W. 112; *Ottoman Bank v. Chakarian* (1930) AC 277

34 See *Usen v. Bank of West Africa Limited* (1965) 1 All NLR 244; compare *Omotayo v. Ojikutu* (1961) 1 All NLR 901

35 See *Miles v. Wakefield Metropolitan District Council* (1987) AC 539

36 See *Osakwe v. Nigerian Paper Mill Limited* (1998) 10 NWLR (Pt. 568) 1

37 See *Maja v. Stocco* (1968) NMLR 372, 379; *Secretary of State For Employment v. ASLEF (No. 2)* (1972) 2 QB 455; *Reading v. Attorney General* (1951) AC 507; *Thomas Marshall (Exports) Limited v. Guinle* (1978) IRLR 174

38 See *Peters of Oron v. Symmons* (1924) 5 NLR 79; *Erabor v. Incar Nig. Limited* (1975) 4 SC 1

39 See *Collier v. Sunday Referee Publishing Co. Limited* (1940) 2 KB 647, at 650 per Asquith, J.; *Langston v. AUEW* (1974) 1 All ER 980

indemnify employee[40]; (iv) Duty to treat employees with respect, trust and confidence[41]; (v) Duty of care[42].

In the determination of the relationship, either party may opt out of the relationship by giving requisite notice (as stated by the contract, otherwise as determined by statute[43] or "reasonable notice" under common law). In the alternative, the party seeking to determine the relationship can make payment in lieu of notice.

Apart from the foregoing, the rules of common law may be found inapplicable, where the contract of employment is adjudged to have a legal or statutory flavour. This is the position where the conditions for appointment or the determination of the contract are governed by the provisions of an enabling statute. In such cases, the law prescribes a strict observance of the provisions of the relevant statute, as they regulate termination of the appointment. Otherwise, the court would declare an order of dismissal or termination as null and void and of no effect, whatsoever.[44]

## Employer and Patient Relationship

In most cases, if not in all, the workers in the employment of the health organisations are regarded as **employees**, implying that they have *contract of service* with their employers. This being so, under certain circumstances, the employer is held vicariously liable for the *tortious* acts or omission of his employees. Thus, the employer is made to answer for the negligence of the employee, occasioned in the course of his employment.[45] However, this is without prejudice to whatever rights the employer may have as against the employee, for example, the right to contribution[46], or indemnity[47], in appropriate cases.[48]

---

40 See *Gregory v. Ford* (1951) 1 All ER 121

41 See *Bliss v. South East Thames Regional Health Authority* (1985) IRLR 308; *Courtaulds Northern Textiles Limited v. Andrew* (1979) IRLR 84

42 See *Paris v. Stepney Borough Council* (1951) AC 367; *Stokes v. GKN Limited* (1968) 1 WLR 1776

43 See section 11 Labour Act

44 See *Fakuade v. O.A.U.T.H.C.* (1993) 5 NWLR (Pt. 291) 47; *Olaniyan & Ors. V. UNILAG* (1985) 2 NWLR (Pt. 9) 599

45 See *UAC Limited v. Saka Owoade* 13 WACA 207

46 See section 9 (2) Civil Liability (Miscellaneous Provisions) Law 1961, Lagos State

47 See *Lister v. Romford Ice & Cold Storage Co. Limited* (1957) AC 555

48 See *Jones v. Manchester Corporation* (1952) 2 All ER 125

The basis of vicarious liability[49] is that, as between the employer and the employee, the former is likely to be in a more viable position to pay any sum awarded as damages, in favour of a third party, for example, a patient. In addition, since the employer takes the benefits of the services of the employee, it is considered only appropriate that he should absorb the outcome of any failure in duty by that employee. Furthermore, only the employer and not the third party could have controlled or influenced what the employee does or how he does it. Again, the employee was able to commit the objectionable act of commission or omission, because of the position the employer put him.

**Employee and Patient Relationship**

Generally, the medical personnel owe a duty of care to the patient in the discharge of their duties towards him. This duty requires that those responsible for the treatment of the patient must exercise reasonable care in the carrying out of their various duties, in relation to the patient. Failure to do this is regarded as a breach of duty. Where this breach occasioned harm or damage to the patient, the law is disposed to awarding damages to him. Damages is an award of a sum of money considered adequate to compensate or assuage whatever damage the negligence of the medical officer may have caused the patient.

The basis of the duty owed by the physician to the patient is said to be contractual. This involves the essentials of *offer, acceptance* and *consideration*. The physician who agrees to treat him accepts the offer of a patient who presents himself for medicare. Consideration by the physician is the deployment of his training and expertise, while the patient undertakes to pay his medical bills. It is instructive to note the decision of the Supreme Court in *Anyah v. Concorde Hotels Limited*[50] to the effect that a breach of contract may give rise to a proper action in negligence.

[49] See *Duncan v. Findlater* (1839) 6 Cl & F. 894
[50] (2002) 12 SCNJ 145

## RIGHTS AND DUTIES OF THE PARTIES

We consider it very important, to consider some of the rights and duties of the parties, particularly as they relate to the patient. However, it should be outside the province of this discourse to do a treatise on the rights and duties of the employer and the employee, *inter se*, that is, as between themselves. (That would be more suited for a work under labour or employment law).

### Duties of the Doctor

The basic duties of a medical practitioner are advice, diagnosis and cure. In specific terms, the Rules of Professional Conduct for Medical and Dental Practitioners in Nigeria imposed some duties on the Doctor, in relation to the patient.

***(i) Duty to preserve life***

At all times, the doctor is expected to bear in mind the obligation of preserving human life.

***(ii) Duty of loyalty***

A doctor owes to his patient complete loyalty and all resources of his science. Whenever an examination is beyond his capacity, he should summon another doctor who has the necessary ability.

***(iii) Duty of secrecy***

A doctor shall preserve absolute secrecy on all he knows about his patient, even after the patient has died, because of the confidence entrusted to him.

***(iv) Duty in emergency situations***

A doctor must give emergency care as a humanitarian duty unless he is assured that someone is available to give such care.

***(v) Duty of care***

Doctors owe a duty of care to their patients in every professional relationship. The particular skill, which training and eventual recognition and registration bestow on a practitioner, is to be exercised in a manner expected of any other member of the profession of his experience and status. It is required that the practitioner upgrades this skill as best as possible in the light of advancing knowledge in the profession.

## PATIENT'S RIGHTS[51]

Strikingly, there appears not to be, any code on the rights of patients, in Nigeria. Albeit, and undoubtedly, a patient who has submitted himself to medical treatment in a health organisation, cannot but have some rights, as well as responsibilities, accompanying the relationship of physician/patient thereby created. In this quest, we shall rely on the common law and such other rights as have become recognised in some other jurisdictions.

*(i)* ***Right to quality medical care:*** Patients have the right to receive quality medical care. This entails considerate, courteous and compassionate care that take care of their personal, spiritual, cultural and religious values and beliefs. All of these should take place in an environment free from all forms of abuse or harassment.

*(ii)* ***Right to refuse treatment:*** The patient has the right to accept or refuse medical care or treatment, prior to and during the course of treatment, and to refuse a recommended treatment or plan of care, to the extent permitted by law and to be informed of the medical consequences of such action.

---

[51] See generally, Riverview Regional Medical Center *"Patients Rights and Responsibilities"*, http://www.riverviewregional.com/getpage.php?name=patientsrights; The California Patient's Guide, Chapter II, *"Your Right to Informed Consent"*, http://www.calpatientguide.org/ii.html ; Duke Health *"Patient Bill of Rights"*, http://www.dukehealth.org/patients_visitors/patient_bill_of_rights.asp ; Veterans Resources *"Patients' Rights and Responsibilities"*, http://www.visn1.med.va.gov/resources/patrights.htm ; Jackson Health System *"Patient's Rights and Responsibilities"*, http://um-jmh.org/JHS/Patient_Rights.html ; Baptist Health of Northeast Florida *"Patient and Visitor Information"*, http://patients.e-baptisthealth.com/info/rights.html ; WMC *"Patient's Rights"*, http://www.wmcnet.org/WMC_2001_Web_Site/Patient_Rights.html

***(iii) Right to informed consent:*** Informed consent is more than merely the agreement to a particular treatment or procedure. Informed consent is agreement to a proposed course of treatment based on clear, understandable information about the treatment's potential benefits and risks. The patient must also be informed about all treatments available for his health condition, and the risks of receiving no treatment. Except in emergencies, this information shall include the purpose and description of the procedure, probable result, significant risks, and alternate courses of treatment.

***(iv) Right to privacy:*** The patient has the right to every consideration of privacy. Case discussion, consultation, examination and treatment should be conducted to protect each patient's privacy.

***(v) Right to confidentiality:*** The patient has the right to expect that all communications and rounds pertaining to his or her care will be treated as confidential by the hospital, except in cases such as suspected abuse and public health hazards when reporting is permitted or required by law. The patient has the right to expect that the hospital will emphasise the confidentiality of this information when it releases it to any other parties entitled to review information in these records.

***(vi) Right in decision-making:*** The patient has the right to actively participate in decisions regarding his medical care, including managing pain effectively by appropriate assessments, interventions, education and assistance. This includes the right to refuse treatment after being informed of the consequences of refusal, the right to leave the care of the entity against physician's advice, except in extraordinary circumstances, or both.

***(vii) Freedom from restraints and seclusion:*** The patient will not be restrained unless clinically justified and only when less restrictive interventions have been determined to be ineffective. Restraints and seclusion are not to be used for coercion, discipline, convenience or retaliation. If the patient has any questions regarding the use of restraints, he should feel free to ask his care nurse or physician.

***(viii) Right to know about the care givers:*** The patient has the right to know who the people are and what they are trained to do for his care, including the name of the doctor who takes care of him. The patient has the right and he is encouraged – to obtain from physicians and other direct care givers, such relevant, current and understandable information concerning diagnosis, treatment and prognosis.

***(ix) Right to visitations and communications:*** Each patient has the right to communicate freely and privately with persons outside the facility of health organisation. To facilitate this, each patient shall be provided the opportunity to meet with visitors during regularly scheduled visiting hours; convenient and reasonable access to public telephone and the opportunity to send and receive unopened mail. However, a patient may refuse visitors.

***(x) Right to give advance medical directives:*** The patient has the right to formulate advance medical directives or to appoint a surrogate to make health care decisions. He should be well-informed about making medical directives such as a living will and health care proxy or durable power of attorney for health care. These documents express the patient's choices for treatment or designate someone to represent the patient in the event the patient is unable to communicate his wishes. The advance directives will be respected to the extent permitted by law.

***(xi) Right to know about entity charges and other policies:*** The patient should be informed of the hospital's charges for services and available payment methods. He also has the right to be informed of hospital policies and practices that relate to patient care, treatment and responsibilities.

***(xii) Right to notice of patient's rights:*** Each patient or his representative should be adequately informed of patient's rights and responsibilities and the complaint resolution process for the organisation. A Statement of Patient Rights should be posted on each inpatient unit and outpatient area. If possible, they should be contained in an informational handbook, readily accessible to the patients. All staff assigned to work with patients should be well-oriented/educated as to these rights.

It is important to note that the list of patient rights outlined above, are by no means exhaustive. At best, they are indicative of those considered almost immutable, in all jurisdictions. We have also found other additions, with variations from one health organisation to another.

## PATIENT'S RESPONSIBILITIES

Aside from the various patient rights, a patient is also invested with certain responsibilities, which he must fulfil to ensure his healing, and health recovery.

***(i) Duty to give information:*** It is the patient's responsibility to give – to the best of his knowledge – accurate and complete information about present complaints, past illnesses, hospitalisations, medications and other matters relating to his health. In addition, he is responsible for reporting unexpected changes in his condition, to the health care provider. He should also report whether he clearly understands a contemplated course of action and what is expected of him; that is, how he will be taken care of and what he needs to do for that care.

***(ii) Duty to follow instructions:*** The patient and family are responsible for following the care, service or treatment plan developed by the health care team. They should express any concerns they have about their ability to follow and comply with the proposed care plan or course of treatment. Every effort is made to adapt the plan to the patient's specific needs and limitations. When such adaptations to the treatment plan are not recommended, the patient and family are responsible for understanding the consequences of the treatment alternatives by not following the proposed course. In other words, if the patient says no to treatment, or do not follow the care, service or treatment plan suggested by his health care team, he is responsible for what happens to him.

***(iii) Duty to keep appointments:*** The patient should keep any doctor or clinic appointments or telephone, or otherwise keep in touch if he cannot keep them.

***(iv) Duty to have respect for others:*** The patient is responsible for being polite and respectful of other patients as well as hospital/clinic employees and property. He should also see that his visitors are polite and respectful.

***(v) Duty to observe rules and regulations:*** The patient should follow the rules and regulations of the establishment, as they affect how patients are cared for and behave.

***(vi) Duty to meet financial obligations:*** The patient has a responsibility to pay his bills promptly or ask questions about them.

## MEDICAL MALPRACTICE/MEDICAL NEGLIGENCE

Medical malpractice, otherwise called medical negligence, in general, is any act or failure to act by a member of the medical profession that results in harm, injury, distress, prolonged physical or mental suffering, or death to a patient, while that patient is under the care of that medical professional. Put differently, it means that a health care provider caused injury or death to a patient by failing to act within the applicable standard of care. Usually, harm must be proven to have occurred. In other words, a physician or other health care provider commits medical malpractice and is negligent when he fails to act reasonably under the circumstances, and his unreasonable conduct causes harm.[52]

Negligence, as a concept, refers to failure to exercise reasonable care, under the circumstances; lack of due diligence or care; omission

[52] See LDHP Medical Review Services Corp. "*Explanation of Medical vs. Legal Malpractice*", http://www.ldhpmed.com/GP_malpractice.htm ; MEDLAW Legal Team "*Medical Malpractice Ques.....: personal injury law*", http://www.medlawlegalteam.com/faqs.html

of duty. In law, negligence requires that there is a duty, a breach of that duty, which is the cause of injury or damage to another.[53] Only then would the negligent person be made to pay damages, to be awarded by a court of competent jurisdiction. Negligence includes both acts of commission and omission.

In the context of health care, legal negligence is the failure to exercise that degree of care or skill practised by other professionals of similar skill and training, under similar circumstances. Such lack of care alone, however, will not result in legal liability; there must be an injury to the patient, and the injury must have been caused by the negligent act. Thus, medical negligence is the failure of a physician or health professional to exercise the degree of skill, prudence and care that would usually and customarily be exercised by other reputable physicians treating the patient in question or a similar patient.[54]

Negligence, *a fortiori*, medical negligence, is largely a civil wrong or *tort*, entailing a civil liability, which finds expression in the award and payment of damages by the *tort-feasor*, that is, the negligent party.

## CRIMINAL LIABILITY

Quite apart from any civil liability that may arise from negligent acts of a medical or health practitioner, there may also arise criminal liability, where his conduct violates any of the provisions of the criminal law of the land. According to the Supreme Court in *Denloye v. Medical and Dental Practitioners Disciplinary Committee*[55].

> ... where the unprofessional conduct of the practitioner amounts to a crime, it is a matter for the courts to deal with....[56]

---

[53] See *Anyah v. Concorde Hotels Limited, supra*; *Koya v. United Bank for Africa Limited* (1997) 1 NWLR (Pt. 481) 251

[54] See generally, The Common Law of Negligence *"Who is at Fault in this Accident?"*, *http://www.ourpeak.com/spatin/negligence.html* ; Glossary *"Negligence"*, *http://www.safetyandquality.org/definition/negligence.htm*

[55] *Supra*

[56] *Ibid.* at p. 312 *per* Ademola CJN

Such a medical practitioner may be charged with any of the following offences: murder; manslaughter; abortion; euthanasia, or killing an unborn child. All of these offences find expression in the Criminal Code[57] and the Penal Code[58]. Except as it is written in these two laws, no conduct may be regarded as criminal under Nigerian laws.[59]

## Murder or Manslaughter

Under the law, any person who unlawfully[60] kills another is guilty of an offence, which is called murder or manslaughter, depending on the circumstances of the case. The offence is murder where the deceased has died, the death resulted from the act of the accused and the act of the accused was intentional with knowledge that death or grievous bodily harm was its probable consequence.[61]

However, a person who unlawfully kills another in such circumstances as not to constitute murder is guilty of manslaughter. Where the consequence of the act or omission of the medical practitioner leads to death, the determination of whether it is murder or manslaughter depends on whether the act or omission was intentionally, negligently or recklessly done.[62]

## Abortion

Generally, every act done to procure or induce a miscarriage of a woman, whether or not she is with child is deemed criminal, under section 228 of the Criminal Code. It is an act punishable with an imprisonment for fourteen years.[63] Equally, anyone who unlawfully supplies to or procures

---

[57] Cap. 77, LFN (being the law regulating criminal conducts in the Southern part of Nigeria)

[58] Cap. 89, Laws of Northern Nigeria, 1963 (being the law which regulates activities regarded as criminal in the Northern part of Nigeria)

[59] See section 36 (12) 1999 Constitution and *Aoko v. Fagbemi* (1961) 1 All NLR 400

[60] It is unlawful to kill any person unless such killing is authorised or justified or excused by law; see section 306 Criminal Code

[61] See *The State v. Ogbunbunjo* 2001 WRN 1; *Ekpe v. The State* (1994) 9 NWLR (Pt. 368) 268

[62] See *R. v. Bateman* (1929) 19 Crim. App. Rep. 8; see generally, sections 306, 308, 315 – 317 Criminal Code; Yakubu, *Medical Law in Nigeria, op. cit.*, pp. 21 - 28

[63] See also section 232 Penal Code

for any person, anything whatsoever, knowing that it was intended to procure the miscarriage of such a woman, is guilty of an offence punishable with imprisonment for three years.[64]

Abortion[65] may only be procured for preserving the life of the mother.[66] This is referred to as therapeutic abortion. According to the World Health Organization, this relates to the health of the mother, suggesting a state of complete physical, mental and social well-being and not merely the absence of disease or infirmity. In any other case, procuring an abortion is a criminal act.

**Euthanasia**

It is a criminal offence for a medical practitioner to terminate the life of another, for showing mercy on the patient, because of his suffering or any unjustifiable cause.[67]

**Killing an Unborn Child**

Under section 328 of the Criminal Code,[68] any person who prevents a child from being born alive (except as provided under section 297, that is, to preserve the life of the mother) is guilty of an offence, punishable with imprisonment for life.

[64] See section 230 Criminal Code

[65] See *Royal College of Nursing of the United Kingdom v. Department of Health and Social Security* (1981) AC 800

[66] See section 297 Criminal Code

[67] See section 311 Criminal Code

[68] See also section 236 Penal Code

## *Chapter 18*

# HUMAN HEALTH AND THE ENVIRONMENT

*Fajewonyomi, B.A. & Bamigboye, A.P.*

**About the Contributors**

Fajewonyomi, a Fellow of the Royal Society for Health is a Professor of Environmental Epidemiology and currently working in the Community Health Department, Obafemi Awolowo University, Ile-Ife. He once served as Commissioner for Health in the old Ondo State (1985-87). He is a member of the Governing Council of University of Ado-Ekiti (Ekiti State) till date. He has published many articles in reputable local and international journals.

Bamgboye is a lecturer in the Department of Community Health, Obafemi Awolowo University, Ile-Ife. He did his Postgraduate work in Community Health and Environmental Health. A member of the Environmental Health Officers Registration Council of Nigeria and the West African Health Examination Board. He is also a Fellow of the Royal Society of Health, London and National President, Environmental Health Officers Association of Nigeria.

## INTRODUCTION

The environment has become a key word reflecting important public issues and thus, across all lands, people are voicing deep concern about environmental abuses and the sequential effects on the health of man. The subject of health and its relationship with the environment has become a major issue in national and international development discourse. In the past, public health approaches are focused on diseases risk factors and behavioural change to attain better health. It took about ten years of research to come to understand that social, economic and environmental 'risk conditions' also have a great impact on health choices. Although much progress has been made in improving the quality of air, water and soil, the situation still remains far from being satisfactory. Many acute environmental problems are being addressed, but much remains to be attended to. In particular, the health implications of chronic exposures are yet to be sufficiently addressed. Little attention is being paid to the interaction of different pollutants in human body as well as in the environment. It is quite disconcerting therefore that understanding of environment and the role it plays in health and disease should remain so poor and out of perspective at this stage of national and international development.

The United Nations and its agencies have made concerted effort at making all countries of the world pay needed attention to environmental issues particularly on the need to prevent their potential effects on health. It is not out of place to state that as beautiful as their strategies are, most countries are just paying lip service to the real issues involved.

Today there is evidence that factors such as particulate matters in air, noise and ground-level ozone damage the health of thousands of people every year. Thousands of man-made chemicals including pesticides persist in the environment, accumulating over time without many people being aware of their presence and their long-term effects.

The poor are the most vulnerable to health and environmental conditions. Environmental factors that affect health are in turn linked to underlying pressures on the environment which are determined by such driving forces as poverty and economic mobility, population dynamics, urbanisation, social and cross-cultural diversity, science and technology, education or lack of it, household wastes, industrialisation, economic development and globalisation of industries.

It has been estimated that about 22-33% of the burden of disease in industrialised countries are attributable to environmental factors with the bulk of it affecting women and children as well as other vulnerable population groups. This has caused serious concern in many parts of the world. In a recent survey in Europe, some 89% of the people are worried about the potential impact of the environment on their health.

Many people living in least developed countries have not come to term with such concerns due to poor awareness as regards the presence of such factors/agents in the environment and the potential problems they cause.

Furthermore, new technology, changing lifestyles, work and life patterns present new and sometimes unexpected impact on the environment and its influence on health.

Tackling environmental health problems therefore requires a better understanding and also identifying their potential health problems so that it will be possible to prevent new health threats linked to environmental pollution (WHO, 1997).

## Relationship between Health and the Environment: The Ecosystem Perspective

The state of health of an individual or population depends on complex interactions of the physical, biological, political and social factors in the ecosystem. The term ecosystem is defined as a system of dynamic interrelationship among living organisms and their physical environment (Annalee Yassi, Kjellstrom, Kok & Guidotti, 2001). It is a bounded entity that has acquired self-stabilising mechanisms and an internal balance that has been evolving over the course of centuries.

The stability of the ecosystem is very fundamental to environmental sustainability and harmony. This stability is maintained when amount of materials and energy being consumed by one species is harnessed without depriving other species, and also without endangering the viability of the entire ecosystem. When this stability is threatened or eroded due to an overwhelmed system, a situation of rapid change or a near total collapse of the system results. Over the past century, human activities have played major role in global environmental change with increases in atmospheric greenhouse gasses, depletion of the stratospheric ozone layer, loss of biodiversity, pollution of water resources and degradation of soils all of which have serious consequences on human health.

Looking at the definition of the environment given by Last (1995), that " all that which is external to the individual human host and which can be divided into physical, biological, social, cultural, any or all of which can influence health status in populations", it is clear that a person's health is largely determined by environmental factors in addition to genetics as well as socioeconomic factors. Whether in natural infections or man-made problems affecting human welfare, the three major factors involved have often been the host (man), the agent (disease agent) and the environment. Epidemiologists particularly in developed countries have thus approached the solution to such problems through efforts directed to each of these factors.

Environmental degradation has a serious impact on people's health. The burden of environmentally related diseases is enormous among all age groups of the population. Several millions of people in many countries of the world particularly in less developed countries suffer from such diseases as respiratory infections, facial-oral infections, vector-borrie diseases, water and sanitation related diseases as well as health problems arising from toxic materials coming from industrial and related activities. Four million infants and children die every year from diarrhoea diseases, largely as a result of contaminated food or water, hundreds of million suffer from intestinal parasitic diseases while two million people die from malaria each year and another 267 million are ill at any given time (Annalee Yassi *et al*, 2001; WHO 1993; 1998a). These health conditions affect children and women in a special way as they are known to bear more of the consequences of environmental abuse and degradation.

For instance, the stratospheric ozone protects the biosphere from potentially damaging doses of ultra-violet-B (UV-B) radiation. Small quantities of the UV-B have been found to be essential to human health acting as a catalyst in the generation of vitamin D. Recent depletion of the stratospheric ozone could lead to significant increased in UV-B reaching the earth's surface. Increased exposure has been found to cause damaging effects on the skin, eye and the immune system (CIESIN 2003). In the same way, an accidental or deliberate abuse of the environment poses a significant threat to the health of present and future population.

From the above, it is clear that, there exists an inextricable link between human health and the environment. This link has been described by the WHO (1992) to consist of an interaction between human activities, the various components of the environment and health. (See Figure 18.1

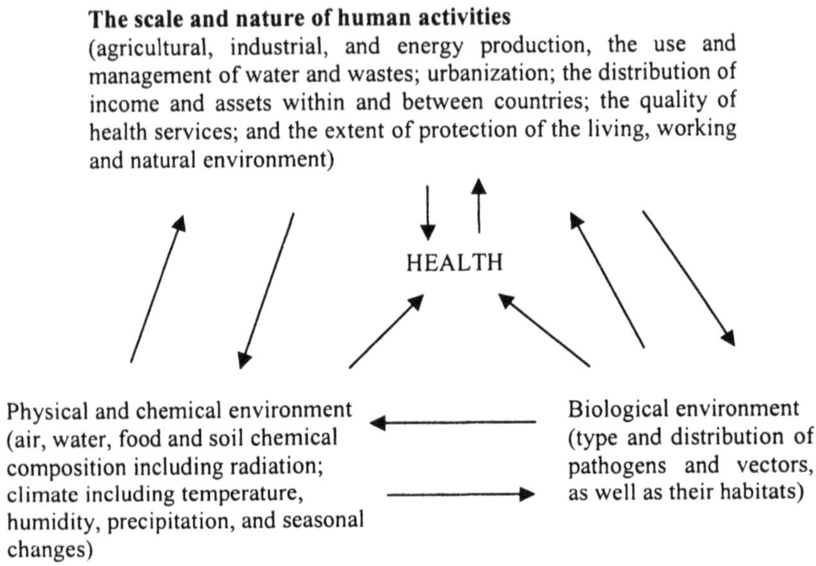


**Fig 18.1: Interaction between Human Activities and Environmental Factors (WHO, 1992)**

## CURRENT ENVIRONMENTAL HEALTH SITUATION IN DEVELOPING COUNTRIES

If we were to accept the World Health Organisation (1948) definition of health, it will be appropriate, therefore, to say that environmental health services are those efforts which are primarily concerned with the physical and mental well-being of people. However, while the big question now is: How much of these services are we providing our people and of what benefit are the services to their health? The answer is that the services provided presently are just very scanty with little or no positive effect on their health.

Despite our long year of sanitary services being provided by governments at various levels, the majority of health problems affecting our people are those arising from our environment. One does not need to be convinced that a people's health depends on services which assure that water, food, shelter, soil and atmosphere are both safe and sufficient. This has been the basis for public health activity and is found to be closely associated with control of serious and widespread epidemics. Thus, public health officials, particularly in the developed countries, continue to recognise that a primary purpose of environmental health programme is to establish, provide, and maintain conditions necessary for the prevention of communicable diseases. This means constant vigilance to see that water supplies are completely safe, milk is pasteurised, food is properly prepared and handled, rodents and insects are kept in check and wastes are disposed of so as not to pollute the environment or promote breeding of insects and rodents. All these are the traditional sanitation activities of public health. However, with man's ceaseless manipulation of his surrounding, it has been recognised that there are other elements in the environment which affect health. These include air free of excessive man-made pollution, control of occupational diseases, regulation of exposure to ionising radiation, accidents, suitable housing in a pleasant, quiet environment, and other items having no direct relationship to sanitation. Even while efforts are being made by our government towards sanitation, the results are not impressive judging from the rates at which a number of communicable diseases continue to affect our people.

Water and food are involved in disease communication where the channel of infection is the mouth and intestinal tract. In most developing countries, water-borne diseases such as typhoid and paratyphoid fever, dysentery, infectious hepatitis, guinea worm, and cholera remain leading cases of illness and death. For example, studies have shown that a greater majority of Nigerians do not have access to safe water supply; in urban communities less than 50% had a domestic supply while 20% use communal water taps, but the supply was often interrupted. In rural areas, the situation is worse as almost 70% of the population rely on unsafe sources of water supply such as streams and ponds.

The overall picture of the sewerage and waster water disposal facilities is even gloomier than that of the water supply. Less than 30%

of the urban populations are served by a public sewerage system while just a little over 40% have their own domestic systems. In rural areas over 60% of the population have inadequate facilities for excreta disposal, and primitive practices of making use of the surroundings for excreta disposal often lead to unnecessary illness, debility and death (UNICEF 2001).

Malaria eradication is still a big, future job in many tropical countries, especially with resistances developing to insecticides and anti-malaria drugs. New dams and irrigation projects are increasing the already high rate of schistosomiasis, an infection from contact with water contaminated by small, free-swimming cercaria which develops in the snails. Rustic and improvised housing is commonly made of the most convenient, locally available materials, such as straw and palm leaves in some regions and mixtures of mud, straw, and bamboo elsewhere. Water may be taken from somewhat distant streams, from dug well subject to contamination, or from ponds or improvised catchments areas to collect rainwater. More cities due to rapid urbanisation are springing up with several industries being established. Changes in the environment require parallel adjustment in environmental health services. The most conspicuous of the forces of change has been modern technology in a rapidly expanding economy. The impact of this force, in consuming forests and minerals and generating waste products and stresses, has been to degrade the environment and deplete the natural resources. The frequent oil spill in the oil producing areas of the country and the attendant effects on the people's health is becoming a problem yet to receive adequate attention.

All these are just a few of the environmental health problems confronting us. Yet how much are our governments addressing themselves to these problems? More efforts are concentrated on the curative aspects at the expense of preventive aspects of health services. Some governments are spending unnecessarily huge amount of money on drug importation believing this step to be the most appropriate to provide health care to the people. The fact is that this amount will continue to multiply annually with less positive result. This will happen as a result of our inability to understand the approach to the solution of our problems. As mentioned earlier, the majority of the disease agents affecting the health of our people emanate from their environment. It is, therefore, to this environment we should direct our attention if success is to be achieved in our attempt to stamp out these diseases.

The number of endemic disease in our community is malaria. A patient treated for this disease is bound to visit the doctor again and for as many times as possible thereafter as a result of infection. This is happening because he goes back to the same mosquito infested environment only to be reinfected by malaria. This is just one of many conditions common in our community. Cholera outbreaks and other gastro-intestinal diseases are becoming an annual event in many parts of the tropics.

A number of studies have shown that the tropical environment is so infested with disease agent and that an average person carries at least one disease agent or the other particularly parasites in his system. There is no way in which these diseases can be controlled without adequate emphasis on environmental health activities.

Unfortunately, one can say that environmental health activities are not given the attention they deserve. Some governments have to be persuaded to even mention something like that in their budgets not to talk of giving adequate funding. This may be due to lack of knowledge as to what environmental health activities involve. To some governments, all that is involved in environment health activities consists of the pulling down of the so called unwanted structures, and sanitation of the environment through garbage collection which in most cases is inadequately planned and poorly executed. However, there is much more involved in environmental health activities than the one presently being carried out by various national, state and local governments.

## ENVIRONMENTAL FACTORS AFFECTING HEALTH

There is hardly any environmental factor that does not have a measurable effect on health either directly or indirectly. It is the characteristic and nature of exposure to each factor that bring about variation in terms of the manifesting health effects. However, some of these factors are examined below:

**Air Pollution**

Air pollution continues to be a widespread problem in many countries causing preventive death, cancer and long-term damage to respiratory and cardio-vascular system. Air pollution also reduces visibility, damages crops and buildings and deposits pollutants on the soil and in bodies of water where they affect the chemistry of the water and the organism living there. Based on the six currently found air pollutants for which health related standards have been established, about 113 million people in the US live in areas designated as no attainment areas by US Environmental Protection Agency.

Automobiles concentration and use increase the chances of air pollution particularly in urban centres. Industrial processes are also a major source of such pollution.

**Water Pollution**

Provision of adequate water supply is fundamental to good health and also to maintaining good sanitation. Water must be available in the required amount so that certain activities for which water would be required could be met. Apart from this, drinking water is expected to meet minimum criteria of purity and potability to render it free from disease-causing agents, whether biological or chemical. This is the primary goal of water supply systems. The problems of water pollution are enormous in many countries. These problems may result from many sources ranging from point to non-point sources. Surface water sources are prone to contamination from run-offs, deposition of pollutants of various characteristics and sources. Underground sources may become polluted due to underground seepage or the dissolution of organic minerals into the water.

The presence of these and many contaminants in water has been known to cause many health problems depending on whether the agent is biological, physical or chemical. Frequently experienced are conditions such as typhoid, and parasitic infections (e.g. dracontiasis, schistosomiasis, etc) among others. The contamination of water sources often time reduces the value to which the water could have been subjected.

## Waste

The problem of waste management has become one of the major challenges of environmental health particularly in many of the least developed countries. Apart from the heaps of waste often found uncollected which constitute an eye saw in many cities of these countries, industrial and commercial activities produce wastes that may be toxic in characteristics which may be collected together with domestic wastes. Toxic and hazardous substances including low level radioactive wastes deposited on land are carried far from their sources by air, surface water, groundwater and runoffs into streams, lakes and seas where they accumulate in the sediments beneath the water. The widespread use of pesticides in agricultural and other uses also increase the concentration of these toxic materials in the environment.

The health implications of defective waste management system are believed to be serious. The main problems, apart from the general unsightliness, include pollution of surface and underground water sources, vermin infestation, possibility of fire outbreak and soil pollution. The effects of these on man are incalculable.

## Unhealthy Homes and Communities

Human shelter and habitation play a significant role in the determination of health and, therefore, houses in which man would live is required under the law to meet specific health and sanitary requirements. The essence of this is to ensure that conditions prevailing within human habitations are those that could promote health and well-being. It is required that such facilities as basic sanitary facilities like adequate sanitary toilets, kitchen, water supply, facilities for waste disposal, adequate ventilation, etc must be provided. The presence of necessary facilities enhances health within individual living premises. Their absence however encourages gross abuse of the immediate living environment resulting into condition such as littering of refuse, indiscriminate defecation, poor ventilation, and soil pollution. The maintenance of the sanitation and hygiene of individual premises promote the hygiene of the entire community which is a prerequisite to effective communal health.

**Animal Health Problems**

Animals have provided man with a source of food, as a means of transportation, as a source for improving farming and hunting, and as a pet. By way of contrast, the disadvantage shows that some animals are a source of direct physical danger to man and indirectly, some serve as reservoirs and transmitters of diseases. It is discovered that well over one hundred diseases of animal are transmissible to man and there is no doubt that the number will continue to increase as investigative methods improve and man does not stop to apply himself to a study of his nature and his environment. Diseases of this nature are termed zoonoses (WHO, 1976; USDHEW, 1973). Success in the control of these diseases particularly in the developed nations has been attained not only by an individual or by a group of individuals of like preparation and training but by the combined skills of a variety of specialists. This is exactly the interdisciplinary cooperation otherwise known as team approach, which is the keystone of public health practice.

The zoonotic diseases constitute a source of ill health and poverty as a result of the acute or chronic infections they cause in human beings, and large economic losses to agriculture and trade. A number of zoonoses result from occupational exposure, such as leptospirosis among rice field workers, anthrax and erysipelas among butchers, or brucellosis among those working with cattle, sheep and goats. Other diseases may result from direct exposure to or bite of companion animals, such as ringworm from dogs and cats, rabies from dogs, toxoplasmosis from cats or psittacosis from some birds. Tuberculosis, hydatidosis, trichinosis and tapeworms are among a number of diseases that man can acquire through ingestion of infected animal tissues.

The prevention and control of the zoonoses in man depend largely on the control of these diseases in animals. It has been observed that these diseases by their nature cannot be eradicated by the separate offers from health and agricultural authorities. The best approach to achieve an effective control of a zoonosis is by coordinating the efforts of public health, agriculture and other groups.

### Poor Care for Food Safety

Food constitutes in no small way a viable medium for disease producing organisms to thrive. Public health standards expect food to be handled in such way as not to expose the consumers to any health risk. Ensuring food safety is a task that goes beyond activities in food selling premises. As a matter of necessity, it should start from the point of production, preparation, sale and till the point of consumption. The objective of food hygiene and safety is to protect food meant for human consumption from any form of contamination in the overall interest of public health. When food and other related products are not adequately protected, the health of the consumers is jeopardised. Many outbreaks of food related diseases have been reported in many parts of the world. Some of these outbreaks have resulted into loss of lives from diseases such as typhoid, salmonelosis, bovine tuberculosis, parasitic infections, among others.

### Global Environmental Health Approach

Environmental health used to be seen as only a local issue or at best a national one and thus, efforts at addressing it were limited to those levels. Increased travel and improved technology, communication and computer technology are making the world a smaller place which has been described as a global community having resources including water, air, soil shared across national and international boundaries.. Activities in one place are really affecting lives at the other places. In this wise, it has become necessary that environmental health is seen beyond a local or national issue. A global approach in planning, implementation and monitoring is required. This approach will accelerate action at controlling the factors and also increase the potential impact of all mitigation measures. This should be the modern day approach to addressing environmental health problems.

## APPROACHES TO IMPROVING ENVIRONMENTAL HEALTH

Improving environmental health has the potential to improve and protect health of billions of people all over the world. This action would require a new approach rather than previous approaches that have failed in many places. The need to create a supportive environment for health and well-being that will focus on the following goal is fundamental. They are:

(i) Ensuring freedom from major health hazards.
(ii) Satisfying the basic needs for health living conditions.
(iii) Facilitates equitable social interactions.

In doing these, there is need to ensure commitment to the *Healthy Peoplė 2010*, environmental health goal which is to **promote health for all through a healthy environment** (Upstill, 2002; CDC 2004). Pursuing the object of this goal will require that commitment is ensured to adequately address issues bothering on all environmental factors affecting health to mitigate against their continued negative impact on health.

In particular, there is need to:

1. Bridge the gap between environmental and public health. This will require strong commitment by public health and environmental agencies and systems to sit at the same planning table. It must be understood at the level that:
   (i) The solution to environmental health problems lies on joint approach. Where environmental health skills are incorporated into multidisciplinary and intersectoral collaboration, significant improvements in quality of life and well-being can be achieved, and these collaborative efforts and support make healthy choices easy, by maintaining improvement and encouraging good personal choices (WHO 1998b).
   (ii) New and innovative approaches are needed to integrate and operationalise concepts of environmental sustainability into economic and community development.
   (iii) Wide range reforms are also needed to deal with the assessment and management of environmental health risks within a framework of mutual collaboration, communication and coordination between environmental and public health.

2. There is need for a stronger public health focus in national planning for sustaining the new frontier (Upstill, 2002). This as a matter of necessity would require:
   (i) That environmental health sub-sector (a major aspect of public health) get serious about highlighting the significance of fundamental determinants of population health.
   (ii) Awareness and understanding about health determinants and population approach in correlation with environmental health.
   (iii) increased health sector involvement at local and state levels to address the health and environmental issues through task forces (as may be necessary) and work groups.
   (iv) That health sector has a key advocacy role to play in highlighting the links between health, environment and sustainable development.

**Specific Measures for Improvement**

Considering all that have been mentioned above and for the purpose of correcting the anomalies in our present health care delivery system in which an almost complete neglect of environmental health services is in existence, there is the need to remind the various governments to be aware of the full areas of coverage of environmental health activity which can have positive effect on the physical and mental well-being of the people.

*Water Supply Control*

It is difficult to figure out the extent of government's commitment in actualising the policy of supplying and guaranteeing safe water to the people. In a well-organised society, effective control of water supply is a major responsibility of the government through a specific ministry. This involves planning, review and approval of proposed sources, treatment, storage, and distribution systems; periodic inspections, and routine laboratory examination. Drinking water standards should be established to take care of water supply sanitation supervision procedures. Among these procedures should be an evaluation by the environmental health department, of the source, treatment process, storage facilities, and distribution system. The standards must suggest the number of samples per month to be collected from various points within the distribution system in order to conduct tests for microorganisms of the coliform group. Standards should also be given for colour, turbidity, odour, taste, total solids, chlorides, and various chemicals and materials which may be toxic and objectionable.

Where there is no pipe borne water, it is the role of the environmental health department to advise on measures to be adopted to purify water obtained from other sources such as rivers, wells and boreholes. For each of the sources, provision must be made to ensure the quality of water and the protection of health of the people.

*Food Hygiene*

It is part of the functions for the Ministry of Agriculture to control those diseases (e.g. tuberculosis and brucellosis) of cattle that are transmissible to man. However, it is at the same time important to prevent transmission of human pathogens from milk handlers to milk.

The main factor in control of milk-borne disease is pasteurisation followed by processing and packaging in a manner to prevent recontamination. Therefore, Public Health Services should provide detailed explanations with adequate consultation or supervision, of all important features of dairy farm and milk-processing sanitation. The most common test is the standard plate count, which indicates, principally, improper clearing of equipment and inadequate refrigeration. Tests which environmental health department should perform on milk samples include: tests to discover watering of milk; butterfat tests; non-fat solid tests; bioassay tests for vitamins; tests for radio nuclides – this is most significant in countries where nuclear bombs are being tested. Other tests are microbiologic growth-inhibiting tests for presence of antibiotics used to treat cows; and insecticide residue tests to determine that milk meets the "zero tolerance" requirement for chlorinated hydrocarbons.

Control of dairy products, other than milk, is also very important. These include ice cream, butter, cheeses, etc. They should be made to meet the standards recommended by the Ministry of Health. Other areas of milk control in which the Ministry of Health should be involved are dairy and plant inspection. Dairy inspection is very important particularly for those close to urban areas. This includes control of manure handling to minimise fly breeding and nuisance as well as proper drainage for mosquitoes control.

As to food sanitation, attention should be given to those foods served at home and those meant for public consumption. The attitude of our people towards the preparation of the food they eat at home leaves much to be desired. The kitchen where the preparation is carried out is often filthy while the processing and utensils used are far from being guaranteed for wholesome food. This can be properly corrected through health education programme of the Ministry of Health.

The governments should be directly concerned with administration of law and ordinances governing foods that are meant for public consumption. This should include preparation, processing, sale, and distribution. The objectives of these efforts are to:

- minimise food poisoning and infection;
- provide clean; sanitary, and vermin-free establishments;
- provide foods that are sanitary, safe, and wholesome;
- provide sanitary utensils; and
- regulate, to a degree, the aesthetic conditions of food establishments as they broadly relate to health and sanitation.

Local food sanitation programme should cover restaurants, markets, bakeries, bakery distributions, caterers, food demonstrators, itinerant restaurants, food service operations at carnivals and festivals, bars and a wide variety of other types of business and establishments. Any food establishment should have design features to exclude rodents; screens or self-closing doors to exclude flies; lighting to facilitate sanitary operation; surfaces and materials which can readily be kept clean; and equipment to protect foods from contamination by leakage by customers.

*Waste Management*

This falls into two major parts – liquid waste disposal and solid waste disposal. The main objectives in liquid waste control are to prevent contamination of surface or underground sources of water supply, to preserve the sanitary quality of waters used for swimming and recreational purposes, to avoid nuisances and health hazards from overflowing septic tank systems and cesspools, and to prevent contamination of water supply sources with chemicals, insecticides, herbicides, or other materials which may be toxic.

Liquid wastes produced by meat-packing plants, breweries, textile plants, oil refineries, paper mills and many other industries are known as industrial wastes. They are growing in volume and constitute an increasingly serious health problem without any attempt to check them.

Control of solid wastes otherwise called refuse is necessary to minimise rodent problem, insect breeding, and nuisances from improper storage and disposal, as well as to abate smoke from burning in improperly designed and operated incinerators or collection points.

It should also be mentioned here that agricultural waste produced by poultry raising in dwelling areas, rearing of cattle and other domestic animals along our streets are causing serious fly problems created by the suitable condition for fly breeding provided by manure from these animal.

Problems emanating from these areas can be competently handled within the province of environmental health activities. The "polluter pay" policy should be adopted while there is urgent need to establish a sound environmental sanitation policy.

*Housing and Environmental Inspection*

The Environmental Health Department ought to be more active in promoting and developing standards for healthful housing in any country. This can be achieved through well-organised environmental health programme. The environmental health department should be charged with providing a guide for designing new housing and for developing codes and evaluation or appraisal procedures for existing housing which cover aspects like facilities, maintenance, occupancy, and environment.

*Vector Control and Control of Animal Reservoirs of Diseases*
These include control of rodents, insects, domestic animals and pets. Rodent is the host for the flea, which is the vector of plague and endemic typhus. Anopheles mosquitoes are the vectors of malaria, an endemic disease in our community while houseflies are responsible for the transmission of a number of gastro-intestinal diseases. The control of these vectors can effectively be carried out through well-planned and well-executed environmental health activities. Involvement of veterinary professionals in the overall public health programmes will go a long way in the control of those diseases associated with lower vertebrate animals otherwise known as the zoonoses which was discussed earlier.

*Other Areas of Environmental Health Activity*
Other areas of environmental health activities to which government should pay attention are air pollution control, radiologic contamination control, occupational health, and injury prevention.

The effects of air pollution range from localised nuisance of smokes, soot, dust and odour to huge area wide fumigations which cause serious physical discomfort, possible injury of health, and sometimes deaths.

Recently, there have been some indications that many least developed countries are warming up to join the nuclear race and evidence abounds that some academic institutions are doing a lot of work at research level in this area. However, no attention is being given to the health implications of such activity. As radioactive pollution is highly hazardous to human health particularly through contamination of water, food and milk, it is the responsibility of environmental health scientist to advise and take the necessary precautions such as monitoring the environment for radioactive substances in food, milk and water.

Occupational health is one of the important areas of activity in environmental health. Health programmes particularly directed towards workers and their families are in the category of occupational health. This includes agricultural and all other kinds of occupations in addition to those found in industry. Studies have shown that workers who were exposed to certain substances, usually over an extended period of time ranging from hours to years, developed specific symptoms which came to be associated with such exposures.

At present, various governments are clamouring for the establishment of industries with little or no concern for the health of those who work in them. The time has come to involve the ministries of health actively in programmes that guarantee good health to workers. The environmental health professional is a potential member of occupational health team that is capable of taking measures that relate to control of the working environment, and control of hazard as well as prevention of occupational diseases to workers.

Injuries of all kinds are becoming a major public health problem in developing countries. It can be said that road accidents, in particular, constitute the leading cause of death in most African countries today. As in natural afflictions, such as communicable diseases the three ecological factors in these "man-made epidemics" are the host, agent and environment. Thus, in road accidents, the host is the road user who may be the pedestrian, the automobile driver and even the passenger, while the agent is the vehicle, whatever its type, its mechanical parts and its equipment, while the environment, natural and social, is the road or highway with all its components and conditioning features. The environmental health professional as a member of public health team is well-placed, particularly through his training and experience in the areas of the third ecological factor (i.e. environment), to contribute immensely to efforts directed toward the prevention of road accidents in our community.

## References

Annalee, Yassi., Tord Kjellstom and Kok de Theo Guido Hi Tee, (2001). *Environmental Health*. Oxford University Press.

CDC (2004). *Healthy People* – 2010. Environmental Health. Association for Toxic Substance and Disease Registry, Centre for Disease Control, Atlanta Ranges.

CIESIN (2003). Human Health and Global Environmental Change. Thematic Guides.

Last, J.M, (ed) (1995). *A Dictionary of Epidemiology* 3rd ed. New York. Oxford University Press.

UNEP (1993). Environmental Data Report. Nairobi. United National Environmental Program.

UNICEF (2001). State of the World Children. UNICEF.

Upstill, Carin, (2002). A Renewed Frontier: Social and Environmental Factors Affecting Health. Turning Point, State Guarantee Management Report.

U.S. Department of Health, Education Welfare (USDHEW) (1973) "Epidemiological aspects of some of the Zoonoses". Publication No. (CDC) 75-8182.

World Health Organisation (1967) Joint FAO/WHO. Expert Committee in Zoonoses Technical Report Series 378.

WHO (1992). Our Planet, Our Health. Geneva. WHO.

WHO (1997). "Health and Environment in Sustainable Development: Five years after the Earth Summit" Geneva. WHO.

WHO (1998). The World Health Report. Life in the 21st Century: A Vision for all. Geneva. WHO

WHO (1998). Problem-Based Training Exercises for Environmental Epidemiology. 901 EHG/98.2 Geneva . WHO

## *Chapter 19*

# GLOBALISATION AND ITS IMPLICATIONS ON HEALTH

*Irinoye, A.I. & Odebiyi, A.I.*

**About the contributors**
Dr A.I. Irinoye is a Principal Medical Officer at the Health Centre, Obafemi Awolowo University, Ile-Ife. His areas of interest are Health Education and Health Management.

Professor (Mrs) Adetanwa Odebiyi is a specialist in Medical Sociology. A former Dean, Faculty of Social Sciences, Obafemi Awolowo University, Ile-Ife, she is a consultant and an international scholar who has published many works widely both in national and international journals. She teaches Medical Sociology in Obafemi Awolowo University, Ile-Ife. Nigeria.

## INTRODUCTION

Globalisation refers to the processes that take place globally. Increased trade across national borders and increased foreign investments combined with free trade are generally considered among the core characteristics of present day globalisation. Information and communication technology, increased and fast travel, migration and culture are part of globalisation. New possibilities arise in the area of health. Health is a salient public good. Good health is a crucial element in human well-being and development. In developing countries, the production is too low to sustain even basic health services. There is a growing concern that globalisation increases marginalisation of the world's poorest.

In this health impact assessment, we use Lee's definition of globalisation (1) as a process of closer interaction of human activity, with spatial, temporal and cognitive dimensions. In addition, globalisation is changing the nature of human interaction across a wide range of spheres e.g. economic, political, socio-cultural, technological and environmental. This definition of globalisation as a process that occurs across different dimensions and spheres can be used to develop a conceptual framework for understanding in greater detail the diverse changes that are being brought about, and provides a basis for developing policy responses.

Globalisation is also the growing worldwide interdependence of people and countries in a close network. Globalisation has been accelerated through advances in technology more so in the last decade. This has led to the collapse of cold wars between nations, trade barriers been broken and human and material movements been cheaper, easier and faster. The world has been more integrated than ever before becoming a "family" in the global village, one family, and one world. However, raising expectations too high could lead to huge disappointment, but the opportunities for substantial improvement in global health are better now than before. For example, the General Assembly of the United Nations, for the first time in year 2002, devoted a session to health topic – HIV and AIDS. Globafund and Globaview, that is the countries contributing to the fight against AIDS, are products of globalisation. The last Summit Meetings of the G8 (the rich countries' club) have included more debates on infectious disease than on nuclear safety, (WHO 1999). The interest of these world leaders in health is being driven by increasing recognition that investment in health is a motor for development and that global security is inextricably intertwined.

Globalisation is the greatest economic event of our era. It is now bringing unprecedented opportunities, challenges and threats to the whole world. This is the global dimensions of health. The work of Dr Kelley Lee, at the London School of Hygiene and Tropical Medicine, notably an analytical framework for thinking about the "Global Dimensions of Health", guided the policy review towards a wider understanding of globalisation as processes reducing the barriers of space, time and ideas between people in the spheres of economy, environment, technology, society, culture and politics. This also represents a reduction in the ability to control many of the determinants of health from an exclusively national or local perspective.

The subsidies granted to farmers in rich countries, the term established by World Trade Organisation agreements are biased against farmers in poor counties where one of their main potential areas of competitive advantage is in the agricultural sector. The worldwide integration has however produced a whole series of consequences in the following areas: economic, political, cultural, social, environmental and health. These consequences have both positive and negative aspects:

> People's lives around the globe are more deeply, more intensely, more immediately than ever before. This opens many opportunities, giving new power to good and bad (Human Development Report, 1999).

Globalisation "has enriched the world scientifically and culturally and benefited many people economically as well" claims Nobel Prize winner in Economics, Amartya Sen. The Human Development Report 1999 points out that globalisation "offers enormous potential to eradicate poverty in the 21st century". This is mainly due to the dramatic increase in prosperity brought about by globalisation. Simultaneously the expenditure of people has also multiplied with multiplier effect on other factors needed to ensure good health e.g. cost of food, food security, cost of ample health etc. Globalisation affects all facets of human life even nature, hence, we have global warming with its attendant consequences:

> The messages of global health are not simple. We cannot say that globalisation is bad for health; neither can we say that it is good for health. We must recognise that globalisation poses threats and opportunities and that we must take responsibility

> as individuals for addressing these threats and taking opportunities to improve health in our global society. This implies being a good citizen of the world community, being informed of global issues and taking personal and collective action. (It is what Kofi Annan called 'responsible globality') (W.H.O. 1999).

Globalisation is a concept familiar to economists, the media and information technologists, but only recently coming to the attention of health professionals. It is not that the international trade of goods, services, money and people along with various diseases is new, but the accelerated speed of human interactions has alarming implications for health and society as well as potentially some great benefits in the new millennium. AIDS is a good example of an illness where the natural history and epidemiology have largely been determined by global travel and other influences such as the inequitable distribution of condoms and retroviral drug treatments because of cost. While many of the movements and forces that create globalisation are transnational, the impact is all too often felt most keenly at local level as individuals and communities become clear winners or losers from globalisation. Globalisation has emerged as a late 20th century phenomenon in response to sweeping political, economic, technological, environmental and social changes. The impact on health and health care is complex, and we are only just beginning to measure that impact on health status. The impacts of local health activities on globalisation have not been studied.

## WORLD HEALTH ORGANISATION GLOBAL HEALTH INITIATIVES

The World Health Organisation has recently initiated a new programme of work, within its Department of Health in Sustainable Development (HSD), as well as a working group on globalisation and health. The two main themes the programme is initially taking forward are global trade and health, and global governance for health.

In May 1999, the World Health Report, *Making a Difference* was published by WHO. The report asserted the goal of reducing the burden of excess mortality and morbidity suffered by the poor, stating that one billion people are entering the 21st century without benefiting from the health revolution that can transform life and health in many parts of the world. It pledges to actively counter potential threats to health, in particular malaria and tobacco.

The Keynote Address of Professor Amartya Sen, the Nobel Laureate in Economics, to the World Health Assembly pointed out that, good health is an integral part of good development and not simply a result of increased Gross National Product (GNP). Health and economic prosperity support one another because healthy people can more easily earn an income and those with an improved income will seek medical care, better nutrition and have the freedom to lead healthier lives. Policies which improve the income of the poor and provide better more appropriate health services can improve health even in the absence of economic growth and equally inappropriate policies will fail to achieve health improvement even if economic growth is achieved. This can be seen as a major restatement of health and economic policy in which health is not simply an outcome of economic development but a goal and integral element of good human development.

The eradication of Polio championed by Rotary Club has gone global; its rejection in any part of the world is a threat to global health for example:

> Leaders in the Nigerian states boycotted the first round of a campaign to immunise 63 million children across West Africa, claiming that the oral vaccine caused sterility and spread AIDS and branding the WHO campaign a US plot to depopulate Africa. *Medi-Link* Journal, Vol. 5.No 4, April, 2004.

The World Health Organisation has recently initiated a new programme of work, within its Department of Health in Sustainable Development (HSD), as well as a working group on globalisation and health. The two main themes the programme is initially taking forward are global trade and health, and global governance for health.

The UN Development Programme (UNDP) has published its *Human Development Report 1999* on globalisation. The UN Children's Fund (UNICEF) is continuing to pursue a programme of work entitled "Children in a globalising world". And the World Bank has contributed policy research to themes related to global health such as the economics of tobacco. European Council meetings have been concerned with issues of food, safety and trade.

## GLOBAL HEALTH: STAKEHOLDERS

The people whose awareness must be raised include:

- Individual citizens, patients and patient /consumer groups,
- Non-Governmental Organisations and the NHS,
- The pharmaceutical and health information industry and the corporate sector, and
- Government and international institutions.

### Globalisation and Poverty

The greatest concern about globalisation is the way it has widened the gulf between the haves and the have-nots. There is increase in global wealth with lopsided concentration in the hands of a few. More and more able-bodied beggars now roam our streets, more and more ex-convicts and those with diseases of malnutrition form public nuisance. Aids are been solicited for on a regular basis for war victims in refugee camps and rehabilitation centres. With abject poverty, household food insecurity ensures, that is, inadequate food to feed the unit family for a day, not to talk of a year. Poverty, unhealthy environment and disease soon form a vicious cycle in such a situation. The multiplier effect of these results in the emergence of chronic diseases out of epidemics, crime, stagnation and economic recession. Globalisation is synonymous with the rat-race for development. Profit maximisation at the expense of other people's lives is the order leaving many jobless and hungry. With globalisation, we now have global poverty.

### Globalisation, Conflict and Wars

Conflicts are necessary evil in any human setting. Many times these conflicts degenerate into wars leading to death, maiming and loss of property. Advances in technology have led to discovery and use of biological and chemical weapons, and other weapons of mass destruction. Globalisation has also helped in checkmating wars. The 1997 International Treaty outlawing landmines was achieved partly by using electronic mails to mobilise diverse pressure and support groups throughout the world. These and many other global humanitarian crises can be tackled with grassroot approach as a new way of conducting international diplomacy with governments and civil societies working in collaboration for common good. Access to people, strategies and information on practically anything, anywhere in the world has become quicker, cheaper and easier. This has made Food Aid, Medical Aid and Emergency Relief materials possible to victims of conflicts and wars. We also have peacekeeping mission of the United Nations coming to the rescue of refugees from war ravaged communities.

**Globalisation and Communicable Diseases**

Globalisation has brought about rapid human connections, distant places can be accessed faster, diseases as well as people can move around the globe with relative ease, including the deadly ones e.g. SARS, HIV/AIDS. "The dramatic increases in worldwide movement of people, goods and ideas is the driving force behind the globalisation of disease", explains Professor Jonathan M. Mann, an expert on epidemics. The Joint United Nations Programme on HIV/AIDS reports that:

> The world has rapidly become much more vulnerable to the eruption and most critically, to the widespread and even global spread of both new and old infectious diseases. Despite millennia of epidemics, war and famine, never before in history have death rates of the HIV-AIDS magnitude been seen among young adults", reports the Joint United Nations Programme on HIV-AIDS.

The AIDS epidemic is so overwhelming in South Africa that some public hospitals are turning infected people away. Globalisation has brought about organisations like AIDS WATCH AFRICA and GLOBAL COALITION FOR AIDS, all in a concerted effort to jointly attack a common health problem. In today's globalised world, globalised diseases need global collective action to safeguard global interests.

Increased travel and trade across borders including human trafficking and prostitution characterise globalisation. Both open for new possibilities; more contact, increased exposure to other cultures, peoples and organisms. At the same time, these contacts open for health-related risks, in the form of exposure to the unknown organisms abroad, or the swift spread of micro-organisms causing communicable diseases to spread. The pandemic and the outbreak of foot and mouth diseases among livestock last year are but the most staggering examples.

## Global Security and Health

There is as yet no commission on global security and health, but security experts are concerned about health, particularly AIDS, malaria and drug resistant tuberculosis. It is common in developing countries to watch corrupt governments use their little resources to feed its law enforcement agents in their bid to stay in power, whereas such funds will have been judiciously utilised to cater for the health of their citizenry, particularly women and children.

The 11 September 2001 Terrorist Attack on the World Trade Centre in USA is the primary reason for the heightened interest in global health issues. The terrorists used the imagery of worsening health profiles in poor countries to win sympathisers. So, the new globalisation on health issues by world leaders appears primarily to counter such terrorist propaganda. This has led to some efforts to improve the public health globally by addressing the problem of poverty and health inequalities across the globe. So far, concerns on global health issues seem to be the residue of world leaders' security policies. The most recent G8 Summit, where Africa was given 10% of its request for development and health assistance while Russia was given over thrice Africa's aid package specifically to destroy or improve the quality of its nuclear arsenals, underscores the priorities of world leaders.(Smith, BMJ 2002).

## Globalisation, Crime and Terrorism

There are laws in every society regulating human behaviours. Punitive measures are also put in place for violators of the law. However, where such punitive measures are too harsh, wrongly applied or at variance with societal expectations, human rights and other pressure groups spring into action to seek redress. Globalisation through advanced technology has provided an avenue for collaborative support from various nations to effect a change. An example of this is that of the Nigerian lady, Aminat Safiyat who the Sharia Court in Nigeria sentenced to death by stoning for adultery while the male partner had no case to answer. Due to global outcry, the said lady's fate was changed. She later found her way to Rome where she is treated like a queen now with full citizenship right.

Another case is that of Amina Lawal, a Nigerian woman of thirty years of age, who was found guilty of adultery after bearing a child outside marriage, and was sentenced to death by stoning. And on March, 2002, an Islamic Appeal Court in Katsina state upheld the death sentence.

Terrorism (bioterrorism and chemoterrorism) are some of the negative aspects of globalisation. The issue of 11 September, 2001 Terrorist Attack in America is a pointer to this. Globalisation has its own soft underbelly which can be exploited for evil machinations by terrorists. The consequences are mass death, multiple disabilities, environmental pollution and degradation. More and more refugees and returnees are seen on a regular basis with no future to look forward to. More rehabilitation camps are needed to accommodate war victims and more prisons and asylums are needed to meet their health needs. "As the multinational corporations have led the drive to globalise the world's economy, so the 'crime internationals' – the organised crime syndicates – have been quick to exploit it", explains the Human Development Report, 1999. Globalisation has accelerated crimes like human trafficking; drug trafficking, and child labour. With globalisation, comes global crime and global criminals.

## Globalisation and Natural Disasters

Natural disasters like landslides, flood disasters, outbreak of epidemics etc are better handled at the global level. When SARS broke out in China in 2003, the world was alerted within minutes and all the required data like incidence rate , attack rate, mortality rate, pattern, symptoms, diagnosis, prevention, prognosis, etc. were available to whoever cared to listen. This enabled individual countries to swing into action, health policing their borders to prevent access to the invading organism. This has gone a long way in curtailing the spread of the disease.

The technological devices of such devices like the seismograph, antiradar, nuclear detectors, scanners, etc. has assisted in no small measure in safeguarding the global environment.

## Globalisation and the Environment

The environmental movement captures the feeling of global responsibility and enables people to express their concern, gain information and take action to reduce pollution and protect endangered species. Global environmental change is beyond the scope of national controls. The environment in which we exist is dangerously polluted. Effluents from large industries do not respect frontiers from their health hazards and it is increasingly difficult to ensure that such polluters pay. Some industrial waste products are toxic and highly injurious to our health. Inordinate dumping of such waste either in the sea, air or land constitutes serious health hazard. Through the enactment of international environmental laws, globalisation has ensured the protection and policing of the environment. The workman's compensation Decree of 1987 was put in place in Nigeria and this followed the dictates of the World Trade Organization (WTO) agreement and is designed to accommodate hazards suffered in the workplace while a host of mandatory safety rules and regulations are instituted to make the workplace safe for human activities. A Global Health Award should be instituted for multinational companies with the aim of raising awareness of the impact of their actions on the health of their workers, and the communities in which they operate.

Another health threat is the global warming. This is both transborder and transgenerational. The long term impacts of this on health are uncertain. It is therefore suggested that a form of global governance and surveillance be put in place which should include some international financial structure in the form of taxation (Tobin or Carbon Taxes) to transfer costs arising from countries suffering from the health impacts of global climatic change to those which are the greatest polluters.

Some of the effects of global warming are depletion of the ozone layer. The medical effect of this is that more solar radiations now reach the earth, so we should be prepared for an increase in skin cancer and other bizarre dermatological conditions. There is also increasing global temperature with a greater potential for heat-related illnesses and deaths as well as the widespread of infectious diseases carried by insects and rodents into areas previously free from them. There is also the resultant effects of melting of the polar ice and flooding of the coastal waters.

**Globalisation and Technology in Medicine**

Technology has revolutionalised medical practice during the past decade. Access to better, faster laboratory investigations and health information system (HIS) practically anywhere in the world has become quicker, cheaper and easier. The globalisation of the media has many implications for health, many of them positive. The effectiveness of the telecommunications industry, especially satellite TV, in penetrating the remotest regions of the world is a health promotion tool that we have not yet begun to exploit. We now have automated and computerised wheelchairs and other effort-saving equipments that are remotely controlled for the disabled in our community. Technology has also provided the physically challenged with vehicles and other tools tailored to accommodate their defect while retaining functionality. Solar energy has become a valuable tool for improving the quality of life and health care for areas that would not have been accessible to quality health. Medical computers are now available, giving the necessary information, making diagnosis, recommending investigations and giving prescriptions on different ailments.

Surgical operations are now technology driven. Diagnosis can be made faster with relative ease; using medical computers with resultant improvement in the quality of patients' care. Medical recordkeeping is better, and quick retrievals, referrals, etc. can be made. Collaborative actions on health can be made via the internet.

However, there has been some untoward use of technology. The controversy surrounding the genesis of HIV as possible fallout from laboratory experimentation is one. Technology is human driven and the human interface can be manipulated for evil machinations. Such manipulations include:

### *1. Genetic Engineering*

The detection of dioxins in the food chain of Belgium producers, had countries such as Myanmar (Burma) imposing an embargo on European food imports and created a major health scare. Food safety has been a prominent issue over the past months due to the dispute with the US over hormone treated beef imports. The World Trade Organisation upheld the US right to impose sanctions in response to European objections to the import of hormone treated beef. This seems to give priority to global trade interests over local health concerns. Meanwhile, in the United Kingdom, public debate on health and the environment has continued to focus on the testing of genetically modified crops. (W.H.O. 1999.)

### *2. Cloning and Assisted Reproduction Techniques*

Cloning, is the method of artificially reproducing a group of cells that have identical genes from a single individual. This process has been widely used to genetically mass-reproduce lower animals. However, due to global outcry, this has not been extended to man. Assisted Reproductive Techniques are various forms of reproduction for infertile couples. This technology has been transferred to various countries courtesy of globalisation. This has brought joy to many childless couples.

## Globalisation and Pharmacy Practice

Pharmacists play a crucial role in the medication use process. They are expected to control the manufacture and distribution of every drug, and dose dispensed or administered to the individual patient. Pharmacists are drug use experts and they have the ultimate responsibility for the control of medication distribution even in cases of emerging pharmacy automation. All these are better enhanced through globalisation.

Drug utilisation studies or drug monitoring programmes are control strategies designed to enhance the standards of medical treatment at all levels of health care delivery system. Global disease pattern, drug usage data and studies thereof are programmed with other patient data and can be used by medical staff to provide a profile of local, national and international drug practices for any period or point in time. This will also suggest changes for the future.

On-line drug purchase, drug monitoring, control and censorship are better done as a result of globalisation. Drug production can be teleguided from the parent company to its distribution channels to the final consumer thereby eliminating fake and counterfeited drugs. There is now a global treaty to tackle the growing international trade in counterfeit drugs. In Nigeria, the National Agency for Food, Drugs Administration and Control (NAFDAC) is doing just this. Packaged foods, drugs and other health-related products are certified for human consumption on a global level via this quality assurance medium.

Globalisation ensures constant updating of new arrivals into the market, elimination of obsolete drugs and control of dangerous drugs e.g. cocaine, heroine, and cannabis. Successful globalisation is meant to improve the quality of life of every inhabitant and that of the global neighbourhood and not to endanger health through the activities of international drug barons. Patent rights from newly patented drugs can also be sought and bought by multinational companies who have the financial muscle to conduct researches and dominate the global market.

### Globalisation and Consumable Goods

There are a host of consumable goods that pose health risks, for instance cigarettes, baby formulas, alcohol, sugared drinks, and genetically engineered foods. The WHO has already instituted a Framework Convention on Tobacco Control (FCTC). This is one of the instruments of global governance required to address such global health issues. Globalisation has enhanced food security in the sense that it allows every nation to realise her food potentials for sustainable development.

## The Impact of Globalisation on Health and Safety at Work

Two departments of the United Nations recently warned that globalisation may considerably increase the number of work-related diseases and injuries in the next century. They said the pressures for deregulation of the basic standards for health and safety is growing, Dr Richard Helmer of the World Health Organization (WHO, 1999) said, "in order to reduce costs, industries with their accompanying occupational hazards are being relocated to developing countries -- home to 75 per cent of the global workforce," There are about 2.6 billion workers in the world as a whole. Dr Jukka Takala, Chief of the International Labour Organization's (ILO, 1999) Health and Safety Programme estimates that there are 250 million accidents in the workplace each year, leading to 335,000 fatalities. One million people die each year from the 160 million illnesses caused by pollution and toxic materials and processes. One hundred thousand chemicals are in use. Of these, 350 are known to be carcinogens and 3,000 are allergenic. Illnesses include respiratory and cardiovascular disease, cancer and reproductive and neurological problems.

In the least developed countries, most workers are involved in production of raw materials — agriculture and mining. This means heavy and noisy physical work, and exposure to pesticide sprays, dusts and parasitic and infectious diseases. In industrialising countries, less advanced and more hazardous technologies are used. The extent of illnesses and injuries is unknown. In industrialised countries and increasingly elsewhere, more than half the workers suffer from psychological stress.

Only 5-10 per cent of workers in developing countries and 20-50 per cent in industrialised countries have access to adequate health care (WHO, 1999).Few small-scale industries across the world are subject to health and safety provisions. The history of occupational health has been that:

> Of a continuous struggle between workers fighting for protection or compensation and their employers seeking to deny or reduce their liability for work-related diseases and injuries. As a result, the burden of disease due to occupational exposures is usually underestimated.

The WHO and ILO (1999) report highlights the terrible conditions facing workers throughout the world. It shows that the poor information about accidents and illnesses is a reflection of the low priority shown by all concerned. It says the solution is to implement "ethically correct and economically sound" measures to improve working conditions and change the existing situation "in the interests of both workers and employers." The WHO and ILO appeal to the World Trade Organization, national governments, employers, trade unions and non-governmental organisations to remedy the situation.

Whilst the WHO and ILO point to some of the implications of globalisation for health and safety, it puts forward the impossible task of changing the situation, "in the interests of both workers and employers". The interests of the working class cannot be reconciled with a system in which production is organised for the benefit of a privileged minority. Only when the mass of working people counterpoise to this an internationalist socialist strategy will a further deterioration in health and safety at work be prevented.

**Globalisation, Health and Foreign Policy**

In October, 1998, a trilateral US/UK/Canada meeting was held in Washington D C on the theme of Global Health. In matters relating to health, there is interdependence between local and global concerns. This was the opinion of Kofi Annan, United Nations Secretary-General, in his address to the World Economic Forum in Davos in January 1999 when he initiated "a global compact" of shared values, this he described as "responsible globality".

The advanced countries are largely concerned with the potential threats posed to their citizens and national interest from migration, the spread of infectious diseases, misuse of antibiotics and other risks arising from an increasing global economy. The advanced countries would buy raw materials for the poor countries at a stipend and later sell the finished product to the same countries at a ridiculously high price. Globalisation while offering many benefits, is also leading to worsening health conditions for certain population groups notably the world's poor, for instance, the subsidies granted to farmers in rich countries are virtually nonexistent to farmers in poor countries. This is one area of competitive advantage in the agricultural sector. Patent right is another issue of global interest. There are situations where medicinal raw materials are obtained from one country at little or no cost and compounded drugs from same raw materials are imported into same country at an astronomically high cost. Rights and resources should follow the demonstration of good governance as well as health need. Health is an important issue in the field of human security, human and economic development, and in relationships between countries and peoples.

## Health Impact of Globalisation on London and Impact of London on Globalisation of Health: Cultural and Social Factors

A library study on the impact of globalisation on London and impact of London on globalisation of health: cultural and social factors were done. Table 19.1 below shows a comparative study of the impact of both.

**Table 19:1 Health Impact of Globalisation on London and Impact of London on Globalisation of Health: Cultural and Social Factors**

| Impact of Globalisation on London | | Impact of London on Globalisation | |
|---|---|---|---|
| **Cultural and Social factors** | **Health Outcomes** | **Cultural and Social factors** | **Health Outcomes** |
| 250,000 Refugees and Asylum Seekers in London. | Mental ill-health, use of health services, social exclusion. | Migration to the rest of UK and overseas. | Isolation of elderly relatives. |
| 25% of London's population are black and ethnic minority communities. | Use of health services, premature mortality from Coronary Heart Diseases etc, for 1.7 million people. | London's health services are centres of excellence in teaching and research. | Setting and monitoring standards, innovation in medicine and technology. |

| | | | |
|---|---|---|---|
| Travel health and infectious diseases for 50 million travellers. | Diarrhoea, Malaria, TB, STDs and HIV. | Export of health knowledge and skills overseas. | Contributes to eliminating world poverty. |
| Poverty and inequalities in health. | Women and children, ethnic communities and the elderly are disproportionately affected by poverty. | Globalisation of financial institutions and other services. Contribution of London to creating poverty. | High mortality rates and low life expectancy in developing countries. |
| Changes in patterns of family size, structure and parenting skills. Loss of "social capital." | Teenage pregnancies Deliberate self-harm Smoking Eating disorders Substance misuse. | Healthy cities initiatives, community development, urban regeneration, all build social capital. | Associated with reduced morbidity, mortality and use of health services. |
| Smoking and the tobacco industry. | Tobacco is estimated to kill 8,000 Londoners per year. | Offices and workplaces concentrated in cities and | Opportunity towns. for effective healthy workplace initiatives. |
| Globalisation of media but loss of local knowledge of health services. | Unwanted teenage pregnancies. Poor use of General Practice services. | London's contribution to the media, entertainments industry, and culture. | Positive and negative effects on mental health e.g. substance misuses. |

**Source**: Bruntland (1999). *Introduction to the World Health Report.* (14)

From Table 19.1 above on the health outcomes of the impact of globalisation on Londoners, the following deductions can be made:

1. Influx of refugees. London has been described as a city of migrants. There was a high influx of refugees necessitating the creation of emergency camps and increase in medical personnel and services especially for malnutrition and mental health care.
2. There was also sporadic increase in communicable diseases like diarrhoea and tuberculosis (TB) to an epidemic proportion.
3. Malaria which was hitherto absent in the community was introduced.
4. There was also increase in teenage pregnancies, sexually transmitted diseases (STDs) and HIV-AIDS.
5. There was perennial search for jobs, better housing and schools which made people to leave relatives and friends behind in the city, thus, contributing to the social isolation of elderly people, often lone female pensioners. The most common health consequences are mental ill-health and poor use of services by the socially excluded.
6. Establishment of a London Health Strategy to minimise the harmful impact of globalisation.

## GLOBAL PROBLEMS: LOCAL SOLUTIONS

Globalisation is no longer an academic concept familiar only to economists, media and information technologists. Now, it is having impact on the health of populations in Britain and, therefore, becoming a local public health issue. However, it is the responsibility of practitioners, planners and politicians to address this issue. Also, it is clear that some of the solutions to globalisation are local.

This health impact assessment identifies health issues where local action in London will have a global impact. It suggests priorities for a programme of policy, action and research that will support the emerging health strategy for London as well as address some of the local implications of globalisation.

Table 19.2 below shows Global Problems, Local Solutions: An example from the London Health Strategy. Nine priorities for a programme of policy, action and research to reduce the negative effects of globalisation are given in the columns "Acting locally." They have been selected from the health impact assessment by using the criteria for "thinking globally" in Bruntland's introduction to the *1999 World Health Report.*(14) Possible targets have been suggested for discussion and adoption by local stakeholders, and the implications for monitoring, surveillance and governance are highlighted.

**Table 19. 2: Global Problems, Local Solutions: An Example from the London Health Strategy**

| Thinking Globally | Acting Locally | Possible Targets | Governance |
|---|---|---|---|
| There is the need to step up ability to deal with the rising toll of non-communicable diseases. Special attention should be given to cancer, and cardiovascular diseases. | Develop and implement a Coronary Heart Disease (CHD). strategy for ethnic minority, communities in London including diabetes and stroke. | Reduction in risk factors, complications and premature mortality from CHD, stroke and diabetes in black and minority ethnic populations. | Ethnic monitoring required. |
| There is the need to be better at responding to increasingly diverse kinds of emergencies and humanitarian crises. | Implement the recommendations in health needs assessment for refugees and asylum seekers. | Co-ordinated action to improve access to services including health advocacy, responsive information systems, partnerships and community participation in service planning. | Better systems for monitoring the numbers, background, needs and use of services. Improved screening and surveillance systems for new entrants (Port Health.) |

| | | | |
|---|---|---|---|
| There is the need to pay more attention to the delivery of high quality health care for children, adolescents and women. | Co-ordinate policies and strategies to promote the health of children young people and women | Reduction in rates of underage deliberate conceptions, suicide and self-harm, child poverty, accidents, smoking and substance misuse. | Co-ordinated surveillance systems to monitor trends of women and children in poverty. |
| There is the need to be committed to reducing the burden of sickness and suffering from communicable diseases." | Improve quality of TB services. Support TB research worldwide. Develop multi-tiered systems of governance. | Reduction in the prevalence of TB, halting the increase in incidence of TB, and preventing resistance to drug therapies. | Global and Clinical governance for TB services. Validated notification and surveillance systems for TB. |
| There is the need for a global commitment to tobacco control, and its success can point the way for effective control of other threats. | Implement and evaluate the London wide Tobacco Control Action Plan. | Reduction in rates of smoking, particularly in the target groups of young people, pregnant and low income groups. Reduction in tobacco advertising and marketing. | Monitor progress by developing city-wide audit and surveys. |

| | | | |
|---|---|---|---|
| The first priority must be to reduce – then eliminate – the debilitating excess burden of disease among the poor. | Racism in the National Health Scheme (NHS) must be acknowledged as a pre-requisite for change. Access to new services for minority ethnic users such as NHS direct should be evaluated. | Reduction in excess inequalities in morbidity and mortality from CHD, stroke, diabetes for black and minority ethnic populations. | Monitoring health outcomes and access to services for black and minority ethnic people will require ethnic monitoring. |
| The tasks (for WHO) should include setting norms and standards, generating and disseminating an evidence and information base. | Supporting and encouraging the development of health promoting settings such as healthy schools and healthy workplaces would be particularly effective in London. | Setting norms and standards, disseminating good practice for health promoting settings, especially the NHS. | Health impact assessments. |
| "There is a need to invest in expanding the knowledge base that made the 20th century revolution in health possible." | Linking WHO healthy city initiatives, and to launch London as a WHO Healthy City. | Partnership with other stakeholders to launch London as a WHO Healthy City. | Health inequalities impact assessment. |
| The tasks (for WHO) should include ensuring that critical research and development for the | Ensure that the health needs of the poor both in London and globally | | |

| | | | |
|---|---|---|---|
| poor receives finance. | are included in the research agenda. Include the health impact of globalisation on R&D agendas. | | |

**Source**: Bruntland (1999). *Introduction to the World Health Report.* (14)

## DISCUSSION

This chapter examines the sphere of cultural and social factors and how they are affected by globalisation, and explains why it is a local issue. It also considers the positive and negative effects of globalisations, i.e. (winners and losers) on population and individuals.

It is not easy to quantify the overall effects of globalisation on a single health outcome such as tuberculosis and identify where good governance at different levels of authority from the individual to the international would minimise the harmful effects of globalisation.

This chapter identifies populations most at risk, i.e. (the "losers" from globalisation) so that appropriate interventions can be targeted. It has also tried to demonstrate that not only globalisation is a local issue, but also local action will make a difference.

## CONCLUSION

Globalisation is a new phenomenon and it is still on trial. It may mean the rich continuing to neglect and exploit the poor, spending huge amount of their resources to keep out the poor, and allowing deterioration in global health and further environmental degradation. In such cases, riot will continue at the meetings of global leaders, and the world may become steadily more unpleasant for all , rich and poor. Alternatively, globalisation through increasing openness and recognition of interdependence could lead to dramatic reductions in poverty and improvements in health. Using the best of modern science and technology and the huge wealth of the rich to improve health would inspire and unite peoples all over the world. The challenge is how globalisation can be better managed to improve the situation of those who are negatively affected and to avoid harm to health and its basic social and environmental determinants. Local solutions can be found if the right to health is linked to the responsibility for good governance of health at all levels, that is, globalisation should be on every health agenda.

## References

Acheson, D. (1999). *Independent Enquiry into Inequalities in Health Report*. Department of Health, London. The Stationery Office.

*Awake*, 22 May 2002, "Globalisation: Curse or Cure".

Awofeso, N., Degeling, P., Ritchie, J., and Winters, M. (2001). Thabo Mbeki and the AIDS 'jury'. *Aust. Health Review:* 74-79.

Black and minority ethnic representatives at an NHS seminar: "Towards a Health Strategy for London: Developing the Vision Together". Connaught Rooms. 19 May 1999.

Brugha, R., and Walt, G. (2001). A Global Health Fund: A Leap of Faith. BMJ.323; 152-154.

Bruntland, (1999). *Introduction to the World Health Report.* (14).

Cornia, A., Jolly, R. and Stewart, F. (1987). *Adjustment with a Human Face*. Oxford: Clarendon.

Dahlgren, G, and Whitehead, M., (1991). Policies and Strategies to Promote Social Equity in Health. Institute of Futures Studies. Stockholm.

Department of Health – Smoking kills: White paper on Tobacco. 1999. London: The Stationery Office.

Gary, Slapper and Steve, Tombs, (1999). *Corporate Crime* Longman.

Habib, N. and Behrens, R. "Global Health: A Local Issue. Travel Health and Infectious Disease". Discussion Paper for a Nuffield Trust Seminar. 14 July 1999.

Health of Londoners Project. Refugee Health in London. Available from: Directorate of Public Health, East London and the City Health Authority, Aneurin Bevan House, 81-91 Commercial Road, London E1 1RD. 1999.

Jacobson, B. (1998). Annual Public Health Report. East London and the City Health Authority.

Kawachi, I., Kennedy, B.P., Lochner, K. and Prothrow-Stith, D. Social Capital, Income Inequality and Mortality. *Am J. Public Health*. 1997; 87:1491-1498.

Kickbusch, I. "Linking the Global and the Local: Healthy Cities for Human Welfare". Paper given to a seminar on globalisation and Health at the 9th Annual Public Health Forum 1999. London School of Hygiene and Tropical Medicine.

Lee, K. "The Global Dimensions of Health". Background Paper for the Global Health, a Local Issue seminar. Nuffield Trust and Templeton College, Oxford University. 17 Feb. 1999.

Lee, K. "Globalisation and Health Policy, A review of the literature and proposed research and policy agenda". Discussion Paper No 1. London School of Hygiene and Tropical Medicine. August 1998.

Lister, G. "Global Health: A Local Issue". Framework Report. The Nuffield Trust. London. 28 February 1999.

*Medi-Link Journal*, April 2004. Vol. 5, No 4. P. 11.

McKee, M. (1999). Sex and Drugs and Rock and Roll. BMJ; 318:1300-1.

Morrow, R.H. (2002).Macroeconomics and health.BMJ. 325:53-54

NHE Exec LRO. London's Health: Developing a vision together. A Newsletter for people working to improve the health of Londoners. Issue 1 June 1999.

NHS Exec The Modernisation Plan for the NHS in London1999-2002.London Regional Office.

Parsons, L. and Whiteman, S. (1998). Bexley and Greenwich School Health Survey. Bexley and Greenwich Health Authority.

Paul, M.(1999). Report issued by the World Health Organisation and International Labour Organisation on Occupational health.

Putnam, R.D. (1993). *Making Democracy Work.* Princeton NJ: Princeton University Press.

Ramsay, S. (2002). Globalfund makes historic first round of payments. Lancet. 359:1581.

Secretary of State for International Development. Eliminating World Poverty: a Challenge for the 21st Century. Command. November 1997.

Sharma, S.S. and Meltzer, M.L. (1999). Final report from the outbreak control committee on the Hepatitis B outbreak associated with Finchley Alternative Medical Centre. Barnet Health Authority.

Sklair L. (2002). *Globalisation – Capitalism and Its Alternatives*. Oxford University Press: 45-57.

Smith, R. (2002). A time for global health. BMJ 325:54-55

United Nations Development Programme (1997). Human development report. Oxford, Oxford University Press: 82.

World Health Organisation (1999). World Health Report - Making a Difference. WHO Geneva.

World Health Organisation (2001). Macroeconomics and health: investing in health for economic development. Report of the Commission on Macroeconomics and Health. Geneva.

# *Chapter 20*

# HEALTH SECTOR REFORM

*Irinoye, A.I., Aderounmu, A.O., Ogunbunmi, P.I. & Abdulahi, M.*

**About the Contributors**

Dr Irinoye is a prolific writer on health matters. He is currently the Physician-in-Charge, R & D, Health Centre, Obafemi Awolowo University, Ile-Ife.

Dr Ogunbunmi, MBBS(Ibadan), MPH (USA), FWACP, has worked as a Consultant Physician/Senior Clinical Tutor in Fiji Island. He is currently the Medical Director of University Health Services, University of Ibadan, Ibadan.

Dr (Mrs) Aderounmu, MBBS(Lagos), MPH(Ibadan), is currently the Medical Director of Medical and Health Services, Obafemi Awolowo University, Ile-Ife.

Dr Mohammed Abdulahi holds MBBS (Maiduguri) and D.TM (USA). He is currently on secondment as the Medical Director of University of Abuja Medical Centre, Abuja. He has worked extensively in various capacities with the Federal Ministry of Health, Nigeria, and has attended and presented papers at both national and international conferences.

## INTRODUCTION

The health care system of Nigeria developed progressively from the colonial medical services that provided free curative medical services to the army and colonial masters, to the era of religious bodies and private agencies establishing hospitals, and later in 1946, the first attempt at proper planning of the health sector took place. In post Independence (1960) era, different health policies have been enunciated either as part of the national development plans or as government decisions on specific health problems.

Health sector reform is not an easy concept to define, as there are many components of reform (institutional, administrative, financing, legislative, health care delivery, among others), and not all of these may be implemented at any one time. Reform generally means to make or become better by removing or putting right what is bad or wrong; that is the removal of vices or imperfections in any system with the view of making the system work better. Health reform therefore, involves changes or modifications in the health system that brings better services and outcomes to the consumers; this can be limited to a sector of the health system or to the health system as a whole. Reform may affect only a particular segment for example, mental health reform, reproductive health reform, etc. One of the recent Nigerian health sector reform projects is *Malaria Bed Net Component*. Future Group was recently selected to manage the implementation of Insecticide Treated Bed Nets. The goal of this social marketing project is to decrease morbidity and mortality due to malaria in pregnant women and children under five years and specifically targeting poor and vulnerable groups. The project purports to increase availability and usage of high quality insecticide treated nets.

Reform can be in the form of quality, quantity or both. It can also be in the form of infrastructure, human resource, logistics, fund disbursement etc. Health is a dynamic entity which is subject to change, hence the need for reforms to meet the challenges of the times.

There is no one best reform for managing the health of a community as one operational setting with positive result in one locality may produce negative result in another. Health system reform can be local, national, regional or international. The sole objective of the reform is equifinality in terms of efficiency and effectiveness, which is, whatever approach that produces optimal result for a given time is deemed to be the best reform.

## WHAT IS A HEALTH SECTOR REFORM?

Health sector is the totality of all the people and actions whose primary and collective purpose is to improved health for all. A reform is intended to redesign the health sector in some respect. Reform is a formally designed package to contribute to or develop an existing sector. Health sector reforms are a combination of changes in the design, management and delivery of health care services in the health sector of a community, state or country. It is a broad-based, purposeful and sustainable fundamental change in the function, structure and performance of health sector in order to deliver efficient, quality, affordable, accessible, effective and equitable health care services to the populace. For a reform to be authentic, it must have the enabling laws to support it. This should state clearly the members of the committee charged with the reform, the need for the reform , the scope, the objectives of the reform, the reform process, the timeframe and how to evaluate, monitor and control the reform.

A health care reform must be holistic (comprehensive) and accommodate the views of all stakeholders including health care professionals, academics, community organisations, political parties, general public and the insurance industry.

Reforms in the provision of health care services must be:

- community driven,
- community mobilised, and
- community empowered.

## WHY REFORMS?

In a dynamic environment where new diseases are emerging and defying medical solutions, it is only necessary that reforms are instituted to accommodate the challenges and opportunities of our times. Reforms occur not only in the health sector but in all sectors where performance per unit time is sub-optimal, hence the need to re-engineer, re-strategise, and re-prioritise right size. The challenge of health reform is to create real partnerships with all stakeholders. Reform can be incremental improvements or radical transformations.

The objectives of health sector reform include:

(i) improving health, even in poor resource settings;
(ii) mobilising resources to improve health status, and ensuring that these resources are allocated efficiently and used effectively;
(iii) ensuring that subsidies benefit poor and vulnerable groups; and
(iv) improving the quality and client-focus of both public and private health services.

Reforms are necessary where the following occur:

- Potential health gains not achieved due to poor performance of many existing health systems,
- Shift from input-oriented approach to one that stresses improving performance in terms of measurable OUTCOMES,
- Movement from State-controlled economies to market economies,
- Insufficient funding for health in times of financial crisis,
- Lack of basic health services for many citizens,
- Poor quality, low accountability and inefficiency of existing health services.
- Lack of adequate managerial skill.

## REFORM MEASURES

Reform measures must consider the following:
1. Financing and resource allocation,
2. Provider payments, incentives & motivation,
3. Organisational change,
4. Laws and regulation,
5. Promotion of healthy behaviour, and
6. Culture.

## GUIDING PRINCIPLES FOR HEALTH SECTOR REFORM

The following are some of the principles which should guide the designing of our various reform proposals:

- Any reform measures must maintain existing strengths of accessible and equitable service, affordable prices and good quality.

- The government must continue to bear a major part of the public health care costs, but with public subsidies targeted at areas of greatest needs.
- The pursuit for better health is a shared responsibility among the individual, the community and the government.
- There must be sufficient safeguards to ensure that no one is denied adequate medical care because of insufficient means.
- The existing dual public and private systems, serving complementary roles, should be maintained, but with better collaboration between them.
- The new health care system should be developed in collaboration with the community and changes must be gradual and evolutionary.
- Public resources should be used efficiently, and targeted at areas of greatest needs. Those who have the means should bear an affordable share of the medical expenses they have incurred.

## PROCESS OF HEALTH SECTOR REFORM

- Begin by identifying desired outcomes that are not being achieved, for example, reduction in maternal mortality,

- Diagnosing components of the health system-instrumental goals or performance criteria that are responsible for deficiencies,

- Prescribe different kinds of intervention to bring about the desired change, and

- Implement the interventions.

The reform initiatives should centre around three main pillars of the health care system namely: service delivery, quality assurance and long-term financing. These initiatives should aim at enhancing the sustainability of the health care system which will be able to continue to meet rising public demands due to an aging population and advances in medical technology.

In implementing the reform proposals, the public should be able to see for themselves quickly the tangible benefits of the reform. The short and medium-term measures should include:

- Revamping the role of the Ministry of Health (MOH) as health advocate and strengthening of prevention care.
- Promoting family medicine with the transfer of general outpatient service from General Hospital to the Community Hospital Authority (CHA).
- Encouraging continuing medical education for all health care professionals.
- Introducing cost containment measures by CHA.
- Revamping of fees structure for public health care services, including the setting up of a safety net for the poor and the needy.
- Setting up working groups to explore ways to improve the interface between the public and private health care sectors.
- Implementing the package of quality assurance proposals to enhance standard.
- Setting up a network of community care programmes to support patients in the community.
- Reducing time wasting bureaucratic bottlenecks in the administration and implementation of health care programmes.
- Reward system should be performance based with staff right-sizing of each unit of health care.

## ELEMENTS OF HEALTH SECTOR REFORMS

The elements of the health sector reform are:

- Ideological Change
  Health services no longer free for all diseases and at all levels,
- Managerial Change
  Improving performance of the Civil Service
  Improving role and function of Ministry of Health,
- Organisational Change

Decentralisation/Local ownership,
- Financial Change
  Broadening health financing options; cost sharing,
- Public-Private Mix
  Introducing managed competition, and
- Health Research
  Providing the evidence base.

## STRATEGIC PLANNING COMMITTEE

A strategic planning committee is an integral part of any reform process and this will sharpen the focus of such a reform.

### Purpose

The purpose of the Strategic Planning Committee is to advise the Board on current and anticipated community and regional health needs, new technology, new medical advances, and to develop or recommend approaches for addressing such needs.

### Responsibilities

The responsibilities of the strategic planning committee are to:
- Attend Annual Strategic Planning Retreat,
- Keep abreast of major trends, issues and technologies in the delivery of health care which may affect health care utilisation,
- Keep abreast and review community health status issues and make recommendations to Board,
- Suggest health sector review, its mission, roles, and vision statements to align with anticipated health needs when deemed appropriate,
- Oversee strategic planning process, approve the Strategic Plan and recommendations to the Board of Directors,
- Monitor progress towards the strategic plans offer at least twice in a year and recommend changes for the strategic direction of the sector,
- Understand long-range options and offer feedback and recommendations to the Board regarding major service delivery

changes,

- Propose investigating partnerships with outside institutions and organisations when appropriate, and
- Review physician supply and demand for Health Sector's service area.

## HEALTH SECTOR REFORM: DRUG UTILISATION AND MANAGEMENT

Until recently, Nigeria use to be a dumping ground for all forms of chemicals in the form of drugs. The National Agency for Food, Drugs Administration and Control (NAFDAC) has brought some sanity into the production, quality control and storage of processed food and drugs for human consumption. This agency should be upgraded to the status of a ministry with various departments and not just a parastatal. Pharmaceutical sector of the organisation, management, procurement, production and quality control, storage and distribution, pharmaceutical financing and pricing are all areas begging for reform.

## HEALTH SECTOR REFORM: GENDER AND EQUITY

Gender is a significant marker of social and economic vulnerability which manifest itself in inequalities of access to health care and in women's and men's different positioning as users and producers of health care. There are two approaches to this, the "gender inequality" approach and the "women's health approach".

Gender equity is one of the major research priorities of the health sector reform programme. Gender is important in the consideration of access to health care services and the impact of health care services on households. Gender and equity issues in the provision of health care services for diseases like tuberculosis, cancer, HIV/AIDS. On the health service provider side, gender is also important in the distribution of males and females at different levels of service personnel. The Human Resource Development work should consider the implications of reform for the management of change and staff development.

Differences in literacy and education levels amongst males and females also have implications for self-medication and care at home and in the community. The development of services to support care in the community must respond to the disproportionate care burden that falls on women. The programme should respond to this issue by contributing to the collaborative work on care and support for people with HIV/AIDS. The value that a society places on male and female roles is often different but whatever the situation is, equity and fairness in health care services must prevail.

## HEALTH SECTOR INFORMATION TECHNOLOGY REFORM

There must be transformation from the manual to electronic health records. This is essential in the health care system as it puts the needs and values of the patient first and gives patients information they need to make clinical and economic decisions in consultation with dedicated health care professionals. Most of our health institutions houses at least one mortuary for outdated, condemned and unserviceable gadgets and appliances.

Health electronic libraries can be established. An electronic health black box can be created for every citizen, this is similar to crew black box in an aircraft. This black box should contain the individual's bio data, national registration number, major health problems or permanent disabilities, criminal records, etc.

## HEALTH SECTOR REFORM AND HUMAN RESOURCES

The relationship between health sector reform and the human resources issues should focus on how the new processes will modify the ways in which health workers interact with their workplace, and the ways in which the workers will influence the reforms. The impact the health sector reform will have on the critical aspects of the health workforce, including labour conditions, degree of decentralisation of management, required skills and the entire system of wages and incentives. Human resources in health, crucial as they are in implementing changes in the delivery system, have had their voices heard in many subtle and open ways – reacting to transformations, supporting, blocking and distorting the proposed ways of action. Individual or collective actions of human resources will shape the reforms, by spotlighting the reform process, the workforce reactions and the factors determining successful human resources participation. This should provide a more powerful way of predicting the effects and interactions in which different "technical designs" operate when they interact with the human resources they affect. Any reform needs human beings for implementation. This leads to the controversial issue of leadership in the reformation process. A few experimentation have been carried out in this respect with varying degrees of successes. Medical experts have held the mantle of leadership of the health sector in most health institutions while managers in the industry have had cause to manage health institutions in some cases. The outcomes of both experiments are far from the ideal. It will therefore be beneficial if the curriculum of training of health care workers is modified to incorporate some managerial skills, and as they progress on the job, management training is made a must for would-be leaders of health establishments. Also, physicians with specialist training should head the various specialities and sub specialities in the health care service provision.

What changes are necessary in human resources (HR) planning and management to improve poor people's access to quality health services? This chapter suggests a balanced effort in four areas of human resources:

- Improving efficiency in the use of HR;
- Enhancing equity in the distribution of HR;
- Improving staff motivation and performance; and
- Improving HR strategic planning and capacity in Ministries of Health.

This chapter details various recommendations for better human resources (HR) management and these are:

- Improvements in efficiency which can result from a number of initiatives such as staff right sizing, changing the skill mix of staff, and making employment arrangements more flexible. Not all of these approaches have been implemented in developing countries, and where they have, they are not always popular.
- Poorer and more remote areas of a country often fail to attract sufficient numbers of well-qualified staff. The solutions to this problem include incentives to employees, and reliance on provision of contracting or other involvement from the private sector.
- A step-forward is to improve the training of health personnel at

various levels. This can be undertaken either through developing training curricula or hiring primary care specific professionals.

- Where the essential needs of staff are met, and incentives are put in place, performance should improve. Financial constraints may count against such approaches.
- Crucial to improved HR management of the health sector is the ability to plan strategically and develop policy. This will require good leadership, staff capacity and collaboration with other sectors and professional bodies.

The management of human resources in the health sectors of developing countries remains poor. A lack of adequate training, low capacity and underfunding continue to hinder the development of this sector. However, it is widely acknowledged that improved HR management is an essential step towards better overall performance of health sectors in both poor and wealthy countries.

**Capacity Building**

The aim of capacity building is to improve management skills of the Community Health Management Teams and implementors of the Health Sector Reforms.

**Advocacy and Coordination**

Reforms in the health sector should be a joint venture comprising the Federal, State and Local Government Civil Service and stakeholders in the private sector. There should be coordination of the reforms in the Health Sector, Civil Service and Local Government, among others to ensure closer collaboration and implementation.

**Partnership**

Partnership should be formed at the community level among Non-Governmental Organisations/Community based organisations, bilateral donors and across communities in planning, monitoring and evaluation of community health plans.

## Strengthening Primary Health Care (PHC)

Primary Health Care (PHC) should be strengthened to be able to carry out documentation, dissemination and coordination of experiences and use them as a basis for replication.

## Legal Framework

There should be meaningful tort legal framework to support the reform process in order to facilitate the acceptability of health financing and management systems. Other areas to be covered by the law are malpractice reform to reduce the number of frivolous suits and medical liability Insurance Coverage.

## Sustainability

Sustainability of the Health Sector Reforms should be in terms of operations and financing. Community Health Management Teams (CHMTs) are a very important component and they should be empowered through capacity building.

## HEALTH SECTOR REFORM FUNDING

Increasing costs and competition in the health care sector requires new and innovative strategies for resource management. As part of the reform in the health sector in Nigeria, the government has put in place the National Health Insurance Scheme (NHIS). This is financed out of tax on wage and salary income and similar tax rate on the income of self-employed, and people living on pension or welfare. This is a form of medical savings account. Social insurance is now internationally accepted as applying to Schemes, which provide benefits to individuals, their employers or both. The NHIS is a new reform in the health sector in Nigeria. The opportunities facing the scheme include:

- Development of the health insurance to a self-sustainable one
- Improving the services at all levels
- Coordination and cooperation system among all health care providers.

### University Health Insurance Scheme

If a social insurance arrangement is made at the university level, it is called University Health Insurance Scheme. The university receives subvention from the authorities that gave birth to its existence and in most cases, provides free medical services for its staff, members of their families and students through their health centres. This is not totally new or lacking in the university system since each university has got at least one form of health insurance arranged partly or wholly for her workers from its inception.

## ROUTE TO IMPROVED HEALTH CARE

Government policies affect health reforms and give the directions of health activities even in other non-health sectors. The health system comprises provision of health services. Other components of the health system, supply in health related factors, household resources and community factors also play major roles in health roles outcomes.

### Good Health Outcomes

The measurement parameters of good health outcomes and effective coverage for the poor are:

- Physical accessibility,
- Availability of human resources,
- Availability of material resources,
- Organisational quality,
- Relevance of services,
- Timing and continuity,
- Technical quality, and
- Social responsibility and accountability.

The framework below can be used for the assessment of the performance of the reforms in the health systems.

- Desired outcomes
  - Reduction in maternal mortality

- improvement in infant/child mortality
- improvement in fertility rates and family planning
- Decrease in HIV/AIDS transmission, etc.

• System Wide Performance
 - Assessibility
 - Equity
 - Quality
 - Efficiency
 - Sustainability
 - Accountability.

• Reform Change Assessment
 - Input
 - Process
 - Output.

• Reform Levers
 - Funding
 - Resource allocation
 - Payment structure
 - Organisational structure
 - Regulatory laws
 - Reformation of healthy behaviours.

• Monitoring and Evaluation.

## CHALLENGES OF HEALTH SECTOR REFORM

The challenge of health sector reform efforts is to determine the appropriate mix of major levers of health sector reforms-financing, organisation, provider motivation, regulation and promotion of healthy behaviour that most effectively influence improvements in the process of health care and in turn health outcomes.

## Challenges of the Reform Measures

### *Financing and Resource Allocation*

- Various financing options have weakness,
- No 'quick fixes',
- Improving impact and distribution of public finance depends on other reforms, for example, strategic purchasing, and
- Additional sources may sometimes offer ways of increasing revenue, but carry important equity risks.

### *Provider Payments, Incentives and Motivation*

- What mechanisms do we currently rely on to motivate providers to provide high quality services?
- What are the problems? Do we need to use the old system better or reform it?
- What can we measure that we can base payments on? How robust are our measures?
- Who is likely to oppose reform (or components of reform) and what actions are they likely to take?

### *Provider Payment Options*

- Fee for service – incentive to increase unit of services or provide more expensive ones, Provider is 'king'; asymmetry is information
- Salary – incentive to serve fewer clients; leave work early; better salary, strong meritocracy, supervision and performance. Monitoring and Evaluation can be used to correct negative incentives.
- Capitation – strong incentive for efficiency and continuity – may cause undersupply of services or sacrifice quality.
- Case per episode – incentive to improve efficiency per case; tend to treat patients in more expensive diagnostic related category-preventive service tend to be neglected.
- Global Budget – if funds run out, incentive to undersupply through rationing; no direct incentive for efficiency.

- Itemised Budget – No direct incentive for efficiency.

***Organisational Change***

Optimal service delivery that:

- Is performance oriented
- Accountability to clients

Changes needed in providers' organisation and management of services from a health system organisation to a client-centred organisation

***Reforming Ministry of Health***

- Decentralisation – deconcentration and devolution of power
- New public-sector management - adoption of private sector management that is result-oriented, manages resources/staff, encourages managers accountability and sets targets
- Separation of Finance from Provision.

***Laws and Regulations***

- Setting priorities
- Creating enabling policies to achieve vision
- All inclusive legal framework-covering public and private including traditional practice.

## GENERALISED COST EFFECTIVENESS ANALYSIS: AID TO REFORM PROPOSAL

Knowledge of Health Economics provides ample evidence for examining the efficiencies in health. Economic appraisal seeks to improve efficiency by guiding policy-makers in how scarce resources can be used to derive the greatest possible social benefit. The current incremental approach to cost-effectiveness (CEA) does not provide decision-makers with sufficient guidance for wide sector priority setting in health. Instead, a broader complementary sectorial approach is proposed via the application of a generalised CEA framework, which allows the examination of existing inefficiencies in health systems. The wide variations in cost-effectiveness ratios observed among interventions that are currently in use, suggests there is considerable room to improve efficiency by moving inefficient interventions to efficient interventions that are underutilised.

## TOOLS FOR EFFECTIVE ENGAGEMENT

Those in charge of health sector reform must be equipped with the following tools:

- Must understand reform process and be able to speak reform language.
- Health must be regarded as a public good.
- Must always assess how changes in any of the reform measures will affect the desired outcomes particularly for the poor.
- Create time to understand how reform measures will affect service provision directly and the health system as a whole.
- Association executives should collect and provide information for members on health reforms.
- Mechanisms for facing some of the challenges that might be posed by the reform process.

## CONCLUSIONS

Health sector reforms are taking place globally in response to the emerging threats of diseases and the opportunities and breakthroughs provided by research and technology. The goal of health sector reform must converge with that of the health care practitioners in order to contribute to the improvements in health outcomes and reduction in disease burden – particularly for the poor. Health care practitioners must acquire medical and managerial skills for effective engagement and also to manage challenges associated with the reform process for optimal results.

## References

Ensor, T. and Cooper, S.(2004). "Overcoming Barriers to Health Service Access: Influencing the Demand Side." *Health Policy Plan.* Mar; 19(2);69-79. Review. PMID: 14982885.

Hall, A. (2004). The Impact and Enforcement of Prudent Laypersons Laws." *Ann. Emerg. Med.* May; 43(5): 558-66. PMID:15111523.

Hutubessy, R.C.,Baltussen, R.M., Torres-Edejer, T.T. and Evans, D.B.(2002). "Generalised Cost-effectiveness Analysis: An Aid to Decision- making in Health." *Global Evidence for Health Policy* WHO, Geneva, Switzerland. Appl. health Econ Health Policy.

Preker, A. and Harding, A. (2003). "The Economics of Hospital Reform: From Hierarchical to Market-Based Incentives." *World Health Serv.* 39(3): 3-10, 42,44, Review. PMID: 14963886.

Rigoli, F. and Dussault, G.(2003). "The Interface between Health Sector Reform and Human Resources in Health." *Human Resource Health* (1):9

Reich, M.R.(2002). "The Politics of Reforming Health Policies." *Promotion Education*; 9(4): 138-142. PMID: 12731117

## AFTERWORD

Health care management is a continuous process. Its usefulness and effectiveness should be directed towards the sustainability of the various categories of health care organisations. However, the topics highlighted in this book are quite generative but not exhaustive, and these include issues on behavioural traits, ethics, information, communication, drugs, finance, population, security, law, marketing, policy formulation and implementation, environmental health and waste management, globalisation and health reform which often pose serious challenges to all stakeholders in the health sector.

The ideas discussed in the book are attempts to kick-start future and further debates, deliberations, talks, seminars, symposia, workshops and researches that will bring about additional contributions to better management of the health sector.

Professor B.M. Ogunbameru was a Consultant for Federal Agricultural Coordinating Unit, Gwagwalada, Abuja for two terms. He had served for three terms as Head of Department, Agriculture and he is currently the Dean, Faculty of Agriculture, University of Maiduguri, Borno State. He has published well over fifty articles in both local and international journals. He has also edited and co-authored several books.

# Name Index

Abdulahi,M, 360
Abiola, Kudirat, 284
Adams, 249
Adebayo,A.A., 159
Adebolajo, S.O., 24
Adegoke, A.A., 46
Ademola, Ade, 239-240, 248, 267
Ademuwagun, Z.A., 13, 20
Aderounmu, A.O. , 360
Adetola, T., 156
Adetunji, J.A., 14, 21
Adeyanju, S.A., 272
Agich, 261
Akiyama, 247
Akinrinsola, Fola, 285,292
Anderson, 254
Andrews, K.R., 68,85
Annalee, Yassi, 316-317,332
Annan, Kofi, 348
Ansoff, H.I., 68,86
Antonocci, 247
Anyanwu, J.C., 138,156
Armstrong, 153
Arojo, Dele, 286
Arnheim, D.D., 277,281
Atchley, R.C., 246-247,252,265
Awe, John, 285,292
Awolowo, Obafemi, 36
Ayeni, O., 9, 21
Azikiwe, Nnamdi, 36

Babangida, Ibrahim, 286
Backett, 252
Baker, D.E., 262, 265
Baksaas, I., 187,208
Bamigboye, A.P., 236,314
Bannerjee, A.M., 138,158
Bauld, 176
Becker, 137
Behman, 162
Belanger, 253
Benner, P., 263,266
Bennett, A.E., 46,64
Berkowiltz, E.D., 253, 266
Berry, T.H., 74, 86
Bixby, 247
Blanks, 165
Blazer, D.G., 253, 266
Bortz, 238
Bowling, 247
Boyd, R., 253, 271
Brodie, D.C., 185, 200, 203, 209
Buchanan, R.J., 252, 266
Buckman, R., 63-64
Buhari, M., 6, 21
Bulatao, R..A, 180
Burnout, 224-226

Callahan, Daniel, 31, 44
Cannon, T., 148-149, 157
Carlson, R.E., 273, 281
Chernichovshy, D., 137, 157
Chisnall, P.M., 147, 157
Clare, A., 49-51, 65
Cleary, P.D., 249, 268
Cleland, D.O., 76
Cooney, 253
Corbin, H.D., 276, 278, 281
Corney, R.H., 48
Cowgill, D.O., 252, 266

Daini, O.A., 101, 107
Davidson, C., 252, 265
Davis, K., 249, 266
Deliganis, S.G., 188, 210
Dickson, Edward, 285, 292
Dikibo, Kala Amunasowi Kala, 286
Diop, F., 136, 157

Ebigbola, J.A., 5, 9, 11, 16, 21
Egbuwalo, M.O., 136
Einstein, Albert, 36
Estes, C., 249, 266
Eston-Smith, 262, 269
Evers, H., 262, 267

Fagunwa, D.O., 239, 267
Fajemilehin, B.R., 235-236, 239-240, 246-248, 254, 260, 265, 267
Fajewonyomi, B.A., 314
Fayose, Ayo, 287
Feachem, R.G.A., 161, 180
Felton, 253
Feyisetan, B., 246, 267
Fishbein, 47, 65
Fletcher, C.M., 47, 65
Fletcher, Joseph, 32-34, 44
Freeling, P., 65
French, B., 264, 268

George, 251-253, 268
Gerard, 249
Gilles, H.M. 16, 21
Gliksman, M.D. 247, 268
Gore, M.S. 246-247, 252-254, 268
Grossman, Michael, 163, 180
Guadagnoti, 249, 268
Guidotti, 316

Hall, J.T., 273, 281
Harris, C.M., 65
Harrison, K., 15,21
Hays, J.A., 253-254, 268
Heaton, I.C., 274,281
Helmer, Richard, 347
Henderson, N.V., 142,157
Hepler, 182
Herman, J.Muller, 45
Hetherlington, 118
Hill, K., 157
Hiris, J., 253, 269
Hobbs, D.A., 165,180
Hobcroft, 162,180
Hollender, 50
Holmes, F.H., 251-252, 268

Ige, Bola, 284
Igun, W.A.,14,21
Ikoku, Chimen, 286
Ilesanmi, L.A., 108
Irinoye, A.I., 1, 117, 360

James, Williams, 25,45
Janning, 248
Jinadu, 246
Jones, J.G.S., 9, 21

Kaplan, M. 273,281
Kelly, Gerald, 30,40,45
King, W.R., 76,86
Kjellstrom, T., 165,180,316
Knapp, D.A., 204,209
Kok, 316
Koplan, J.P., 165,180
Korpela, M., 107
Kotter, P., 147,157
Kotter, J.P., 83, 86
Koutsoyiannis, D., 141-142,157
Kraus, R., 274, 281
Kuper, A., 68-69, 86
Kuper, J., 68-69, 86
Kure, Alhaji, 287

Laroche, Mireille, 160,162,180
Larson, L.E., 250,268
Last, J.M., 316,333
Latimer, 262
Lawal, Amina, 342
Lawler, J., 261, 269
Lazarus, R., 247, 268
Leader, S.R., 247,268
Lederberg, Joshua, 35,45
Lee, Kelley, 139,157,336
Lucas, A.O., 16, 21, 88,99

Maclean, U., 13,21
Maddox, 251
Maguire, P., 59,65
Makanjuola, R.O.A., 101,107
Manley, K., 263-264, 269
Mann, Jonathan, M., 340
Marshall, Harry, 249, 284, 286
McCormack, B., 261, 263-265, 269

Mcnell, B.J., 249, 268
Michael, A. Simpson, 45
Mills, A., 139,157
Monekosso, 161, 180
Mor, V., 253, 269
Morrison, Robert, 39, 45
Muller, 36-37
Murray, 253
Myerscough, P.R., 55,57-58, 64-65

Neun, S.P., 139,141,158, 163, 165, 181
Northon, D., 262,269

Obasanjo, President, 287
Odusola, 161
Ogunbameru, O.A.,66,74,86
Ogunbunmi, P.I., 360
Ogunjuyigbe, P.O., 5, 11, 22
Ogunlade, J.O., 211, 233-234
Ojeme, Sunday, 285, 292
Ojo, A.A., 246, 267
Ojo, J.O., 101
Oladeji, Bayo, 286, 292
Oladeji, S.I., 159
Oladipo, Dotun, 286-287, 292
Olorunfemi, Steven, 287
Olorunnipa, Phillip Kayode, 287
Olorunsola, H.K., 272
Olowo, T., 148, 151, 158
Olson, L.K., 249, 269
Oni, J.B., 247, 269
Onyibe, Magnus, 286, 292
Oribabor, P.E., 87
Orifowomo, O.A., 294
Orubuloye, I.O.,.12-15, 22
Oyeneye, O.Y., 239, 270
Oyewole, Dare, 286, 292

Pasteur, Louis, 36
Pategi, Ahmed, 286
Patterson, 183
Pearce, J.A., 71, 78, 81, 83-86
Phillips, M.A., 180
Porter, M.E., 78
Prasad, L., 138, 158
Psacharopoulos, G., 136-137, 158
Purtilo, R.B., 49, 65

Quandt, 142

Rahe, R.H., 251-252, 268
Rakowski, W., 253, 269
Ramsey, Paul, 29, 45
Ransome-Kuti, O., 89, 97, 99
Raymond, D. Garrett, 115
Restrepo, H.E., 246, 248-250, 270
Rewane, Alfred, 284
Richman, V., 274, 277, 281
Robinson, R.B., 71, 78, 81, 83, 84-86
Rogers, 253
Ronald, Yezzi, 45
Rothenbery, R.B., 165, 180
Rowland, 249
Rozental, M., 246, 248-250, 270
Runyon, K.E., 147, 158

Safiyat, Aminat, 342
Santerre, R.E., 139-141, 158, 163, 165, 181
Schenider, 252-253
Schultz, J.H., 246-247, 270
Schultz, T.P., 162, 181
Segun, James, 287, 293
Sen, Amartya, 336, 338
Siegel, J.S., 236, 247, 270
Sirageldin, I., 157
Skeet, M., 255, 257, 259, 270
Smith, R., 341, 359
Smith, S.C., 162, 181
Smith, W.E., 185, 200, 203, 209
Soriyan, H.A., 107
Spitzer, W.O., 184, 210
Spivey, 44-45
Stokes, J.P., 251, 270
Stolar, M.H., 185, 189-190, 196, 200,210
Strand, 182
Strauss, J., 162, 181
Streib, 252-253
Swan, 249
Szasz, 50

Takala, Jukka, 347
Talley, C.R., 185, 210
Taubman, 162

Tense, M., 276, 281
Thomas, D., 162, 181
Thorestenson, C.T., 274, 281
Todaro, P.M., 162, 181
Tooley, Michael, 31, 45
Townsend, 249
Turner, J.G.S., 9, 22

Uhlenberg, P., 253, 271
Upstill, C., 326-327, 333
Urberson, 247
Uyanga, J., 13, 23

Van Beukeson, J.A.H., 62-63, 65

Wareham, D.U., 188, 210
Warmer, M., 74, 86
Warren, Marjorie, 261
Weinberg, 264
Weiskopt, D.C., 276, 281
Wells, T.J., 262, 271
Wilcox, V., 253, 269

# Subject Index

Abortion, 25, 28-33, 64, 312-313
- and Infanticide, 31
- (freedom, sanctity of life), 31-32
- laws, 31
- medico-legal perspective on, 33
- utilitarian perspective on, 32

Action plans and short-term objectives, 70, 72
Activity/passivity type of doctor/client relationship, 50
Adjunctive therapy, 276
Adult
- literacy rate, 127
- mortality, 17, 137

Adverse Drug Reactions (ADR), 206
African
- health care system, 114
- syncretic and Pentecostal churches, 12

Age related changes, 241
Ageing, 238
- population, 258
- social impact of, 246-264

Aging, 238, 246, 248-249, 255, 260
- population, 250-251, 255
- life events and stress in, 251-253
- process, 252
- studies, 249

Agricultural waste, 330
Aid to reform proposal
- cost effectiveness, 375-376

AIDS, 341
- epidemic, 340
- WATCH AFRICA, 340

Air
- pollutants, 322
- pollution, 322
  - control, 331

Alarm stage, 227
Alternative
- health financing, 6
- medicine, 48

Ambulatory surgery centres, 296
American Marketing Association, 147
Animal
- Health Problems, 324
- Morbidity and Mortality Statistical Reports, 106

Appropriate Use of Silence, 57
Armed Forces hospitals, 276
Armed robbery, 285
Artificial insemination, 25, 36
Assassinations, 285
Assisted Reproduction Techniques, 345
Atmospheric greenhouse gases, 316
Audience variable, 47

Behaviour and lifestyle of people, 174
Behavioural commitment, 154
Better Health in Africa, 90
Biodiversity
- loss of, 316

Biological engineering, 35
Birth
- control measure, 33
- defects, 32, 35, 37
- rates, 7, 9-10, 20, 236

Census figures, 235
Centre for
- African Settlement Studies and Development (CASSAD), 171
- Recreation and Disability Studies, 278

Chartered Institute of Marketing, United Kingdom, 147

Child
- labour, 342
- mortality, 16
- rate, 8

Childhood
- diseases, 160
- killer diseases, 174

Children (under five years) social Health Insurance Programme, 123
Children's Hospitals, 276
Cholera outbreaks, 321
Christian
- Health Association of Nigeria, 12
- literature, 34
- medical missions, 12
- missionaries, 13

Christianisation, 13
Cloning, 25
- and Assisted Reproduction Techniques, 345

Colonial medical services, 360
Communal health, 323
Communication
- definition of, 46
- principles of, 47-48
- skills, 48

Communicable diseases, 319, 332, 341
- prevention of, 122

Communicator variable, 47
Community
- based organisations, 370
- Health Management Teams (CHMIs), 370-371

Community Health
- nurses, 258-259
- organisations, 3

Community
- Hospital Authority (CHA), 365
- Hospitals, 188, 191
- programmes, 41
- project, 259

Company mission, 70, 72, 75-76
Comparative Drug Study, 206
Competitive
- health care, 142
- secrecy, 82

Competitors
- identification and mistakes of identification, 78-79

Compulsory sterilisation, 34-35
Computer
- Literacy level of pharmacists, 115
- medical records system, 113

Computerised medical records systems, 102
Concurrent Drug Utilisation Review (CDUR), 192
Conflict between Work and Non-Work, 218
Consultation, 52-53, 171
Contraceptives
- use of, 174

Cost of Treatment
- estimates of, 205

Creative technological adaptations, 76
Crime
- internationals, 342
- rate, 285

Criminal liability, 311-313
Crude death rate (CDR), 8
Cultism, 287
Cultural Environment, 77
Curative medical services, 360

Daily Bed Statistics, 102
Dairy Inspection, 329
Database, 105
Death
- and Dying, 38
- rates, 7-8

Defective children, 34
Defined daily dose (DDD), 205
Degenerative diseases, 223
Demographic
- and Operational Characteristics, 201
- factors, 235-238
- statistics, 160

– transition model, 9
Dental Hospital, 69
Department of Health in Sustainable Development, 337-338
Descriptive Contextual Information, 207
Diagnostics and Operations Codes, 102
Diarrhoea diseases, 166, 317
Direct therapeutic abortion, 30
Disease
– communication, 319
– control, 11
Diseases associated with overcrowding, 16
Dispensaries, 167, 299-300
Doctor/Client Relationship, 49-54
Doctor/patient relationship, 41
Doctors Anxieties
– problem of, 62
Domestic wastes, 323
Down's syndrome, 38
Downsizing, 74
Drug
– budget planning, 186
– daily dosage (DDD), 187
– data, 113
– importation, 320
– Incompatibility, 111-113
– Information (D.I), 112-113
– Service, 108
– (DIS) Development, 114
– inventory, 113
– Control Information, 110
– monitoring programmes, 183, 346
– peddlers, 14
– performance, 183
– procurement and inventory control, 110
– Procurement Information, 109-110
– related problems, 204
– selection, 183
– supply management, 108
– Information, 109
– use of computer, 110-111
– therapy, 111, 114-115, 182, 184-185, 187-188, 192
– audit
– use of computer, 113
– trafficking, 342
– usage data, 183, 346
– usage
– review of, 200-202
– use, 184
– control, 108
– Information, 111
– data, 185
– problems in, 205
– Profile, 201
– Review programmes, 190
– utilisation, 183
– and management, 367
– evaluation (DUE), 185
– Research Group (DURG), 184
– review (DUR), 184-185, 190
– methodology, 190-192
– Studies (DUS), 183-190, 197, 199, 203-206, 346
Dry drug stalls, 14

Early age at marriage, 8-9
Ecological factor
– (of health), 76, 332
Economic environment, 76-77
Ecosystem
– definition of, 316
Effective Communication
– facilitation of, 54-64
– obstacles to, 57-64
Elderly Abuse and its socioeconomic implications, 253-255
Electronic health records, 368
Emergency
– medical relief organisations, 1
– Relief materials, 340
Emotional Experience, 275
Employee
– and Patient Relationship, 304

– assistant programmes (EAPs), 232
– Development, 154
Employer
– and Employee Relationship, 301
– Patient Relationship, 303-304
End-stage Renal Disease Centres (ESRD), 296
Environment
– definition of, 109, 316
Environmental
– abuse and degradation, 317
– agencies, 326
– degradation, 317
– factor, 176-177
– factors affecting health, 321-325
– Health, 325-326
– activities, 321, 330-331
– goal, 326
– improvement of, 325-352
– problems, 316, 320, 325-326
– professional, 332
– programme, 319, 330
– risks, 326
– services, 318, 320, 327
– situation
– in developing countries, 318-321
– legislation, 76
– policy, 77
– pollution, 177, 316
– and degradation, 342
– protection and sanitation programme, 176
– sanitation, 122
– policy, 330
– stability, 316
Environmentally related diseases, 317
Ethical
– choices, 24
– implications, 35-37
– issues
– moral cautions on, 37-41
– perspectives and principles, 25-28
– Problems
– types of, 28-37
Eugenic sterilisation, 34
Euthanasia, 25, 313
Extended family, 239
– structure, 17
– system, 120, 256
External Environment, 70, 72, 76-77

Facial-oral infections, 317
Facility Utilisation Review, 196-197
Fairness and Justice, 154
Faith
– and spiritual healing, 12
– healing, 12-13
– churches, 13-14
– Homes, 3
Fake drugs, 15
Family
– history, 239
– planning, 10, 17-19
– programmes, 20
– service, 179
– support, 238
– supportive practice, 232
Federal
– Environmental Protection Agency (FEPA), 176
– Medical Centres, 174
– University Teaching Hospitals, 174
Fellowship, 275
Fertility, 7
– rates, 9-10, 165
Financing health care
– methods of, 121
Foetal
– loss, 17
– tissue in research
– use of, 25
Food
– Aid, 340
– Hygiene, 328-329
– and safety, 325

- related diseases, 325
- safety, 325, 345
- sanitation, 329
- programme, 329
- security, 336, 346

Foot and mouth diseases, 341
Forced option, 25
Framework Convention on Tobacco Control (FCTC), 346
Free
- market-oriented economy, 90
- trade, 334

Freedom of
- choice, 31
- women, 31

Freestanding Substance Abuse Facilities, 296
Frozen embryos, 25
Functional Tactics, 72, 80
Fundamental human rights, 154
Funding of Health, 171-173

Gastro-intestinal (G.I) – bleeding, 208
- diseases, 321, 331

Gender
- equity, 367
- inequality approach, 367

General Hospital, 167, 171, 288, 298, 365
Generic and Grand Strategies, 70, 72, 75
Genetic
- control, 36-38
- ethnics of, 35
- counselling, 38
- diseases, 37-38
- Engineering, 37, 345

Geriatric
- medicine, 262
- Social Health Insurance Programme, 123

Gerontological Nursing, 238, 263-264
Gerontology, 238
Global
- Coalition for AIDS, 340
- community, 325
- disease pattern, 346
- environmental change, 316
- Environmental Health Approach, 325

Globalfund, 358
Global
- economic recession, 93
- Health, 338-339, 348
- Award, 343
- stakeholders, 339-351
- humanitarian crises, 340
- leadership, 83
- performance of Health system, 88
- poverty, 339
- Problems–local solutions, 351-355
- Security, 335
- and Health, 341
- treaty, 346
- village, 335
- warming, 336, 343-344
- wealth, 339

Globalisation, 334-356
- and
- Communicable Diseases, 340-341
- Consumable Goods. 346
- Natural Disasters, 343
- Pharmacy Practice, 345-346
- Poverty, 339
- Technology in Medicine, 344-345
- the Environment, 343-344
-, Conflict and Wars, 339-340
-, Crime and Terrorism, 343
-, Health and Foreign Policy, 348-349
- of Health
- Impact of London, 349-351

Good health outcomes, 372-373
Government Hospitals, 142, 144. 152

Guidance – cooperation type of doctor/ client relationship, 50-51

Harvard
- Business School, 68
- Medical School, 39

Health
- afflictions
  - causes of, 160
- and Environment, 316-318
- and Population Policy, 17-18
- and Safety at Work
  - impact of globalisation, 347-348
- care delivery, 121, 295
  - policy response, 174
  - system, 19, 108-109, 183, 296-297, 327, 346
    - components of, 296
    - parties involved in, 299-301
- care
  - institutions, 258
    - /Organisations
      - establishments of, 298-299
  - Organisation
    - quality assurance activities, 196
  - practitioners, 376
  - provider, 1-2, 14, 48, 131, 179, 197, 310
    - client/relationship, 48, 64
  - services, 6, 139, 362
    - cost of, 170-171
    - demand and supply analyses, 139-146
    - major defects of, 119-120
    - marketing strategies, 152
    - state of, 119-120
    - system, 2, 166
- system
  - funding of, 90-95
  - of Nigeria, 360
- ways of management, 121-122
  - workers, 24
- consumers, 131
- Economics, 375
- education, 258
  - and services, 10
  - programme, 329
- electronic libraries, 368
- establishments, 168-169
- expenditure, 11, 162, 172-173
- for All, 6
- funding, 118
- gain, 264
- hazards, 330
- /Health care
  - concept of, 138-139
- Human Capital Accumulation, 161, 166-177, 179
- indices, 127
- information system (HIS), 344
- institutions, 64, 107, 284-285, 288-291, 368
- Insurance Scheme
  - need for, 121
- monitoring, 258
- policy, 18, 172, 361
  - formulators and implementors, 42
- promotion activities, 257
- promotion strategies, 241
- protection measures, 138
- reform, 361
- related risks, 341
- revolution, 338
- Sector Information Technology Reform, 368
- Sector
  - Reform, 361-366 and Human Resources, 368-371
- challenges of, 373-375

– drug utilisation and management, 367
– gender and equity, 367-368
– services in Nigeria, 89
– statistics, 119, 164
– status in Nigeria, 88-89
– system reform, 361
– team, 3-4
Healthy Homes and Communities, 323
Heat-related illnesses, 344
High fertility rate
– factors associated with, 8-9
Hippocratic Oath, 25
Home
– for the Aged persons, 277
– Health Agencies, 296
Hospice, 296
Hospital
– /clinical setting, 57
– formulary, 109
– Information System (HIS), 101-107
– Management Board, 89
– Management Policy, 109
– Pharmacy, 109-115
– information needs, 108-115
Hospitals
– classification of, 68-69
Household wastes, 315
Housing and Environmental Inspection, 330
Human
– capital accumulation, 159-179
– capital investment, 161
– Development Index (HDI), 166
– evolution, 37
– health capital – accumulation, 172
– structure, 164
– Immunodeficiency Virus/ Acquired Immune Deficiency Syndrome (HIV/AIDS), 1, 18, 20, 152, 160, 284, 335, 340, 351, 367-368
– Resources Development, 367
– trafficking, 342
– and prostitution, 341
Humanistic nursing, 265

Ife State Hospital (ISH), 102, 104-106, 113
Illegal abortions, 31
Immunisation, 19, 131-132, 174
Indirect therapeutic abortion, 29
Individual's rights, 32
Industrial
– waste products, 343
– wastes, 330
Industrialisation, 315
Infant
– and childhood mortality, 236
– mortality, 16
– rate (IMR), 8-9, 120, 127, 131, 160, 164, 166, 170
Infanticide, 31
Infectious diseases, 223, 335, 344, 348
Informal or unwritten policies, 82
Information and Communication Technology, 334
Injury prevention, 331
Insecticide Treated Bed Nets, 361
Insurance
– principle, 121
– schemes, 19
– system, 122
Interactive marketing strategies, 152, 154-156
Internal
– Analysis, 70, 72
– marketing strategies, 152-154
– migration, 17
International
– Environment, 77-78
– environmental laws, 343
– Labour Organisation (ILO) Health and Safety Programme, 347-348
– migration, 7, 9, 16
– Network for Rational Utilisation of Drug (INRUD), 192
– Treaty outlawing landmines, 1977, 340
Intestinal parasitic diseases, 317
Ionising radiation
– exposure to, 319

Job-related stress, 218
Joint United Nations Programme on HIV/AIDS, 340

Killing an Unborn Child, 313

Laws and Regulations, 375
Leadership and Culture, 83-84
Legal Environment, 78
Leprosy, 160
Life expectancy, 7-8, 18, 120, 123, 127, 137, 160-161, 164, 166, 169-170
Life insurance policy, 232
Liquid waste disposal, 329
Literary rate, 166, 174-175
Local Health Organisations, 3
London
- Health strategy, 351-352
- School of Hygiene and Tropical medicine, 336
Long-Term objectives, 70, 72
Low literacy rate, 9
Low utilization of modern contraceptives, 9

Malaria, 160, 317, 321, 338, 341, 351
- Bed Net Component, 361
- eradication, 320
Malnutrition, 17
Man-made epidemics, 332
Man-made pollution, 319
Management
- definition of, 138, 296
- Information System (MIS), 102
Managing stress
- organisation based strategies, 232
Manufacturer Association of Nigeria (MAN), 16
Market forces, 144
Marketing
- definition of, 147
- milk, 148-152, 155-156
- of medical services
  - concept of, 147-156
- of services, 149-150
Maternal
- and child health, 18
  - care, 20
- health, 165
- mortality, 17-18
Maternity, 167
- care, 174
- centres, 299
Medical
- administration system, 102
- Advisory Committee (MAC), 199
- Aid, 340
- alternatives, 41
- and Dental Council of Nigeria, 300
- and Dental Practitioner Act, 300-301
- and Dental Practitioners Disciplinary Tribunal, 300
- care, 139-141, 156, 163, 165
  - evaluation (MCE) study, 199
- communication, 48
- computers, 344
- consumables, 171
- diagnosis, 59
- education policy, 41
- ethics in Medical Education, 41-43
- Health Centres, 167
- injuries, 184
- malpractice, 310-311
- management, 272-280
- market, 137
- Negligence, 310-311
- recordkeeping, 344
- records, 102
  - Department, 102-106
- Rehabilitation Therapists (Registration, etc) Act, 301
- services, 144-146
  - market, 142
- technological advancement, 11
- technology, 236
Medicare, 150
Medication errors, 111

Medicine stores, 14
Medico-moral problems, 30
Mental health
- disability, 278
- reform, 361
Mental power
- use of, 275
Message variables, 47
Migrant population, 9
Migration, 7
Military incursions and civil wars, 20
Milk-borne diseases, 328
Mission - Clinics, 171
- Health Organisations, 3
- hospitals, 12
Monetary Incentive, 153
Moral obligations, 28
Morbidity Data, 206
Mortality rate, 9, 98, 187
- reduction of, 10, 19
Motivating strategies, 153
Motivation, 153
Murder, 285
- Manslaughter, 312
Mutual participation, 51

National
- Agency for Food, Drugs and Control (NAFDAC), 174, 346, 367
- Council of Health, 18
- Drug Formulary, 110
- drug policy, 109
- Essential Drugs List, 110
- Formulary and Essential Drugs List, 109
- Health Insurance Scheme (NHIS), 6, 98, 117-134, 174, 371
- Health
- Organisations, 3
- Policy, 88-89, 117
- Insurance, 121
- Policy on HIV/AIDS and STIs, 18
- Population Policy, 7, 18
- security, 284
- Therapeutic Recreation Association of America, 276
Natural
- disasters, 343
- law, 30, 34
- selection, 36
Neurology Hospital, 69
New Drugs
- research on, 206
Nigeria
- health sector reform projects, 361
- Indigenous Pharmaceutical Manufacturers Association (NIPMA), 123
Nigerian Health Care System, 11, 89-90
Non-governmental
- agencies, 12
- Organisations (NGOs), 3, 90, 152, 339, 370
- health care centre, 171
Non-monetary Incentive, 153
- steroidal anti-inflammatory drugs, (NSAIDS), 208
- verbal, 55-56
Nursing
- and Midwifery Act, 301
- and Midwifery Council of Nigeria, 301
- assessment, 241
- care system, 260
- Homes, 120, 277
Nutritional deficiencies, 136

Obafemi Awolowo University Teaching Hospitals Complex (OAUTHC), 101-106, 111, 113-115, 289
Obstetrics and Gynaecology Hospital, 69
Occupational
- Demands, 218
- diseases, 319, 332
- exposure (to diseases), 324
- hazards, 347
- health, 347
- team, 332
- therapy, 197

Optimal Management
- definition of, 138
Organisation
- Behaviour, 225
- building of, 83
- structure
  - shaping of, 83-84
Organisational
- Action
  - initiation of, 80-81
- Change, 331, 375
- Culture, 84
- downsizing, 74
- efficiency and performance, 74
- strategy, 83
Orthodox
- health system, 6
- medical institution, 15
- medicine, 184
Orthopaedic Hospital, 69
Out-of-Stock (O/S) Syndrome, 111
Outdoor
- air quality, 322
Outpatient care, 174
Ozone layer
- depletion of, 344

Pain, Suffering and Death
- problem of, 59-61
Parasitic
- and infectious diseases, 177
- diseases, 160
Patent
- medicine vendors, 14
- right, 346, 349
Patient
- care, 208
  - Audits (PCA), 196-199
- education, 184
Patients, 300-301
- Emotional Reactions, 63
- Responsibilities, 309-310
- right to life, 26
- Rights, 306-309
Permanently Disabled Person Social Health Insurance Programme, 123
Personality
- issue of, 26
Pharmaceutical
- care, 182
- inventory, 114
Pharmacy
- Ancillary Service Review, 199-200
- Audit Committee (PAC), 187-188
- automation, 182
- operators, 14
- Priorities, 114-115
Physical
- Evidence, 156
- Medicine and Rehabilitation, 279
- Well-being, 275
Policies that Empower
- creation of, 81-82
Polio
- eradication of, 338
Polluter pay policy, 330
Population
- and Health, 16-17
- Census, 8
- Dynamics, 7-9, 315
- explosion, 6, 9
- growth, 17
  - rate, 7-8, 16
- related issues, 18
Poverty, 176
- and economic mobility, 315
- rate, 178
Practising physicians
- attributes of, 43-44
Prescription records, 206
Primary Health Care (PHC), 4, 6, 20, 88, 90, 117, 171, 371
  - and sanitation, 19
  - organisations, 4
  - programmes, 89, 98
  - services, 89
Primary
- Health Organisations, 3
- level health care, 139
- level medical care, 69
Prison Inmates Social Health Insurance Programme, 123

Private
- Hospitals, 139, 142-143, 152, 171
- medical practice, 11-12
Productive ages, 9
Production theory, 164
Professional Conduct for Medical and Dental Practitioners in Nigeria
- rules of, 305
Prospective Drug Utilisation Review (PDUR), 191-192
Protein Energy Malnutrition (PEM), 259
Psychiatric Hospital, 69
Psychological support, 259-261
Public Health, 314, 324, 326-327, 341, 351
- activities, 319
- and community medicine, 10
- programmes, 9, 11, 331
- services, 328
- standards, 325
Public Hospitals, 178-179, 340

Quack doctors, 4, 176
Qualitative
- Drug Utilisation Studies, 187-190
- Overload, 218
Quality assurance programmes, 193-200
Quantitative
- Drug Utilisation Studies, 186
- Overload, 218

Radioactive
- pollution, 331
- wastes, 323
Radiologic contamination control, 331
Recreation, 272-280
- characteristics of, 274
- concept of, 273-274
- therapist, 276
- therapy services, 279
- Therapy Interactions
- for Persons with Development Disabilities, 278-280
- values of, 273-275
Recreational activities, 276, 278
Reengineering, 74
Referral medicare, 139
Reform Measures, 363
Refugee camps, 14
Regional Health Organisations, 3
Reintegration through Recreation (RTR), 279
Relationship model, 51
Religious
- foundations, 26
- riots, 287
Remote environment, 76
Reproduction - age, 36
- health reform, 361
- health policy
- draft of, 18
- period, 17
Resistance stage, 227
Respiratory infections, 17, 160, 317
Retirement
- incomes, 248
- planning schemes, 232
Retrospective Drug Utilisation Review (RDUR), 190-191
Retroviral drug treatments, 337
Reward system, 83-84
Rewards
- designing effective ones, 83
Right of
- confidentiality, 41
- death with dignity, 26-27
- to health care, 26-28
Rights and Responsibilities, 26-28
- relationship between, 27-28
Rights
- of non-interference, 27
- of opportunity, 27
- of the mentally ill, 26
- of the retarded, 26
- of the unborn, 26
Ritual killing, 285
Role Ambiguity, 218
Role Conflict, 218
Roman Catholic View

- on abortion, 30
Routinised geriatric care, 262
Royal College of Nursing (RCN), 264
Rural
- Communities, 119
- Community Social Health Insurance Programme, 122
- Health Clinics, 299
Rural - urban migration, 9, 17, 256

Sanitary Services, 318
SARS, 340, 343
Schools of
- Health Technology, 288
- Nursing, 288
Secondary Health
- Centres, 4
Secondary level
- health care, 139
- medical care, 69
Security in Health Institutions, 288-292
Security
- definition of, 282
Self
- development, 154
- managed learning, 154
- medication, 122
Sense of Achievement, 275
Services
- characteristics of, 150-152
Sexual
- functions, 55
- Harassment, 219
Sexuality
- problem of, 61-62
Sexually transmitted
- diseases (STDs), 16, 160, 351
- infections, 16
Skilled Nursing Facilities, 296
Social and
- community service, 171, 178
- cultural diversity, 315
- environment, 246-247
- gerontologists, 252
- Gerontology perspective, 248-251
Social
- Health Insurance Programme. 122
- Insurance, 120-121, 133, 371-372
- Organisation
- impact of, 250-251
- psychologists, 47
- relationship, 249
- impact of, 251
- support, 219
- system, 1-2
Socio-Demographic studies and Health
- association between 247
Socio-economic
- determinants, 11
- factors, 11
- on health, 317
- status (SES), 165, 246
Soil pollution, 323
Soils
- degradation of, 316
Solar energy, 344
Solid waste disposal, 329
Spiritual
- churches, 13
- healing
- homes, 15
- services, 13
- homes, 13-14
Staff Development, 154
Standard drug use indicators, 193
State
- Environmental Protection Agencies (SEPA), 176
- Hospitals, 298
- Neuropsychiatric Hospitals, 276
- of Health, 9-16
- or Sectorial Health Organisations, 3
Sterilisation, 33-35
Stillbirth, 16
Strategic
- Analysis and Choice, 70,72
- Control and Continuous Improvement, 74-75

– intent, 83
– management
– benefits of, 85
– formulation, 75-79
– key components, 70
– model, 71-72
– planning for health, 172
Strategy Implementation, 74, 79
Stratospheric Ozone, 317
– layer
– depletion of, 316
Stress – Control, 230-232
– management Programmes, 232
– management Unit, 232-233
– meaning of, 213-217
– work-related causes of, 217-221
Stressful Life Events, 219
Stressors, 213-214, 227
Structural Adjustment Programme (SAP), 15, 90, 170
System Architecture, 103-106

Taiwan Universal Health Insurance Programme, 19
Teaching Hospital Complexes, 288
Teaching Hospitals, 167, 170-171, 298-299
Technological factors, 76
Teenage pregnancies, 351
Terrorism (bioterrorism and chemoterrorism), 342
Tertiary
– health care, 90
– delivery, 6
– Health Centres, 4
– health institutions, 183
– level health care, 139
– medical care, 69
Therapeutic
– compliance, 206
– recreation, 273, 275-276
– objectives, 273, 277
– programme, 273, 277-278
– specific uses of, 278-280
– sterilisation, 34
Time
– problem of, 58-59
Total
– fertility rate (TFR), 8
– life stress, 220
Toxic materials, 317
Trade barriers, 335
Traditional
– education, 41
– extended family system, 260
– family system, 238
– farming system, 238
– healers, 13, 163, 171
– Healing Homes, 3
– health care practitioners, 13
– health facilities, 13
– medicine, 13, 15
– sanitation activities, 319
Trado-medical practice, 6

Ultra-violet-B (W-B) radiation, 317
Unit dose dispensing method, 108, 114-115
United
– House Conference on Aging, 253
– Nations Children's Fund, 338
– States Environmental Protection
– Agency, 322
University
– College Hospital (UCH), Ibadan, 288
– Health Insurance Scheme, 372
– of Kupio, Finland, 103, 105-106
– Teaching Hospitals (Reconstruction of Boards etc) Act, 299
Unresolved Personal Problems, 63-64
Urban
– populations, 320
– Self-employed Social Health Insurance Programme, 123
Urbanisation, 251, 315

VA MUMPS/FileMan technology, 101, 103
Valuing Employees, 154
Vasectomies, 33
Vector-borne diseases, 317
– Control and Control of Animal Reservoirs of Diseases, 331

Veterans hospitals, 276
Veterinary professionals, 331
Vocabulary, 55
Voluntary organisations, 12

Warri communal clashes, 287
Waste Management, 323, 329-330
- system, 323
Water
- and sanitation related diseases, 317
- borne diseases, 319
- pollution, 322
- resources
    - pollution of, 316
- supply, 322
    - control, 327-328
Wesley Guild Hospital, 106
Westernisation, 13
Witchcraft, 13
Woman's
- right to control her body, 26
- right to pregnancy,33
Women's health approach, 367
Work
- related diseases and injuries, 347
- stress
    - experience of, 221-222
Workman's Compensation Decree, 1987, 343
World
- Bank - IMF program,12
- Development Report, 90
- Health Assembly, 338
- Health Organisation (WHO), 3, 8, 15, 19, 87-88, 91, 184, 192-193, 234, 253, 255, 316-318, 326, 333, 335, 337-338, 345-348
    - Essential Drugs Policy, 109
    - global health initiative, 337-339
- Trade Organisation (WTO), 345, 348
    - agreement, 336, 343

Written
- or formal policies, 82
- policies
    - advantages of, 82-83

Zoonoses, 324, 331
Zoonotic diseases, 324

www.ingramcontent.com/pod-product-compliance
Ingram Content Group UK Ltd.
Pitfield, Milton Keynes, MK11 3LW, UK
UKHW041141300926
15471UKWH00011B/75

9 789780 295370